D0813581

The Spirit and the Church

The Spirit and the Church

Peter Damian Fehlner's Franciscan Development of Vatican II on
the Themes of the Holy Spirit, Mary, and the Church—*Festschrift*

EDITED BY

J. Isaac Goff,
Christiaan W. Kappes,

AND

Edward J. Ondrako

☙PICKWICK *Publications* · Eugene, Oregon

THE SPIRIT AND THE CHURCH
Peter Damian Fehlner's Franciscan Development of Vatican II on
the Themes of the Holy Spirit, Mary, and the Church—*Festschrift*

Copyright © 2018 Wipf and Stock Publishers. All rights reserved. Except for
brief quotations in critical publications or reviews, no part of this book may be
reproduced in any manner without prior written permission from the publisher.
Write: Permissions, Wipf and Stock Publishers, 199 W. 8th Ave., Suite 3, Eugene,
OR 97401.

Pickwick Publications
An Imprint of Wipf and Stock Publishers
199 W. 8th Ave., Suite 3
Eugene, OR 97401

www.wipfandstock.com

PAPERBACK ISBN: 978-1-5326-5140-3
HARDCOVER ISBN: 978-1-5326-5141-0
EBOOK ISBN: 978-1-5326-5142-7

Cataloguing-in-Publication data:

Names: Goff, J. Isaac, editor. | Kappes, Christiaan W., editor |
Ondrako, Edward J., editor.

Title: The Spirit and the church : Peter Damian Fehlner's Franciscan develop-
ment of Vatican II on the themes of the Holy Spirit, Mary, and the church—
Festschrift / edited by J. Isaac Goff, Christiaan W. Kappes, and Edward J.
Ondrako.

Description: Eugene, OR : Pickwick Publications, 2018 | Includes bibliographi-
cal references.

Identifiers: ISBN 978-1-5326-5140-3 (paperback) | ISBN 978-1-5326-5141-0
(hardcover) | ISBN 978-1-5326-5142-7 (ebook)

Subjects: LCSH: Fehlner, Peter D. | Holy Spirit. | Church.

Classification: BJ1251 .H72 2018 (print) | BJ1251 .H72 (ebook)

Manufactured in the U.S.A.   09/27/18

Contents

Part One: The Church, the Dignity of the Person, and Creation

v

Contributors

Arthur B. Calkins is a retired priest of the Archdiocese of New Orleans. In 1985 Calkins was named a corresponding member of the Pontifical International Marian Academy and, in 1995, a corresponding member of the Pontifical Roman Theological Academy. He served as an official of the Pontifical Commission "Ecclesia Dei" from 1991 to 2010. In 1997 Calkins was named a Monsignor at the rank of Chaplain of His and was promoted to be a Prelate of Honor in 2010. His doctoral study, written Peter Fehlner's direction, *Totus Tuus: John Paul II's Program of Marian Consecration and Entrustment* (2017), has gone into four printings and a second edition is now in print. In 2006 Edizioni Cantagalli of Siena, Italy published his anthology on the Marian Magisterium of Pope John Paul II entitled *Totus Tuus. Il Magistero Mariano di Giovanni Paolo II.*

Jeremy Daggett currently teaches music at a Great Hearts Academy, a Classical Education Charter School. He is beginning studies in Canon Law in the Archdiocese of San Antonio.

Gloria Falcão Dodd is Director of Academic Programs, International Marian Research Institute. Dodd serves on the Administrative Council of the Mariological Society of America and is president of her Legion of Mary *praesidium*. She is the author of *The Virgin Mary, Mediatrix of All Grace: History and Theology of the Movement for a Dogmatic Definition from 1896 to 1964* (2012).

Robert Fastiggi is Professor of Systematic Theology at Sacred Heart Major Seminary in Detroit, MI and a former president of the Mariological Society of America. He is the co-editor of the English translation of the 43rd edition of the Denzinger-Hünermann *Compendium of Creeds, Definitions, and Declarations on Matters of Faith and Morals* (2012).

Jonathan A. Fleischmann is an assistant professor of mechanical engineering at Marquette University, Milwaukee, WI. Dr. Fleischmann has written peer-reviewed articles on a wide range of subjects, including engineering mechanics, mathematical logic, and Mariology. He is the author of the book *Marian Maximalism* (2016), with a foreword by Cardinal Raymond Burke and an afterword by Fr. Peter Fehlner as well as over twenty articles on Marian subjects, appearing in journals such as the *Homiletic and Pastoral Review* and the *Missio Immaculatae International* magazine.

John T. Ford, CSC, recently retired from teaching at The Catholic University of America, Washington DC, is the recipient of the Paul Wattson Christian Unity Award from the Franciscan Friars of the Atonement (2014), the Ecumenism Award (2015) of The Washington Theological Consortium (2015), and the Gailliot Award of the National Institute for Newman Studies (2016). He served as editor of Newman Studies Journal (2004–2013); he is the author of Saint Mary's Press Glossary of Theological Terms (Saint Mary's Press, 2006) and editor of John Henry Newman: Spiritual Writings (Orbis, 2012), as well as the numerous essays, book chapters and articles.

Angelo Geiger, OFM Conv., is a STD student at the Catholic University of America in Historical Theology. He has contributed several studies to the series, *Mary at the Foot of the Cross* (2000–2002, 2005, 2009).

T. Alexander Giltner is currently an undergraduate instructor of theology at Saint Louis University in St. Louis, MO. He has taught on a number of topics of Christian theology, and has presented and published on thinkers ranging from Bonaventure to John Scottus Eriugena to Gregory Palamas. He is currently preparing a manuscript on Saint Bonaventure's epistemology and metaphysics called *The Lightness of Being*.

J. Isaac Goff is an instructor in theology at Ss. Cyril and Methodius Seminary. He has published on Bonaventure, John Duns Scotus, Gregory Palamas and Catholic/Orthodox ecumenical theology. His recent publications include: *Caritas in Primo: A Study of Bonaventure's Disputed Questions on the Mystery of the Trinity* (2015), co-editor of *A Companion to Bonaventure* (2014).

David Bentley Hart is currently a fellow at the Notre Dame Institute for Advanced Study. His specialties are philosophical theology, systematics, patristics, classical and continental philosophy, and Asian religion. His most recent work has concerned the genealogy of classical and Christian metaphysics, ontology, the metaphysics of the soul, and the philosophy of mind. At present he is working on a book on the nature of consciousness and the classical metaphysics of the soul. Hart's principal scholarly books are *The Beauty of the Infinite* (2003); *The Doors of the Sea* (2005); *In the Aftermath* (2007); *Atheist Delusions* (2009); *The Experience of God* (2013); *A Splendid Wickedness* (2016); *The Dream-Child's Progress* (2017); and *The Hidden and the Manifest* (2017).

J.A. Wayne Hellmann, OFM Conv., is professor of Historical Theology at Saint Louis University, St. Louis, MO. He has taught and published in the area of St. Francis and early Franciscan sources as well as in the theology of St. Bonaventure.

Christiaan W. Kappes is a priest currently serving the Byzantine Archeparchy of Pittsburgh as the academic dean of Ss. Cyril and Methodius Byzantine Catholic Seminary. His latest publications include "Gregorios Palamas' Reception of Augustine's Doctrine of the Original Sin and Nicholas Kabasilas' Rejection of Aquinas' Maculism as the Background to Scholarios' Immaculism." *Byzantinisches Archiv: Series Philosophica* (2017), and "A New Narrative for the Reception of Seven Sacraments into Orthodoxy: Peter Lombard's Sentences in Nicholas Cabasilas and Symeon of Thessalonica and the Utilization of John Duns Scotus by the Holy Synaxis." *Nova et Vetera* (2017).

James McCurry, OFM Conv., is the Minister Provincial of the Franciscan Friars Conventual of Our Lady of the Angels Province, which encompasses the east coast of the United States; Ontario, Canada; Rio De Janeiro, Brazil; Ireland and Great Britain. He is a past President of the Mariological Society of America, and an appointee to the Pontifical International Marian Academy. During the past forty years, he has lectured, conducted retreats, led pilgrimages, and preached in all fifty states of the US, as well as sixty countries of the world, on all seven continents. He authored *Maximilian Kolbe: Martyr of Charity* (2013). He has published numerous articles and booklets, and has appeared on radio, television, and video broadcasts. His "Mariology" series on the Eternal Word Television Network was syndicated for several years.

John-Mark L. Miravalle is assistant professor of Theology at Mount St. Mary's Seminary. He is author of *The Drug, the Soul, and God: A Catholic Moral Perspective on Antidepressants* (2010).

Edward J. Ondrako, OFM Conv., is currently Research Fellow at the Pontifical Faculty of St. Bonaventure, Rome and Visiting Scholar at the McGrath Institute for Church Life at the University of Notre Dame. He completed a doctoral program and dissertation in the Humanities at Syracuse University in 1994 on Newman and Gladstone in relation to Vatican II; and a second doctoral program in theology at the University of Notre Dame in 2017. His dissertation was on Fr. Peter Damian Fehlner's Appropriation and Development of the Ecclesiology and Mariology of Vatican II. He edited and contributed to *The Newman-Scotus Reader* published in 2015.

Trent Pomplun is associate professor of Theology at Loyola University Maryland, author of *Jesuit on the Roof of the World: Ippolito Desideri's Mission to Tibet* (2010), and assistant editor of *John Duns Scotus: The Report of the Paris Lecture (Reportatio IV-A)* (2016). He is currently at work on a critical edition of the Tibetan works of Ippolito Desideri, S.J.

Homage to Fr. Peter Damian Fehlner

Fr. James McCurry, OFM Conv.

ON BEHALF OF THE Franciscan family, I pay homage to Fr. Peter Damian Fehlner. Moreover, on behalf of the Franciscan family, I express gratitude to all of you who are honouring him at this symposium. Together we are expressing our mutual esteem for his brilliant contributions to the Catholic intellectual tradition of the Church and the Franciscan Order. Praised be Jesus Christ and His Immaculate Mother—now and forever!

Our honoree, Fr. Peter Damian, joined the Franciscan Order 70 years ago in 1945, when he was merely 14 years of age. From the small down of Dolgeville in upstate New York, he journeyed to the metropolis of New York City, where he enrolled in St. Francis Minor Seminary on Staten Island. There he soon developed a passion for classical studies. It has been my personal privilege as a friar to have known and loved Fr. Peter Damian for 45 of those 70 years. He served as my Rector, Professor, Confessor, Spiritual Director, Mentor, Consultant, Colleague in the Apostolate—and throughout all of those decades, my cherished friend and brother.

His parents, Mary Elizabeth Considine and Herman Joseph Fehlner, had five sons, whom they imbued with the staunch Catholicism of their Irish and German ancestors. The faith of their ethnic forebears had been chiseled on the anvil of political and religious persecution during the upheavals of nineteenth-century secularism and liberal evangelism which wracked the European continent. I can recall visiting many years ago with old Mrs. Fehlner, Fr. Peter's mother. In her own gentle Irish way, the family matriarch lived, prayed, and breathed the truth of her Catholic tradition. Even in the nursing home where she spent her final years, Mary Elizabeth evangelized her fellow patients, and convinced her 110-year-old roommate to make the act of total consecration to Our Lady the Immaculata. She was indefatigable!

Indeed, the acorn does not fall far from the tree! Her son Herman Joseph Jr. was given the religious name "Peter Damian" when he was invested as a novice in the Immaculate Conception Province of the Franciscan Friars Conventual in 1951. He professed his First Vows as a friar in 1952 in Albany, New York. Subsequently he was sent to the Assumption Seminary of the Franciscan Province of Our Lady of Consolation in Chaska, Minnesota, where he completed two years of philosophy studies, before being sent to Rome, Italy for the continuation of his Franciscan and priestly formation. In 1955 he professed his Final Vows at the Basilica of the Twelve Holy Apostles in Rome, and was ordained to the priesthood at San Alessio in Rome on the fourteenth of July 1957.

While in Rome, he obtained three pontifical decrees from the Seraphicum-Pontifical Theological Faculty of St. Bonaventure: an STB in 1956, an STL in 1958, and an STD in 1959. His doctoral dissertation entitled "The Role of Charity in the Ecclesiology of St. Bonaventure" established new benchmarks, in the days before and during the Second Vatican Council, for understanding the relevance of the Seraphic Doctor to the theological, metaphysical, historical, and cultural issues of the Church in the modern world. Indeed, Fr. Peter Damian, a Franciscan to the core, forged such a kinship with St. Bonaventure that the rest of his life to this present day would be colored by an overriding Bonaventurian optic. I have often maintained that, if the *Opera Omnia* of Bonaventure were to be obliterated from this earth, his writings could be reconstructed from the memory of Fr. Peter Damian Fehlner. I doubt that there is any scholar in this world whose brilliant mind has memorized and stored the Bonaventurean opus as profoundly as Fr. Peter Damian. Indeed, his brain might well be considered a PDF file of Bonaventure.

St. Bonaventure's disciple and heir, Blessed Friar John Duns Scotus, proffered his notable PDF argument in behalf of Our Lady's Immaculate Conception—*Potuit, Decuit, Fecit.* So too our modern-day scholar and honoree, Fr. PDF, a modern heir to the Franciscan intellectual tradition of Bonaventure and Scotus, embodies what the Seraphic and Subtle Doctors proffered. In computer parlance, PDF means "portable document format"—an ordering system developed in the 1990s to encapsulate, store, and present documents in an intelligible manner independent of various applications and operating schemes. Building upon that metaphor, I think we can say with confidence that God has transformed little Herman Joseph Fehlner into a walking PDF—and for that we give God thanks and praise!

St. Bonaventure loved the number 3—in honor of the Most Holy Trinity, of course. His triplets and triads are the stuff of legend. Even in this numeric vein, Fr. Peter Damian often resembles his holy mentor. I can recall sitting in several of Fr. Peter Damian's classes forty years ago, marveling and puzzling over the fact that he kept talking in 3s—"triad-talk," I called it. He taught us friars the A,B,Cs of God's Divine Plan of Salvation. Said Fr. Peter Damian: "It's as simple as A,B,C—from birth (A) through Justification at Baptism (B) through works of charity to Salvation (C)." Further, putting theology at the service of spirituality, Fr. Peter Damian lived and taught Bonaventure's "triple way" to holiness—purgative, illuminative, and unitive. On the personal level, he lived a triad of vows—poverty, chastity, and obedience—and thereby thrice offered himself in dedicated service to the Church and its mission.

One day about thirty years ago, Fr. Peter Damian and I were walking together through the streets of Rome, and we kept stopping to look at some of the ancient Roman inscriptions. Three letters kept predominating and punctuating our walk: D.O.M.—an acronym originally paying homage to the Emperor and to the pagan Jove, but transformed by early Christians as homage to the One True God: *D.O.M.*—"*Deo. Optimo. Maximimo*"—"To God, the Best, the Greatest"! That acronym could well be the motto of Fr. Peter Damian's life. His one and only goal as a friar has ever been the honor and glory of God—the Best, the Greatest. Surely the only reason he has permitted this *Festschrift* of scholarly tributes these days is so that all may redound to the best and greatest honor and glory of God.

The intellectual and spiritual journey of Fr. Peter Damian, in tandem with the mission he has embraced, have never brooked mediocrity. Mediocrity is compromise worked out into a system, a leveling of ideals down to the lowest common denominator. For God, the Best and Greatest, Fr. Peter Damian has ever striven for the highest common denominator. Fr. Peter Damian has always recognized that high ideal in the Bonaventurian ethos of early Franciscanism, which found pristine expression in the Order's Conventual tradition. Historically it was the Conventual Franciscans who fostered large communities, wherein friars strove to achieve harmony between contemplation and action, study and evangelization, poverty and obedience, whilst living naturally and supernaturally in a radical commitment the Rule of St. Francis. This older form of Franciscan "conventuality" would come under zealous attack by the secular movements of the French Revolution onwards through the nineteenth and early twentieth centuries. Ever the Bonaventurian student of history, Fr. Peter Damian recognized the Vatican Council II as a new moment for "conventuality" in the Church and in the Order—a time for reinforcing the ideals of St. Francis through Franciscan community life. Fr. Peter Damian lived in Rome through those glory days of Vatican II, and became imbued by its authentic call of radical commitment to the ideals of one's religious founder. Accordingly, he sought to reclaim St. Bonaventure's understanding of St. Francis. Ever since those days of his Roman formation, Fr. Peter Damian's lens on Franciscan life—indeed his hermeneutic on Christ and the Church—can be summed in one word: *Bonaventure!*

Eventually Fr. Peter Damian was reassigned to the United States. In the early 1980s, while on the faculty at St. Anthony-on-Hudson Theological Seminary in Rensselaer, New York, Fr. Peter Damian undertook an intensive study of the writings of the newly canonized Conventual Franciscan martyr of Auschwitz, Saint Maximilian Kolbe. The impact of this Kolbean study proved incalculable. For Fr. Peter Damian, St. Maximilian's writings demonstrated the "golden thread" of Mary's coherent presence and continuing influence in the Franciscan tradition. St. Maximilian asserted that in the earliest days of the Order's foundation, in the intentions of St. Francis of Assisi himself, God was putting Mary Immaculate to work. Fr. Peter Damian grasped with a new clarity the coherent, consistent, unbroken axis of Marian ideals inherent in the Franciscan tradition, beginning with St. Francis and continuing through Bonaventure, Scotus, and the Franciscan School, all the way through Kolbe.

The key to this new synthesis of insight for Fr. Peter Damian was the Divine Will and Plan that Mary *qua* Immaculate—and thereby "spouse" of the Holy Spirit, and thereby "Virgin made Church"—would be God's chosen instrument for gathering the friars and their flocks to implement God's Plan for the Kingdom, building a Divine civilization of love. For Fr. Peter Damian, this was pure Bonaventure—seen all the more clearly when refracted through the Marian optic of Kolbe—who, by the way, was an alumnus of the same Pontifical Faculty of St. Bonaventure in Rome, which later educated Fr. Peter Damian.

Gradually Fr. Peter Damian's intellectual excitement about the link between Saints Francis, Bonaventure and this Marian-Franciscan synthesis of St. Maximilian Kolbe became more palpable. He even grew a beard. I recall visiting him in Rensselaer back in the 1980s with my parents. My Irish mother, never at a loss for words, remarked: "Father Peter, you look very distinguished with the beard." He chuckled and said to Mother in his deep baritone: "I bet you thought I looked like Saint Joseph." "No," said she, "You look like Saint Maximilian Kolbe!"

Following the Marian-Kolbean ideal within the Franciscan charism, Fr. Peter Damian discovered a new branch of Franciscans, the Friars of the Immaculate, who professed a fourth vow of Total Consecration to the Immaculate. The fourth vow would not disturb all of those Bonaventurian triads in Fr. Peter Damian's life. Perish the thought! Rather, he understood that the fourth vow would reinforce the first three by making explicit Mary's place in God's plan for the Franciscan Order and its mission of evangeliza-tion. With no prejudice or judgment towards those who freely chose not to take the fourth vow, he himself made a crucial decision. After many years of association with the Friars of the Immaculate, Fr. Peter Damian formally transferred into their jurisdiction in 1996.[1] At that moment, he explicitly offered himself to Our Lady, so that she could use his Franciscan memory, intellect and will wherever in the world God wanted him to be. The rest is history! We praise God and the Immaculate for letting him be an instrument of the Divine Plan. If St. Bonaventure is called the "Seraphic Doctor," and Blessed John Duns Scotus the "Subtle Doctor": perhaps we might unofficially confer on Fr. Peter Damian the title "Doctor Immacula-tus"—Immaculate Doctor!

Let me conclude with two Scripture quotations dear to our honoree: When Fr. Peter Damian teaches in a classroom or lectures from a podium, there is one verse from the Gospel of St. John which he very frequently quotes. In fact, I can never remember a single class of his without his repeating the phrase at least once: John 15:5—"Apart from me you can do nothing." Imbedded in Jesus' last supper discourse about the Vine and the Branches, these words of our Savior give summary to the vocation of Mary Immaculate in God's Plan, to the vocation of Francis of Assisi, the vocation of Bonaventure, the vocation of Maximilian Kolbe, and indeed to the vocation of Peter Damian Fehlner. All of these disciples realized that their works of charity could bear fruit only when grafted to Christ the Vine in his primacy.

As inevitable as it is that we shall often hear John 15:5 quoted in Fr. Peter Damian's theological disquisitions, there is another quote that you will nearly always hear in his homilies. In fact, I have never heard a single sermon of his without this other quote or its equivalent insinuating its way: 1 John 3:2—"We know that when Christ appears, we shall be like him, for we shall see him as he is." The finality, teleology, and goal of all our theological probings, spiritual yearnings, and apostolic endeavors ultimately leads to the beatific vision of God Himself, who is Good, All Good, Supreme Good.

We give thanks to you, Fr. Peter Damian, for being, like the Immacu-late herself, not just a PDF file, but a living *hodegetria*—pointing our way to the eternal vision of Christ, His Father, and Their Holy Spirit, gloriously overflowing with Divine goodness, now and forever. Amen.

---

1. Fr. Peter, since this paper's writing, has returned to the Conventual Franciscans.

Editors' Acknowledgments

THE EDITORS WOULD LIKE to acknowledge the essential role in bringing this *Festschrift* together of Fr. James McCurry, OFM Conv., Minister Provincial of the Province of Our Lady of Angels in the USA. His beautiful homage at the beginning of this volume brilliantly captures the "golden thread" running through the entirety of Fr. Peter Fehlner's life and work. Without his assistance this book would not have been published. We are grateful, too, for patience of Matthew Wimer, RaeAnne Harris, and others at Wipf and Stock as they awaited the completion of this volume. Above all, we are thankful to God for Fr. Peter Damian Fehlner who has inspired us.

Introduction

EDWARD J. ONDRAKO, OFM CONV.,

AND

J. ISAAC GOFF

IT HAS BECOME EVIDENT in the seventy years since the *Universal Declaration of Human Rights* (December 10, 1948) that the experience of freedom has been increasingly brought to the fore on a global scale. In 1945, Herman Fehlner began his formation as a Franciscan Conventual. As a novice, he assumed the religious name the Franciscans gave, Peter Damian. In 1957, he was ordained a Catholic priest in Rome and completed his doctoral studies in sacred theology at the Pontifical Faculty of St. Bonaventure, the Seraphicum, Rome, and, in 1965, published his dissertation: *The Role of Charity in the Ecclesiology of St. Bonaventure*. Ecclesiastical authorities immediately recognized his gifts and guided him on a journey as teacher, researcher, spiritual guide, mentor, and pastor. The Homage at the outset of this *Festscrift* by the Very Reverend James McCurry, OFM Conv., Minister Provincial of the Province of Our Lady of Angels in the USA, masterfully underscores high points in Fr. Fehlner's life.

The essays in this *Festschrift* fall into three main areas that touch upon the many profound contributions Fr. Fehlner has made. Group one is organized around creation, the dignity of the person, and ecclesiology. The essays in group two deal with Mariology and Pneumatology. Group three's essays seek to advance along scholarly avenues either suggested by or building upon Fr. Fehlner's theological efforts.

Fr. Fehlner engages the Marian Franciscan vision begun by St. Francis of Assisi through his theologian disciples, St. Bonaventure, Bl. John Duns Scotus, and St. Maximilian M. Kolbe. Of particular interest and remarkable originality is Fr. Fehlner's critical investigation of a unity of concern and larger agenda pointing to the Christology, metaphysical precision, and

theology of Bl. John Henry Newman and its commonalities with St. Bonaventure and Bl. Duns Scotus. Newman identified a "new" theology during his Anglican period and Fr. Fehlner carries his tone forward to how to
conduct the renewal of the Church, the "new" theology today.

The Church, the Dignity of the Person, and Creation

Arthur Calkins surveys Catholic magisterial teaching from 1854 to 2007
on the question of the so-called "Franciscan Thesis," which teaches that the
incarnation of Jesus Christ was planned or predestined by God, in a Marian
mode, in a manner that was ultimately unconditioned by sin's entry into the
world. In his engagement with Papal teaching on the question of the motive
for the Incarnation, Calkins interacts with the contributions of the towering
figures of Carlo Balić, OFM and Juniper Carol, OFM, arguing that Fr. Fehlner, in line with Balić and Carol, has done more than anyone else to present this key aspect of Franciscan Christology and Mariology to the present
generation. Calkins further contends that in the light of Fr. Fehlner's own
research and exposition of this theme, the "Franciscan Thesis" should not so
much be considered a unique position to Franciscans, but rather represents
a fundamental contribution of the Franciscan tradition to Christology and
Mariology that is best understood as a well-developed doctrinal conclusion
common to all Christians.

David Bentley Hart focuses his attention on the question of the relationship between love and knowledge, intellect and intentionality. Occasioned by his reading of Fr. Fehlner's lengthy essay on John Duns Scotus
and John Henry Newman, Hart situates his reflections in this volume
within his own larger project dealing with the metaphysics of the soul
and the philosophy of mind. Noting convergences and points of overlap
between Duns Scotus and the Eastern Patristic tradition, Hart addresses
the perennial, now reinvigorated, disagreements between Duns Scotus and
certain forms of Thomism on the order and relationship between intellect
and will, which naturally extend into profound questions touching upon
the transcendent finality of reason and the will, the human person as *capax
Dei*, and the relationship between nature and grace. Hart concludes that
Duns Scotus, among medieval systems or schools, preeminently offers resources to modern theologians and philosophers to recognize the final love
towards which intentionality and the will are ordered and to formulate an
account of rational philosophy that is logically coherent, consistent with
the phenomenological analysis of knowledge and answers problems that
have arisen in modern philosophy.

John Ford considers John Henry Newman's understanding of the assent of faith. Interacting with Fr. Fehlner's essay on Newman and Duns Scotus, Ford frames his discussion within the context of the new evangelization. Ford argues that Newman's approach at once emphasizes the uniquely personal aspect of belief as well as the manner in which believers and unbelievers share a great deal of common ground in the actual process of gathering and apprehending data, making inferences, and arriving at personal judgments about such information and the manner in which this concretely impacts their lives and decisions. Ford concludes that Newman, in his *Grammar of Assent*, offers both a theoretically insightful and pastorally adaptable analysis of the assent of faith. By offering a careful description of the process of assent, Ford argues, that Newman provides an effective framework, disclosing where the assent of faith, namely belief, can be derailed. Ford, in common with Fr. Fehlner, suggests that Newman's analysis highlights the *real* over the *notional* when it comes to evaluating complex realities such as assent and faith. Ford argues that, according to Newman, believers and non-believers have much in common and, thus, much room for irenic discussion in coming to grips with the process of assent. Ford, quoting Pope Francis, concludes: "realities are greater than ideas."

Jonathan Fleischmann discusses Fr. Fehlner's developing position on questions concerning origins and the debate over creationism versus evolutionism. Fleischmann argues that Fr. Fehlner's position must be understood as falling neither into the camp of fundamentalist creationism nor materialist evolutionism. Drawing upon Fr. Fehlner's writings, Fleischmann argues that both extremes, in terms of common metaphysical presuppositions, risk falling into forms of the common error of monergism, which, in the end, deny synergistic secondary causality. On the analogy between creation and re-creation, Fleischmann contends that Fr. Fehlner presents a balanced position that guards both God's goodness and initiative in creation and salvation, but also allows for true creaturely cooperation in the development and working out of the plan God has willed to be ultimately realized in and through Christ in a Marian mode and the unique operation of the Church, which redounds upon creation and draws all creation back to the Father in the Spirit.

Angelo Geiger believes that Fr. Fehlner has made an important contribution to the understanding of the relationship and role of Mary, considered as the Immaculate Conception, to the overall charism and mode of life of the Franciscan order, in general, and, especially, the intellectual component of the Franciscan vocation. Building upon St. Maximilian Kolbe's understanding that the dogma of the Immaculate Conception is not merely a truth to be believed, but, also, and more importantly, a reality to be integrated into the mind and hearts of all believers, Geiger argues that Fr. Fehlner presents a way of understanding the Franciscan way of life that carries over into the form of life of individual believers and the Church as a whole. Geiger shows how Fr. Fehlner articulates a manner in which to understand the need for Mary to act in the life of the Order and the Church and how through the integration of the Immaculate Conception into the entire life of Franciscans, one discovers the means to sanctify the intellect and thus carry out theological inquiry in order that individual friars, believers in general, and the Church as a whole might become good: like the Immaculate Mary.

Mary and the Holy Spirit

The essays in this second group interact with Fr. Fehlner's contributions to the theology of Mary and the Holy Spirit. Fr. Fehlner's contributions to the study of a Christian mode and Marian mode of theology and philosophy are extensive and continue to influence a devoted group of scholars and researchers, many of whom joined in honoring him at the University of Notre Dame in June 2015. For Fr. Fehlner, we cannot do theology except to the degree that we enter the economic Trinity in a Bonaventurian manner of *exitus* or going forth of all creatures from God, how this culminates with the Immaculate Conception, and through her the Incarnation, which initiates the return of all creation to the Father. In sum, theology, echoing St. Bonaventure, is pursued "that we might become good" (*ut boni fiamus*). In developing his own theological approach, Fr. Fehlner explicates as a contemporary disciple of Bonaventure and John Duns Scotus, Maximilian Kolbe, whose original contribution refers to Mary as the created Immaculate Conception and to the Holy Spirit as the uncreated Immaculate Conception.

A central idea of Fr. Fehlner's reflection and writing is Mary's divine maternity and its theological and philosophical implications. Robert Fastiggi argues that Fr. Fehlner's theology of Mary's divine maternity contains important and lasting contributions to the field of Mariology and "manifests a richness of spiritual insight and synthesis." In laying out Fr. Fehlner's treatment of this topic, Fastiggi points out the ways in which Fr. Fehlner links a proper and adequate understanding of Mary's maternity to other theological questions, such as her predestination to be the mother of God, the virginal conception of Christ, her own perpetual virginity and her Immaculate Conception. Fastiggi contends that Fr. Fehlner's multifaceted presentation of the divine maternity, integrating and ordering a wide range of Mariological questions, helps provide greater clarity and understanding of the central and integral role that Mary, as Mediatrix of Grace, plays in the context of the Church's sacramental and doctrinal mission. According to Fastiggi, Fr. Fehlner's presentation of the divine maternity helps explain why Catholic theology understands Mary as having a key part in the Eucharistic worship of the Church, and why Mary is seen as the spiritual mother and, thereby, teacher of all Christians.

John-Mark Miravalle focuses on Fr. Fehlner's reception and interpretation of the theology of Maximilian Kolbe concerning Mary's relation to the Holy Spirit. Miravalle notes how Kolbe's terminology and theological expressions often present difficulties for those unfamiliar (as well for some who are familiar) with the systematic distinctions present in the Franciscan spiritual and theological tradition—following Francis, Bonaventure and Duns Scotus—out of which Kolbe preached and wrote. Miravalle shows how Fr. Fehlner opens a way to understanding and receiving Kolbe in the light of Kolbe's Franciscan theological antecedents that unlocks many theological questions concerning Mary's relation to the Holy Spirit, Christ and the Church. Miravalle argues that, if rightly contextualized along the lines of Fr. Fehlner's exposition, Kolbe's insights and terminology are not inherently problematic, but rather communicate fundamental truths about God's plan of salvation as it pertains to Mary as the special locus in and through which the Holy Spirit manifests himself and operates.

Fr. Fehlner has been, at least for the past thirty years, one of the world's leading and most profound voices, articulating the theological and doctrinal rationale for understanding Mary's unique role in the economy of salvation as Coredemptrix and Mediatrix of All Graces. Fr. Fehlner has been unwavering in his support of these two doctrines and has given a great deal of his scholarly work to explaining and defending, in a Franciscan key, these two privileges of Mary as essential and logical out-workings of Christian belief and practice from its beginnings to the present. Gloria Dodd presents a bird's eye view of Fr. Fehlner's contributions to this topic. Dodd first wrestles with the difficulties in defining and applying the terms *coredemptrix* and *mediatrix* to Mary, and skillfully shows how the terms as defined by Fr. Fehlner, do not derogate from the uniqueness of Christ as redeemer nor from the Holy Spirit as the source of grace. Next, Dodd, in scholastic fashion presents Fr. Fehlner's main arguments in favor, followed by objections against his position and then Fr. Fehlner's own replies. Through the course of her essay Dodd's purpose is to note the strength and coherence of Fr. Fehlner's position. However, Dodd offers constructive critiques to Fr. Fehlner in relation to her understanding of competing schools of thought. Dodd concludes with a recognition of Fr. Fehlner's importance for current and future Mariological discussion and research, noting the impact he has already made as well as the importance of his use and development of the concepts of "liberative redemption" and "liberative mediation" that could further clarify the proper understanding and use of the term *coredemption* and the title *Mediatrix of All Graces* with respect to Mary in her cooperation with her Son for the salvation of the world. Fr. Fehlner, in reply to Dodd's paper, understood her line of reasoning and was able to reply to her criticisms and suggested several further avenues of research on this topic.

The final essay in the second group is thematically related to the first three under the strikingly original banner of Fr. Fehlner's rediscovery and articulation of a "Marian Metaphysics." While Fastiggi, Miravalle and Dodd, pinpoint and discuss specific, yet interrelated topics of Mariology, J. Isaac Goff addresses Fr. Fehlner's theological metaphysics—emphasizing the person and exemplarity—which informs all of his theological and philosophical speculation, writing, and teaching. Clearly present in the first stages of Fr. Fehlner's career, a developing thought form was planted early on that sought to articulate an integrated wisdom in terms of the theology of the Trinity, Christology, and Ecclesiology. This project has borne fruit in what Fr. Fehlner himself has termed a "Marian Metaphysics." While some might consider this title exotic, Fr. Fehlner, as Goff shows, contends that his understanding of Marian Metaphysics is simply the logical fruit of a consistent understanding of perennial Catholic teaching on Mary's central role in the economy of salvation. Mary, in different modalities, is seen as essential in the process of creation and salvation that begins in the Trinity itself, reaches a terminus in the Incarnation and sacrifice of her Son through the power of the Holy Spirit, and through the Spirit-filled Church draws all creation through the Son back to the Father in the unity of the Holy Spirit. Goff shows how, for Fr. Fehlner, Mary, through her free acceptance and cooperation with God, has a privileged and unique role in both effecting this order of salvation and in aiding our coming to a proper understanding of the development and perfection of creation and re-creation in terms of the absolute goodness of God, the divine will in predestining the grace of the primacy of Jesus Christ in the Incarnation and its divinely-willed Marian Mode in each stage of development and recapitulation.

Scholarly Explorations in the Spirit
of Fr. Peter Damian Fehlner

The essays in group three open upon many further dimensions of the vast field of research and creative theological imagination that have sound guidance in method and content from Fr. Fehlner. Always respecting a scholar's exercise of freedom, Fr. Fehlner exemplifies and constructs his ideas for renewal, as did Newman, based on continuity with tradition and the conviction that a theological or philosophical insight to be new must first be old, as St. Augustine's *Beauty* that is the Lord, ever ancient and ever new. Moreover, Fr. Fehlner qualifies that God is known, not directly as the subject of a science called theology, but as a conclusion of a study known as metaphysics or ontology whose object is simply being as common to all that exists. John Henry Newman's seven notes about true development of doctrine have massive importance for Fr. Fehlner. These developmental principles include: preservation of its type; continuity of its principles; its assimilative power; its logical sequence; anticipation of its future; conservative action on its past; and its chronic vigor. In a word, Fr. Fehlner has been prayerfully attentive all of these Newmanian principles, which underscores the axiom: to alter the type is to change the type.

Jeremy Daggett offers an exposition of John Duns Scotus' argument for the existence of God that complements Allan Wolter's magnificent treatment of the subject in his translation and commentary on the *De primo principio*. Daggett contends that Duns Scotus' argument takes the most important, yet disparate, demonstrations from his predecessors for the necessary being of God as infinite, and weaves them together into a single metaphysical proof that transcends and strengthens many of the weak points of earlier attempts. In the process of his presentation of Duns Scotus, Daggett also provides illuminating rebuttals to more recent objections to Duns Scotus argument. Daggett contends that Duns Scotus' use of essentially ordered causality as distinct from accidentally ordered causes, when applied to the analysis of the notion of efficiency, finality and eminence, provides a powerful and convincing inference to a God that is absolutely one, intellectual, volitional and infinite in every way.

Christiaan Kappes's contribution builds on his monograph *Why Thomas Aquinas Denied, While John Duns Scotus, Gregory Palamas, and Mark Eugenicus Professed the Absolute Immaculate Existence of Mary*. What is not generally known is that Fr. Peter Damian Fehlner acted as an advisor, if not a supervisor, of Kappes's thesis during each stage of its writing. In honor of Fr. Fehlner, Kappes's contribution expands Fr. Fehlner's fundamental insight that the Immaculate Conception, albeit by means of other methodologies and modes, was present in both the East and the West in the first millennium. Taking to heart his reading of the Fehlnerian corpus, this study that manages to show exactly the points at which a Marian bridge was established between the Greek speaking and Latin speaking portions of the Roman empire. So much is it the case that a common Marian heritage compenetrated both environs that Kappes has located the famous ecclesiastics of history and shown that Gregory the Theologian was properly and beneficially translated and engaged by famous Latins of the Late Roman Empire, such as Rufinus and Augustine. What is more, when John Cassian's and Leo Magnus's writing are read in continuity with their unnamed sources that Kappes has uncovered it becomes plainly obvious that their development of phraseology and theology marked an attempt plainly to overcome Augustine's misconceptions of what is likely an imperfect read of Gregory the Theologian's doctrine of Mary immaculate. Augustine was absorbed into the works, whether directly or indirectly, of Sophronius of Jerusalem and Maximus Confessor, who developed Mary's title of "prepurified" into a more explicit notion of "Mary immaculate." The tradition of linking Mary's immaculate flesh to her description as "purified" was carried on by their successor Theodore of Tarsus, who as archbishop of Canterbury clearly established the doctrine of the purified virgin in the Canterbury school of theology. Elsewhere, papal promotion of Lateran 649 and preparation for Constantinople III led not a few popes to promote Mary's aforementioned titles in not only England, but even in Spain. Thus, Gregory the Theologian's defense of Mary's all-holiness reached the far side of the empire by the seventh century. As Kappes shows, this provided the foundation for an explicitly theological defense of what is clearly Mary's conception in Anna's womb as something entirely immaculate by the seventh century in Byzantium and by the ninth century in Latindom. John Damascene and Paschasius Radbertus marked the culmination of Mariology by defending Mary's untainted conception in utero by recourse to her status as a "prepurified virgin," otherwise known as Mary immaculate. The implications of Kappes's study clearly require a rewriting of the narrative of Immaculate Conception in the first millennium of the Catholic Church. Furthermore, they cause one to question whether or not traces of this doctrine survived in the Latin Church in the second millennium before Scholastic culture of the universities by and large contested the feast of Mary's conception since it presented a puzzle to them in how to reconcile the universal curse of original sin with Mary's natural mode of conception.

T. Alexander Giltner, following a suspicion Fr. Fehlner has long held, provides what he has called a "think-piece" in which he explores not merely possible, but very likely lines of influence linking the Carolingian theological master and translator, John Scottus Eriugena, to St. Bonaventure. Giltner argues that an Eriugenian inspiration is present in Bonaventure, not only as a main source for Bonaventure of translations of Greek Patristic texts and ideas, but also, and more interestingly for Giltner, Eriugena likely stands behind thought patterns and conceptual structures emblematic of the Seraphic Doctor. Giltner explores the likelihood that Bonaventure's famous "cosmic exemplarism" goes beyond the recognized Bonaventurian sources,

East and West, and notes the similarity between Bonaventure's position and that of Maximus the Confessor. Bonaventure, Giltner notes, never explicitly cites Maximus on such points. However, Bonaventure (almost) certainly knew key texts of Eriugena wherein Eriugena interacted a great deal with Eastern Patristic sources, including Maximus, which shaped Eriugena's own metaphysics of Christic exemplarism. If this supposition is correct, Giltner thinks many questions that have appeared to divide East and West could be further resolved. Bonaventure's excellent understanding of both Greek and Latin theological and metaphysical positions, if properly understood, have massive purchase for future research and ecumenical dialogue between Eastern and Western Christians.

Fr. Fehlner, like many of his Franciscan forebears over the past three hundred or so years, has had a longstanding interest in the life and writings of Sor María de Jesús de Ágreda (†1665). Fr. Fehlner has publicized his favorable stance towards Sor María through his work in translating from Spanish into England some of the more important scholarly works in defense of Sor María and in various lectures and talks over the years. Sor María is famous for reports of bilocating from her convent in Spain to the American Southwest in order to evangelize the native peoples. Such reports alone would be enough to establish a lasting reputation for most historical figures.

However, Sor María is also known for her massive *Mística ciudad de Dios* (*Mystical City of God*), which purports to be a kind of spiritual biography of Mary, dictated to Sor María by the Blessed Virgin herself. It is this work that has spurred the greatest controversy surrounding María de Ágreda. Early on disputes arose between Thomists and Scotists over the very strong Scotistic presentation Sor María provides, putatively under the direct guidance of Mary. Related to theological turf wars between competing schools, many criticized Sor María and the work as a forgery concocted by Scotist theologians and confessors of Sor María, who were using the less educated Sor María as a mouthpiece for their theological agenda. Trent Pomplun uses historical-theological scholarship and provides English speaking readers with an evocative treatment of questions pertaining to the influences and sources behind Sor María's *Mystical City of God* and heretofore vexing questions over its authenticity. As a result of his careful analysis of primary and secondary literature, Pomplun contends that the arrangement, technical precision, and clarity of Sor María's writings are truly her own. Although she was influenced by Scotistic theologians, Pomplun shows how Sor María manifests a unique theological creativity and genius.

Wayne Hellmann's essay serves as a fitting final contribution to this *Festschrift*. Hellmann turns our attention back to Fehlner's early work on the place of charity in the life of the Church. In developing and applying insights from Fehlner's 1965, *The Role of Charity in the Ecclesiology of St. Bonaventure*, to the question of the Eucharist, Hellmann argues that, if, as Fehlner has shown, for Bonaventure, charity is the radical principle of unity in the Church, it is by prayerful participation in the Eucharist that this Charity is most fully manifested and accomplished. Hellmann concludes: "Eucharist takes us to the heart of an ecclesiology of charity. It is where the ecclesiology of charity is fully realized and thus the 'realization of salvation itself.'"

Conclusion

To those who met at the University of Notre Dame in June 2015, to his readers, and to those who know and love him, Fr. Fehlner's appropriation of Franciscan theology since Vatican II is uncontested. We have come to see that he has followed faithfully St. Bonaventure: theology begins where philosophy leaves off. He has kept sacred his vocation of being entrusted with the Christian intellectual formation of youth and those seeking Christ the one Teacher of All. With Bl. John Duns Scotus, he knows the importance of the disjunctive transcendentals and the problem of collapsing the infinite into the finite, making the Creator and creature equal. With St. Maximilian Kolbe, he radiates the discovery of the basis for genuine metaphysics and dogmatic theology in the contemplation of Mary and her intellectual and affective humility. Finally, with Bl. John Henry Newman, he is convicted: God is the *summum bonum* in itself, rather than for us. With St. Francis of Assisi, our primary relation to the Trinity is praise.

That is why, in time, we, Fr. Fehlner's theologian disciples, are confident that he will be recognized as carrying the Franciscan torch further in perfect fidelity to the initial insights and inspirations of St. Francis of Assisi and to the correct understanding and interpretation of St. Bonaventure, Bl. John Duns Scotus, St. Maximilian Kolbe and the trajectory of the Franciscan Order in the service of the irreplaceable Vatican II.

The Writings of Peter Damian Fehlner, FI/OFM Conv. (1960–2018)

Books (Monographs, Translations, Edited Volumes, and Journals)

Bl. John Duns Scotus and His Mariology: Commemoration of the Seventh Centenary of His Death: Acts of the Symposium on Scotus' Mariology, Grey College, Durham—England. Ed. Peter Damian Fehlner. New Bedford: Academy of the Immaculate, 2009.

Bonaventure of Bagnoregio. *The Triple Way.* Trans. Peter Damian Fehlner. New Bedford: Academy of the Immaculate, 2012.

Domanski, Jerzy. *For the Life of the World: St. Maximilian and the Eucharist.* Trans. Peter Damian Fehlner. New Bedford: Academy of the Immaculate, 1999.

Kolbe, Saint Maximilian. *Roman Conferences of St. Maximilian M. Kolbe.* Trans. Peter Damian Fehlner. New Bedford: Academy of the Immaculate, 2004.

Llamas Martinez, Enrique. *Venerable Mother of Agreda and the Mariology of Vatican II.* Trans. Peter Damian Fehlner. New Bedford: Academy of the Immaculate, 2006

Manelli, Stefano. *All Generations Shall Call Me Blessed.* 2nd edition. Trans. Peter Damian Fehlner. New Bedford: Academy of the Immaculate, 2005.

Mariological Studies in Honor of Our Lady of Guadalupe—1. Ed. Peter Damian Fehlner. New Bedford: Academy of the Immaculate, 2013.

Mariological Studies in Honor of Our Lady of Guadalupe—3. Ed. Peter Damian Fehler. New Bedford: Academy of the Immaculate, 2016

Mary at the Foot of the Cross—I: Millennium with Mary. Ed. Peter Damian Fehlner. New Bedford: Academy of the Immaculate, 2000.

Mary at the Foot of the Cross—II: Marian Coredemption. Ed. Peter Damian Fehlner. New Bedford: Academy of the Immaculate, 2002.

Mary at the Foot of the Cross—III: Maria, Mater Unitatis. Ed. Peter Damian Fehlner. New Bedford: Academy of the Immaculate, 2003.

Mary at the Foot of the Cross—IV: Mater Viventium (Gen. 3, 20). Ed. Peter Damian Fehlner. New Bedford: Academy of the Immaculate, 2004.

Mary at the Foot of the Cross—V: Redemption and Coredemption Under the Sign of the Immaculate Conception. Ed. Peter Damian Fehlner. New Bedford: Academy of the Immaculate, 2005.

Mary at the Foot of the Cross—VI: Marian Coredemption in the Eucharistic Mystery. Ed. Peter Damian Fehlner. New Bedford: Academy of the Immaculate, 2007.

Mary at the Foot of the Cross—VII: Coredemptrix, Therefore Mediatrix of All Graces. Ed. Peter Damian Fehlner. New Bedford: Academy of the Immaculate, 2008.

Mary at the Foot of the Cross—VIII: Coredemption as Key to a Correct Understanding of Redemption. Ed. Peter Damian Fehlner. New Bedford: Academy of the Immaculate, 2008.

Mary at the Foot of the Cross—IX: Mary: Spouse of the Holy Spirit, Coredemptrix and Mother of the Church. Ed. Peter Damian Fehlner. New Bedford: Academy of the Immacuate, 2010.

Miles Immaculatae: Rivista di Cultura Mariana e di Formazione Kolbiana. Ed. Peter Damian Fehlner (1985–1989).

Quaderni di studi Scotisti. Ed. Peter Damian Fehlner (2004–2012).

Rosini, Ruggero. *Mariology of Blessed John Duns Scotus.* Trans. Peter Damian Fehlner. New Bedford: Academy of the Immaculate, 2008.

Ruotolo, Dolindo. *Come, O Holy Spirit.* Trans. Peter Damian Fehlner. New Bedford: Academy of the Immaculate, 2007.

Schneider, Johannes. *Virgo Ecclesia Facta: The Presence of Mary in the Crucifix of San Damiano and in the Office of the Passion of St. Francis of Assisi.* Trans. Peter Damian Fehlner. New Bedford: Academy of the Immaculate, 2004.

St. Maximilian Kolbe, Martyr of Charity: Pneumatologist. New Bedford: Academy of the Immaculate, 2004.

The Role of Charity in the Ecclesiology of St. Bonaventure. Rome: Editrice "Miscellanea Francescana," 1965.

The Theologian of Auschwitz: St. Maximilian M. Kolbe on the Immaculate Conception in the Life of the Church. Forthcoming.

Thomas Aquinas. *Aquinas On Reasons for Our Faith Against the Muslims, Greeks and Armenians.* Trans. Peter Damian Fehlner. New Bedford: Academy of the Immaculate, 2002.

Articles (listed by ascending date)

1960

"Teilhard de Chardin: Ambiguity by Design." *Homiletic and Pastoral Review* 50 (May 1960) 709–17.

"Exchange on Teilhard de Chardin: Pro/Con." With Robert Francoeur. *Homiletic and Pastoral Review* 50 (October 1960) 34–47.

1961

Response to Owen Bennett, OFM Conv., "The Point of Departure of Metaphysics According to Gabriel Marcel." *Inter-Province Conference of the Friars Minor Conventual: Report of the Thirteenth Annual Meeting* 13 (1961) 89–91.

"Theology at the Service of Piety." *Inter-Province Conference of the Friars Minor Conventual: Report of the Fourteenth Annual Meeting* 12 (1961) 69–85.

1964

Review Essay of *De Scriptura et Traditione*. *Miscellanea Francescana* 64 (1964) 103–19.

1965

"Mary, Mother of the Church according to the 'Constitutio De Ecclesia.'" In *Miles Immaculatae* 1 (1965) 31–39.
"Person und Gnade nach Johannes Duns Scotus." *Wissenschaft und Weisheit* 28 (1965) 15–39.

1966

"Poverty in Christ—A Christian Sign." *The Role of Religious in the Church Today: Report of the 47th Annual Meeting of the Franciscan Education Conference, vol. XCVII*, 147–92. Burlington, WI: Franciscan Educational Conference, 1966.

1969

"The New Constitutions—Chapter One: On the Life of the Franciscan Brotherhood: Introduction and Commentary." *Inter-Province Conference of the Friars Minor Conventual: Report of the Fourteenth Annual Meeting* (1969).

1974

Foreword to Bonaventure, *Rooted in Faith: Homilies to a Contemporary World*. Translated by Marigwen Schumacher, ix–xv. Chicago: Franciscan Herald, 1974.

1975

"Bonaventure and Contemporary Thought: Comments on the Convocation Address of Ewert H. Cousins." *Cord* 24/4 (1975) 99–102.

1981

"Meditations." *Francis: St. Francis of Assisi–Eighth Centenary*, October 1981–June 1982.
"Maria nella Tradizione Francescana: 'la Vergine Fatta Chiesa.'" *Miles Immaculatae* 17 (1981) 180–98.

1982

"Community, Prayer and Apostolated in the Conventual Tradition." *Inter-Province Conference of the Friars Minor Conventual: Report of the Annual Meeting* 29 (1979) 34–54.

"Consacrazione totale, battesimo e ideale francescano." *Miles Immaculatae* 18 (1982) 60–92.

"Life in the Spirit and Mary." *Cord* 32/10 (1982) 301–6.

"Our Lady and St. Francis." *Cord* 32/5 (1982) 142–47.

"Saint Francis and Mary Immaculate." *Miscellanea Francescana* 82 (1982) 502–19.

"Vir Catholicus Et Totus Apostolicus: St. Francis and the Church." *Inter-Province Conference: Conventual Franciscans, USA* (1982).

1983

"The Conventual Ideal and Franciscanism," *Cord* 33/8 (1983) 225–26, 256.

Review article of Hans Urs von Balthasar, *First Glance at Adrienne von Speyr*, in *Faith and Reason* 9 (1983) 69–75.

1984

"St. John Neumann C.S.S.R and the Friars Minor Conventual in the U.S.A.: A Critical Edition of Eight Letters." *Miscellanea Francescana* 84 (1984) 317–29.

"Una tesi di S. Massimiliano su S. Francesco e l'Immacolata alla luce della ricerca recente." *Miles Immaculatae* 20 (1984) 165–86.

1985

"The Immaculate and the Mystery of the Trinity in the Thought of St. Maximilian Kolbe." *Miscellanea Francescana* 85 (1985) 382–416.

"Complementum Ss. Trinitatis." In *Miles Immaculatae* 21 (1985) 177–204.

"Healing an Ancient Schism: Theological Reflections." *Social Justice Review* (September–October 1985) 148–53.

"Mary in the Franciscan Tradition: 'The Virgin Made Church.'" *Civitas Immaculatae* 1 (March 1985) 1–18.

"Niepokalanow in the Counsels of the Immaculate." *Miles Immaculatae* 21(1985) 309–81.

"The Immaculate and the Mystery of the Trinity in the Thought of S. Maximilian Kolbe." *Miscellanea Francescana* 85 (1985) 382–416.

"Vertex Creationis. St. Maximilian and Evolution." *Miles Immaculatae* 21 (1985) 236–59.

1986

"Hereditas Kolbiana: Novus Impetus Influxus Mariae Immaculatae in Ordinis Spiritualitate." *Capitulum Generale Extraordinarium* 7 (February 1986) 1–17.

"The Immaculate and the Extraordinary Synod 1985." *Miles Immaculatae* 22 (1986) 1–4.

"St. Francis Anthony Fasani of Lucera and the Mystery of the Immaculate." *Civitas Immaculatae* 4 (March 1986) 4–35.

1987

"La Marologia di San Francesco Antonio Fasani nel 'Mariale' e nelle '7 Novene Mariale.'" In *San Francesco Antonio Fasani, Le 7 Novene Mariane*, edited by Francesco Costa, 265–304. Padua: Edizione Messagerro Padova, 1987.

"Madre del Redentore i Redemptoris Mater." *Miles Immaculatae* 23 (1987) 223–38.

"Thesis of St. Maximilian Concerning St. Francis and the Immaculate in the Light of Recent Research." *Civitas Immaculatae* 6 (August 1987) 1–23.

1988

"A Proposal." *Miles Immaculatae* 24 (1988) 16–18.

"Geografia mariana della fede prospettive Kolbiane." *Miles Immaculatae* 24 (1988) 259–63.

"In the Beginning." *Christ to the World* 33 (1988) 56–72; 150-64; 237–48.

"Kolbe, Maximilian. 1894–1941." In *Marienlexikon*, 3:600-601. Archabbey St. Ottilien, EOS, 1988.

"Marian Geography of Faith, the Kolbian Perspective." *Miles Immaculatae* 24 (1988) 264–67.

"Marian Slavery. Slavery of love." *Miles Immaculatae* 24 (1988) 10–15.

"Schiavitù mariana. Schiavitù d'amore." *Miles Immaculatae* 24 (1988) 1–6.

"The Other Page." *Miles Immaculatae* 24 (1988) 512–31.

"Unaproposta." *Miles Immaculatae* 24 (1988) 7–9.

1989

"'*Miles Immaculatae*' dopo il primo congresso internazionale Kolbiano: 19-5-1989." *Miles Immaculatae* 25 (1989) 290–324.

"Mulieris Dignitatem." *Miles Immaculatae* 25 (1989) 1–9.

"The Immaculate Conception: Outer Limits of Love." *Miles Immaculatae* 25 (1989) 537–48.

1991

"Marian Doctrine and Devotion: A Kolbian Perspective." In *De cultu mariano saeeulis XIX-XX*, 4:303–21. Rome: Pontificia Academia Mariana Internationalis, 1991.

1992

"Fr. Juniper Carol: His Mariological and Scholarly Achievement." *Marian Studies* 43 (1992) 17–59.

1996

"A Chaste and Celibate Priesthood Is an Apostolic Tradition." *Christ to the World* 41 (August 1996) 202–7.

"Immaculata Mediatrix—Toward a Dogmatic Definition of the Coredemption." In *Mary Coredemptrix, Mediatrix, Advocate: Theological Foundations II: Papal, Pneumatological,* Ecumenical, edited by Mark Miravalle, 259–329. Santa Barbara: Queenship, 1996.

"Maria SS.ma e la verginità nel parto." *Corredemptrix: Annali mariani, santuario dell'Addolorata, Castelpetroso* 1 (1995) 73–97.

"Sense Knowledge and Error." *Christ to the World* 61 (October 1996) 291.

1997

"Jesus, Peter and the Keys." *Christ to the World* 42 (June 1997) 125.

"On Practical Zeal for True Faith." *Christ to the World* 42 (August 1997) 280–88.

"Rehabilitation in the True Faith." *Christ to the World* 42 (October 1997) 344–52.

"Reflections on the Life of St. Francis in a Marian Key." In *Virgo facta Ecclesia: The Life and Charism of St. Francis of Assisi,* 87–171. New Bedford: Academy of the Immaculate, 1997.

"A Special Providence for Winning, Keeping God's Friendship." With Alphonsus M. Sutton. *Christ to the World* 42 (February 1997) 57–69.

"The Truth about Mary." *Christ to the World* 42 (August 1997) 233–34.

1998

"Current Errors and Their Refutation : Difficulties about Penance and Related Matters." *Christ to the World* 43 (December 1998) 445–50.

"A Review of Moral Theology and Canon Law." With Alphonsus M. Sutton. *Christ to the World* 43 (October 1998) 356–63.

1999

"Current Errors and Their Refutation: Cooperation in Sacrilege." *Christ to the World* 44 (June 1999) 154–68.

"Current Errors and Their Refutation : Population Control vs Divine Revelation." *Christ to the World* 44 (December 1999) 442–56.

"Mensura Christi Maria." In *Maria Corredentrice: Storia e Theologia II: Scuola Francescana,* 9–16. Frigento: Casa Mariana Editrice, 1999.

"Il mistero della Corredenzione secondo il dottore serafico san Bonaventura." In *Maria Corredentrice: Storia e Theologia II: Scuola Francescana,* 11–91. Frigento: Casa Mariana, 1999.

2000

"The Case for Mary as Coredemptress." *Christ to the World* 45 (February 2000) 78–81.

"The Sense of Marian Coredemption in St. Bonaventure and Bl. John Duns Scotus." In *Mary at the Foot of the Cross–I*, 103–18. New Bedford: Academy of the Immaculate, 2000.

2001

"De metaphysica mariana quaedam." *Immaculata Mediatrix* 1/2 (2001) 13–42.
"Mater et magistra apostolorum." *Immaculata Mediatrix* 1/1 (2001) 15–95.
"Scientia et pietas." *Immaculata Mediatrix* 1/3 (2001) 11–48.

2002

"The Divine Primacy of the Bishop of Rome and Modern Eastern Orthodoxy." *Christ to the World* 47/5 (October 2002) 378.
Introduction to *Mary at the Foot of the Cross–II*, viii–xxiii. New Bedford: Academy of the Immaculate, 2002.
"Io sono l'Immacolata Concezione: adhuc quaedam de metaphysica mariana." *Immaculata mediatrix* 2 (2002) 15–41.
"Mary Coredemptrix: Doctrinal Issues Today." *Christ to the World* 47/2–3 (June 2002) 186.
"Miles Immaculatae." *Immaculata Mediatrix* 2 (2002) 105–17.
"Virginitas in partu." *Immaculata Mediatrix* 2 (2002) 241–46.

2003

"Mater Unitatis." In *Mary at the Foot of the Cross–III*, 1–24. New Bedford: Academamy of the Immaculate, 2003.

2004

"Bibliografia mariana-bonaventuriana." *Immaculata Mediatrix* 4 (2004) 241–56.
"Communicatio in Sacris." *Christ to the World* 49 (August 2004) 360–64.
"Communicatio in Sacris." *Christ to the World* 49 (October 2004) 454–63.
"Il discorsi mariani di san Bonaventura." *Immaculata Mediatrix* 4 (2004) 17–65.
"Immaculate to Be Coredemptrix." *Christ to the World* 49 (December 2004) 524–29.
Introduction to St. Maximilian Kolbe, *Roman Conferences of St. Maximilian M. Kolbe*, iii–viii. New Bedford: Academy of the Immaculate, 2004.
"Maria Coredemptrix–Mater Viventium (Gen 3, 20)." In *Mary at the Foot of the Cross–IV*, 1–16. New Bedford: Academy of the Immaculate, 2004.

2005

Introduction to Caroli Francisci de Varesio, *Promptuarium Scoticum: Scripta Scotistica Antiqua*, i–vi. Frigento: Casa Mariana Editrice, 2005.

"Mariae Advocatae Causa: The Marian Issue in the Church Today." In *Maria "Unica Cooperatrice alla Redenzione,"* 529–78. New Bedford: Academy of the Immaculate, 2005.

"Mary and the Eucharist in St. Bonaventure." *Immaculata Mediatrix* 5 (2005) 311–38.

"Opening Address—Symposium 2004." In *Mary at the Foot of the Cross V*, v–xvi. New Bedford: Academy of the Immaculate, 2005.

"Redemption, Metaphysics and the Immaculate Conception." In *Mary at the Foot of the Cross–V*, 187–262. New Bedford: Academy of the Immaculate, 2005.

"Theistic Evolution or Special Creation." *Christ to the World* 50 (June 2005) 243–53.

"Theistic Evolution or Special Creation." *Christ to the World* 50 (August 2005) 329–40.

"Theistic Evolution or Special Creation." *Christ to the World* 50 (October 2005) 427–37.

2006

Foreword to Beato Giovanni Duns Scoto, *Prologo dell'Ordinatio*, i–xiii. Frigento: Casa Mariana Editrice, 2006.

"Marian Minimalism on Coredemption: Marie corédemptrice?: débat sur un titre marial controverse." *Immaculata mediatrix* 6 (2006) 397–420.

"Neo-patripassionism From a Scotistic Viewpoint." *Quaderni di studi Scotisti* 3 (2006) 35–96.

"Pope Benedict XVI on Intelligent Design." *Christ to the World* 51 (February 2006) 55–60.

2007

"Angelus Domini: 14 October 2007." *Missio Immaculatae* 1 (January 2008) 5–6.

"The Dual Fiat." *Missio Immaculatae* 5 (June 2007) 5–6.

"Frei Anthony of St. Anne Galvao: a Marian-Franciscan Saint, Part 1." *Missio Immaculatae* 8 (October 2007) 5–6.

"Frei Anthony of St. Anne Galvao: a Marian-Franciscan Saint, Part 2." *Missio Immaculatae* 9 (November 2007) 5–6.

"Frei Anthony of St. Anne Galvao: a Marian-Franciscan Saint, Part 3." *Missio Immaculatae* 10 (December 2007) 5–6.

"The Marian Principle of the Church: Pope Benedict XVI on Mary." *Missio Immaculatae* 1 (January 2007) 6–7.

"Mary: Bridal Chamber of the Espousal of the Christ and the Church: Pope Benedict XVI on Mary." *Missio Immaculatae* 2 (February–March 2007) 7–8.

"Nostra Signora d'America." *Immaculata Mediatrix* 7 (2007) 270–81.

Opening Address in *Mary at the Foot of the Cross–VI*, 1–9. New Bedford: Academy of the Immaculate, 2007.

"Predestined by One and the Same Decree, Part 1." *Missio Immaculatae* 3 (April 2007) 5–6.

"Predestined by One and the Same Decree, Part 2." *Missio Immaculatae* 4 (May 2007) 4–5.

"The Two Great Marian-Christological Councils: Part 1: Ephesus." *Missio Immaculatae* 6 (July–August 2007) 7–9.

"The Two Great Marian-Christological Councils: Part 2: Chalcedon." *Missio Immaculatae* 7 (September 2007) 7–9.

2008

Appendix to Rugero Rosini, *Mariology of Blessed John Duns Scotus*, 255–83. New Bedford: Academy of the Immaculate, 2008.

"The Concept of Redemption in the Franciscan-Scotistic School: Salvation, Redemption, and the Primacy of Christ." With Alessandro Apollonio. In *Mary at the Foot of the Cross–VIII*, 111–56. New Bedford: Academy of the Immaculate, 2008.

"De Deo Uno et Trino ad mentem Caroli Rahner." In *Karl Rahner.Un'analisi critica: Le figure, l'opera e la recensione: Teologia di Karl Rahner (1904–1984)*, edited by Serafino Lanzetta, 73–161. Siena: Cantagalli, 2009.

"The Franciscan Mariological School and the Coredemptive Movement." *Marian Studies* 59 (2008) 59–88.

"Mary's Vow of Virginity." *Missio Immaculatae* 2 (February 2008) 4–5.

"Opening Address in *Mary at the Foot of the Cross–VIII*, 1–14. New Bedford Academy of the Immaculate, 2008.

"Pope Benedict XVI on Lourdes and Marian Mediation." *Missio Immaculatae* 6 (June–July 2008) 7–8.

"The Predestination of the Virgin Mother and Her Immaculate Conception." In *Mariology: A Guide for Priests, Deacons, Seminarians, and Consecrated Persons*, edited by Mark Miravalle, 213–76. Goleta: Queenship, 2008.

"The Richest of the People Seek Thy Smile (Ps 44, 13)." *Missio Immaculatae* 8 (October 2008) 7–8.

"Santa Chiara: Dei Matris vestigium : (Legenda S. Clarae, prol.)." *Immaculata Mediatrix* 8 (2008) 321–46.

"The Virginal Marriage of Mary and Joseph, Part 1." *Missio Immaculatae* 4 (April 2008) 5–6.

"The Virginal Marriage of Mary and Joseph, Part 2." *Missio Immaculatae* 5 (May 2008) 6–7.

"The Vow of Virginity and the Immaculate Conception." *Missio Immaculatae* 3 (March 2008) 5–7.

2009

"The Great Sign (Apoc 12:1)—The Virginal Maternity and Maternal Virginity of Mary's Virginity: Before, During and After Childbirth." *Missio Immaculatae* 1 (January–February 2009) 4–5.

"The Great Sign (Apoc 12:1)—The Virginal Maternity and Maternal Virginity of Mary: Fitting Sign of God and Salvation, Part 1." *Missio Immaculatae* 2 (March–April 2009) 8–9.

"The Great Sign (Apoc 12:1)—The Virginal Maternity and Maternal Virginity of Mary: Mary's Virginity: God's Gift and a Pledge of Eternal Glory." *Missio Immaculatae* 3 (May–June 2009) 8–10.

"The Great Sign (Apoc 12:1)—The Virginal Maternity and Maternal Virginity of Mary: The Dawn of Salvation Herald of the Savior." *Missio Immaculatae* 4 (July–August 2009) 8–10.

"The Great Sign (Apoc 12:1)—The Virginal Maternity and Maternal Virginity of Mary: Mother in the Order of Grace." *Missio Immaculatae* 5 (September–October 2009) 7–8.

"The Great Sign (Apoc 12:1)—The Virginal Maternity and Maternal Virginity of Mary: Mother in the Order of Grace." *Missio Immaculatae* 6 (November–December 2009) 4–5.

Opening Address in *Bl. John Duns Scotus and His Mariology: Commemoration of the Seventh Centenary of His Death, Acts of the Symposium on Scotus' Mariology, Grey College, Durham–England*, edited by Peter, D. M. Fehlner, 13–17. New Bedford: Academy of the Immaculate, 2009.

"Sources of Scotus' Mariology in Tradition." In *Bl. John Duns Scotus and His Mariology: Commemoration of the Seventh Centenary of His Death, Acts of the Symposium on Scotus' Mariology, Grey College, Durham–England*, edited by Peter D. M. Fehlner, 235–94. New Bedford: Academy of the Immaculate, 2009.

2010

Concluding Reflections in *Mary at the Foot of the Cross–IX*, 521–25. New Bedford: Academy of the Immaculate, 2010.

"The Magisterium of the Immaculate: Ad Jesum per Mariam." *Missio Immaculatae* 1–2 (January–April 2010) 7–8.

"The Magisterium of the Immaculate: The Singer of Charity." *Missio Immaculatae* 3 (May–June 2010) 6–7.

"The Magisterium of the Immaculate: The Kindness and Humanity of God." *Missio Immaculatae* 4–5 (July–October 2010) 6–7.

"Marian Magisterium: The Faith of the Martyrs and the Mother of God." *Missio Immaculatae* 6 (November–December 2010) 4–5.

Opening Address in *Mary at the Foot of the Cross–IX*, 1–8. New Bedford: Academy of the Immaculate, 2010.

2011

"The Beatitude of Faith." *Missio Immaculatae* 2 (2011) 9–11.

"Mary in the Mystery of Christ." *Missio Immaculatae* 5 (September–October 2011) 19–23.

"The Mother of God and the Paschal Mystery." *Missio Immaculatae* 1 (Lent–Easter 2011) 4–6.

"The Mother of God, Bl. John Paul II and Mariology." *Missio Immaculatae* 3 (May–June 2011) 23–25.

"*Redemptoris Mater*: Magna Carta of Contemporary Mariology." *Missio Immaculatae* 2 (2011) 29–31.

"War, Peace and Our Lady." *Missio Immaculatae* 4 (July–August 2011) 3–4.

"Who is the Marian Doctor?" *Missio Immaculatae* 6 (November–December 2011) 17–24.

2012

Appendices to Bonaventure, *The Triple Way*, 195–229. New Bedford: Academy of the Immaculate, 2012.

Introduction to Bonaventure, *The Triple Way*, 1–94. New Bedford: Academy of the Immaculate, 2012.

"Maternal Mediation." *Missio Immaculatae* 2 (March–April 2012) 4–6.

"Pentecost: On the Praying Presence of Mary." *Missio Immaculatae* 3 (May–June 2012) 28–29.

"Pentecost: On the Praying Presence of Mary." *Missio Immaculatae* 4 (July–August 2012) 25–26.

"The Presence of the Mother of God at the Center of the Pilgrim Church." *Missio Immaculatae* 1 (January–February 2012) 31–32.

2013

"Believing in Charity Calls Forth Charity." *Missio Immaculatae* 3 (May–June 2013) 11–15.

"Coredemption and Assumption in the Franciscan School of Mariology: The 'Franciscan Thesis' as Key." In *Mariological Studies in Honor of Our Lady of Guadalupe*, 1:163–249. Academy of the Immaculate, 2013.

"The 'Franciscan Thesis' and Pope Benedict XVI." *Missio Immaculatae* 1 (January–February 2013) 12–22.

"Mother of Faith." *Missio Immaculatae* 6 (November–December 2013) 13–15.

"Under the Sign of the *Protoevangelium*." *Missio Immaculatae* 4 (July–August 2013) 13–17.

"Total Consecration to the Immaculate Hearts and the Mariology of St. Bonaventure." In *Mariological Studies in Honor of Our Lady of Guadalupe*, 1:251–330. New Bedford: Academy of the Immaculate, 2013.

2014

"A Blessed New Year." *Missio Immaculatae* 1 (January–February 2014) 4–5.

"Mother and Mediatrix." *Missio Immaculatae* 4 (July–August 2014) 16–20.

"Saving Mediation and the Blessed Trinity." *Missio Immaculatae* 5 (September–October 2014) 27–29.

"Spouse of the Holy Spirit, Therefore Mediatrix of all Graces." *Missio Immacualatae* 3 (May–June 2014) 29–33.

2015

"Mary and Theology: Scotus Revisited." In *The Newman-Scotus Reader: Context and Commonalities*, edited by Edward J. Ondrako, 111–80. New Bedford: Academy of the Immaculate, 2015.

"Newman and Scotus in Dialogue." In *The Newman-Scotus Reader: Context and Commonalities*, edited by Edward J. Ondrako, 243–389. New Bedford: Academy of the Immaculate.

Significant Unpublished Manuscripts (listed by descending date)

The Origin of Human Knowledge and The Theory of Illumination According to Saint
  Bonaventure, 1953, Unpublished Manuscript, Collected Papers of Peter Damian
  Fehlner.
The Dogmatic Constitution *Lumen Gentium de Ecclesia.* (1966) This is a long detailed
  outline, originally a basis for a series of conferences, but which I may incorporate
  as a new chapter in my revised dissertation.
On Getting Our Theological Bearings in a Time of Renewal: Ubinam Gentium
  Sumus?, 1967, Unpublished Manuscript, Collected Papers of Peter Damian
  Fehlner.
Mission: A Dogmatic Approach, 1968, Unpublished Manuscript, Collected Papers of
  Peter Damian Fehlner.
Treatise on Grace (Latin), 1968, Unpublished Manuscript, Collected Papers of Peter
  Damian Fehlner.
Reflections on Religious Renewal, 1972, Unpublished Manuscript, Collected Papers of
  Peter Damian Fehlner.
Trinitarian Dynamic in Our Lives, 1973, Unpublished Manuscript, Collected Papers of
  Peter Damian Fehlner.
De Vitalitate Provinciae Minorum, 1975, Unpublished Manuscript, Collected Papers of
  Peter Damian Fehlner.
Comments on the conference of Rev. James O'Connor at 1981 meeting of Mariological
  Society, entitled: *Modern Christologies and Mary's Place Therein: Dogmatic Aspect,*
  1981, Unpublished Manuscript, Collected Papers of Peter Damian Fehlner.
Casus Conscientiae ex Regula et Constitutiones, 1983, Unpublished Manuscript,
  Collected Papers of Peter Damian Fehlner.
The Impact of the Kolbian Heritage on Relaunching the Influence of Mary Immaculate
  in the Spirituality of the Order, 1986, Unpublished Manuscript, Collected Papers
  of Peter Damian Fehlner.
The Conventual Charism: A Historical and Contemporary View, 1987, Unpublished
  Manuscript, Collected Papers of Peter Damian Fehlner.
Fundamental Theology, 2000, Unpublished Manuscript, Collected Papers of Peter
  Damian Fehlner.
Dogmatic Theology: Trinity, 2000, Unpublished Manuscript, Collected Papers of Peter
  Damian Fehlner.
Dogmatic Theology: Christology, 2000, Unpublished Manuscript, Collected Papers of
  Peter Damian Fehlner.
Marian Coredemption and the All-Male Priesthood, 2002, Unpublished Manuscript,
  Collected Papers of Peter Damian Fehlner.
Mariology Manual, 2003, Unpublished Manuscript, Collected Papers of Peter Damian
  Fehlner.
'I am the Immaculate Conception': Redemption and Coredemption, Recirculation
  and Recapitulation in the Light of Metaphysics: Bonaventurian Exemplarism and
  Scotistic Univocity," 2003, Unpublished Manuscript, Collected Papers of Peter
  Damian Fehlner.
Transcendental Thomism and Bl. John Duns Scotus, 2003, Unpublished Manuscript,
  Collected Papers of Peter Damian Fehlner.

Trojan Horses in the City of God: Theistic Evolution and Special Creation, 2003, Unpublished Manuscript, Collected Papers of Peter Damian Fehlner.

Mater et Magistra Theologorum: The Immaculate Conception and the Notion and Method of "Our Theology" according to Bl. John Duns Scotus, 2004, Unpublished Manuscript, Collected Papers of Peter Damian Fehlner.

Patripassionism, 2004, Unpublished Manuscript, Collected Papers of Peter Damian Fehlner.

Virgo Mater–Signum Magnum, 2004, Unpublished Manuscript, Collected Papers of Peter Damian Fehlner.

Introduction to an Ecumenical Dialogue in the Spirit of Prayer and Devotion, 2005, Unpublished Manuscript, Collected Papers of Peter Damian Fehlner.

On the Philosophical Theology of Immanuel Kant, 2007, Unpublished Manuscript, Collected Papers of Peter Damian Fehlner.

The Love of Learning and the Desire of God: Reflections on the Critical Question and its Resolution in Practice in the *Itinerarium mentis in Deum* of St. Bonaventure Understood as the Structure of What Cardinal Newman Understands by the Personal Conquest of Truth, 2007, Unpublished Manuscript, Collected Papers of Peter Damian Fehlner.

Marian and Charismatic Movements, 2007, Unpublished Manuscript, Collected Papers of Peter Damian Fehlner.

Marian Citadel Immaculatum, 2007, Unpublished Manuscript, Collected Papers of Peter Damian Fehlner.

Marian Charismatic Contemplation, 2008, Unpublished Manuscript, Collected Papers of Peter Damian Fehlner.

Organ Transplant and the Criteria of Death, 2008, Unpublished Manuscript, Collected Papers of Peter Damian Fehlner.

The Words of Institution of the Eucharist: In the New Testament and in the Liturgy, 1966, revised 2014, Unpublished Manuscript, Collected Papers of Peter Damian Fehlner.

Notes on Univocity, nd., Unpublished Manuscript, Collected Papers of Peter Damian Fehlner.

Our Lady of America and the Present US Situation, nd., Unpublished Manuscript, Collected Papers of Peter Damian Fehlner.

Our Lady of Guadalupe and the Immaculate Conception, nd., Unpublished Manuscript, Collected Papers of Peter Damian Fehlner.

The Sanctification of the Intellect, nd., Unpublished Manuscript, Collected Papers of Peter Damian Fehlner.

The Church, the Dignity of the Person, and Creation

The Franciscan Thesis as Presented by Father Peter Damian Fehlner and the Magisterium

Arthur B. Calkins

I. The Franciscan Thesis as Articulated by Father Peter Damian

In the course of almost thirty years I have learned a great deal about Mariology from Father Peter Damian Fehlner. He is a disciple and master of that uniquely Franciscan approach to the doctrine of the joint predestination of Jesus and Mary known as the Franciscan thesis. His exposition of this doctrine on the Mariology and scholarly achievement of Father Juniper B. Carol (1911–1990) at the convention of the Mariological Society of America in 1992[1] made a deep impression on me. In introducing the contribution of Juniper Carol, he found it appropriate to treat of the accomplishment of Father Juniper's master and guide in the field of Franciscan Mariology, Father Carlo Balić (1899–1977):

> Fr. Balić's contribution to Mariology is, therefore, unabashedly Franciscan in inspiration. It takes its cue from the so-called Franciscan thesis: the absolute primacy of the Word Incarnate (Kingship of Christ) and his Blessed Mother's association *uno eodemque decreto* in that primacy (qua Immaculate Queen of heaven and Earth), an association particularly evident at three points in the life of the Virgin: her conception, her cooperation in the work of salvation, her triumph in heaven or put doctrinally: the Immaculate Conception; the universal maternal mediation of Mary; and her glorious Assumption and Coronation in heaven as Queen of the Universe.[2]

1. Fehlner, "Fr. Juniper B. Carol, O.F.M.," 17–59.
2. Ibid., 22.

The allusion, of course, to *uno eodemque decreto* is a shorthand reference to the famous text wherein the Franciscan thesis passed into the papal magisterium in Blessed Pius IX's Apostolic Constitution *Ineffabilis Deus* in which he solemnly declared the dogma of the Immaculate Conception. In that authoritative document Pius stated that God

> by one and the same decree, had established the origin of Mary and the Incarnation of Divine Wisdom [*ad illius Virginis primordia transferre, quæ uno eodemque decreto cum divinæ Sapientiæ incarnatione fuerant præstituta*].[3]

This is to say that from all eternity in willing the Incarnation of the Word, the second person of the Most Blessed Trinity, God also willed Mary. This may seem to be a simple and obvious statement in itself until one begins to realize that God could have brought the Incarnation about in any way that he wished since he needed no one to accomplish it, but he willed to "need" Mary. This position in based on the union of the woman of Genesis 3:15 with her offspring. Together, though not on an equal par, they will overcome the serpent. But first of all, they are willed for themselves as the crown of the material creation. Thus, as Father Peter Damian tells us, the joint predestination of Jesus and Mary is "at the very center of the divine counsels of salvation"[4] and for this reason "the mode of the Incarnation is Marian, not only in its first moment, but in every moment, above all the last."[5] This statement, then, by Blessed Pius IX in *Ineffabilis Deus* marks the first time that this position, long sustained and taught by Franciscan theologians, entered into the papal magisterium. This theological conviction in fact is not original to Franciscan theologians because, as Father Peter Damian explains, its roots

> antedate both Scotus and Francis himself. It is Franciscan, not by reason of origin (in this it is rather Catholic), but by reason of its promotion, of its being rendered more explicit and then more effectively incorporated into the life of the Church, as St. Maximilian Kolbe would say.[6]

The statement that Father Peter makes in parenthesis is very important. This position is ultimately **Catholic** and we owe our gratitude to the

---

3. *Pii IX Pontificis Maximi Acta* I, 599; *Our Lady: Papal Teachings* [= OL] #34].

4. Fehlner, "Immaculata Mediatrix," 285.

5. Ibid., 284.

6. Fehlner, "Fr. Juniper B. Carol, O.F.M.," 27. In his last major work, *Why Jesus Christ? Thomistic, Scotistic and Conciliatory Perspective*, Fr. Carol carefully documented the sustainers of this position from earliest times.

Franciscan family for having consistently sustained it and taught it. Ultimately, as he explains:

> Mary in some intrinsic manner pertains as no other person to the order of the hypostatic union, the grace of graces and source of all order and intelligibility both in the economy of salvation and in creation. To this fact and to the special place enjoyed by Mary in the economy of salvation, both in relation to the mystery of Jesus and of the Church (cf. *Lumen Gentium*, ch. 8, title), the whole of revelation affords abundant witness (as sketched out in *Lumen Gentium*, nn. 55ff).[7]

In the first part of his magisterial article, "The Predestination of the Virgin Mother and Her Immaculate Conception" in the *Mariology* volume edited by Mark Miravalle Father Peter laments the fact that treatment of the predestination of Mary has all but disappeared from Mariological study.[8] We are grateful that his study in that volume once more presents it to a wide audience. From the perspective of Blessed John Duns Scotus (c. 1266–1308), whose faithful disciple Father Peter has ever remained, he explains that

> Whereas the fullness of grace in Mary is in view of the foreseen merits of her Son, the participation in grace by all others is in view of the mediation of Jesus and Mary. Because of the fact of sin on the part of Adam and Eve, that mediation of Christ, when realized historically after the tragic event of original sin and the fall of the angels, is in fact redemptive as well as saving: preservatively in Mary (and in a subordinate way in the angels who did not fall) and liberatively in all others. In Mary redemption is her Immaculate Conception; in us it is our liberation from sin. In both cases redemption is the term of divine mercy: more perfectly, however, in Mary than in us, and in us dependently on its realization in the Immaculate.[9]

Father Peter goes on to underscore a point often overlooked by the critics of Scotus.

> In the joint predestination of Jesus and Mary, the distinctive personal roles of Jesus and Mary are not confused, nor does their coordination with a single work of mediation put Mary on a par with Jesus, any more than the capacity of the blessed to think and love in the mode of divine persons (a kind of coordination,

7. Fehlner, "The Predestination of the Virgin Mother," 218.

8. Cf. ibid., 213.

9. Ibid., 225.

anticipated in the divine indwelling by grace) put them on a par
with the divine persons. Such coordination, heart of the supernatural order of grace, rests ever on a radical subordination. In
this joint predestination Jesus is ordained absolutely for his own
sake, and Mary for the sake of Jesus and no other, not even herself. Yet in virtue of the very grace of the Immaculate Conception whereby she totally belongs to Jesus and to the Church as
Mother, she is ennobled in a most personal way, thereby revealing how grace transforms and perfects the person.[10]

While it would be possible to outline Father Peter Damian's thought
on this topic more extensively, I trust that this serves as a useful foundation.
One can find more in the vast number of his Mariological works, especially
in his article in *Mariology*.

II. The Confirmation of the Thesis in the Magisterium

Since the statement by Blessed Pius IX that by one and the same decree,
God established the Incarnation of Divine Wisdom and the origin of
Mary, this conviction has been restated on numerous occasions in the papal and conciliar magisterium. It is true that they have not all been stated
at the highest level of the magisterium such as in a doctrinal definition
or an encyclical, but nonetheless, each restatement is in concord with the
others while enriching the doctrine with further valuable nuances. I will
present here what is more common knowledge as well as what I have subsequently discovered. I make no pretense of having discovered all of the
restatements of this theme in the papal magisterium, but simply of providing data that confirm that the so-called "Franciscan thesis" is no longer a
thesis, but is truly "the Catholic position."

1. The most important restatement of the position stated by Blessed
Pius IX occurs in the Apostolic Constitution of the Venerable Pius XII, *Mu-
nificentissimus Deus* of 1 November 1950, in which he solemnly defined the
bodily Assumption of the Blessed Virgin Mary into heaven. In Apostolic
Constitution he referred to Blessed Virgin Mary as

> The revered Mother of God, from all eternity joined in a hidden
> way with Jesus Christ in one and the same decree of predestina-
> tion [. . . *Idcirco augusta Dei Mater, Iesu Christo, inde ab omni
> æternitate, «uno eodemque decreto» prædestinationis, arcano
> modo coniuncta*].[11]

10. Ibid., 226.

11. *Acta Apostolicæ Sedis* [= *AAS*] 42 (1950), 768; OL #520.

2. The next three restatements occur in *Lumen Gentium*, the Dogmatic Constitution on the Church promulgated on 21 November 1964. As statements of an Ecumenical Council they cannot be dismissed as lacking in doctrinal weight. The first is found in #53:

> Redeemed by reason of the merits of her Son and united to Him by a close and indissoluble tie, she [Mary] is endowed with the high office and dignity of being the Mother of the Son of God, by which account she is also the beloved daughter of the Father and the temple of the Holy Spirit. Because of this gift of sublime grace she far surpasses all creatures, both in heaven and on earth. [*Intuitu meritorum Filii sui sublimiore modo redempta Eique arcto et indissolubili vinculo unita, hoc summo munere ac dignitate ditatur ut sit Genitrix Dei Filii, ideoque prædilecta filia Patris necnon sacrarium Spiritus Sancti quo eximiae gratiæ dono omnibus aliis creaturis, coelestibus et terrestribus, longe antecellit*].[12]

Insofar as I am aware, this is the first time in a magisterial document that the term *indissolubilis nexus* or "indissoluble bond" is used to describe the inseparable relationship between Jesus and Mary. This is also, of course, the same term used in the Church's Code of Canon Law to describe the union between husband and wife in a valid sacramental marriage.

3. The second reference occurs in *Lumen Gentium* #56:

> The Father of mercies willed that the incarnation should be preceded by the acceptance of her who was predestined to be the mother of His Son, so that just as a woman contributed to death, so also a woman should contribute to life. [*Voluit autem misericordiarum Pater, ut acceptatio prædestinatæ matris incarnationem præcederet, ut sic, quemadmodum femina contulit ad mortem, ita etiam femina conferret ad vitam*].[13]

We note here that Mary is referred to as the *prædestinatæ matris* or "predestined mother."

4. The third occurrence of this doctrine in the same Dogmatic Constitution is to be found in #61 where the Virgin Mary is described as:

> Predestined from eternity to be the Mother of God by that decree of divine providence, which determined the incarnation of the Word [*Beata Virgo, ab æterno una cum divini Verbi*

---

12. *AAS* 57 (65), 58-59.
13. *AAS* 57 (65), 60.

*incarnatione tamquam Mater Dei praedestinata, divinae Provi-
dentiæ consilio*].[14]

5. Another important conciliar text on this matter is that stated in *Sacrosanctum Concilium*, the Second Vatican Ecumenical Council's Constitution on the Sacred Liturgy, #103.

> In celebrating this annual cycle of Christ's mysteries, holy
> Church honors with especial love the Blessed Mary, Mother of
> God, who is joined by an inseparable bond to the saving work of
> her Son. In her the Church holds up and admires the most ex-
> cellent fruit of the redemption, and joyfully contemplates, as in
> a faultless image that which she herself desires and hopes wholly
> to be. [*In hoc annuo mysteriorum Christi circulo celebrando,
> Sancta Ecclesia Beatam Mariam Dei Genetricem cum peculiari
> amore veneratur, quae indissolubili nexu cum Filii sui opere
> salutari coniungitur; in qua præcellentem Redemptionis fructum
> miratur et exaltat, ac veluti in purissima imagine, id quod ipsa
> tota esse cupit et sperat cum gaudio contemplatur*].[15]

6. Recognizing the chaos that was overcoming the Church after the
Second Vatican Council, Blessed Paul VI made a clear and concise profession of faith on 30 June 1968, that decisive year of contestation in the
Church and in the world. This *Professio Fidei* is often referred to as the *Credo
of the People of God*. In it Blessed Paul VI in recapitulating the fundamental
teaching of the Church on Mary, states that she is

> joined by a close and indissoluble bond to the mystery of the
> Incarnation and Redemption [*Arcto et indissolubili vinculo mys-
> terio Incarnationis et Redemptionis coniuncta*].[16]

We note here that in the footnote to this text the Pope cites *Lumen
Gentium* #53 in which we find the term *indissolubilis nexus*. Here we find
that same term again.

7. In his general audience address of 30 May 1973 Blessed Paul VI
referred to Mary in this way:

> And what human cooperation has been chosen in the history of
> our Christian destinies, first in function, dignity and efficiency,
> not purely instrumental and physical, but as a predestined,
> though free and perfectly docile factor, if not that of Mary? (cf.

14. *AAS* 57 (65) 63.

15. *AAS* 56 (64) 125.

16. *AAS* 60 (1968) 438; *The Pope Speaks* 13:278

Lumen Gentium, 56). [*E quale cooperazione umana è stata eletta nella storia dei nostri destini cristiani, prima per funzione, per dignità, per efficienza, non puramente strumentale e fisica, ma come fattore predestinato, ma libero e perfettamente docile, se non quella di Maria?*].[17]

This, indeed, is a rhetorical question packed with weighty dogmatic facts. Effectively Paul VI indicates that our Christian destinies are interwoven with the destiny of Mary, who is not merely an instrumental or physical factor in the work of our redemption. She was predestined for her role, but at the same time completely free. Without her docility to God's will, we would not be saved.

8. Our final text from Blessed Paul VI also appears in a document of high doctrinal import, his Apostolic Exhortation *Marialis Cultus*, of 2 February 1974, #25:

> It likewise seems to us fitting that these expressions of devotion should reflect God's plan, which laid down "with one single decree the origin of Mary and the Incarnation of the divine Wisdom." [*Nobis tamen videtur potissimum convenire . . . ut referatur ad ipsum consilium Dei, quo illius Virginis primordia . . . cum divine Sapientiae incarnatione fuerant praestituta*].[18]

Here we observe that the Pope encourages us to venerate Mary precisely because God himself has honored her in linking her with the predestination of the Eternal Word.

9. The first texts that I want to present from the magisterium of Pope Saint John Paul II come from his Marian Encyclical, *Redemptoris Mater* of 25 March 1987. His mode of presentation in this document is not linear, but rather circular in that he presents truths and then returns to them, each time with further developments. In #8 of that encyclical he makes this statement:

> In the mystery of Christ she [Mary] is *present* even 'before the creation of the world,' as the one whom the Father 'has chosen' *as Mother* of his Son in the Incarnation. And, what is more, together with the Father, the Son has chosen her, entrusting her eternally to the Spirit of holiness. In an entirely special and exceptional way Mary is united to Christ, and similarly she is eternally loved in this "beloved Son," this Son who is of one

17. *Insegnamenti di Paolo VI* XI (1973) 474; *Mary—God's Mother and Ours*, 90.

18. *AAS* 56 (1964), 135–136. Attached to the text is this footnote: (*Pius IX, Litt. Ap. Ineffabilis Deus: Pii IX Pontificis Maximi Acta, I, 1, Romae 1854, 599; cf etiam V. Sardi, La solenne definizione del dogma dell'immacolato concepimento di Maria Santissima. Atti e documenti . . . Roma 1904–1905, vol. II, 30.*

being with the Father, in whom is concentrated all the "glory of grace." [*In mysterio Christi ea est præsens iam «ante mundi constitutionem», utpote quam «elegerit Matrem Filii sui in incarnatione et cum Patre elegerit Filius, eam Spiritui sanctitatis ex æternitate permittens. Maria ratione omnino singulari et extraordinario iuncta est Christo, et item inaeternitate amatur in hoc «Filio dilecto», in hoc Filio consubstantiali Patri, in quo tota continetur «gloria gratiæ*].[19]

In this text John Paul speaks of Mary as "present in the mystery of Christ even 'before the creation of the world,'" that is to say in the Divine mind. She only began to exist in time, but in the Trinitarian counsels she is already present. This way of speaking was understood for centuries in the Church when the readings for Marian Masses were often taken from the Sapiential Books of the Bible. Here is an example from the Mass of the Immaculate Conception in the 1962 Roman Missal, which testifies to ancient liturgical tradition and whose first reading comes from the Book of Proverbs:

The Lord possessed me in the beginning of His ways, before He made anything, from the beginning. I was set up from eternity, and of old, before the earth was made. The depths were not as yet, and I was already conceived neither had the fountains of waters as yet sprung out. [*Dominus possedit me in initio viarum suarum, antequam quidquam faceret a principio. Ab æterno ordinata sum, et ex antiquis, antequam terra fieret. Nondum errant abyssi, et ego jam concepta eram: necdum fontes aquarum eruperant*].[20]

Of course, this reading has to be understood in an accommodated sense. Its first reference is to the Divine Wisdom, which the Fathers of the Church applied to the Son, the Eternal Word, one with the Father from all eternity, who in time became flesh in the womb of the Virgin Mary. In a secondary and subordinate sense, it was also understood of Mary through whom the Word became flesh. So explains Abbot Prosper Guéranger (1805–1875) commenting on this reading for the Feast of the Immaculate Conception:

She that was to be His Mother was eternally present to the thought of God, as the means whereby the Word would assume the human nature. The Son and Mother are therefore united in the plan of the Incarnation: Mary, therefore, existed, as did Jesus, in the divine decree, before creation began. This is the

19. *AAS* 79 (1987), 370.
20. Proverbs 8:22–24.

reason of the Church's having, from the earliest ages of Christianity, interpreted this sublime passage of the sacred volume of Jesus and Mary unitedly, and ordering it and analogous passages of the Scriptures to be read in the assembly of the faithful on the solemnities or feasts of the Mother of God.[21]

Thus the great abbot and liturgist explains the appropriateness of these readings from the Books of Wisdom on Marian feasts, underscoring how Mary is *present* "in the mystery of Christ" . . . "even 'before the creation of the world.'"

In #9 of the encyclical John Paul continues his explanation:

> If the greeting and the name "full of grace" say all this, in the context of the angel's announcement they refer first of all to the election of Mary as Mother of the Son of God. But at the same time the "fullness of grace" indicates all the supernatural munificence from which Mary benefits by being chosen and destined to be the Mother of Christ. If this election is fundamental for the accomplishment of God's salvific designs for humanity, and if the eternal choice in Christ and the vocation to the dignity of adopted children is the destiny of everyone, then the election of Mary is wholly exceptional and unique. Hence also the singularity and uniqueness of her place in the mystery of Christ. [*Si salutatio et nomen «gratia piena» hæc omnia indicant, in contexta oratione angelici nuntii ante omnia spectant ad electionem Mariæ uti Matris Filii Dei. Sed simul «plenitudo gratiæ» totam largitionem supernaturalem indicat, qua Maria fruitur, eo quod electa et constituta est, ut Christi Mater esset. Si hæc electio fundamentalis est ad perficienda Dei salvifica consilia quoad humanum genus; si æterna electio in Christo et destinatio ad dignitatem filiorum adoptivorum ad omnes homines pertinet, electio Mariæ est omnino singularis et unica. Hinc etiam «locus» proprius et unicus quem obtinet in mysterio Christi.*][22]

Here the pope strives to draw out the meaning of *kecharitomene*, the term rendered in Latin as *gratia plena*. This, he says, "indicates all the supernatural munificence from which Mary benefits precisely because she was chosen and destined to be the Mother of Christ." Then he goes on to argue that "if the eternal choice in Christ and the vocation to the dignity of adopted children is the destiny of everyone, then the election of Mary is wholly exceptional

---

21. Guéranger, *The Liturgical Year*, 400–401. On this theme cf. also Bouyer, *The Seat of Wisdom*, 20–28; Manelli, *All Generations Shall Call Me Blessed*, 104–7.

22. *AAS* 79 (1987), 371.

and unique." Father Peter Damian's commentary, which we have already heard above, illustrates beautifully what Saint John Paul says here:

> Because of the fact of sin on the part of Adam and Eve, that mediation of Christ, when realized historically after the tragic event of original sin and the fall of the angels, is in fact redemptive as well as saving: preservatively in Mary (and in a subordinate way in the angels who did not fall) and liberatively in all others. In Mary redemption is her Immaculate Conception; in us it is our liberation from sin. In both cases redemption is the term of divine mercy: more perfectly, however, in Mary than in us, and in us dependently on its realization in the Immaculate.[23]

Mary's place in the mystery of Christ has been ordained from all eternity. Finally in #10 of *Redemptoris Mater* continues his argument.

> From the first moment of her conception—which is to say of her existence—she belonged to Christ, sharing in the salvific and sanctifying grace and in that love which has its beginning in the "Beloved," the Son of the Eternal Father, who through the Incarnation became her own Son. Consequently, through the power of the Holy Spirit, in the order of grace, which is a participation in the divine nature, Mary receives life from him to whom she herself, in the order of earthly generation, gave life as a mother. [*A primo temporis momento suæ conceptionis, seu suae exsistentiæ, ea pertinet ad Christum, eius gratiam salvificam et sanctificantem communicat eumque amorem, qui initium habet in «Dilecto», in æterni Patris Filio, qui per Incarnationem factus est proprius eius filius. Idcirco, Spiritus Sancti virtute, in ordine gratiæ, id est consortionis divinae naturæ (cfr. 2 Peter 1:4), Maria ab eo vitam accipit, cui ipsa, in ordine generationis terrenæ, vitam dedit ut mater.*][24]

From the first moment of her existence, the Pope argues, Mary belongs to Christ—and yet Christ does not yet exist in his humanity because he has not yet taken flesh in her womb. The mystery is great: "Mary receives life from him to whom she herself, in the order of earthly generation, gave life as a mother." All of this simply draws out the statement of Blessed Pius IX about the "one and the same divine decree."

10. In his general audience address of 23 November 1988 Saint John Paul II once again touched on the joint predestination of Jesus and Mary. He said

---

23. Fehlner, "The Predestination of the Virgin Mother," 225.

24. *AAS* 79 (1987), 372.

In this gift made to John and, through him, to Christ's followers and to all mankind, there is as it were a completion of the
gift, which Jesus made of himself to humanity by his death on
the Cross. Mary is as it were "entirely one" with him [Jesus],
not only because they are mother and son "according to the
flesh", but because in God's eternal plan they are contemplated,
predestined and situated together at the center of the history of
salvation. [*In questo dono fatto a Giovanni e, in lui, ai seguaci di
Cristo e a tutti gli uomini, vi è come un completamento del dono
che Gesù fa di se stesso all'umanità con la sua morte in Croce.
Maria costituisce con lui come un "tutt'uno," non solo perché sono
madre e figlio "secondo la carne," ma perché nell'eterno disegno
di Dio sono contemplati, predestinati, collocati insieme al centro
della storia della salvezza.*][25]

Here the Pontiff begins with reference to the gift of Mary's spiritual motherhood of John and to all of Jesus' followers. Then he makes the statement
that Mary is "entirely one," *un "tutt'uno"*[26] with Jesus. *They are indissolubly
united, even if at different levels; they are one in God's eternal plan. They are
predestined to be "at the center of the history of salvation." This is indeed a very
clear confirmation of the Franciscan thesis.*

11. In #78 of his Apostolic Letter *Dies Domini* of 31 May 1998 John
Paul II made this statement:

Likewise, "in celebrating this annual cycle of the mysteries of
Christ, the holy Church venerates with special love the Blessed
Virgin Mary, Mother of God, united forever with the saving
work of her Son." [*Æquabiliter "in hoc annuo mysteriorum
Christi circulo celebrando, Sancta Ecclesia Beatam Mariam Dei
Genetricem cum peculiari amore veneratur, quæ indissolubili
nexu cum Filii sui opere salutari coniungitur."*][27]

A close examination of this text will indicate that it is a direct quote from the
conciliar Constitution on the Sacred Liturgy, *Sacrosanctum Concilium* #103.

12. On December 8, 2004 Pope Saint John Paul II celebrated the 150th
Anniversary of the Dogma of the Immaculate Conception. It was his last
earthly celebration of the Feast of the Immaculate Conception. In his homily on that occasion he said:

25. *Insegnamenti di Giovanni Paolo II* XI/4 (1988), 1636; *L'Osservatore Romano*,
weekly edition in English. First number signifies cumulative edition number; second
number signifies page [= *ORE*] 1061:16.

26. The weekly English edition of *L'Osservatore Romano* rendered this "all one," but
I believe that "entirely one" renders the idea better.

27. *AAS* 90 (1998), 761.

The *predestination of Mary*, like that of each one of us, is linked to the *predestination of the Son*. Christ is that "seed" that was "to bruise the head" of the ancient serpent, according to the Book of Genesis (cf. Gen. 3:15); he is the Lamb "without blemish" (cf. Ex. 12:5; 1 Pt. 1:19), immolated to redeem humanity from sin. *With a view to the saving death of the Son,* Mary, his Mother, was preserved free from original sin and from every other sin. The victory of the new Adam also includes that of the new Eve, Mother of the redeemed. The Immaculate Virgin is thus a sign of hope for all the living who have triumphed over Satan *by the blood of the Lamb* (cf. Rev. 12:11). [*La predestinazione di Maria, come quella di ognuno di noi, è relativa alla predestinazione del Figlio. Cristo è quella "stirpe" che avrebbe "schiacciato la testa" all'antico serpente, secondo il Libro della Genesi (cfr. Gn 3,15); è l'Agnello "senza macchia" (cfr. Es 12,5; 1 Pt 1,19), immolato per redimere l'umanità dal peccato. In previsione della morte salvifica di Lui, Maria, sua Madre, è stata preservata dal peccato originale e da ogni altro peccato. Nella vittoria del nuovo Adamo c'è anche quella della nuova Eva, madre dei redenti. L'Immacolata è così segno di speranza per tutti i viventi, che hanno vinto satana per mezzo del sangue dell'Agnello (cfr. Ap 12,11).*][28]

In this homily he clearly states that the predestination of Mary is linked to that of Christ, as is our predestination.[29] The joint predestination of Jesus and Mary, however, is prior to ours in God's plan. Here John Paul links the joint predestination to the very fundamental scriptural text of Genesis 3:15, the Protoevangelium, and accepts the present prevailing interpretation that it is the seed of the woman who crushes the serpent as opposed to the Vulgate translation of Saint Jerome, which has the woman crushing the head of the serpent[30]. On another occasion John Paul pointed out that Genesis 3:15 must still be understood as referring to Mary's sharing in the conflict with Satan and her sharing in the victory of Christ albeit in a secondary and subordinate way, totally dependent on Christ.[31] He does that also in the text just cited.

28. *Insegnamenti di Giovanni Paolo II* XXVII/2 (2004), 669–70; *ORE* 1873:3.

29. The fact is that the only predestination known in the New Testament and in the teaching of the Catholic Church is predestination to glory. We can choose against that, but God predestines no one to hell.

30. Cf. Manelli, "The Mystery of the Blessed Virgin Mary in the Old Testament," 5–14; Manelli, "Genesis 3:15 and the Immaculate Conception," 263–322.

31. Cf. his general audience address of 24 January 1996 in *Insegnamenti di Giovanni Paolo II* XIX/1 (1996) 116–17; *ORE* 1426:11.

Here it may also be helpful to indicate that John Paul's primary optic was that of Calvary so there are numerous texts in which he discusses the joint predestination of Jesus and Mary primarily in terms of the joint suffering on Calvary of Jesus, the new Adam, and Mary, the New Eve.

13. We move now to the 8th of December 2006, to Pope Benedict XVI's Prayer to Mary Immaculate in the Piazza di Spagna.

> *"Full of grace"* are you, Mary, full of divine love from the very first moment of your existence, providentially predestined to be Mother of the Redeemer and intimately connected to him in the mystery of salvation. [*Piena di grazia" Tu sei, Maria, colma dell'amore divino dal primo istante della tua esistenza, provvidenzialmente predestinata ad essere la Madre del Redentore, ed intimamente associata a Lui nel mistero della salvezza.*][32]

Here we note, too, that Benedict continues where John Paul II concluded. Mary is predestined to be the Mother of the Redeemer in both the Incarnation and the Redemption.

14. In his Angelus address of the 15th of August 2007 Benedict stated

> *Today, we are celebrating the Solemnity of the Assumption of the Blessed Virgin Mary. This is an ancient feast deeply rooted in Sacred Scripture: indeed, it presents the Virgin Mary closely united to her divine Son and ever supportive of him. Mother and Son appear closely bound in the fight against the infernal enemy until they completely defeat him. This victory is expressed in particular in overcoming sin and death, that is, in triumphing over the enemies which St. Paul always presents as connected (cf. Rom 5:12, 15–21; I Cor. 15:21–26). . . . He [the Venerable Pope Pius XII] declared: "Hence, the revered Mother of God, from all eternity joined in a hidden way with Jesus Christ in one and the same decree of predestination, immaculate in her conception, a most perfect virgin in her divine motherhood, the noble associate of the divine Redeemer who has won a complete triumph over sin and its consequences, finally obtained, as the supreme culmination of her privileges, that she should be preserved free from the corruption of the tomb and that, like her own Son, having overcome death, she might be taken up body and soul to the glory of Heaven where, as Queen, she sits in splendor at the right hand of her Son, the immortal King of the Ages" (Apostolic Constitution Munificentissimus Deus: AAS 42, [1950] 768–69). [Celebriamo quest'oggi la solennità dell'Assunzione della Beata Vergine Maria. Si tratta di una festa antica, che ha il suo fondamento ultimo nella Sacra*

---

32. *Insegnamenti di Benedetto XVI* II/2 (2006) 772; ORE 1973:12.

Scrittura: questa infatti presenta la Vergine Maria strettamente unita al suo Figlio divino e sempre a Lui solidale. Madre e Figlio appaiono strettamente associati nella lotta contro il nemico infernale fino alla piena vittoria su di lui. Questa vittoria si esprime, in particolare, nel superamento del peccato e della morte, nel superamento cioè di quei nemici che san Paolo presenta sempre congiunti (cf. Rom 5:12, 15–21; 1 Cor 15:21–26). . . . Egli dichiarava: "In tal modo l'augusta Madre di Dio, arcanamente unita a Gesù Cristo fin da tutta l'eternità con uno stesso decreto di predestinazione, Immacolata nella sua Concezione, Vergine illibata nella sua divina maternità, generosa Socia del Divino Redentore, che ha riportato un pieno trionfo sul peccato e sulle sue conseguenze, alla fine, come supremo coronamento dei suoi privilegi, ottenne di essere preservata dalla corruzione del sepolcro e, vinta la morte, come già il suo Figlio, di essere innalzata in anima e corpo alla gloria del Cielo, dove risplende Regina alla destra del Figlio suo, Re immortale dei secoli"].[33]

Once again it is worthy of note that in quoting his predecessor, the Venerable Pius XII, who was effectively repeating his predecessor Blessed Pius IX on "one and the same decree of predestination," Benedict is also reaffirming on his own that "the Virgin Mary" was intimately and completely "united to her divine Son." In stating that "Mother and Son appear closely bound in the fight against the infernal enemy until they completely defeat him," he is effectively linking the Protoevangelium to Calvary and Jesus' Resurrection and Ascension to Mary's Assumption.

15. The final text that I cite in this florilegium is from Benedict XVI's homily on 7 September 2008 at the Shrine of Our Lady of Bonaria in Cagliari, Sardinia.

The predestination of Mary is inscribed in the predestination of Jesus, as likewise is that of every human person. The 'here I am' of the Mother faithfully echoes the 'here I am' of the Son (cf. Hebrews 10:6), as does the 'here I am' of all adoptive children in the Son, that of us all, precisely." [*Nella predestinazione di Gesù è inscritta la predestinazione di Maria, come pure quella di ogni persona umana. Nell'"eccomi" del Figlio trova eco fedele l'"eccomi" della Madre (cfr Eb 10,6), come anche l'"eccomi" di tutti i figli adottivi nel Figlio, di tutti noi appunto.*][34]

---

33. *Insegnamenti di Benedetto XVI* III/2 (2007) 136–37; *ORE* 2007:4.

34. *Insegnamenti di Benedetto XVI* IV/2 (2008) 227; *ORE* 2060:3.

He puts the matter nicely: "The predestination of Mary is inscribed in the predestination of Jesus." It is a statement of the priority of their joint predestination, which at the same time is meant to include that of all believers. Here, as we found in the last text, which I cited from Saint John Paul II, Benedict makes a deliberate connection with the predestination to glory of all the faithful.

III. Conclusions

While this survey of the Franciscan thesis, as presented by Father Peter Damian and confirmed in the papal and conciliar magisterium from 1854 to 2007 has been a relatively brief one, I believe that it is possible to draw some conclusions.

1. The period of the magisterium, which I have briefly analyzed covers over 150 years. While what I have presented here may not be exhaustive, it is definitely representative. Anyone contesting the concept of the joint predestination of Jesus and Mary at this stage in history would be opposing a well-established development of doctrine grounded in Genesis 3:15. Authentic Catholic doctrine develops, but does it does not go backwards; it does not negate.

2. For this reason I do not think it necessary any longer to speak of the Franciscan thesis because the thesis has been confirmed by the magisterium many times over with consistency and further nuances. Shall we call it a fundamental Franciscan contribution to Christology and Mariology?

3. The doctrine of the joint predestination of Jesus and Mary provides very significant corroboration of the dogma of the Immaculate Conception as it has ever since it passed into the magisterium in *Ineffabilis Deus* in 1854. It also upholds the primordial significance of Genesis 3:15 (the Protoevangelium) in the history of salvation and the doctrine of Marian coredemption.

4. After Fathers Carlo Balić, OFM, Juniper Carol, OFM and their colleagues of the past, I believe that Father Peter Damian Fehlner, OFM Conv has done more to make the present generation aware of this Franciscan contribution to Christology and Mariology than anyone else, especially in the English-speaking world. In what is perhaps his single major contribution on this matter he tells us candidly that "treatment of the predestination of Mary has disappeared from Mariological study,"[35] but largely thanks to him that is no longer the case.

---

35. Fehlner, "The Predestination of the Virgin Mother," 213.

Bibliography

Acta Apostolicæ Sedis I (1909–).

Bouyer, Louis. *The Seat of Wisdom: An Essay on the Place of the Virgin Mary in Christian Theology.* Translated by A. V. Littledale. New York: Pantheon, 1962.

Carol, Juniper B. *Why Jesus Christ? Thomistic, Scotistic and Conciliatory Perspectives.* Manassas, VA: Trinity Communications, 1986.

Fehlner, Peter Damian. "Fr. Juniper B. Carol, O.F.M.: His Mariology and Scholarly Achievement." *Marian Studies* 43 (1992) 17–59.

———. "Immaculata Mediatrix—Toward a Dogmatic Definition of the Coredemption." In *Mary Coredemptrix, Mediatrix, Advocate, Theological Foundations II: Papal, Pneumatological, Ecumenical,* edited by Mark I. Miravalle, 259–329. Santa Barbara, CA: Queenship, 1997.

———. "The Predestination of the Virgin Mother and Her Immaculate Conception." In *Mariology: A Guide for Priests, Deacons, Seminarians, and Consecrated Persons,* edited by Mark Miravalle, 213–76. Goleta, CA: Seat of Wisdom, 2008.

Guéranger, Prosper. *The Liturgical Year.* Vol 1. Translated by Laurence Shepherd. Westminster, MD: Newman, 1948.

Insegnamenti di Benedetto XVI, I–IX (2005–2013). Vatican City: Libreria Editrice Vaticana. 2006–2013.

Insegnamenti di Giovanni Paolo II, I–XXVIII (1978–2005). Vatican City: Libreria Editrice Vaticana. 1979–2006.

Insegnamenti di Paolo VI, I–XV (1963–1978). Vatican City: Libreria Editrice Vaticana. 1965–1979.

Mary—God's Mother and Ours. Boston: St. Paul Editions, 1979.

Manelli, Settimio M. "Genesis 3:15 and the Immaculate Conception." In *Mary at the Foot of the Cross—V: Redemption and Coredemption under the Sign of the Immaculate Conception. Acts of the Fifth International Symposium on Marian Coredemption,* 263–322. New Bedford, MA: Academy of the Immaculate, 2005.

Manelli, Stefano M. *All Generations Shall Call Me Blessed: Biblical Mariology.* Translated by Peter Damian Fehlner. New Bedford, MA: Academy of the Immaculate, 2005.

———. "The Mystery of the Blessed Virgin Mary in the Old Testament." In *Mariology: A Guide for Priests, Deacons, Seminarians, and Consecrated Persons,* edited by Mark I. Miravalle, 1–6. Goleta, CA: Seat of Wisdom, 2008.

L'Osservatore Romano, weekly English edition of Italian daily edition of *L'Osservatore Romano,* Vatican newspaper.

Our Lady: Papal Teachings. Edited by the Benedictine Monks of Solesmes. Translated by Daughters of St. Paul. Boston: St. Paul Editions, 1961.

Pii IX Pontificis Maximi Acta I. Graz, Austria: Akademische Druck–n. Verlagsanstalt, 1971.

The Pope Speaks (1954–1998).

2

Love and Knowledge

On Intellect and Intentionality[1]

DAVID BENTLEY HART

THANK YOU FOR INVITING me. It's been about a year since I've been able to participate in many things of this sort. So, to quote a once-famous vice-presidential candidate: Who am I and why am I here?

I'm not normally someone who writes much about Scotus or about Western scholasticism in general. I'm an Eastern Orthodox scholar. The thoughts in this paper, however, were occasioned by reading Fr. Peter Damian Fehlner, principally on John Duns Scotus and John Henry Newman. The title of my paper reflects the broader project that I'm working on these days: a project on the metaphysics of the soul and on the philosophy of mind, and whether we can give up on the latter and get back to the former. This work has brought me into conflict not only with persons in neuroscience and various parts of the analytic philosophical world, but also (curiously enough) with some scholars of that robustly reviviscent style of Baroque Thomism whose detractors like to call it "two-tier Thomism," and that I will call "two-tier Thomism." Needless to say, I regard many in those numbers as friends—though, perhaps, also a few as enemies, of a cordial kind—and I am a frank admirer of their barnacle-like pertinacity in debate, and even feel a kind of grudging admiration for their proud indifference to other Christian traditions (such as patristic thought, modern Catholic systematic theology, the whole of Eastern Christianity in every epoch, and arguably even much of the thought of Thomas Aquinas himself). My encounters within them have also made me able to appreciate those aspects of

---

1. This paper is a transcript of a keynote address given by Dr. Hart at the symposium in honor of Peter Damian Fehlner, *Sursum actio!* at the University of Notre Dame, 15 June 2015.

the Scotist tradition that perhaps coincide with much of Eastern tradition, such as its approach to the mystery of the relationship of intellect and will. I am obviously not an expert here on Scotus, and so this paper is inspired by certain of Fr. Fehlner's readings of that tradition, as well as by my own inept, maladroit, and tentative ventures into Scotus's writings. I've come away with certain reflections, but forgive me if it takes me a while to get to anything that actually sounds relevant to this conference.

Let me explain that some of my problems with the renewal of the "Commentary Tradition" in Thomism have to do with what strike me as certain theological problems or deficiencies, some of which it is not necessarily controversial in this company to criticize. To wit: the infralapsarian displacement, for some of them, of the incarnation of the Logos from the center of the divine rationale in creation, so that the incarnation is reduced to a sort of superaddition to the economy of a natural and human order entire in itself, which leads even more basically to a sort of curious logical displacement of the divine Logos as the only rational illumination of nature *as* nature. By this I mean that there is a certain tendency to embrace the idea that the gratuity of grace can be properly affirmed only through a distinction between nature and grace, or between nature and supernature, so absolute that one must posit a sphere of nature perfectly complete in itself, containing within itself all the ends sufficient for all creatures, even rational creatures, such that even the intellectual appetite of a rational spirit could come wholly to rest *satis* in the purely natural terminus. Now, the reason that this ties into the work I have been doing on the philosophy is of mind is that, perfectly consistent with this view of nature and grace is the belief that that what makes the human being *capax Dei* (unless extrinsically superelevated by the gracious superaddition of a certain light of glory, a *lumen gloriae*) extends no further than an "elicited" desire for God, which is only a kind of secondarily evoked curiosity in regard to the ultimate causal explanations of nature. And this certainly cannot have as its natural end the supernatural vision of God. (I hope I don't sound like I am lampooning the tradition. I am actually quoting, more or less verbatim, things that Larry Feingold said to me in private conversation a few weeks ago, and has said in his book on these issues.) Because they are trying to preserve a vital partition between nature and supernature in such a way precisely—so they imagine—as will preserve the gratuity of grace, for them even the desire for God as *God*, the love of God as *God*, is a gracious, unmerited, and in a sense *unnatural* supernatural addition to human nature.

To put the matter very simply, theologically I regard much of that as disastrous if followed through to its logical consequences. But I also believe that when applied to the question of rational consciousness, it produces a

picture that is logically incoherent and that even the most basic phenomenology of the act of rational awareness shows to be false. The problem for
me lies not only in the very notion of a created nature so complete in itself
that the incarnation is not necessitated, with the incarnation understood as
a supplement in a sense to the to the gracious act of creation. The problem
for me lies also in the logical consequence that follows from this, which
presents the revelation of God's Logos in nature not as being also, simultaneously, the revelation of the logos of nature and of the human being. For,
of course, both world and humanity could be known within their natures
without any reference to the God-man. And it is surpassingly strange to
think that grace can be grace only if something prior and very nearly anti-
nomous to grace is first secured, something that we can call "pure nature"
that is an absolute immanence, so that we can then draw a clear demarca-
tion between the first and the second gifts of grace. Now, a certain exercise
of subtlety here is necessary; but, just as a general, global observation, the
doctrine of creation from nothingness is from the first an assertion that
everything, of course, is already unmerited gratuity, a perfect donation in
both its essence and its existence, and we need no more insist upon the
category of pure nature to secure the freedom of the supernatural and of
sanctifying grace than we would need the notion of "pure nothingness" to
ensure the sovereignty of God's work in creation. All of created being is in its
most primordial nature an ecstasy from nothingness towards God: *ex nihilo
in infinitum*. Being has in its inmost essence the shape of a movement of love
and this is especially obvious in the case of spiritual creatures.

This is the crux of the issue for me when I think about just the phenomenology of consciousness. As I say, that is my chief concern: the structure of
rational consciousness, and especially of the act of consciousness, understood as being irreducibly intentional. It is here that I find not only that the
traditional Thomist system is inadequate, but also that the more Augustinian
account of memory, intellect, and will preserved within the Scotist tradition
points towards a model of consciousness that is genuinely intentional. How
we think it through in the light of later philosophical questions is a different
matter. But, I find it impossible to avoid the force of that famous question
Henri de Lubac addressed to Maurice Blondel, in a private letter that has
become famous. De Lubac asks: "How can rational spirit be anything other
than an absolute desire for God"? And, to be honest, it is a question that
does not even require a theological premise, even if it is posed in reaction to
a theological enigma. If, even for rational creatures, the supernatural vision
of God—this is the theological issue—is a wholly gratuitous superaddition,
and if the natural status of rational creatures as *capax Dei* can be exhausted
by an elicited curiosity secondary to concrete experience, and, if it is taken

for granted that there is a necessary proportionality between created apti-
tudes and their natural final causes, and if the will always and only follows
the intellect, all of this means that rational consciousness can function as a
finite orientation towards a finite final causality, correctly grasping reality
within a perfectly finite range of intelligibility, through a desire that can be
sated by coming to rest in a finite object. We know this cannot be true, not
for theological reasons, at least not only for theological reasons, but because
of simple logical problems that the notion raises.

I do not have a great deal of patience for much modern philosophy of
mind, but one of the refreshing developments of recent years has been the
greater attention being paid to intentionality as a special problem in our
understanding of rational consciousness: the mind's capacity for "about-
ness," by which it thinks, desires, believes, means, represents, wills, imagines, or otherwise orients itself towards a specific object, purpose, or end.
Intentionality is present in all perception, conception, language, cogitation,
imagination, expectation, hope, and fear, as well as in every other determinate act of the conscious intellect—even the barest most minimal instance
of cognition. To know is to intend meaning, to interpret concrete experiences as having *this* determinate content, answering to *this* orientation of
the mind. Not that this was not a topic of scholastic thought. It certainly
was. But I think it can be said fairly that for modern philosophy it was not
until Franz Brentano in the nineteenth century declared intentionality the
very mark of the mental and of its nature, something entirely absent from
merely material mechanical physical order, that the question began to make
itself felt as a special problem—logical and then phenomenological—in the
philosophy of conscious acts. And it was perhaps not until the twentieth
century phenomenological schools (and I don't mean here just Husserl—
certain writings of Edith Stein are very fascinating on this this topic) began
to make more than a marginal impression upon philosophers of mind that
the full dimensions of the problem started to be appreciated.

My particular interest, moreover, is in the necessarily *transcendental*
structure of reason. I mean to say, consciousness obviously does not merely
passively reflect the reality of the world. It is necessarily a dynamic movement of reason and will towards reality. It becomes actual only through
intentionality, and intentionality is, however else we understand it, a kind
of agency directed towards an end. We could never know the world from a
purely receptive position, obviously. To know anything the mind must be
actively disposed towards things outside itself, always at work interpreting
experience. The world is intelligible to us because we reach out towards it or
reach beyond it, coming to know the endless diversity of particular things
within the embrace of a more general and abstract yearning for knowledge

of truth as such, and by way of an aboriginal inclination of the mind towards reality as a comprehensible whole. In every moment of awareness,
the mind at once receives and composes the world, discerning meaning in
the objects of experience precisely through its power of conferring meaning upon them. Thus, consciousness lies open to and enters into intimate
communion with the *forms* of things. Every venture of reason towards an
end, moreover, is prompted by a desire of the mind—a rational appetite.
Our knowledge is born out of a predisposition, also, and predilection of
the will towards beings, a longing for the ideal comprehensibility of things
and a natural orientation of the mind towards that infinite horizon of intelligibility that is Being itself. Thus, the mind never simply submissively
registers sensory data, like wax receiving the impression of a signet, and all
scholastic schools agree upon the agency of the of the mind in abstraction.
The mind is constantly at work, organizing what it receives from the senses
into form and meaning. This it does because it has a certain natural compul-
sion to do so, a certain interestedness that exceeds most of the individual
objects of knowledge that it encounters because we are driven by a prior
and consuming interest in reality as such. So, there is simply no such thing
as knowledge entirely devoid of desire. I am sorry if I am saying something
we all already know, but I have to trace out my steps to show where I'm
going. You could not make cognitive sense of a glass of water or a tree on a
hill apart from the action of your mind towards some end found either *in*
that thing or *beyond* that thing, and so all knowledge involves an adventure
of the mind beyond itself. Desire, moreover, is never purely spontaneous.
It does not arise without premise out of some aimless nothingness within
the will, but always moves towards an end, real or imagined, which draws
it on towards the Good. Will is, moreover, of its nature teleological, and
every rational act is intrinsically purposive, prompted by some final cause.
One cannot freely stir a finger without the lure of some aim, proximate or
remote, great or small, constant or evanescent. But what is it that the mind
desires, then, or even that the mind loves, when it is moved to seek the ideal-
ity of things—the intelligibility, I mean, of experience as a whole? What is it
that continues to compel thought onward whether or not the mind happens
at any given moment to have some attachment to the immediate objects
of its cognizance, of its experience? What is the horizon of that limitless
directedness of consciousness that allows the mind to define the limits of
the world it knows? Whatever it is, its end lies always further beyond what
is ever near at hand, and it excites in the mind a need not merely to be aware
but truly to know, to discern meaning, to grasp hold of being, to embrace
it under the aspect of intelligible truth or of a desirable goodness or beauty.
So, there is always a kind of deferral of finite desire towards ultimate ends,

and there is always a greater and more remote purpose for the sake of which one wants whatever one wants. All concretely limited aspirations of the will are sustained within formally limitless aspirations of the will, which is to say, movements of the will towards transcendent perfections. These transcendentals constitute an absolute orientation for thought, that horizon of being of which I spoke above, towards which the mind is always turned and against which every finite object is set off in clear and distinct outlines in the great middle distance of the phenomenal world.

Now, clearly, we are not speaking here about one or another mood or private disposition of which one is continuously conscious. Neither, obviously, are we only speaking of will in the sense just of a choice made after a process of deliberation. This vocation of the mind to absolute ends is not a simple psychological state. It is a transcendental condition of thought, which is in some sense logically prior to the finite identity and diverse impulses of the ego. To wax unnecessarily but only momentarily Kantian, the vanishing point of the mind's inner coherence and simplicity is met by the vanishing point of the world's highest values. The gaze of the apperceptive "I" is turned towards a transcendental "that" which is forever beyond. And any mental experience of the self or of the world outside the self takes shape in the relation between these two transcendental polls. The rational mind is able to know reality with the fullness it does because of its singular ability to go beyond each object of experience and therefore to comprehend that object within more capacious conceptual categories. Ultimately, the mind knows the world as a whole because it has always already in its intentions exceeded the world. Consciousness contains nature as a complete and cogent reality because it is always gone beyond nature. It has a *supernatural* end. The mind possesses the capacity to understand and to judge because it is obedient to absolute values that appear as concrete realities nowhere within the physical order. Yet I am most definitely speaking of an act of willing, in its way as primordial as any act of the intellect, and indeed logically prior to every finite discovery of the intellect.

Another way of saying this is that the intellect is the ward of a primordial movement of love. If reason's primordial orientation is indeed towards total intelligibility and perfect truth (and I think that it obviously is, as otherwise we would not have a desire to know at all—we would not know), then it is essentially a kind of ecstasy of the mind towards an end beyond the limits of nature. It is an impossibly extravagant appetite, a longing that can be sated only by a fullness that can never be reached in the world, but that instead ceaselessly opens the world to consciousness. Thus, the restless heart that seeks its repose in God, to use Augustine's language, expresses itself not only in the exaltations and raptures of spiritual experience, but also in the plain persistence of awareness. The unquenchable *eros* of the soul for the divine of which the mystics speak is the acute manifestation of the love that, in a more chronic and subtle form, underlies all knowledge, all openness of the mind to the truth of things. This is because in God the fullness of being is also a perfect act of infinite consciousness that, wholly possessing the truth of being in itself, forever finds its consummation and boundless delight. The Father knows his own essence—here one can work from within either the Augustinian realm or Cappadocian. The Father knows his own essence perfectly in the mirror of the Logos and rejoices in the Spirit who is the bond of love or bond of glory in which divine being and divine consciousness are perfectly joined. The ecstatic structure of finite consciousness, then, this inextinguishable yearning for truth that weds the mind to the being of all things, is simply a manifestation of the metaphysical structure of all reality; and that is because all created reality reflects the *ordo amoris* that is the life of God.

One might reasonably ask, then, what does all this have to do with the topic of this symposium? Maybe nothing. But I should at this point mention Bernard Lonergan. He became impatient in his later years with what he called the "faculty psychology" tradition of scholastic thought, and with the regularity with which many of his colleagues continued to demand he explain his thinking in a way consonant with what he saw as an oddly static conception of intellect and will as two discrete powers almost literally *related* to one another, almost as if separate components within a mechanism, and in a very specific order of priority and sequacity. He came to realize, I think, that simply to say that the will follows the intellect can be nearly as meaningless as to say that the day follows the night. But that very recognition perhaps allows one to see how the Scotist understanding of the faculties of the soul is already a movement beyond any confiningly (for want of a better word) "automatic" relation between them. Between intellect and will there exists only a formal distinction of what, in the life of the soul, is a dynamic unity, as both faculties are rational and, in fact, are rational only to the degree that the will is engaged in the act of understanding from the first. I mean, yes, considered as an entirely static arrangement, one can say with some assurance that will must follow intellect, in the fairly trivial sense that any predilective act must be directed towards the end that the mind has conceived. Conversely, however, considered as an event—as the actual dynamic action of the soul towards knowledge or resolve and hence, transcendentally, towards truth as such or the good as such—every act of the mind must be intentional, and intentionality must be from the first the turning of the mind towards the real inspired by a prior consuming love for the whole of being *as* the true and the good. This desire for the whole of being simply *is* the original structure of knowing, and this structure seems to me to necessitate at least two affirmations that the Scotist tradition encourages and that certain other traditions (we need not name them) might deny. First, the primary object of the intellect is *ens*, not simply *quidditas* or *species*, at least in the sense that no essence or form is comprehensible as the sufficient or final cause of thought, but must be embraced within an orientation of the mind that is nothing less than the total intentionality towards the inexhaustible transcendental desirability of being itself. Hence, what is spoken of as an apprehension of being as being, and therefore some intellectual intuition of any given object as first *existing*, seems a necessary prerequisite for any intellectual act. And this means, second, that one can posit of rational spirit a natural aptitude that is *capax Dei*, teleologically proportioned to the vision of God naturally, rather than by a superaddition, and not merely an elicited curiosity about the causal origins of nature that could satisfactorily terminate in some formal definition of God as first efficient cause, or in an analogical postulate regarding that cause. One must posit this, moreover, not only as some edifying affirmation of the wonderful spiritual capacity of rational creatures, but rather as an indispensable logical premise for any coherent attempt to explain rational consciousness as the phenomenon it so resplendently obviously is.

Yes, will must follow intellect, but so also must intellect follow the rational will, and from the very first. To love, one must know what one loves. This is also true. But again, to know, one must love what one knows first under the transcendental aspects of being: within the horizon, that is, of those transcendental aspirations that allow every finite object of knowledge to appear as an instance, in some greater or lesser degree, of what is supremely rationally desirable. To seek a simple priority between distinct faculties here, then, is to attempt to reduce the movement of thought to a bare static structure of relations. But, in the infinite orientation of the concrete action of thought, the distinction is always already resolved in the simplicity of the created spirit's openness to the God who is himself love and knowledge.

At the very least there is a phenomenological plausibility to the Scotistic account of the will's agency as the soul's most purely rational aptitude, and not merely because it is not bedeviled by the kind of automatism of the will that seems to be the consequence of a purely thoroughgoing intellectualism. No analysis of finite freedom can ever satisfactorily present us with a picture of the wellsprings of the will. No one has ever succeeded at this, no one will. We can nevertheless see with a certain immediacy that the will cannot only fail to follow intellect with its assent—that mysterious power of *non velle* that somehow seems indispensable to any model of creaturely freedom even in situations where it would actually be impossible to withhold assent, at least as a formal possibility—but that the will has the power to inhibit the intellect's power of understanding by a willful withholding of assent or of desire or of love. And it seems to me that the specter of a pure voluntarism rears up behind this thought only if one fails to think of the will as rational of its nature and so conceives of it merely as spontaneous in employment. The will is free not because it can deliberate, but because it can assent or refuse assent; but that does not mean it can spontaneously reject the Good when it is truly perceived. Even if, admittedly, it is difficult to understand how the will acts or declines to act, even if one understands the will as inflected through—or perhaps stalled by the tension between—the *affectio commodi* and *affectio iustitiae*, still, at a purely phenomenological level, we know this power to be real. We know that there are instances when the failure to know something is truly a moral failure: not merely a refusal to follow, but a true refusal to see, because of a withholding of love. Even to know what we know requires not only the initial natural volition of the soul towards the transcendental perfections of being, but a final surrender, affirmation, or assent, by which knowledge becomes actual in the movement of rational freedom.

This, I suppose, is what I find most suggestive and attractive, for the work I am doing now, in the Scotist understanding of knowledge, specifically the knowledge of God. What I find somewhat lacking in certain other traditional scholastic accounts is the recognition that knowledge, arising from an irrepressible loving desire, is made complete in the freely given loving delight that completes the primordial movement of intellect and will as an accomplished act of supreme freedom, the loving Yes to the God from whom the eyes of the soul will never turn: given not simply as the inevitable affective consequence of active knowledge already complete in itself and so an automatic response, but as the actual attainment of the deepest and highest knowledge without which the intellect does not yet truly know the truth as *truth*. What begins as eros ends in eternal bliss, and logically must do so. This is the most Augustinian and most Trinitarian aspect of what I understand to be—admittedly defectively—the Scotist understanding of intellect and will: that the creaturely knowledge of God completes itself in a final love, and *only* there, just as the Father's knowledge of himself and the Son is complete only in the delight of the Spirit. Just as the Father's knowledge of himself, moreover, is complete only in the Spirit as the divine *vinculum amoris*, so the creature's knowledge of God is fulfilled within that same Spirit, when the concord of intellect and will become the joy of final love as a supremely rational act of assent (to use Newman's term). Creatures, no less than God himself, are joined to the truth of God's being by the bond of love. Of course, this act, no matter how actually impossible it might be for the soul that knows God to turn from him, is no more "unfree" (to use a troubling expression popular in certain redoubts) than is God's Trinitarian life itself: any more, that is, than it would be appropriate say that God's eternal joy in the love of the Spirit is *either* simply arbitrary *or* somehow externally necessitated.

Here, however, I am straying somewhat beyond my topic, which is somewhat humbler in prospective range. As I said, my real interest, just at the moment at least, is an account of rational consciousness that is both logically coherent and consistent with any rigorous phenomenology of the act of knowledge, and one that therefore answers problems that have arisen in modern philosophy. (And there has been philosophy since the sixteenth and seventeenth century, of which I can't convince some of my friends, that really has raised important questions on these issues.) In that respect, the Scotist tradition enjoys, among medieval systems or schools or streams of thought, a certain undeniable preeminence and conceptual solvency.

3

John Henry Newman's *Grammar of Assent*

Some Lessons for the "New Evangelization"

JOHN T. FORD, CSC

PETER DAMIAN FEHLNER'S ESSAY in *Newman and Scotus* presents numerous opportunities for discussion and dialogue.[1] One obvious option would be a brief appraisal of each of the topics treated by Fehlner. While this approach would provide a summary over-view and evaluation of his essay, the result might resemble an itemized shopping list: Christology and Mariology, apologetics and dogmatics, metaphysics and epistemology, etc. Another option would be to examine one specific theme—which would allow treatment in more detail and depth; yet if one is going to consider a single theme—the problem is: which one to choose? Among the attractive choices are Newman's idea of education, his view of spirituality and his discussion of the illative sense.

My choice for this presentation is the assent of faith—a topic that is perennially fascinating not only because of its intrinsic merits but also because of its contemporary relevance in light of the Church's current call for a "New Evangelization"[2]—a call related to the findings of a recent survey that more than one-fifth of the American population self-identifies as "NONEs"—people who are unaffiliated with any religion—a percentage larger than the membership of any single denomination in the U.S.[3] An important sub-set

1. Fehlner, "Scotus and Newman in Dialogue," 243–391.

2. A Google check of "New Evangelization" produced 424,000 results; for an official statement, see: www/usccb.org/beliefs-and-teachings/how-we-teach/new-evangelization.

3. In surveys of religious affiliation, "None" is typically the last choice, though, ironically, more favored than any single denomination. According to a survey (2014) of the Pew Research Center (www.pewresearch.org), respondents self-identified as: Evangelical Protestant (25.4%), Unaffiliated (22.8%), Catholic (20.8%), Mainline Protestant (14.7%).

of NONEs are STEMs—people involved in "science/technology/engineering/mathematics"; usually their education does not include any study of religion and, not surprisingly, many STEMs do not believe in God: some are atheists,[4] others agnostics.[5]

Belief in God was central both to Newman's pastoral ministry and to his philosophical/theological thought. From a pastoral perspective, faith was a topic that resounded in his hundreds of sermons; from a theoretical perspective, faith was the basic concern of his most analytical work: *An Essay in Aid of a Grammar of Assent* (1870).[6] Newman's description of the assent of faith is predicated on the way we humans actually think—in contrast to the way we humans claim to think or the way we purportedly should think—*pace* those philosophers who have diligently described how the mind *should* operate, Newman's approach was: how does your mind *really* work?

Newman's approach to assent might well provide a model for the New Evangelization: instead of telling people what they should believe or how they should think, new evangelists might ask people; how do you think? New evangelists should then be able to ascertain: (1) how their way of thinking might allow for an assent of faith; and (2) what are the disconnections that short-circuit the process to belief? What are the derailments that prevent people from arriving at an assent of faith? What are the potential detours in the journey of faith?

For such a conversation, one needs common ground and in that regard, Newman's description of the way humans actually think is both comparatively commonplace and presumably universal, even undeniable: we ask questions, we consider evidence, we make decisions. Newman implicitly asks his readers whether they utilize the same process in their decision-making—whether we are making the numerous mundane decisions of daily life—or whether we are making decisions of life-changing importance: where to live, what work to do, what to believe, etc. In our daily lives, as well as in STEM professional activities, do we not ask questions, consider data, evaluate options,

---

4. See, for example, Baggini, *Atheism*, which discusses atheist ethics, meaning, purpose, as well as its history and relation to religion; unfortunately, the treatment of religion tends to be superficial.

5. See, for example, LePoidevin, *Agnosticism*, which provides a clearly written, well organized discussion of the history and rationale for agnosticism as an appropriate stance in the STEM world; the book's treatment of religion is both knowledgeable and fair.

6. Among the many editions of Newman's *An Essay in Aid of a Grammar of Assent* is one with a useful Introduction by Nicholas Lash; hereafter cited: *Grammar*; a helpful companion for reading Newman's *Grammar* is James W. Lyons, *Newman's Dialogues on Certitude*.

and arrive at decisions? The steps of the process are basically the same, even though the content and context are quite varied.

In this respect, Newman distanced himself from those who put this-world decisions into one compartment and religious decisions into a completely separate compartment, like those fundamentalist Christians who do not allow an historical-critical reading of Scripture. In contrast, Newman claimed that reason functions the same way in both religious matters and in every day matters. This point seems crucial for "New Evangelization"; if new evangelists begin with "spiritual" or "supernatural" language in contrast to "worldly" or "natural" language, the conversation runs the risk of trying to converse with NONEs and STEMs in a language they probably do not understand, much less accept.

Insofar as the New Evangelization needs to contact people where they are, another advantage to Newman's approach is that it utilizes a process that is widely, if not universally, shared. For Newman, the fundamental differences in human decision-making are not in the process, but in the person: in other words, actual decision-making, while part and parcel of everyday life, is inherently personal and inevitably problematic. First, the fact that decision-making is inherently personal means that every person is going to have problems in making appropriate decisions—at least in some areas of life; colloquially stated: "that's not my problem." This response seems characteristic of NONEs: "God is not my concern." Second, the fact that decisions unavoidably involve problems means that every person must take responsibility for the decisions that one makes. One has the impression that NONEs want to avoid any responsibility that might emerge from a God-relationship; in Facebook terms, one simple way of doing this is "not to friend" God.

If decision-making as a process is standard, the content of human decisions is wide-ranging: (1) from simple mathematical equations (e.g., 1+1=2), which always have the same solution to (2) complex decisions that affect the life of an individual, a family, a nation, the earth or even the universe.[7] In real-life decisions, the outcome is always problematic, mistakes are always possible; as John Greenleaf Whittier (1807–1892) poignantly observed in his poem, "Maud Muller":

For of all sad words of tongue or pen,
The saddest are these: "It might have been."

7. The effects of self-centered individual, institutional and governmental decisions on the wellbeing of the world is a recurrent theme in Pope Francis, *Laudato Si'* (24 May 2015).

Yet, however complicated the content, however personalized the decision, however much time is taken, however problematic the outcome, the steps in the process are simple and consistent: apprehension, evaluation, decision; in Newman's terms: question, inference, assent.

Generally speaking, this reasoning process works—indeed it usually works quite well: I ask a question, I consider the evidence and weigh my options, I arrive at a reasonable conclusion—at least one that seems reasonable to me. Nonetheless, in practice, the process can easily be disconnected or derailed: I ask the wrong questions, I do not find appropriate evidence, I misread the data, I hastily jump to an inappropriate conclusion, I make a disastrous decision. Most of us, like both the judge and Maud Muller in Whittier's poem, have experienced a number of disconnections and derailments—even disasters—in our decision-making.

Not only are some of our decisions inappropriate, even unreasonable; even when the evidence is the same, why does one person make one decision, while another person make a quite different decision? In contrast to mathematics—if a=b and b=c, then a=c—where everyone comes to the same conclusion, why doesn't the process work in other areas of life? Given the same data, why don't people come to the same conclusion? For example, if all jurors view the same evidence, why aren't verdicts unanimous? The short answer is that we evaluate the evidence differently. Similarly, we all live in the same universe, why does one person (theist) conclude that God created the universe? Why does another person (atheist) insist that the universe came into being on its own? Why does a third person (agnostic) think that this question is unanswerable?[8]

The process of decision-making—moving from question, via inference, to a conclusion—implicitly is an attempt to "bind together" a variety of data in a meaningful way.[9] We are frustrated when we can't fit the pieces together in a jig-saw puzzle; we are happiest when the available data fall into place, like the clues in a Sherlock Holmes mystery. Similarly, we feel frustrated when we cannot prove the existence of God but we feel relieved when we have received blessings that seemingly can come only from God. However, sometimes we encounter "recalcitrant data": our attempts at problem-solving are unsuccessful, we cannot make any connection; the data remain disconnected—like items waiting to be packaged that somehow don't fit the container. Sometimes in the attempt to tie things together, the

8. Although many scientists are atheists or agnostics, many other scientists are theists, for example, the head of the Human Genome Project, Francis S. Collins, *The Language of God.*

9. See *syndesis* = "binding together," like "connecting the dots."

data come untied.[10] In decision-making, there are always potential points of disconnection/derailment (*asyndesis*) where connections seemingly cannot be made or where connections are made but subsequently break down or where we find it impossible to get things on the right track.

Five Potential Disconnections

Reflection about the steps in the decision-making process indicates at least five points where the process can disconnect or derail at the discretion (or indiscretion) of each person. Sometimes a specific disconnection occurs unconsciously and inadvertently, but sometimes a derailment is conscious and deliberate. (Some people seem to relish life most when things go wrong: "I told you so.") Succinctly stated, the first place where decision-making can be disconnected or derailed is in apprehension; then there are three potential disconnection-points in regard to inference, and a fifth in regard to assent.

Such disconnections can and do occur in everyday matters; a fortiori, they can occur in the process leading to an assent of faith. Just as every decision-maker needs to be aware of potential disconnections and possible derailments and their likely effect on personal or communal life, new evangelists need to be alert to: where a person's faith-journey can be detoured, where and why our contemporaries are likely to disconnect from God and religion, where faith-decisions can easily be derailed.

1. *Apprehension* as a Point of Possible Disconnection

For Newman, the initial step in the intellectual process is apprehension, which he understood as a dialogue between the mind and reality; as a result of apprehension, I give meaning to an "object." Newman's dialogical understanding of apprehension contrasted with those who view apprehension as the impression that an object imposes on me (like a signet ring making an impression on hot wax) on the one hand; and the conformity of my mind to an object (like calculating one's taxable income with complete accuracy) on the other.

For Newman, apprehension is historically, culturally, and socially conditioned in a uniquely personal way. For example, Eskimos have multiple words for "snow." Since their survival depends on coping with different types of snow, their "real" apprehension of various types of "snow" is much more

10. Kuhn, *The Structure of Scientific Revolutions* (1962) maintained that when problems can no longer be solved within a customary paradigm, scientists search for a new paradigm where the problem can be more adequately, if not definitively, resolved.

differentiated than people who live in the tropics. In contrast, Hawaiians may be content with a "notional" idea of snow, since it has scant reference to their daily lives. Similar to "snow" for Hawaiians, for STEMs, "God" is a notion both unnecessary for, and unrelated to, their scientific endeavors—there is no Catholic science, Hindu technology, Moslem engineering, Jewish mathematics. Thus, insofar as STEMs focus on "observable phenomena" or "mathematical quantity" and God is neither observable nor quantifiable, "God" is an unnecessary notion, irrelevant to the task at hand.

This is not so say that STEMs are not curious about God, but it does mean that the "God-question" does not enter their horizon of meaning *ex professo*, though it may be prompted by various extraneous factors, ranging from simple curiosity to an unexpected crisis: a family tragedy or death, a business failure, a national calamity, etc. Similarly, STEMs' interest in God may be prompted by an inexplicable event that is considered "miraculous," or by a scientific conundrum: where did the material for the "Big Bang" originate? STEMs may become interested in God simply out of curiosity, for example, why are some people religious and others not? In other words, some personal experience may bring "God" into STEMs' area of apprehension. Nonetheless, though the "God-question" may engage some STEMs existentially, it is collateral, even coincidental, rather than essential to their endeavors. The "God-question" may tantalize one STEM, but not another.

Every apprehension is uniquely individual: the way I apprehend a specific reality at this point in my life differs from that of other people, although our apprehensions may be basically similar. In addition, apprehension has a cumulative dimension, like an hermeneutical spiral: my apprehension of this datum builds on my previous apprehensions. For example: an adult apprehends in a different way from the way a child apprehends. Likewise, my previous apprehensions influence my current ones, but sometime my previous apprehensions block my apprehension of new data. For example, in the 18th century, when a group of English scientists examined a stuffed platypus, they thought it was a clever fake because there was nothing in their previous experience that enabled them to imagine a furry animal with a duck's beak.[11] Similarly, many STEMs seem inclined to categorize God as "a clever fake" due to the limitations of their apprehension.

The summation of my personal apprehensions at any particular point of time provides me with a view—a view that may be static like a CAT-scan of the body—yet the body is living and so constantly changing; similarly, my view of life is continually under construction, revision, enlargement, expansion. My view provides a window for looking out on life that is sometimes

11. See: bioscience.oxfordjournals.org/content/49/3/211.full.

clear and lucid, at other times smudged and dirty depending on a specific viewer (like a cornea with cataracts) at a specific time and place (a view may be obstructed). Accordingly, a critical faith-question is: can God come within your view?

The relationship of apprehension to God can then be illustrated by three different views: for a theist: God is clearly in view (from creation, revelation); for an agnostic: God may be there, but it is too cloudy to tell; for an atheist: the reason that God is not in sight is that there is no God. Thus, insofar as apprehension as a hermeneutical process can include an enlargement of mind or an expansion of horizon, the faith question at the level of apprehension is whether my view can be enlarged or expanded to include God. And so the correlative challenge for new evangelists is: How can I bring God within the view of contemporary STEMs?

2. *Inference:* Dealing with Data

The second step in decision-making is dealing with data: inference. While inference can be a simple step when dealing with notions—if a=b and b=c, then a=c—in dealing with reality, three different but inter-related steps can be identified: (a) data *collection*; (b) data *analysis*; and (c) data *hypothesis*. While these steps can be distinguished conceptually, in fact, they are often simultaneous; e.g., I collect (a) and analyze (b) particular data because of (c) a "working hypothesis." In other words, from the very beginning of considering a question, I am looking—at least implicitly—for a hypothesis that will furnish an answer, resolve my problem. Thus, my (implicit) hypothesis influences both my choice of data and the way that I evaluate that data.

By occupation, if not by instinct, STEMs are habituated to collect and examine data; and if STEMS are prompted to ask the "God-Question," they are likely to follow a rather standard three-step methodology in answering this question: (a) data *collection*: is there any evidence (for God)? (b) data *analysis*: does this evidence say anything about God? (c) data *hypothesis*: does the evidence, collectively considered, suggest a "God-hypothesis"?[12] Since the contours of scientific methodology are fairly standard, STEMs know from experience—especially from experiments gone wrong—that disconnections are possible at every stage of this process.

---

12. See, for example: Stannard, *The God Experiment.*

2a. Data Collection

Like the proverbial pack rat, STEMs are avid collectors of data; however, a crucial question in data-collecting is: what evidence is pertinent? Unlike pack rats, whose collection of things seems opportunistic and arbitrary, implicit to scientific data collection is a "working hypothesis": that provides the rationale for collecting this set of data (rather than some other set). Consequently, even at the initial stage of data collecting, a preliminary hypothesis (stage 2c) is implicitly operative. In other words, every investigator has implicit criteria for data inclusion/exclusion and failure to acknowledge and critique one's "working hypothesis" often leads to error. An investigator may fail to collect or may discard some data on the basis that they don't matter and he may be tempted to collect only data that fits his (implicit) hypothesis, thereby "fudging" the data.

Accordingly, a person whose premise is that only visible and quantifiable data should be collected tends a priori to exclude God from consideration insofar as God is invisible and non-quantifiable. Insofar as data collection is unavoidably selective and arbitrary, the data that a STEM so diligently selects may be misleading or counterproductive. For example, "Who wants to believe in a God who sends plagues to punish people?"[13] Consequently, a person excludes God from history in particular and life in general.

In addition to selectivity, another formidable challenge in data collection is a result of excessive data. Data collection can be an unending process—like the gerbil endlessly running on a wheel. An investigator can experience data fatigue or data paralysis, overwhelmed by the sheer amount of data available. In order to cope with a mind-boggling information-overload, an investigator may refuse to make any decision at all or may make a tentative decision on the basis of some data but disregard other data—with the haunting awareness that the non-considered data may really be the most relevant and important.

Data paralysis seems to be experienced by those agnostics who postpone a faith decision because "I need more information about God." Insofar as God is infinite, there is infinitely more data available than there is time to collect and process it and places to categorize and store it; and so no faith-decision is forth-coming. At this point in their data collecting, STEMs may be sympathetic to the "wager" of Blaise Pascal (1623–1662):

---

13. Some Gnostic groups in the second century gave a dualistic answer to such questions: the God of Evil is the author of the Old Testament with its horrendous events, while the God of Good is the author of the New Testament.

Let us weigh the gain and the loss in wagering that God exists. Let us estimate these two chances. If you gain, you gain all; if you lose, you lose nothing. Wager, then, without hesitation that God exists.[14]

2b. Data Analysis

Each specific datum may tell me something different than its neighbors; each datum can easily have a fascination all of its own, like a kid watching a pet grow. Data analysis has then a way of producing a kind of near-sighted-ness. First of all, modern science has become so specialized that scientists are prone to restrict their findings to a narrow sliver of specialization and are reluctant to make generalizations. In effect, "not only can I not see the forest, I am overly focused on a particular tree or even a particular branch or single leaf"; thus, while I can say something about a specific branch or tree or leaf, I can't generalize about the forest. The opposite may also be the case: a scientist may extrapolate from a particular datum and generalize about its implications: "I cannot see God in this datum, therefore God does not exist." For example, Charles Darwin (1809–1882) was seemingly haunted by wasps that deposited their eggs in a caterpillar who became their food-supply: "I cannot persuade myself that a beneficent and omnipotent God would have designedly created parasitic wasps with the express intention of their feeding within the bodies of Caterpillars."[15]

In data-collection, there are two recurrent disconnections: (1) an over-specialization that prevents STEMs from seeing beyond a limited set of particular data to examine a larger view; (2) an over-generalization which prompts some STEMs to extrapolate from the distressing presence of evil and/or the apparent absence of God in specific data to a denial of God altogether. Unfortunately, some apologists in the past trapped themselves by attempting to correlate biblical passages with scientific data or historical interpretation—for example, by attempting to correlate the "days" of creation with specific eons or by trying to justify the murderous deeds of an apparently vengeful god. Hopefully, new evangelists will avoid such hermeneutical mistakes by taking a more comprehensive biblical view, while encouraging STEMs to amplify their scientific view beyond the merely materialistic.

---

14. Pascal, *Pensées* 233.

15. See: imperial.ac.uk/college.asp?P=2753.

2c. Data Hypothesis

From the very start of their data collecting, STEMs are continually asking themselves: what do the data mean? How are the data connected? What may not be initially apparent is that every attempt to explain data is per-sonal to some extent—it is this STEM's hypothesis about the data. However, this hypothesis may, or may not, be accepted by others. In addition, every explanation is provisional—rarely does any hypothesis explain all the data: hypotheses are often modified during an investigation; a better hypothesis may emerge in the future. Science then relies on a process of evaluating hypotheses—sometimes accepting, sometimes abandoning them, while at-tempting to fine-tune them.

Data are not self-explanatory. STEMs construct hypotheses to explain data; sometimes these explanation gain wide-spread acceptance, as is the case with the theory of evolution.[16] However, the history of science has a long list of discarded theories—for example, the once popular phlogiston theory is now consigned to history books.[17] Constructing a hypothesis from a collection of data usually follows a prosopograhical method: I sort the data to see whether a pattern emerges.[18] However, the cubby holes or cat-egories for that sorting, as well as the assessment of the value of both data and categories, depend on my discretion; thus, a STEM's pre-determined categories may effectively distort the data.

Newman's example of widely variant historical interpretations of Greek city-states[19] suggests that historical explanations and scientific hy-potheses involve the personal perspective of STEMs and so their hypotheti-cal reconstruction, however notionally convincing, may later turn out to be dead wrong. The provisionality of scientific hypotheses is exemplified by the transition from geocentrism to heliocentrism to relativity; geocen-trism, for example, was a convincing hypothesis until the invention of the telescope. In regard to an assent of faith, this step of data *hypothesis* has both advantages and disadvantages. On the one hand, the proposal that "God is a provisional hypothesis" seems in accord with both STEM-methodology and STEM-mentality. On the other hand, the "God-hypothesis" is tenuous, since like every hypothesis, it is "always in play" and with the arrival of a more attractive hypothesis, it may be discarded. Thus, while new evangelists

---

16. For an eloquent description of evolution, see Johnson, *Ask the Beasts*.

17. See: britannica.com/science/phlogiston.

18. See: prosopography.modhist.ox.ac.uk/images/01%20Verbiveb%20pdf.pdf.

19. Newman, *Grammar*, 284–90.

may need to gear their apologetics to current scientific theories, they need to realize that scientific hypotheses may or may not last.

3. *Assent*

The process of considering data should eventually lead to a conclusion: the purpose of inference is to arrive—sooner or later—at an assent. Ordinarily, this easily happens in most cases of notional assent: who is going to dispute: if a=b and b=c then a=c? In the case of real assent, sometimes the inferential process is labor-intensive: should I buy this house? Should I make this commitment? Should I get married? Et cetera. However, there is nothing inherent in the process that guarantees that a person will make an assent, much less a reasonable assent because: (1) I may postpone an assent; (2) I may decline to make an assent; (3) I may make the wrong decision.

First, since assent depends on the way a person sees the data, I may decide that I need more data; yet the quest for more data may be unrealistic: proverbially, the person seeking the perfect spouse never marries. Second, I can decline to make an assent not only on the grounds that the data are insufficient, but simply out of sheer stubbornness: *homo sapiens est homo pertinax.* For example, in spite of all evidence to the contrary, the Flat Earth Society still exists.[20] Third, on the basis of the data available, I make what seems to be a reasonable decision, only later to realize that my decision was wrong. For example, a jury may convict an innocent person on the basis of the evidence presented only later to learn that the evidence was tainted. But is there really any evidence that is not tainted by the investigator? In broader terms, is it ever possible really and totally to avoid uncertainty?[21]

A major difficult in assenting about matters in the real world, is that notional assent does not inevitably or necessarily translate into real assent: good ideas are often difficult to implement. For example, a student, wanting to learn a foreign language, may spend hours memorizing vocabulary and grammatical rules, yet never quite manage to speak the language. Or for example, a thoracic surgeon, who is scientifically convinced that smoking causes lung cancer, may nonetheless be a smoker. In traditional theological terminology, the *motiva credenditatis* may provide me with a basis for notional assent, but such apologetical arguments cannot ensure real assent. "I may be intellectual convinced that I should believe; but I

20. See: theflatearthsociety.org/cms.

21. For example, see Heisenberg's "uncertainty principle" that it is impossible simultaneously to know the exact position and the momentum of a particle (aip.org/history/exhibits/Heisenberg).

may really find it impossible to believe." In the case of real assent, purely intellectual reasons are usually insufficient motivations for action: notional assent does not necessarily result in real assent; at some point, the human will must enter the process. As Newman astutely remarked: "I do not want to be converted by a smart syllogism."[22]

By its very nature, real assent in general and the assent of faith in particular are subject to disconnection and derailment. A person may consider all the philosophical arguments for the existence of God; that person may find those arguments persuasive and reasonable, but still withhold real assent. STEMs, for example, by training are prone to carefulness in advancing conclusions; they may be afraid of making a mistake; they may fear that the evidence is insufficient to make a commitment. Not surprisingly, STEMs may hesitate about making long-term commitments—for example, they covet the latest technological instruments, they tend to change jobs with relative ease, they search for cutting edge procedures, they casually abandon outmoded styles. etc. STEMs are quite willing to consider new options and discard older ones—for example, in arriving at a new city, they may go "church-shopping."[23] STEMs are well aware that hypotheses have a "shelf-life"—like the latest computer that is obsolete even before it leaves the factory. If STEMs are willing to consider (and perhaps adopt) the latest religious trend, they tend to do so on a provisional basis, reserving the right to discard it later or replace it with a seemingly better option.

Humanly speaking, STEMs have a good case because there are often advantages to keeping options open: a new and presumably better hypothesis may come along. At that point, STEMS do not want to be held back by long-term obligations that prevent them from opting for the new and hopefully better. Last but not least, there is the very human tendency, even among believers, to make God according to their own image and likeness. Such a tendency has a double implication as far as STEMs are concerned: (1) traditional views of God (or religion or church, etc.) may be unattractive and so summarily rejected; (2) a STEM-constructed God may be notional but not real; i.e, the "God" whom STEMs would like, does not exist.

22. Newman, *Grammar*, 330.

23 The era is past when newcomers regularly attend the nearest parish church; since many people today "church-shop" via the internet, parishes should have attractive up-to-date websites.

Faith: Analysis and Reality

Newman's *Grammar of Assent* provides both a theoretically insightful and a pastorally adaptable analysis of the assent of faith. Yet as Thomas Huxley (1825–1895) back-handedly complimented, the *Grammar* can be read as a *Primer of Infidelity*.[24] Although neither Newman nor New Evangelists would presumably read the *Grammar* that way, the *Grammar*'s description of the process of assent simultaneously provides a framework that shows where an assent of faith may be effectively disconnected, where belief may be derailed. Such an awareness at least provides new evangelists with some possible "talking points" for dialogue with NONEs and STEMs. While an epistemological analysis may frame such prospective conversations, there is no guarantee that a conversation will be productive; a logical analysis is only a cardboard figure of a complex reality: the very human process of questioning, examining and evaluating data, and then coming to a reasonable conclusion. Conversations about ideas tend to be notional, the assent of faith must be real. As Pope Francis has emphasized: "realities are greater than ideas."[25]

Bibliography

Baggini, Julian. *Atheism: A Very Short Introduction*. Oxford: Oxford University Press, 2003.

Collins, Francis S. *The Language of God: A Scientist Presents Evidence for Belief*. New York: Free Press, 2006.

Crosby, John F. "A 'Primer of Infidelity' Based on Newman? A Study of Newman's Rhetorical Strategy." *Newman Studies Journal* 8/1 (Spring 2011) 6–19.

Fehlner, Peter Damian. "Scotus and Newman in Dialogue." In *The Newman-Scotus Reader: Contexts and Commonalities*, edited by Edward J. Ondrako, 243–391. New Bedford, MA: Academy of the Immaculate, 2015.

Godfray, Charles. "Darwin's Nightmare: What Parasitoid Wasps Can Tell Us about Ecology and Evolution." 2001. www.imperial.ac.uk/college.asp?P=2753.

Hall, Brian K. "The Paradoxical Platypus." 1999. bioscience.oxfordjournals.org/content/49/3/211.full.

Johnson, Elizabeth A. *Ask the Beasts: Darwin and the God of Love*. London: Bloomsbury Academic, 2014.

Kuhn, Thomas S. *The Structure of Scientific Revolutions*. Chicago: University of Chicago Press, 2012.

LePoidevin, Robin. *Agnosticism: A Very Short Introduction*. Oxford: Oxford University Press, 2010,

Lyons, James W. *Newman's Dialogues on Certitude*. Rome: Catholic Book Agency, 1978.

24. See Crosby, "A 'Primer of Infidelity' Based on Newman? A Study of Newman's Rhetorical Strategy," 6–19.

25. *Laudato Si'*, 201; *Evangelii Gaudium*, 231.

Newman, John Henry. *An Essay in Aid of a Grammar of Assent.* Introduction by Nicholas Lash. Notre Dame: University of Notre Dame Press, 1979.

Pascal, Blaise. *Pensées.* https://www.gutenberg.org/files/18269/18269-h/18269-h.htm.

Francis. *Evangelii Gaudium.* November 24, 2013. www.vatican.va/evangelii-gaudium/en/files/assets/basic-html/index.html#1.

———. *Laudato Si'.* May 24, 2015. https://laudatosi.com/watch.

Stannard, Russell. *The God Experiment: Can Science Prove the Existence of God?* Mahwah, NJ: Hidden Spring, 1999.

United States Conference of Catholic Bishops. "New Evangelization." www.usccb.org/beliefs-and-teachings/how-we-teach/new-evangelization/index.cfm.

Verboven, Koenraad, Myriam Carlier, and Jan Dumolyn. "A Short Manual to the Art of Prosopography." prosopography.modhist.ox.ac.uk/images/01%20Verbiveb%20pdf.pdf.

Whittier, John Greenleaf. "Maud Muller." www.bartleby.com/102/76.html.

4

Special Creation, Theistic Evolution, and Marian Mediation

Jonathan A. Fleischmann

Quaestiones Disputatae

THIS PRESENTATION TAKES AS point of departure the following insightful quotation of Peter Damian Fehlner regarding two contemporary and highly popular counter-visions to the fully Catholic view of the 'one mediation' of Christ (1 Timothy 2:5), and in particular the mode of our cooperation within that mediation:

> Two objections to the Catholic theology of cooperation with the Creator implied in the mediatory vision of the world and of its development, in particular with the Savior as that is fulfilled in extraordinary fashion by the Immaculate, are often heard. One commonly stems from those protestant circles which, while often rejecting all theories of evolution, also insist in such wise on the uniqueness of Christ's mediation as to exclude the possibility of any cooperation with Him on the part of creatures in the work of salvation. . . . The other proceeds from exactly the opposite stance, one inclined to give full credence to theories of evolution, because these seem to sustain the proper autonomy of the world.[1]

In this quotation, we are presented with three views regarding the supernatural order of grace and the natural human order; and, within the context of the latter, regarding the material and spiritual dimensions proper to human nature. On the one hand, we have the "evolutionary" view, which in any of its more extreme forms (e.g., atheistic or pantheistic) is in obvious contradiction to perennial Catholic tradition, as clarified by the Fourth Lateran and First

1. Fehlner, "*Vertex Creationis*," 236-59.

41

Vatican Councils, and therefore clearly heretical. However, even in its more moderate forms (e.g., so-called "theistic evolution"), the evolutionary mind-set is essentially a form of neo-Pelagianism, since it relegates to mankind a sort of causal or natural self-determinism ("survival of the fittest"), even if this autonomy is subsequent to some initial creation event.[2]

On the other hand, we have the "Christus solus" view, as exemplified by Calvinism and Jansenism, which has also been declared heretical by the Catholic Magisterium. Once again, however, this point of view is not un-common within the Catholic Church itself, appearing in varying degrees as Gnosticism or one of its more "practical" variants (e.g., voluntarism and nominalism), all of which can be understood as forms of "theistic" or supernatural determinism, and frequently infect otherwise well-meaning theories of so-called "special creation."

In striking contrast to these two views, both of which are erroneous even in their more "moderate" (or perhaps more subtle and insidious) forms, is "the mediatory vision of the world and of its development, in particular with the Savior as that is fulfilled in extraordinary fashion by the Immaculate," which is a vision that supports both mankind's absolute dependence on God (i.e., our non-autonomy) as well as the absolute pos-sibility of mankind's cooperation with God (i.e., our freedom to love), both in the natural order and in the order of grace. This fully Catholic view is perhaps most coherently presented in the Marian Metaphysics of the Fran-ciscan school, as exemplified by St. Bonaventure, Bl. John Duns Scotus, and St. Maximilian Maria Kolbe, of which Peter Damian Fehlner is certainly one of the greatest teachers.

In the following sections, we propose to follow the analyses of Peter Damian Fehlner regarding these views of "theistic evolution" and "special creation" (as these terms are commonly understood), which, though they purport to be mutually exclusive and mutually exhaustive options regarding the origin of species in fact share much in common, not least of which being the fact that both are examples of erroneous mindsets that lead to heresy, and which both exclude the *true* third option, which is the oft-ignored but indispensible Catholic doctrine of *Marian Mediation*, admirably explained by the Franciscan thesis on the Absolute Primacy of Christ and the joint predestination of Jesus and Mary. Or, in the words of Peter Damian Fehlner, we will consider these

> Trojan horses in the City of God: Evolutionism and Creation-
> ism as explanations of, or as sufficient reason for the origin of
> the species versus Marianization: the law of perfect freedom [. . .

---

2. Fehlner, "In the Beginning," 56–72; 150–64; 237–48.

which is] progressive creation by way of differentiation of species so as to permit recapitulation in man first in Adam (male
and female) and then in the new Adam—Man-God (Head and
Body) [. . . which is the] joint mystery of Word Incarnate and
Virgin Mother wherein uncreated and created, male and female
meet in perfect spousal love.[3]

Special Creation

When we speak of "Creationism" or "Special Creation," it is imperative that
we avoid a simplistic understanding of the terms that we are using. This is
not because simplicity is a bad thing *per se*, but rather because a simplistic
understanding of these terms, and in particular a misunderstanding of the
way these terms are used by others, will lead to a tautological treatment of
the disputed questions, which will be neither enlightening to ourselves nor
convincing to others. Thus, in the words of Peter Damian Fehlner:

> What is called evolutionism and historicism has been con-
> demned by the Church. From this it does not follow that his-
> tory has been condemned. May we raise a parallel consideration
> in reference to claims, first articulated in the English speaking
> world by Cardinal John Henry Newman on the publication of
> Darwin's anti-Christian classic, that while atheistic evolution-
> ism is false, the concept of evolution is radically positive and
> imbedded in Christian tradition and revelation itself. Tradition-
> alism is bad; tradition is eminently good and holy. Pietism is to
> be shunned; piety cultivated. So, too, with the notion of evolu-
> tion in connection with the origin of species. This is clearly the
> view of the reigning Pontiff [Benedict XVI].[4]

Similarly, the first article of our Creed affirms: "I believe in God, the
Father Almighty, Creator of heaven and earth. . . . " If we do not subscribe to
"creationism" in this sense, then we are not Christian, much less Catholic!
However, in both contemporary and historic discourse (especially polemic
and apologetic), the terms creationism and special creation frequently imply considerably more than literal Biblical truth. In fact, popular notions
of special creation *ex nihilo sui et subiecti* of every living species, though
almost certainly based on a commendable desire to defend the truth of the

---

3. Fehlner, "Trojan Horses in the City of God: Evolutionism and Creationism"
(hereafter cited as "Trojan Horses").

4. Ibid.

first article of the Creed, are often inextricably bound to the error of "literal-ism" regarding Biblical exegesis, which, as we will see, is an error common among creationists and evolutionists alike.

Here we must make yet another critical clarification regarding termi-nology. As Catholic Christians, we are indeed bound by our faith to a *literal* belief in Sacred Scripture, which is the inspired word of God himself. This is forcefully illustrated in the famous exchange of letters between Augus-tine and Jerome regarding Bible translations. However, while *literal* is good when it comes to Biblical exegesis, *literalism* is and always has been bad. Peter Damian Fehlner explains:

> When the great Fathers and Doctors of the Church refer to the *inspired* literal meaning of a text of Scripture, basis of its *in-spired* spiritual or mystical sense, what they mean dogmatically and theologically by literal and spiritual must be carefully dis-tinguished from what is meant by the same or matching terms in logic (univocal and analogical) and in philology or gram-mar (literal and metaphorical). Use of these terms at different levels: theology-metaphysics, logic and grammar involves no necessary contradiction. Indeed, theological use in Biblical exegesis presupposes logic and grammar (because God reveals mysteries beyond our natural ken and speech in concepts and language drawing on logic and grammar). But by the very fact that he communicates to us mysteries beyond our natural powers of thought and speech, the technical use of literal and spiritual in the study of the inspired text must be carefully dif-ferentiated from that of similar terminology in logic and gram-mar. Literal sense of a biblical text is not synonymous either with univocal in logic nor with literal in grammar, but may also be analogical and/or metaphorical. Similarly, spiritual or symbolic sense of a biblical text is not synonymous either with analogical or with metaphorical.[5]

The fact that Sacred Scripture is *literally true* and at the same time *symbolic* is the basis for the entire Catholic doctrine of type and anti-type, which can be traced at least to St. Paul, and includes the entire system of typology by which the Old Testament prefigures the New Testament. On the other hand, far from defending reality, the error of *literalism* is closely allied with the error of *nominalism*, since both deny that in the mind of God the particular can have an eternal (or universal) archetype. The Biblical system of typology is wonderfully illustrated in the Blessed Virgin Mary, who in Catholic theology is understood as the eternal archetype of the feminine

5. Ibid.

in the mind of God,[6] but who was also a particular woman who lived at a particular time in history, and from whose virgin womb was drawn the new Adam, Jesus Christ, just as the old Adam was drawn by God from the virgin earth. In the words of Peter Damian Fehlner:

> When St. Augustine states that Genesis tells us precious little directly bearing on empirical science either in the ancient or modern sense, he does not mean it tells us nothing about the essence of the Creator or creature metaphysically or analogically. All the holy Doctor means is that our metaphysical and revealed theology is in this vale of tears no substitute for the study of empirical science, even if the latter can only be successfully conducted over the long haul in harmony with the truths of faith. Precisely because theological analogy as defined by Lateran IV rather than mythical or purely symbolic discourse is entailed in the account of creation and the work of the six days, the metaphorical style employed to explain this does indeed "literally" tell us something about the world which science prefers to explain "literally" in another style. Evidently, "literal" is not at all a term free of ambiguity, viz., is not univocal. . . . Error arises when one claims that the literal sense of any passage of Scripture is confined to what is meant by literal in grammar, in which case (as many modern philosophers erroneously maintain) not only theology in the Catholic sense, but Christian metaphysics based on the analogy of being becomes, as it does in Kantian inspired thought, meaningless, except as a way of interpreting the literal or real symbolically or mythically.[7]

To obtain a correct hermeneutic regarding Biblical exegesis, it is crucial to meditate constantly and prayerfully on the fact that God in his infinite and tender love for his creatures throughout history is continually communicating to us truths about himself, and even truths about his creation, that are *essentially unspeakable*, and sometimes *essentially unknowable*. As St. John Damascene tells us:

> It is necessary, therefore, that one who wishes to speak or to hear of God should understand clearly that alike in the doctrine of Deity and in that of the Incarnation, neither are all things unutterable nor all utterable; neither all unknowable nor all knowable. But the knowable belongs to one order, and the utterable to another; just as it is one thing to speak and another thing to know. Many of the things relating to God, therefore, that are

6. Cf. Pope Benedict XVI (then Cardinal Joseph Ratzinger), *Daughter Zion.*
7. Fehlner, "Trojan Horses."

dimly understood cannot be put into fitting terms, but on things above us we cannot do else than express ourselves according to our limited capacity.[8]

This is especially true in the sublime mystery of the Absolute Primacy and joint predestination of Jesus and Mary (the Franciscan or Scotistic thesis), which Pope Pius IX affirmed when he stated in his declaration of the dogma of the Immaculate Conception that "from the very beginning, and before time began, the eternal Father . . . by one and the same decree, had established the origin of Mary and the Incarnation of Divine Wisdom."[9]

To give one's rational *assent* to unspeakable and even unknowable truths in no way forces one to subscribe to the error of *Fideism*, as shown by John Henry Newman.[10] On the contrary, via the analogy of being, the existence of such truths opens up a truly vast realm of thought to which empirical science can meaningfully contribute. For example, the phenomenon that true propositions can exist that are unspeakable or essentially indefinable can be studied in the relatively mundane subject of mathematical logic via the phenomenon of countable incompleteness in proof theory; and one can gain considerable insights regarding the Franciscan notion of recapitulation, and especially the place of Mary, the Created Immaculate Conception, as the "Vertex of Love" in the return of all things to God the Father (John 13:3, 16:28) via an analogy with the "equal and contrary" action and reaction forces predicted by the third law of Newtonian physics, as was done by Maximilian Kolbe.[11] But as useful and necessary as science and mathematics are, to equate the "literal" meaning of Genesis with that which is measurable or even definable, not only shortchanges the uncreated order (e.g., God, the person and divine nature of Jesus), but also shortchanges the created order (e.g., the human nature of Jesus, the Blessed Virgin Mary, humankind in general, animals, plants . . . even incompleteness in mathematical logic and uncertainty in the laws of physics). In the words of Peter Damian Fehlner:

> It is perfectly true that the revealed account of the origin of the world as we know it is historical, and contains true information both about the material as well as the spiritual. But what this account means when translated from theological to scientific language using the same words, e.g., species, kind, day, etc., is very difficult and sometimes impossible at present to determine, as it has always been recognized to be difficult by great Fathers

8. John of Damascus, *An Exact Exposition of the Orthodox Faith*, bk. 1, ch. 2.
9. Pius IX, *Ineffabilis Deus*, Apostolic Constitution, Dec. 8, 1854.
10. See Newman, *An Essay in Aid of a Grammar of Assent*.
11. Cf. Fleischmann, "The Vertex of Love."

> (St. Augustine) and Doctors (St. Thomas, St. Bonaventure). For this reason the Church, even when condemning philosophical evolutionism denying the first article of the Creed, has always refused to define the exact sense of day in the work of the six days, thus acknowledging that something is to be said for each of the divergent opinions of such great Saints and thinkers as Augustine, Bonaventure and Thomas Aquinas . . . . Literalistic reading of the Scriptures, a failing shared both by evolutionists and creationists, equates the literal meaning of Genesis with "the sensible and scientifically measurable." What is not literal in that sense is mythical or fictional. The only difference between both warring camps is one of faith: the creationist believes the literal sense of the Genesis account of the *Hexaemeron* tells us something immediately relevant to scientific theory and practice. The evolutionist holds, that because it does not, therefore it is pure fiction or myth bearing only on the way we think or do not think about the material. Both are wrong.[12]

In fact, regarding the question of whether or not the first member of every species was created *ex nihilo* by God, while we may not know absolutely whether or not this is true in the cases of plants and animals, we certainly know that this is *not* true in the case of man!

On the contrary, we know that "the Lord God formed man of the slime of the earth" (Genesis 2:7). For the Marian biblical exegete, this passage is quite literally pregnant with meaning, since the contribution of the virgin earth to the body of the first man, Adam, who was made in the image and likeness of God, foreshadows the active, virginal contribution of the Blessed Virgin Mary to the body of the new Adam, Jesus Christ, who is that very God Incarnate. In the order of grace, the denial of Mary's active cooperation in the Incarnation, and consequently the denial of her active cooperation in the Mediation of Christ and His objective redemptive sacrifice, is the greatest danger of the position known as special creation, and why it often tends toward the heresy of "Christus solus," as exemplified by Calvinism and Jansenism.

Theistic Evolution

As we have already noted, terminology is important. Thus, while many versions of "evolution" and even "theistic evolution" may indeed be heretical, the abstract term "evolution" cannot be condemned *per se*, as is sometimes

---

12. Fehlner, "Trojan Horses."

claimed by special creationists. This is obviously true if "evolution" is taken to mean something as straightforward and innocuous as motion or temporal change, which are both measurable and so empirically verifiable in nature: as in the "time evolution" of dynamical systems in physics. To go further, the positive development of species of plants or animals within certain bounds, sometimes called "micro-evolution," can be observed over the course of a single human lifetime, and is therefore indisputable. Even when "evolution" refers to major developments in the history and development of the human race, it is equally indisputable that God can make use of the free choice of an individual to significantly change the course of the future, as in the case of the *Fiat* of the Blessed Virgin Mary to become the Mother of Jesus. Unsurprisingly, the Catholic Church condemns none of these notions of evolution; and this with good reason, as Peter Damian Fehlner explains:

> There is found in the solemn decisions of Lateran IV and Vatican I condemnation of atheistic evolution: viz., of the false and heretical claim that the world, material and spiritual, did not originate with a simple act of the Creator's will calling this world and each distinct species in it into existence immediately out of nothing, but by way of an immanent evolution out of an eternally existing matter. This condemnation, it is claimed [by special creationists], translates automatically into a condemnation of the abstract term "evolution" as atheistic by definition, whether applied to the origin of the world as a whole, or to the differentiation of the species. On such grounds any theory of theistic evolution as an explanation of the origin and differentiation of the species in the work of the six days would be *a priori* contrary to the faith. Such a claim is dangerous, because it tends of itself to a denial of the very possibility of creaturely cooperation in the work of recreation, and of the return of all things to God by whom they were first made. That denial is the basis for repudiating the title of our Lady as Immaculate Mediatress of all graces, Mother of God and Mother of the Church, Mother indeed of the Creator and so able to cooperate with Him in the salvation of the world. In a word, it is a denial of the classic thesis formulated by St. Anselm, of the very possibility that the *Fiat* of the Creator might be complemented by that of the Immaculate Virgin in the formation of the New Adam and work of recreation, remotely envisioned (typologically) in the work of six days leading to the formation of the first Adam.[13]

13. Ibid.

Not only are some forms of evolution *not* condemned by the Catholic Church, some form of evolution *cannot be* condemned by the Catholic Church without contradicting certain basic theological premises of our Faith, having nothing to do with empirical science.

It is in this sense that recent popes (e.g., Francis, Benedict XVI and St. John Paul II) have referred to (theistic) evolution as something "more than a hypothesis,"[14] or at very least as something "not opposed to the notion of creation."[15] In fact, it can be argued on a philosophical level, and independently of any scientific observation, that some form of "creative evolution" is necessary to deal with the problems of determinism versus indeterminism in the philosophy of science, as well as the physical space-time continuum.[16] It can also be argued that some form of progressive or "continuing creation," which would better be called "recreation" or "recapitulation," is necessary to allow the cooperation of the creature in the work of his or her own justification, which is the crux of the Catholic theology of grace and merit as opposed to the Lutheran *solus*.

Nevertheless, the recreation or recapitulation of the created order can only be understood as an evolutionary process if the *end* or final cause of evolution (micro, macro, or otherwise) has a pre-determined structure, or *hierarchy* in the terminology of Bonaventure (or sacred order in the terminology of Pseudo-Dionysius), which was absolutely prescribed by God *from the beginning*. In this sense, God's work of creation was, in fact, finished on the "sixth day" of Genesis, and all subsequent "recreation" or development in the created order, including Mary's monumental *Fiat* and the Incarnation of the God-Man Jesus Christ, are a *conservation* or realization of the work of creation accomplished by God alone "in the beginning." This conservation is not deterministic, but rather contingent on the will of creatures; yet ordered toward the return of all things to the Eternal Father by our membership in the Mystical Body of Christ, through the maternal mediation of the Virgin-Mother of God. This is the content of the Franciscan thesis of the Absolute Primacy of Christ and the joint predestination of Jesus and Mary, and the basis for St. Bonaventure's doctrine of recapitulation. Peter Damian Fehlner expounds:

> Translated into a discussion of finality this means that the finite or created world was created in a way to make possible a return of all things to the Father via mediation and recapitulation of the lower by the intervention of the higher. The so-called immanent

14. John Paul II, Address to the Pontifical Academy of Sciences, Oct. 22, 1996.

15. Francis, Address to the Pontifical Academy of Sciences, Oct. 27, 2014.

16. Cf. De Koninck, "The Philosophy of Sir Arthur Eddington," 99–233.

finality to be observed in the operation of the cosmos is not that of evolution, but supernatural mediation, ultimately of God himself, based on the absolute supremacy of the divine will and divine freedom, a sovereignty not to be confused with the immanent finality of natural processes. For that is what stands at the heart of the supernatural: the intervention of the higher or super-agent in a lower order limited by the species defining that order. Recapitulation does not proceed from the action of the lower producing the higher or truer. Theistic evolutionists in trying to meet the charge that evolution as such is merely a matter of chance fail to allow for this key distinction and so end by excluding the natural substratum of a world created for the sake of hierarchical mediation. Simply put, evolution and mediation are two completely opposed versions of how the world functions: the first insisting on the absolute priority of the natural, the other on the absolute priority of the transcendent divine will in explaining the differentiation of the species.[17]

It follows that the Franciscan-Bonaventurian-Scotistic-Kolbean notion of return or recapitulation is radically opposed to what is usually meant by the term "evolution," since the latter almost invariably implies a progression from a lower order to a higher order by some autonomous action of the lower order itself: random in the case of atheistic evolution; or given some (usually loose) guidance from God in the case of theistic evolution. In the words of Peter Damian Fehlner:

> One of the major problems of evolutionary theory is its inbuilt proclivity to divorce any concept of final causality from the operation of efficient causes, agents of change. All change, macro and micro, is therefore arbitrary or blind, a matter of chance . . . . This points to a second mistaken premise, one absolutely fatal for theistic evolution, that the finality which can be observed in the order of the world and in the disorder resulting whenever that finality is not respected, is inherent in the natural processes as autonomous. Translated this means that the creature at a lower level of existence, e.g., non-living, can actively elevate itself to a higher level, e.g., living, or in its most radical form to the very level of divine existence as in the Teilhardian notion of Christogenesis: Thus, God himself in some way is not only the author, but becomes the end product of natural processes. Theistic evolutionists often point to this "immanent" finality in the evolutionary process, as touching all aspects of finite existence

17. Fehlner, "Trojan Horses."

including the religious, as the "global" approach to all reality as the outcome of process [leading to the so-called "process theology" of Whitehead and Hartshorne], first fully articulated by Teilhard de Chardin, as opposed to the "reductive" Darwinian approach attempting to justify evolution on scientific certitudes. This "global" approach, they claim, renders irrelevant the older patristic-scholastic notion of fixed or changeless species as the basis for change or development in individuals, or in more general terms process is dependent on and limited by the priority of reality or essence. In order to make this transposition (essentially Hegelian) from *being* into *becoming* as the first ground of reality it is necessary to understand priority merely in temporal terms and, as Scotus would say, in terms of an "accidentally" ordered series. That is just what genuine Christian metaphysics in terms of the notion of being, and theology on the basis of the first article of the Creed, deny. The priority here is that of the eternal, of the exemplars in the mind of God according to which the Creator has determined the essence or *ratio* or species of each created type, and which in the material, organic order has been endowed with the power (seminal) to reproduce [in the case of plants and animals; to *procreate* in the case of man and woman created in the image and likeness of God]. The priority is "not accidental, but essential," as Scotus so neatly puts it, thus asserting the fixity of the species and of being, not in a phenomenological way, but metaphysically *a parte rei*.[18]

Rather than divorcing the notions of efficient causality and final causality, which are favored by the special creationists and the theistic evolutionists, respectively, the Franciscan-Bonaventurian-Scotistic-Kolbean notion of recapitulation hinges on the contingent, *personal*, mediatory (or terminal) causality of John Duns Scotus. Peter Damian Fehlner illustrates this mediatory causality with a very relevant example:

We might pinpoint the relevance of these formal subtleties by noting the distinction between biological reproduction and personal procreation. The first is a purely physical procedure, as Aristotle so accurately noted, directed to the preservation of the species via the multiplication of individuals, who never attain the level of personal existence and never exist for their own sake, but merely to conserve a species or essential type, so long as this is useful to the cosmos as a whole . . . . What is primary and principal in procreation is not the production of a new individual nature similar to that of the parents. Rather in the communication

18. Ibid.

> of a part of the father's nature to the child through the mother
> there is established a relationship of paternity-filiation, that is,
> the begotten is a *person* . . . . The essence of marriage, unlike
> reproduction, consists not in its use, but in the mutual vow of
> fidelity effecting an unbreakable covenant "until death do us
> part." Infidelity to spousal love, rendered totally efficacious in
> contraceptive form, nullifies entirely the procreative action dif-
> ferentiating human begetting from animal breeding.[19]

As Maximilian Kolbe humorously notes in his "non credo" to Darwinian evolution, progress and change are not the same. While variation may
exist, for example, among chimpanzees, this change does not alter their level
of perfection. Thus, these "children of Darwin" do not exhibit any progress.[20] In the case of humans, however, there is a possibility of real spiritual
change or transformation, precisely because of the hierarchy of created being, which has as its apex the created Human Nature of the God-Man Jesus
Christ, followed by the most perfect created Person, the Virgin-Mother of
God, and so on, eventually arriving at ourselves:

> In a Kolbian perspective, then, theistic evolution fails to take
> account of the order of grace, because though recognizing the
> origin of the world in a creative act of God, it fails to note the
> term of that act is not, without further intervention of God as
> Mediator, capable of a reaction equal and contrary to that of the
> divine action, or of autonomously advancing in perfection so
> as to be capable of such. . . . This vision of creation can aptly be
> described as hierarchical, one entailing the recognition not only
> of the difference (and inequality) between Creator and creature,
> but of the relative difference (and inequality) between creatures
> in perfection. Further, that vision includes a recognition that the
> source of that difference in perfection is an act of the Creator,
> the premise of progress, not its fruit; and that the purpose of
> that differentiation is precisely to make possible a higher and
> higher level of progress, or return to Him from whom all cre-
> ation originally came. That such a return should be by "steps"
> rests on the fact that such a return is a passage from the less
> perfect to the more perfect. Each grade of being represents a
> step, whose limits are passed, not by natural evolution, but by
> an ever more special act of divine love, a grace, terminating at
> an ever more perfect kind of being. That love, at heart a media-
> tion between the less perfect and the more perfect, finds in the

19. Ibid.

20. Fehlner, "*Vertex Creationis*."

"reaction" of the creature a cooperation, to the extent that such a "reaction" is informed by obedience. In relation to its own immediate finality that creature in reacting is the principal cause of its action. In relation to the higher purposes of God, that agent is a potential instrument, whose potential is realized to the extent its obedience is perfect in responding to an ever special love on the part of the Creator. Finally, in respect to less perfect agents, that cooperation itself is mediatory, for the lower creation is fulfilled not in becoming the higher, but in serving the higher in attaining its perfection.[21]

Marian Mediation

As we have seen, in marked contrast to the forms of "evolutionism" and "creationism" already discussed, which bear marked resemblances to the old heresies of Pelagianism and Jansenism, stands the perennial Catholic doctrine of Marian mediation and the unique grace of the immaculate conception, which form a vision for a complete understanding of grace and merit that includes the possibility of our cooperation with God as creatures. In the words of Peter Damian Fehlner:

> The Bible, the Fathers, the Scholastics, the Magisterium of the Church have always insisted on the mediatory vision in the functioning of the cosmos, created for the sake of Jesus and Mary. It is clearly apparent in the priority of grace over nature and explains St. Augustine's horror for the errors of Pelagius. Evolution as a substitution of becoming for being in general, and the being of the species or *ratio seminalis* in particular, in any form, is but a version of the opposite: naturalism, or pelagianism. A view of the world based on the mediation of the Incarnate Word postulates an origin of the world, not by way of neo-platonic devolution, nor Hegelian evolution, but one created, structured and coordinated by the Creator alone in the work of six days . . . . A full presentation of the Catholic doctrine of creation must give due consideration both to the origin and to the end of the world: to the last week (Holy Week) as well as the first week. In that doctrine the origin of the world, or its *exitus* (coming forth) from the hand of God out of nothing, the differentiation and coordination of the various species is the exclusive work of the Creator. The cooperation of creatures, of each of the species in a certain order of subordination of one to the other in the *reditus*

21. Ibid.

(return) of all things to the Father through the Son in the Holy
Spirit, is the work both of the Creator and of the creatures, [and]
is not a work of evolution, but of mediation by which the lower
is recapitulated in and by the higher and the highest (angels and
man) is elevated by the mediation of the Incarnate Word of God
to communion with the Blessed Trinity. Recapitulation, recirculation (as it is described by the early Fathers such as Justin and
Irenaeus) is the mind-set of the Lord himself.[22]

It is *no coincidence* that both Pelagianism and Jansenism (old and new)
are hostile to the unique grace of Mary's immaculate conception. According to the Pelagians, Mary's immaculate conception is unnecessary, because
they believe that human nature is untainted by original sin. According to
the Jansenists, Mary's immaculate conception is impossible (a "pious ex-
aggeration"), because they believe that human depravity is absolute and
irrevocable after the fall. Thus, when discussing merit and grace, it is the
Catholic doctrine of Mary's active cooperation with Christ, as co-redemptrix, mediatrix of all graces, and advocate, that guides the Barque of St. Peter
with a sure rudder to the *true* "catholic middle-ground" between "the two
shoals of despairing of man's native powers because of the fall, or ignoring
original sin and so exalting human nature that nothing is supposed to be
impossible to man."[23] In fact, the Catholic "middle-ground" between the
shoals of neo-Pelagianism and Jansenism, or of natural and theistic determinism, or of evolutionism and literalism, is not a kind of average point
between two extremes.

Rather, it is more like the pinnacle of Mt. Everest when viewed as a
topographical map from above. It is the meeting point of heaven and earth.
In the words of Maximilian Kolbe:

> In the union of the Holy Spirit with her, not only does love bind
> these two beings, but the first of them [the Holy Spirit] is all
> the love of the Most Holy Trinity, while the second [the Blessed
> Virgin Mary] is all the love of creation, and thus in that union
> heaven is joined to earth, the whole heaven with the whole
> earth, the whole of Uncreated Love with the whole of created
> love: this is *the vertex of love.*[24]

Thus, the mediatory view of creation, as opposed to the strictly evolutionary or strictly literalist creationist views, allows for the possibility of
our adequate return of love to God the Father, despite the fact that He

22. Fehlner, "Trojan Horses."

23. Cf. Hardon, *History and Theology of Grace.*

24. Maximilian Kolbe, quoted in Fleischmann, "The Vertex of Love."

is infinite and uncreated and we are poor finite creatures, specifically through the perfection of the Created Immaculate Conception, who is the *Vertex Creationis*, and who holds in herself all the love of creation. Peter Damian Fehlner expounds:

> In such a scheme the most perfect creature, the one in whom the reaction to divine love in creating is equal and contrary, is the one in whom the mediatory grace of the Savior is fullest, the one who is the "perfect fruit of a perfect redemption," the Immaculate, preserved free of all stain of sin, spouse of the Holy Spirit, Mother of God, first-born daughter of the Father, perfect cooperator with the Redeemer, mediatrix of all graces and perfect instrument of the Holy Spirit in the sanctification of sinners. The perfection of her love, viz. of her "reaction" is evident in the fruit of her womb, the Word Incarnate, the humanization of God, the divinization of man. And in such a scheme the progressive purification effected by the Immaculate as Mediatrix of all graces in all those who have become her "property" is but the complement of that "divinization" or "infinitization" effected by the Savior in recapitulating all things and offering them to His Father. That action on her part is not the result of our progress at any level, but its premise.[25]

The metaphysical possibility of the return of all created things to God the Father through the mediation of the Immaculate is based on the hierarchization of creation according to the eternal design of the Father from *before time began*, and it is *not* the result of any progressive evolution on our part, as has been postulated, for example, in the theistic evolution of Teilhard de Chardin.[26] God created with a purpose, and that purpose was the most perfect reciprocal love between God and Man, via the God-Man Jesus Christ, through the Maternal Mediation of the Immaculate Virgin-Mother of Jesus Christ. Though God created the world in a free act of unselfish love, Peter Damian Fehlner explains that

> The world, however, did not simply come forth from the hand of God; it was made to return to God. In Kolbian terms the creative action of God is designed to find a reaction in the creature. Except in the most perfect of creatures, that reaction is never "equal and contrary," i.e. could always be more perfect. It is a reaction always contained within the limits of creaturely powers, limits not determined by the creature, but

25. Fehlner, "*Vertex Creationis.*"

26. Cf. Von Hildebrand, *Trojan Horse in the City of God.*

principally by the Creator, and only within the power of the Creator to modify. A more perfect return to God, a greater immediacy and intimacy with the Creator, with Father, Son and Holy Spirit, is only possible to the degree that higher grades of perfection are introduced into the world. That is a work of the Creator, mediating rather than making. The differentiated structure of the world, the varied strata of perfection, though not necessarily the fruit of a creative act in the strict sense, are not the term of a natural evolutionary process.[27]

The realization of our ultimate destiny, which is perfect intimacy with our Creator, is found in our recapitulation in Christ, since it is through Him, with Him, and in Him that we are able to return to God, the almighty Father. This, however, is not to be taken in the sense of theistic evolution, which would result in what Peter Damian Fehlner has called the "orgy of pseudo-mysticism" of Teilhard de Chardin. Rather, our recapitulation in Christ is realized precisely in our membership in His Mystical Body, which we cannot obtain by our own autonomous power, but by grace. Further, our membership in Christ's body can *only* be realized by our rebirth by the Holy Spirit, the Uncreated Immaculate Conception. Moreover, this rebirth in the likeness of Christ is accomplished *only* through the maternal mediation of the Virgin-Mother of God, our dear co-redemptrix and advocate. In the words of Peter Damian Fehlner:

> In the context of such thought patterns there is evident the mystery and genius of the Immaculate Conception: the spouse of the Holy Spirit, the fruit of the mutual love of the Father and Son in the economy of salvation as the Holy Spirit is the fruit of that love in eternity, the personification of their mercy and love for a race of sinners, the perfect fruit therefore of a perfect redemption because preserved from sin so as to be Mother of God and mediatrix of all grace, the vertex of creation's love for its Creator, a reaction equal and contrary to the love of the triune God, whose perfection as such is evident above all in her love for sinners and in the power of her prayer and obedience to work the conversion even of the worst of these provided he is capable and willing to respond to this Mother's love, something every person short of a sin against the Holy Spirit, i.e. a deliberate and final repudiation of such love of the Immaculate, is capable of doing. In such a vision the doctrine of Mary's absolute predestination with Christ, and of her cooperation with Him as Mediatrix in the work of redemption from beginning to end, is inextricably

27. Fehlner, "*Vertex Creationis.*"

linked to the mystery of the Immaculate Conception, her preservation from all stain of original sin.[28]

Bibliography

De Koninck, Charles. "The Philosophy of Sir Arthur Eddington." In *The Writings of
Charles de Koninck*, 99–233. Notre Dame: Notre Dame University Press, 2008.

Fehlner, Peter Damian. "In the Beginning." *Christ to the World* 33 (1988) 56–72; 150–
64; 237–48.

———. "Trojan Horses in the City of God: Evolutionism and Creationism."
Unpublished manuscript, Collected Papers of Peter Damian Fehlner. 2014.

———. "*Vertex Creationis*: St. Maximilian and Evolution." *Miles Immaculatae* 21
(1985) 236–59.

Fleischmann, Jonathan A. "The Vertex of Love." *Homiletic and Pastoral Review* (October
8, 2012).

Hardon, John A. *History and Theology of Grace*. Ave Maria, FL: Sapientia, 2002.

John of Damascus. *An Exact Exposition of the Orthodox Faith*. Translated by S. D. F.
Salmon. New York: Scribner's, 1899.

Newman, John Henry. *An Essay in Aid of a Grammar of Assent*. London: Longmans,
Green, 1903.

Ratzinger, Joseph. *Daughter Zion: Meditations on the Church's Marian Beliefs*. San
Francisco: Ignatius, 1983.

Von Hildebrand, Dietrich. *Trojan Horse in the City of God*. Chicago: Franciscan Herald,
1967.

28. Ibid.

5

"In the Counsels of the Immaculate"

Peter Damian Fehlner's Contribution to the Renewal of Franciscan Immaculatism

ANGELO M. GEIGER, OFM CONV.

It is not so much a question of what place Mary has in our lives, as what place we occupy in hers that is the starting point of any discussion. Only when the correct starting point from which to begin any study of the distinctive relations between Mary and our Order has clearly been identified, do we find ourselves in a position to assess the claims and implications of the Militia Movement within the Order.[1]

IN THIS WAY, FR. Peter Damian Fehlner has formulated the importance of the heritage of St. Maximilian Kolbe left to the Franciscan Order. The question is not what is the place of the Immaculate in plans of the Order, but where does the Order fit into the plans of the Immaculate?

For Fehlner, this has been a burning question for a great many years of his intellectual life. Indeed, what is the Order's place "in the counsels of the Immaculate"? And what do we need to do to execute Her plans? In this essay I hope to provide a sense of the enormous contribution that Fehlner has made to answer this question. I will do this in two parts: first, in an examination of Fehlner's views on Franciscan charism in the light of St. Maximilian, which he developed during the postconciliar period;[2] secondly, in a

1. Fehlner, "Mary in the Franciscan Tradition," see note 2, infra.

2. The following are Fehlner's published articles on the Franciscan Order's relation to the Immaculate: "Poverty in Christ: A Christian Sign," 147–92; *The New*

consideration of Fehlner's vision concerning the way in which Franciscan life contributes to the intellectual vocation.

On a personal level I would like to say that I am very grateful for the opportunity to present on this topic, because Fr. Peter has shaped my own journey within the Franciscan Order more than anyone else. He has been a spiritual father to me since the day in 1985 when I was first given a copy of the conference quoted above, "Mary in the Franciscan Tradition: the Virgin Made Church." It was that conference which opened my eyes the nature of the Marian-Franciscan vocation. For this, his friendship and his fatherly guidance I will be eternally grateful.

Part One: Franciscan Life and the Kolbean Heritage

1. St. Maximilian's Interpretation of Franciscan History

In a letter of 1933 to the clerics of the Order, St. Maximilian Kolbe proposed "the cause of the Immaculate" as the "golden thread," of Franciscan history running continuously throughout, from the beginning with the foundation of the Order by St. Francis, to the present day with the promotion of the spirituality of total consecration to the Immaculate.[3] The standard division of Franciscan history posits two periods: the first, from the foundation of

---

Constitutions—Chapter One: On the Life of the Franciscan Brotherhood. Introduction and Commentary, access only to manuscript form; "Community, Prayer and Apostolates in the Conventual Tradition," *Inter-Province Conference 1979*, 34–54; "Our Lady and St. Francis": access only to manuscript form; "Life in the Spirit and Mary," 301–6; "Consacrazione totale, battesimo e ideale francescano," 60–92; "Vir Catholicus et Totus Apostolicus: St. Francis and the Church": access only to manuscript form; "St. Francis and Mary Immaculate," 502–19; "Mary in the Franciscan Tradition: The Virgin Made Church"; "Niepokalanów in the Counsels of the Immaculate"; "Two Testaments," 354–81; "St. Francis Anthony Fasani of Lucera and the Mystery of the Immaculate," 1–36; "Hereditas Kolbiana: Novus Impetus Influxus Mariae Immaculatae in Ordinis Spiritualitate," 1–17; "Conventual Charism: a Historical and Contemporary View:": access only to manuscript form; "Thesis of St. Maximilian Concerning St. Francis and the Immaculate in the Light of Recent Research," 1–23; "The Other Page," 512–31; "Marian Geography of Faith, the Kolbian Perspective"; "Marian Doctrine and Devotion: A Kolbean Perspective." I include here several unpublished manuscripts as well: *S. Clara: Dei Matris Vestigium*, 1–17; *Virgo Ecclesia Facta: The Immaculate Conception, St. Francis of Assisi and the Renewal of the Church*, 1–19. There are many other works in which Fehlner speaks of the topic of the place of the Order in the plans of the Immaculate, some of which I refer to throughout this essay; however, I include in this note only those works explicitly dedicated to the question.

3. Kolbe, *The Writings of St. Maximilian Maria Kolbe*, 486; cf. also ibid., 586. The numbering of the citations to this work refers not to page numbers, but to entry numbers, which are continuous in the two volumes. Henceforth, references to this work will be abbreviated KW.

the Order in 1209 to its juridical division in 1517; and the second, from 1517 to the present. Because of the central date of 1517, the point of view of this historical account is the controversy in the Order concerning the observance of poverty, which was ultimately resolved by juridical division of the Order.

St. Maximilian saw Franciscan history much differently: instead of focusing on what has traditionally divided Franciscans, he emphasized on what united them, namely, the Cause of the Immaculate. This is the golden thread. Hence, he saw two phases or "pages" in Franciscan history: the first page begins with the foundation of the Order at the little Church dedicated to Our Lady of the Angels and extends to the proclamation of the dogma of the Immaculate Conception in 1854 by Bl. Pope Pius IX.[4] It is characterized by the Order's defense of the doctrine of the Immaculate Conception and epitomized by the teaching of Bl. John Duns Scotus. The second page begins with the dogma in 1854, when this truth of about Our Lady, which is of the highest certitude, becomes a pattern for rebuilding the Church. Hence, in the second phase of Franciscan history the Cause of the Immaculate takes the form of the incorporation of the dogma into the life of the Church through total consecration to the Immaculate.[5] Thus, if St. Maximilian's claims are true then Fehlner's formulation of the question about the relationship between the Immaculate and the Order is the correct one. The question is not where does Our Lady fit into our plans, but where do we fit into Hers.

2. St. Maximilian as Eschatological Sign

Fehlner's point of departure consists in the presuppositions of the Franciscan way of doing theology. According to St. Bonaventure, thinking about divine things begins with the assent of faith, proceeds forward by rational approval and is consummated by means of apprehension of truth through charity.[6] In other words, mystical theology is above the symbolic or speculative modes of theology.[7] This is the reason St. Bonaventure believed that the life of St. Francis could be utilized as theological source.[8] He saw the stigmatized St. Francis as an eschatological sign given by God. Fehlner

4. Cf. KW 486

5. Cf. ibid.; Fehlner, "Other Page."

6. Cf. Fehlner, "Introduction," in *The Triple Way of by St. Bonaventure of Bagnoregio*, 63. Fehlner is referring here to Saint Bonaventure, *Sermo IV, Christus unus omnium magister* [V, 567b].

7. Cf. Bonaventure, *Itinerarium Mentis in Deum*, c. 1, 7 [V, 298a].

8. Fehlner, "Mary in the Franciscan Tradition," 13.

sees the Marian Martyr of Auschwitz also as an eschatological sign in this modern age, especially in respect to the Franciscan Order and its vocation to rebuild the Church:

> If the miracle of the stigmatization of St. Francis reveals the depth of his love for the Crucified and the degree of conformity of his heart to that of Jesus, then the miracle of the martyrdom of St. Maximilian reveals the way to the attainment of that ulti- mate objective for which St. Francis was inspired to found.[9]

In this, Fehlner merely presupposes that both St. Francis and St. Maximilian had an enlightened point of view. Essentially, Fehlner's position, which he has cogently defended for many years, is that St. Maximilian both formu- lated the question correctly and gave an answer that is theologically rigor- ous, i.e., it is consistent with the faith, confirmed by rational discourse, and the fruit of a deep contemplative life.

3. Fehlner's Postconciliar Interpretation of the Franciscan-Kolbean Heritage

Thus, between the late sixties and the early part of this century, Fehlner wrote approximately twenty articles on the subject of the Order in the counsels of the Immaculate for various journals, such as *Miscellanea Francescana* and *Miles Immaculatae*, the latter founded by St. Maximilian himself and edited by Fehlner between 1983–1989.[10] The context of his endeavor was the postconciliar implementation of the renewal of religious life, which had not proven itself to be uniformly successful. But Fehlner rightly viewed St. Maximilian as the apostle of our difficult age and a true son of St. Francis, whose mission was to rebuild the Church in the moment of crisis. It was in this context that Fehlner saw and continues to see St. Maximilian as an eschatological sign.

Further, Fehlner's insight was particularly pertinent in respect to shift- ing ecclesial models, which pitted Our Lady's ecclesiotypical place in the Church against the christotypical understanding of Her role. St. Maximilian believed that Our Lady as Immaculate Conception is a blueprint for the rebuilding of the Church and did so because this understanding was trace- able to St. Francis. To quote Fehlner:

> The intimate relations between the mysteries of Mary and of the Church there revealed also illumine the ecclesial dimension of

9. Fehlner, "Niepokalanów," 324; cf. also, Fehlner, "Two Testaments," 369.

10. Cf. note 2, pg. 58, supra. Fr. Fehlner was assistant editor under Fr. George Domanski between 1983-1984 and then editor from 1985-1989.

Francis' vocation to "rebuild the Church," thereby underscoring the Marian foundations of Francis' love for the immaculate bride of Christ (Eph. 5, 27), his reverence for Churches where the mystery of the real presence is to be discovered, as in his tabernacle, analogous to that original tabernacling in the womb of the Virgin Mother . . . .[11]

In a prophetic manner, St. Maximilian addressed the problems of modernity with what he believed was the antidote for our times, viz., the Immaculate Conception. Through prayer and reflection St. Maximilian concluded that the key to St. Francis' ecclesial vocation was precisely to be found in She whom he understood to be the mistress of history, because the history of the Order like that of the Church itself was locked in the struggle between the Ancient Serpent and the New Eve.[12]

In seeking to maintain a strict observance of the Franciscan Rule, St. Maximilian was actually situating the Order in the counsels of the Immaculate in respect to the reform of the Church. Thus, in Fehlner's view, the fundamental reason why St. Maximilian resisted all attempts to level the observance of the Rule of St. Francis in Niepokalanów was to secure it as the property of the Immaculate and had nothing to do with "divisive" or "sectarian" pracitices, or with "pragmatic considerations."[13] There was "nothing of the sanctimonious about it, for the discipline observed [was] not an end in itself, but a means to an end, in this case ever closer union with and ever more zealous service of her who is the zenith of humility and simplicity, the Immaculate."[14] St. Maximilian understood the Immaculate to be the Mistress of history and of the Order. It was this truth that he defended. The traditional observances of the Order at Niepokalanów were the fruit of unlimited consecration to the Immaculate.

4. Implications for Ecclesiology

According to Fehlner, this is because the form of life given to St. Francis is both Marian and Petrine, i.e., rooted in the evangelical poverty of Christ and His Holy Mother, and characterized by a committed ecclesiality, meaning that the friars as individuals and in their corporate identity are to be "subject and submissive to the Holy Roman Church."[15] These two aspects, Marian and

11. Fehlner, "St. Francis and Mary Immaculate," 509.

12. Cf. Fehlner, "Niepokalanów," 319–20.

13. Ibid., 314.

14. Ibid., 338–39.

15. Cf. Francis of Assisi, "The Later Rule"; Fehlner, "Vir Catholicus," 8, 11, 14–15.

Petrine, cannot be separated. By entrusting the Order to the Immaculate as Advocate, St. Francis was also choosing the Church.[16]

In fact, there were a number of evangelical reform movements in the thirteenth century, and many of them, like the Joachimists, were characterized by a profound anti-ecclesial spirit. Fehlner points out that by instituting a form of life in which both priests and brothers have a true common life and yet the structure of authority is hierarchical, that is, clerical, St. Francis was choosing as the form of life for his order the Church herself. To put it as Fehlner does in his doctoral thesis on charity in the ecclesiology St. Bonaventure, authority in the Church is to be exercised in the service of communion and not the other way around.[17] And in an essay on the Catholicity of St. Francis, Fehlner writes: "For the first time in a sense a religious founder consciously and deliberately embraced an ecclesiology as the cornerstone of his form of observing the Gospel."[18]

Thus, with this Marian and ecclesial form of life in mind, St. Maximilian effectively began a renewal of Conventual Franciscan life by way of unlimited consecration to the Immaculate, and in so doing reestablished the tradition of the great friaries, like that of the Sacred Convent in Assisi,[19] and the *magna domus* of Paris.[20] In the former, the life of prayer and work was organized around the presence of the relics of St. Francis, and in the latter the great Franciscan theological tradition was developed by men like Alexander of Hales, St. Bonaventure and Duns Scotus. It was in Paris, of course, that Scotus defended the doctrine of the Immaculate Conception.

In other words, in the City of the Immaculate the friars were committed the *"vita perfecte communis"* (perfect common life) after the example of St. Francis,[21] as well as to the study of theology in the light of the Immaculate, and the execution of a large apostolate carried out in such a way as not to quench the spirit of prayer and devotion.[22] Fehlner has shown that according to St. Maximilian's formula we see that Conventual life does not have to be a compromise with the life of prayer and poverty. Rather, when the life of the friars is considered "in the counsels of the Immaculate," it becomes a means for the renewal both of the Order and the Church.[23]

16. Cf. Fehlner, "Vir Catholicus," 8.

17. Cf. Fehlner, *The Role of Charity*, 164.

18. Fehlner, "Vir Catholicus," 8.

19. Cf. Fehlner, "Conventual Tradition," 34, 50.

20. Cf. ibid., 49; idem, "Mary in the Franciscan Tradition," 16; idem, "Conventual Charism," 20.

21. Fehlner, "Conventual Charism," 19.

22. Cf. ibid., 8–9.

23. Cf. ibid., 20.

5. Fehlner's Confirmation of St. Maximilian's Insights

St. Maximilian wished also to establish an academy to study the mystery of the Immaculate, in particular, the basis for his claim that the Immaculatist tradition of the Order begins with St. Francis himself.[24] In 1993 he wrote to the eminent Franciscan scholar Fr. Ephrem Longpré asking for recommendations of sources to accomplish this task: "I would like to explore more critically the relationship of our Father St. Francis, of his followers, and of the Order to the Blessed Virgin Mary, particularly with regard to her privilege of the Immaculate Conception."[25] The existence of a fully formed institutional academy is a desire of the Saint yet to be realized, nevertheless it was in view of a first step toward this goal that Fehlner founded and continues to edit our books under the auspices of the Academy of the Immaculate.[26] Beyond this, it is fair to say that no one has done more to fulfill St. Maximilian's desire in this regard than Fehlner.

In fact, in his Franciscan essays, such as "Mary in the Franciscan Tradition: 'The Virgin Made Church,'" "Our Lady and St. Francis," "Total Consecration, Baptism and the Franciscan Ideal," "St. Francis and the Immaculate Conception," "Thesis of St. Maximilian Concerning St. Francis and the Immaculate in the Light of Recent Research," "Niepokalanów in the Counsels of the Immaculate," "The Other Page," "*Virgo Ecclesia Facta*: The Immaculate Conception, St. Francis of Assisi and the Renewal of the Church," Fehlner has done the lion's share of the foundational work that St. Maximilian saw as so necessary to the Order's correspondence to the counsels of the Immaculate.[27]

Among the lines of thought developed by Fehlner in these essays are the following (this is a very brief summary of many converging lines of thought which Fehlner develops at length): First, early Franciscan sources corroborate St. Maximilian's claim that St. Francis, "not implicitly alone, but also formally and explicity knew, honored, and served the Immaculate."[28] Basing himself on recent research, but going well beyond it, Fehlner shows that authoritative early biographies of St. Francis and his writings give evidence of the Immaculatist orientation of the Seraphic Founder. Even if he did not explicitly use the title of the Immaculate Conception, his appelatives "Virgin Made Church," and "Spouse of the Holy Spirit" both express the characteristic

24. Cf. KW 508, 564, 647; Fehlner, "Other Page," 524.

25. KW 564.

26. Cf. http://academyoftheimmaculate.com/blog/about-the-academy-of-the-imm aculate/.

27. Cf. note 8, pg. 61, supra.

28. Fehlner, "Thesis of St. Maximilian," 1–2.

nature of his Marian devotion and qualify it as ecclesisal and Immaculatist.[29] In fact, St. Maximilian's quintessential contribution to the understanding of the Immaculate Conception is precisely accessed through the concept of Spouse of the Holy Spirit, which he took from St. Francis.

Secondly, Fehlner shows that St. Maximilian did not formulate his persective on the history of the Order wholeclothe, posterior to the foundation of Niepokalanów. Nor did he come to a theory about the origins of the Immaculatist tradition in the Order in the light of his own commitment to Marian consecration, but rather the other way around. In fact, he was studying the work of a little known Ubrian friar by the name of Filippo Rossi, during his years of formation in Rome, who articulated precisely this position. Fehlner writes:

> . . . [B]efore St. Maximilian "wrote" the first page as a prelude to the second, he had already read that page elsewhere, explained in such detail from a marian perspective that one may justly say it was the first page which initially suggested to him the second, not the second to originate a marian-immaculatist reading of the first as the justification for making the Cause of the Immaculate the central concern of the Franciscan Order.[30]

Thirdly, Fehlner highlights the importance of a Franciscan-Marian "geography of faith" by which he utilizes an insight expressed by St. John Paul II in his encyclical *Redemptoris Mater*, viz., that the historical interventions of the Immaculate in a specific place, where her "maternal presence is exercised and felt in a special way complements and reinforces the perception of the objective and supernatural character" of the mystery celebrated there.[31] Thus, corresponding to the two pages of Franciscan history are two historical centers: the first is the Portiuncula, the little Church dedicated to Our Lady of the Angels, where St. Francis chose to found the Order and where he laid himself down to die because of his great love for the Woman of the Apocalypse; the second is Niepokalanów, where the Cause of the Immaculate is executed in the mode of the incorporation of the dogma into the life of the Church.[32] In both places, there is a special active and exemplary presence of Our Lady, and there is the perfect common life patterned on the gospel, whose form is the Church and whose purpose is ecclesial renewal.

29. Cf. ibid., 9; idem, "Mary in the Franciscan Tradition," 9.

30. Fehlner, "Other Page," 514–15.

31. Fehlner, "Marian Geography," 264, 66; cf. John Paul II, *Redemptoris Mater*, 28.

32. Cf. Fehlner, "Other Page," 513.

6. The Development of Fehlner's Thought on the Order

A most interesting feature of Fehlner Damian's thought on this subject is its evolution. It began in the late seventies with a desire to see balance achieved within the Conventuals in regard to the implementation of the conciliar reforms of religious life.[33] And it developed into an ever more explicit conclusion that the Kolbian Heritage was both the solution to the renewal of Franciscan religious life in obedience to the Council and the recovery of the greatest features of the Conventual tradition. This work culminated in 1986 with the presentation of a paper to the extraordinary general chapter of the Conventuals on the Kolbian Heritage entitled: "The Impact of the Kolbian Heritage on the Relaunching of the Influence of Mary Immaculate in the Spirituality of the Order."[34]

Peter Damian's insights have proved to be prophetic. In several general audiences of 2010, Pope Emeritus Benedict placed the early Joachimite controversy within the Order in parallel with the post-Vatican II crisis of implementation, and proposed St. Bonaventure's wise and prayerful response as an answer.[35] We can say, then, between the extremes of secular worldliness and anti-ecclesial sectarianism there is the sanctification of the intellect according to the mode of *sentire cum ecclesia*, which corresponds with a sapiential way of doing theology. St. Maximilian exemplified this tradition in response to the growing crisis of modernity, and Fehlner has urged this solution in and throughout our own period of crisis.

That the Order should be destined to swing between the poles of secular worldliness and sectarian apocalypticism is the irony of the Franciscan phenomenon, whose mission it is to repair the Church. But the extremes are not inevitable, especially when divine providence has provided us the formula over and over again in saints like Bonaventure and Maximilian. St. Francis was given a vocation whose very nature was to embrace and embody an ecclesiology and an ecclesiality. As Fehlner has written, this was the cornerstone St. Francis' "form of observing the gospel," viz., the Church repaired according to the pattern of the Immaculate.[36]

The realization of this ecclesiology and ecclesiality involves at its most fundamental level an assimilation of the teaching of Christ at the level of prayer and devotion. St. Francis wished to live an evangelical way of life, i.e., "to follow the life and poverty of our most high Lord Jesus

---

33. Cf. e.g., Fehlner, "Conventual Charism."; idem, "Conventual Tradition."

34. Fehlner, "Hereditas Kolbiana."

35. Benedict XVI, *General Audience: Bonaventure (1)* (Rome: March 3, 2010); *General Audience: Bonaventure (2)* (Rome: March 10, 2010).

36. Fehlner, "Vir Catholicus," 8.

Christ and of His most holy Mother."[37] However, according to Fehlner, this is not the pietistic, anti-intellectual project that some Franciscanists make it out to be. And the reoccurrence of the extremes among the followers of St. Francis makes the precise dimensions of the Franciscan intellectual commitment a critical question. We might say that the precision can be defined as "the counsels of the Immaculate." This is what we intend to deal with in the second part of this paper.

Part Two: Fehlner on Franciscan Intellectual Life

1. The Sanctification of the Intellect

Anyone who has listened at any length to Fr. Fehlner's conferences or homilies has heard him use the phrase "sanctification of the intellect" more than once. For the friars who have long been the beneficiaries of his wisdom, especially those of us who have been blessed to be his students in theology, the sanctification of the intellect is known to be a theme of particular importance to him. In my study of the foregoing material it became clear how the Marian dimension of the Order, the form of life chosen by St. Francis for the Order and the sanctification of the intellect are integrally connected in Fehlner's mind.

The context is St. Bonaventure's broad vision of theology, which includes not only the speculative work of the academic, but also the simple assent of the faithful as well as the prophetic vision of the mystic. Fehlner writes:

> Without in any way denigrating the value of what St. Bonaventure (*Itinerarium*, 1, 7) calls intellectual [or speculative] theology, one may with the Seraphic Doctor regard this kind of spiritual contemplation of the truths of faith a mode of theologizing more truly theological than that which is characteristic of the classroom or lecture-hall. While it is surely necessary that the conduct of prayer be guided by the truths of faith it is also a fact that those truths are never so fully and profoundly grasped as when the activity called "theologizing" is thoroughly imbued with the spirit of prayer and devotion, is carried out, i.e., in a contemplative rather than academic mode.[38]

The phrase above "the spirit of prayer and devotion," are the words of St. Francis to St. Anthony by which the Seraphic Founder laid down the

37. Francis of Assisi, *The Last Will Written for Saint Clare and Her Sisters*, 46.
38. Fehlner, "Marian Geography," 264.

conditions for the teaching of theology to the brothers.[39] St. Francis is quoting the *Rule* in regard to way the friars ought to conduct their work in the service of God.[40] Thus, Fehlner sees the Bonaventurian mode of doing theology to be an integral development of the understanding of Franciscan religious life. St. Francis himself is the ideal of the pious assent of the simple faithful. Yet he also exemplifies the prophetic vision of the mystic and sums up in his clear simple, evangelical manner of life what the academic hopes to achieve speculatively.

In fact, through Bonaventure, the friars learned to read Francis like a book. The *Legenda Minor*, in fact is a liturgical text, a "choir legend," which reinforced Franciscan identity in the context of the liturgical *lectio*.[41] What in fact the friars learned in choir was Francis' way of reading and assimilating sacred scripture, viz., as a mode an illuminating descent into the sacred page and ascent into the blinding source of that illumination.[42] The form of life of the friars demands the pious assent of faith expressed in fidelity to the teaching of the gospel as interpreted by the Holy Roman Church. The observance of this form, linked inextricably to the instrumentality of Christ and the sacred page, is particularly oriented toward the fruitful reception of divine revelation achieved in supernatural wisdom. Bonaventure also expresses the symbolism of ascent and descent in the *Legenda Major*. There he writes of St. Francis:

> . . . [A]lthough he had no skill in Sacred Scripture acquired through study, his intellect, illumined by the brilliance of eternal light, *probed the depths* of Scripture with remarkable acumen. Free from all stain, his genius penetrated the hidden depths of the mysteries, and where the scholarship of the teacher stands outside, the affection of the lover entered in.[43]

Reading this we must be careful to understand Bonaventure's point is not to radically distinguish the scholar from the lover, or to suggest that pious assent is surpassed by academic theology only later to be superseded by the mystical life. In fact, symbolic, speculative and mystical theology are three spheres of the same order, not sequential but conjunctive. They may

---

39. Francis of Assisi, "A Letter to St. Anthony," 79.

40. cf. Francis of Assisi, "The Later Rule," c. 5, 140; also, Fehlner, "Mary in the Franciscan Tradition," 12.

41. Cf. Johnson, "The Legenda Minor," 436–37; Bonaventure, *Legenda Minor S. Francisci* [VIII, 565–79].

42. Cf. Johnson, "The Legenda Minor," 442–43.

43. Bonaventure, *Legenda Major*, c. 11, 1 [VIII, 535b–d, quoting Job 28:1]. English translation is from "Life of St. Francis."

or may not all be realized in the same person, but to the extent that the contemplative aspect is absent from theological endeavor, to that extent it fails to reach its potential height. In his introduction to Bonaventure's *Triplici Via* Fehlner writes:

> the goal of all intellectual activity is to make present to the will, or to the person, the good: being as goodness, to be loved. The love of learning so connatural to the created person is rooted in the desire for God, a desire which cannot reach fulfillment except via the sanctification of the intellect in the Word of God made flesh.[44]

Bonaventure integrates the new mendicant charism with the monastic-scholastic tradition. The monastic practice of *lectio divina* and the academic *lectio* of the scholastic masters were both an attachment to the text of sacred scripture and to the commentaries of the fathers. In fact, they were not altogether distinct. Pope Benedict XVI has called it the "culture of the word," eschatologically oriented, i.e., toward the "definitive" lying behind the "provisional."[45] According to Bonaventure, the starting point of all theology is the assent through faith to the objective content of what God has revealed, and the end point is contemplative wisdom. Strictly speaking, the *medium* is theology properly so called, which in the first place is *lectio*. Only after this does it become *quaestio* or *disputatio*.

Bonaventure sees this *lectio* realized in a preeminent way in the Poverello of Assisi who called himself *simplex et idiota*.[46] The Seraphic Patriarch was not a pious literalist, but a man full of zeal, who received the scriptures from the Church piously and understood them contemplatively. He attached himself to the sacred text by meditation, prayer and contemplation, or what Fehlner has called "Franciscan *lectio divina*."[47] It is an ecclesial reality, which St. Francis came to embody in his evangelical form of life. Benedict XVI has said that the culture of the Word is not a "purely individual path of mystical immersion," but one that leads to the "pilgrim fellowship of faith."[48] It was rooted in pious assent to the literal and spiritual senses, as read by the Church, but open to the deeper meanings to be found there in contemplation. Through Bonaventure's *lectio* of St. Francis, which was presented in the form of *legenda* to be read in a liturgical context, he attached the friars to Francis' *lectio* of the gospel.

44. Fehlner, "Introduction," 52.

45. Benedict XVI, *Meeting with the Representatives from the World of Culture*.

46. Francis of Assisi, "The Testament," 29.

47. Fehlner, "Introduction," 48.

48. Benedict XVI, *Meeting with the Representatives from the World of Cuture*.

2. The Conventual Charism

Thus, there is an intellectual trajectory of the Franciscan vocation. This does not mean that all Franciscans are called to be academics, but that the intellectual vocation is integral to the evangelical life. Fehlner defines conventualism, the style of Franciscan life centered on the large friary, such as exemplified by St. Maximilian's Niepokalanów, in relation to the sanctification of the intellect. Its purpose is

> to realize in a Franciscan way an orderly interior life of prayer and mortification, to integrate the intellectual life into the context of prayer and devotion, thereby sanctifying the intellectual life and exorcizing from Franciscan piety the vice of ignorance, to cultivate the apostolate of penance and missions of the Order more fruitfully, and above all by providing solid programs of formation, spiritual and intellectual to insure the stability and continuity of the Order and the presence within it of prudent friars capable of guiding it amidst a variety of circumstances and trials.[49]

By this definition Fehlner answers the usual objections to Conventual life, viz., that it amounted to the clericalization and monasticization of the Order, ultimately leading to relaxation of the observance in disregard of Francis' insistence on evangelical simplicity and poverty.[50] There is no question that the Conventual mode of life occasioned the opportunity to institutionalize dispensations and relaxations in favor of the intellectual life and to pave the way not only for temporal prosperity and careerism among the *magistri*.[51] However, to reduce Conventualism to this problem is to oversimplify the reality. From the beginning there were different styles of life within the Order and it was not only possible but necessary to have larger more institutional type friaries existing along side the smaller hermitages.[52] On the one hand, where Conventualism simply formalized compromise the smaller hermitages had no place, but on the other, the health of the Franciscan reform movement had a real need of the larger houses.[53]

Fehlner's point is that without the Conventual life there would be no fundamental commitment to the sanctification of the intellect which would leave unchecked the "basic risk of Franciscanism," viz., that the radical

49. Fehlner, "Conventual Charism," 1.

50. Cf. ibid., 2–3.

51. Cf. ibid., 11.

52. Cf. Fehlner, "Conventual Tradition," 39.

53. Cf. ibid., 40.

evangelical commitment of St. Francis "degenerate into either an ignorant pietism or ideological zealotry."[54] In fact, according to Fehlner, true conventualism navigates a middle way between "the repudiation of the intellect in the name of devotion" and "the cultivation of the intellect apart from the authority of Christ and his Church," precisely by the common and ecclesial identity of Franciscan intellectual life.[55]

Both these extremes remain real dangers today within the Franciscan movement, and the *via media* is a matter of careful precision. In his day, Bonaventure was guarding against the extremes of radical Averroism with secularist tendencies and reform theology of Joachim of Fiore. Within the Order this dichotomy represented itself in the secularist and laxist tendencies of the *magistri* and anti-ecclesial temper of the spirituals. But the tendencies have always been there and so remain. Benedict XVI has proposed Bonaventure's notion of theology as a means of avoiding both extremes of viewing the second millennium as a "gradual decline," or of renewal in the Church after the manner of an "anarchic utopianism."[56]

This being said, it is important to note that in his postdoctoral dissertation, Joseph Ratzinger famously has interpreted Bonaventure's critique of the masters of Paris as an anti-intellectual attack on philosophy itself.[57] There Ratzinger also opined that Bonaventure bifurcates revelation into one content for the mass of men and another for only a few[58]—a division that orients the Church toward a future in which *ratio* will be completely supplanted by *auctoritas*.[59] But Bonaventure does not see the threefold theology as a sequence but as a conjunction, in which speculative theology holds the mediating position, under the influence of the gift of understanding between the pious assent of faith and the apprehension of truth in the gift of wisdom.[60] If faith, as the beginning, is consummated in wisdom without ever ceasing to exist this side of eternity, then there must also always be a *medium*, which is academic theology. Conventual life guarantees that that *medium* will always exist in the Order, not as an end in itself, but as a

54. Fehlner, "Conventual Charism," 7.

55. Ibid., 6.

56. Benedict XVI, *General Audience: Bonaventure (2)*.

57. Cf. Ratzinger, *The Theology of History in St. Bonaventure*, 156.

58. Cf. ibid., 61–62.

59. Cf. ibid., 156.

60. Cf. Bonaventure, *Commentaria in Quatuor Libros Sententiarum Magistri Petri Lombardi: In Tertium Librum Sententiarum*, dist. 35, a. 1, q. 3, conc. [III, 778bc]; *Collationes in Hexaëmeron*, col. 3, 1–4 [V, 342–4]; *Collationes de Septem Donis Spiritus Sancti*, col., 8, 5 [V, 494d–95a].

guarantee that the endeavor to achieve evangelical wisdom never become either simply an enthusiasm or an impersonal ideology.

3. Teacher of Evangelists and Apostles

Fehlner sees the permission of St. Francis to St. Anthony to teach the brothers theology as indicating that the "proximate aim of the Order" is an intellectual one. This is because for the Order to fulfill its "ultimate aim" to rebuild the Church and lead it to its final consummation in Christ and the final defeat of the ancient dragon it would need a blueprint.[61] The Order's "spiritual potential" could only be "fully activated" in the light of the Immaculate, whose counsels could only be adequately understood in view of the dogmatic definition of the Immaculate Conception.[62] Hence, St. Maximilian's organization of Franciscan history into two pages has their corresponding spiritual-intellectual centers: the "*magna domus studiorum*" at the University of Paris in respect to the proximate goal of the dogmatic definition, and Niepokalanów in terms of living and bringing to fulfillment the mystery of the Immaculate in the Church.[63]

This is a great synthesis, which St. Maximilian saw intuitively and began to flesh out in terms of a rethinking of Franciscan history. As already said, Fehlner has undertaken to tighten that synthesis and trace it more completely to its sources, especially in the person of St. Francis who had begged Our Lady to become his "advocate," and through whom he had conceived and gave birth the "the spirit of evangelical truth."[64] If Francis is a book to be read because of his prophetic reading of sacred scripture, even more so is the Immaculate who embodies in Herself the fullness of evangelical truth. Hence, the critical importance of the founding of the Order, so dedicated to poverty, not only according to Her counsels, but at Her Church which is called Her *Portiuncuala*, or "little portion."[65]

This evangelical reading of Francis becomes the scholastic *lectio* of Bonaventure in which the Seraphic Doctor says the Blessed Virgin is referred to everywhere in sacred scripture as one of the principle allegories of the spiritual understanding.[66] Thus, he calls Her "teacher of Apostles and

---

61. Fehlner, "Mary in the Franciscan Tradition," 12.

62. Ibid., 11–12.

63. Ibid., 12.

64. Bonaventure, *Legenda Major*, c. 3, 1 [VIII, 510a]; cf. Fehlner, "Mary in the Franciscan Tradition," 2.

65. Cf. Fehlner, "Mary in the Franciscan Tradition," 7.

66. Cf. Bonaventure, *Collationes in Hexaëmeron*, col. 13, 20 [V, 391a].

Evangelists."[67] He refers to Her as an order unto Herself, above all the choirs of angels.[68] She crowns the created hierarchical order of illumination and is the great sign in heaven of the role of the hierarchized soul in the growth of the Church in wisdom, and her role is unique as Mother of Christ.[69] In the order of illumination and spiritual hierarchy the Blessed Virgin stands above all other creatures.

Thus, for Fehlner, Bl. John Duns Scotus does not so much correct Bonaventure, as "polish" his synthesis with the absolute primacy of Christ and his defense of the Immaculate Conception:

> What the latter day Franciscan beneficiary of the work of Scotus and so many others after him wonders is why Bonaventure did not see the full implications of St. Francis' understanding of Mary. Whatever the reason, the fact that he did not may well explain why he failed to appreciate the practical import and Franciscan character of the arguments for the absolute primacy of Christ that he formulated so well. Therein we can identify the exact manner in which Scotus, despite the unfinished character of his theological opus, gave definite form to the Franciscan theological synthesis, thereby completing the theological foundation for the achievement of Mary's first goal for the Order: the explicit formulation and eventual definitive proclamation of the truth of the Immaculate Conception.[70]

St. Maximilian Kolbe inherited this synthesis and implemented it in the light of the Immaculate in order to incorporate this mystery into the life of the Church. He renewed the importance of the *magna domus* in which the sanctification of the intellect and its practical consequences executed in the form of a large common apostolate at the service of the Church hold pride of place. Hence, the original question posed under the aegis of Fehlner at the beginning of this paper takes on new significance. It is not only a question of the place the Order has in the counsels of the Immaculate, but

67. Cf. ibid., col. 9, 13 [V, 374c].

68. *II Sent.*, op. cit., d. 9, q. 7, 1 [II, 253b].

69. In his sermon *De Sancto Stefano Martyre*, Bonaventure interprets the Woman of Revelations 12 as the Blessed Virgin and says that the crown of stars upon her head represent the doctors of the Church, *Sermo* 2, [IX, 448]; Cf. *De Assumtione B. Virginis Mariae, Sermo II* [IX, 689d-670a], and *De Assumtione B. Virginis Mariae, Sermo V* [V, 699-700], where Bonaventure speaks of three coronations: glorious, luminous and precious, corresponding to her conformity to each of the persons of the Blessed Trinity. The luminous crown, corresponding to Her conformity to the Son, is bestowed upon Her because She taught the Apostles.

70. Fehlner, "Mary in the Franciscan Tradition," 14.

of Her own wisdom as the triumph of the Church over ignorant pietism and ideological zealotry. Our Lady is the personal form of the Church because She realizes in Herself, from the first moment of Her Immaculate Conception, the full measure of evangelical perfection. Her project is an intellectual one, precisely because it must be consummated in love for the Word made flesh.

Conclusion

Father Peter Damian Fehlner has asked the right question concerning the relationship of the Franciscan Order to the Immaculate. And in answering it he does not say that every Franciscan friary needs to be a City of the Immaculate, but that the Order needs the City of the Immaculate, because, to put it simply, the Order needs the Immaculate Herself. For Fehlner, there is a great deal that rides on what happens to St. Maximilian's Franciscan patrimony. It is a question of recognizing the proximate and ultimate ends of the Order as an intellectual project to understand and defend the doctrine of the Immaculate Conception and then to implement it into the life of the Church. It is a patrimony in which Franciscan piety passes into wisdom through the *medium* of theology under the title of the sanctification of the intellect.

If I were to dare to summarize the thought of Fehlner in this matter, I would use an insight from Joseph Ratzinger that "the personal figure of Mary becomes transparent to the personal form of the church herself."[71] It is Our Lady that guarantees that the Church is not turned into some sort of abstraction, or that faith is not reduced to an enthusiasm or personal experience. In choosing the Immaculate, St. Francis chose the Church, and in choosing the Church, St. Francis chose the Immaculate. In this way, Franciscan ecclesiality steers clear of the extremes without denying or minimizing either *auctoritas* or *ratio*.

In sum, the personal form of the Church is the Immaculate, and the form of life of the Franciscan Order is the Church. In the light of St. Maximilian, and most especially, "in the counsels of the Immaculate," the rebuilding of the Church means that the form of the Immaculate must be impressed upon the members of the Church by means of total consecration, and the chosen instrument for this work is the Order, especially the City of the Immaculate.

71. Ratzinger and Von Balthasar, *Mary*, 27.

In the end, it is not that Our Lady needs us, but that we need Her. And the realization of this truth is something for which we will be ever grateful to Fr. Peter Damian.

Bibliography

Benedict XVI. *General Audience: Bonaventure (1)*. Rome, March 3, 2010.

———. *General Audience: Bonaventure (2)*. Rome, March 10, 2010.

———. *Meeting with the Representatives from the World of Culture*. Paris, September 12, 2008.

Bonaventure. *Collationes De Septem Donis Spiritus Sancti*. Opera Omnia. 10 vols. Florence: Quarracchi, 1891.

———. *Collationes in Hexaëmeron*. Opera Omnia. 10 vols. Florence: Quarracchi, 1891.

———. *Commentaria in Quatuor Libros Sententiarum Magistri Petri Lombardi: In Tertium Librum Sententiarum*. Opera Omnia. 10 vols. Florence: Quarracchi, 1887.

———. *Itinerarium Mentis in Deum*. Vol. 5. Opera Omnia. Florence: Quarracchi, 1891.

———. *Legenda Major S. Francisci*. Vol. 8. Opera Omnia. Florence: Quarracchi, 1898.

———. *Legenda Minor S. Francisci*. Vol. 8. Opera Omnia. Florence: Quarracchi, 1898.

———. "Life of St. Francis." In *Bonaventure: The Soul's Journey into God, the Tree of Life, the Life of St. Francis*. Edited and translated by Ewert Cousins, 179–327. Mahwah: Paulist, 1987.

———. *Opera Omnia Ed. Studio Et Cura Pp. Collegii a S. Bonaventura Ad Plurimos Codices Mss. Emendate, Anecdotis Aucta, Prolegomenis Scholiis Notisque Illustrata*. 10 vols. Florence: Quarracchi, 1882–1902.

———. *Sermo IV, Christus Unus Omnium Magister*. Opera Omnia. 10 vols. Florence: Quarracchi, 1891.

Fehlner, Peter Damian. "Community, Prayer and Apostolates in the Conventual Tradition." *Inter-Province Conference 1979* 29 (1982) 34–54.

———. "Consacrazione Totale, Battesimo E Ideale Francescano." *Miles Immaculatae* (1982) 60–92.

———. "Conventual Charism: A Historical and Contemporary View." *Inter-Province Conference: Conventual Franciscans, USA* (1987).

———. "Hereditas Kolbiana: Novus Impetus Influxus Mariae Immaculatae in Ordinis Spiritualitate." *Commentarium Ordinis* (1986).

———. "Introduction." In *The Triple Way* by St. Bonaventure of Bagnoregio. New Bedford: Academy of the Immaculate, 2012.

———. "Life in the Spirit and Mary." *The Cord* 32/10 (1982) 301–6.

———. "Marian Doctrine and Devotion: A Kolbean Perspective." *De Cultu Mariano Saeculis* 19–20/4 (1991) 301–21.

———. "Marian Geography of Faith, the Kolbian Perspective." *Miles Immaculatae* 24 (1988) 264–67.

———. "Mary in the Franciscan Tradition: The Virgin Made Church." *Civitas Immaculatae*, March 25, 1985.

———. *The New Constitutions—Chapter One: On the Life of the Franciscan Brotherhood. Introduction and Commentary*. Inter-Province Conference: Conventual Franciscans, USA, 1969.

————. "Niepokalanów in the Counsels of the Immaculate." *Miles Immaculatae* 21 (1985) 309–52.

————. "The Other Page." *Miles Immaculatae* 24 (1988) 512–31.

————. "Our Lady and St. Francis." *The Cord* 32/5 (1982).

————. "Poverty in Christ: A Christian Sign." *Report of the 47th Annual Meeting of the Franciscan Educational Conference* 47 (1966) 147–92.

————. *The Role of Charity in the Ecclesiology of St. Bonaventure*. Rome: Editrice "Miscellanea Francescana," 1965.

————. *S. Clara: Dei Matris Vestigium*. New Bedford, MA: Academy of the Immaculate, 2000.

————. "St. Francis and Mary Immaculate." *Miscellanea Francescana* 82 (1982) 502–19.

————. "St. Francis Anthony Fasani of Lucera and the Mystery of the Immaculate." *Civitas Immaculatae*, March, 1986.

————. "Thesis of St. Maximilian Concerning St. Francis and the Immaculate in the Light of Recent Research." *Civitas Immaculatae*, August, 1987.

————. "Two Testaments." *Miles Immaculatae* 21 (1985) 354–81.

————. "Vir Catholicus Et Totus Apostolicus: St. Francis and the Church." *Inter-Province Conference: Conventual Franciscans, USA* (1982).

————. *Virgo Ecclesia Facta: The Immaculate Conception, St. Francis of Assisi and the Renewal of the Church*. New Bedford, MA: Academy of the Immaculate, 2004.

Francis of Assisi. *The Last Will Written for Saint Clare and Her Sisters*. In *Francis and Clare: The Complete Works*. New York: Paulist, 1982.

————. "The Later Rule." In *Francis and Clare: The Complete Works*, 136–45. New York: Paulist, 1982.

————. "A Letter to St. Anthony." In *Francis and Clare: The Complete Works*. New York: Paulist, 1982.

————. "The Testament." In *Francis and Clare: The Complete Works*, 153–56. New York: Paulist, 1982.

John Paul II. *Redemptoris Mater*. Rome, March 25, 1987.

Johnson, Timothy J. "The Legenda Minor." In *A Companion to Bonaventure*, edited by Jay M. Hammond, J. A. Wayne Hellmann, and Jared Goff, 435–51. Boston: Brill, 2014.

Kolbe, Maximilian. *The Writings of St. Maximilian Maria Kolbe*. 2 vols. Edited by Antonella Di Piazza. Lugano: Nerbini, 2016.

Ratzinger, Joseph. *The Theology of History in St. Bonaventure*. Translated by Zachery Hayes. Chicago: Franciscan Herald, 1971.

Ratzinger, Joseph, and Hans Urs Von Balthasar. *Mary: The Church at the Source*. San Francisco: Ignatius, 2005.

Part 2

Mary and the Holy Spirit

6

Fr. Peter Damian Fehlner
on Divine Maternity

ROBERT FASTIGGI

IN THIS ESSAY, I will explore the theme of the Blessed Virgin Mary's divine maternity in the Mariology of Father Peter Damian Fehlner, OFM Conv.[1] For Fr. Fehlner, Mary's divine maternity is not simply an affirmation of her status as the Mother of God as defined by the Council of Ephesus in 431.[2] In a much fuller sense, Mary's divine maternity means she is the *predestined* Mother of God, the *ever-virgin* Mother of God, and the *immaculate* Mother of God. Mary's predestination, her perpetual virginity, and her preservation from all sin are all intimately connected to her divine maternity. Each of these deserves individual treatment.

Mary as the Predestined Mother of God

Father Fehlner, following Bl. John Duns Scotus (c. 1265–1308) affirms the "Franciscan thesis" of the "absolute primacy of Christ as Head of those predestined jointly in him."[3] Because of the absolute primacy of Christ, Mary is predestined along with her divine Son. As Fr. Fehlner writes:

> The Incarnation of the Savior is willed absolutely prior to any consideration of sin or of creation, in that sense independently of both. On the other hand both creation, and afterwards the

1. When the *Sursum Actio* Symposium took place at the University of Notre Dame, IN on June 8–9, 2015, Fr. Fehlner was a member of the Franciscan Friars of the Immaculate. He has since re-joined the Franciscan Conventuals.

2. See Heinrich Denzinger and Peter Hünermann, eds. *Compendium of Creeds, Definitions, and Declarations on Matters of Faith and Morals* 43rd ed. [henceforth D-H], n. 251, where Mary is defined as *Theotokos*, the birth-giver or Mother of God.

3. Fehlner, "The Virgin Mother's Predestination," 222.

redemption of mankind, are willed dependently in view of the
Incarnation, the central mystery of salvation, effected through
the divine-virginal maternity. Hence, within the one act of
jointly predestining all in Christ, there is a more restricted sense
of joint predestination, viz., that of one of the elect to be the
Mother of the incarnate Head Savior, and so Mediatrix of all
graces, viz., the person through whom the Mediator comes to us
and through whom we are incorporated into Christ.[4]

Mary's predestination as the Mother of God, therefore, follows from the
predestination of the Incarnation itself. It is impossible to exclude Mary's
divine maternity from divine predestination. The joint predestination of
Jesus and Mary is also affirmed by the Magisterium of the Catholic Church.
In his papal bull, *Ineffabilis Deus* of Dec. 8, 1854, Bl. Pius IX taught that
"God ineffable . . . from the beginning and before the ages (*ab initio et
ante saecula*) chose and ordained a mother for his only begotten Son, from
whom he would become incarnate and be born in the blessed fullness
of time."[5] The joint predestination of Jesus and Mary was likewise taught
by the Second Vatican Council, which states: "Predestined from eternity
(*ab aeterno*) to be the Mother of God by that decree of divine providence
which also determined the Incarnation of the Word, the Blessed Virgin
was in this earth the virgin Mother of the Redeemer and, above all others
and in a singular way, the generous associate (*generosa socia*) and humble
handmaid of the Lord."[6] Both Pius IX and Vatican II explicitly teach the
predestination of Mary's divine maternity. They leave open, however, the
question whether the Incarnation was predestined because of God's fore-
knowledge of the fall.[7]

The joint predestination never confuses the distinct roles of Jesus
and Mary. Jesus is the Eternal Word of God who becomes incarnate in
the womb of the Blessed Virgin Mary. Mary, as the Mother of the Word
Incarnate, is always subordinate to her divine Son. As Fr. Fehlner writes:
"In this joint predestination Jesus is ordained absolutely for his own sake,

4. Ibid., 222–23.

5. D-H, 2800.

6. Vatican II, *Lumen gentium*, 61; D-H, 4176.

7. In the opening paragraph of *Ineffabilis Deus*, this clause is left out via ellipsis
in the text cited in D-H, 2800: "[God ineffable] having foreseen from all eternity the
lamentable wretchedness of the entire human race which would result from the sin of
Adam, decreed, by a plan hidden from the centuries, to complete the first work of his
goodness by a mystery yet more wondrously sublime through the Incarnation of the
Word." The text of *Ineffabilis Deus* in English translation can be found at: http://www.
papalencyclicals.net/Pius09/p9ineff.htm.

and Mary for the sake of Jesus and no other, not even herself."[8] Mary's entire being and all her activity are "totally related to Christ and the work of salvation and redemption."[9]

Even prior to the fall, the joint predestination of Mary and Jesus was willed by God in the very the act of creation. Father Fehlner notes that "almost all the Fathers of the Church" held that the words of Gen 1:1, "in the beginning" refer not to "a first moment of time, but "the first point in [God's] eternal counsels, namely the incarnate Word, Son of Mary."[10] This means that "God created heaven and earth for the sake of Jesus and Mary."[11] Jesus, as the Incarnate Word, is "the image of the invisible God" (Col 1:15). He could only be an image (icon) by virtue of his incarnation. If "all things in heaven and on earth" were created "in him" (Col 1:16), then Mary's divine maternity is essential to the work of creation, especially the creation of the human race. Fr. Fehlner points out that man and woman constitute the high point of the six days of creation, and they "were formed before the fall in a spousal context."[12] In this context, we must recognize marriage "as a divinely instituted covenant between Adam and Eve," which typifies "Christ and Mary, and through Mary, Christ and the Church."[13] It's important then to realize that "the absolute primacy of Jesus and Mary so indicated in the work of the six days constitutes the ontological basis both for the possibility of redemption from the tragedy of the fall and for the perfection of that redemptive work, namely, its character as most perfect (Bl. Duns Scotus) or quasi-infinite (St. Thomas)."[14]

Fr. Fehlner believes that joint predestination of Jesus and Mary, as articulated by St. Bonaventure and Bl. John Duns Scotus, is an expression of "the Marian contemplative theology of St. Francis."[15] In this theology, the Incarnation and Mary's divine maternity are expressions of the same mystery "because we cannot talk about the Son without the Mother, or the Mother without the Son."[16] We must realize that "the mode of the Incarnation and redemption is Marian."[17] Fr. Fehlner notes that "the joint predesti-

---

8. Fehlner, "The Virgin Mother's Predestination," 226.

9. Ibid., 227.

10. Ibid., 217.

11. Ibid.

12. Ibid.

13. Ibid.

14. Ibid.

15. Fehlner, "The Sense of Marian Coredemption," 110.

16. Ibid., 111.

17. Ibid.

nation of Jesus and Mary constitutes the order of the hypostatic union, the very center of the Gospel."[18]

Fr. Fehlner clearly sees Mary's divine maternity as intimately linked to her joint predestination with her divine Son. The Franciscan-Scotist doctrine of the absolute primacy of Christ necessarily includes the joint predestination of Jesus and Mary. Mary is not only the Mother of God; she is the *predestined* Mother of God.

Mary as the Ever-Virgin Mother of God

Fr. Fehlner believes Mary's perpetual virginity is intrinsically connected to her divine maternity. His words on this matter are lucid and insightful:

> Mary remained "ever Virgin." Indeed, it means that the great sign of salvation is Mary herself as Virgin Mother. It means that at the core of her interior life, of her consent to the Incarnation, to the primary decree of God's will, of her *Fiat*, of her association in Christ's ministry and of her work as Mediatrix of all grace, is the integrity of her soul and body. Here we see the perfect integration of grace and nature.[19]

Fr. Fehlner's reference to the integrity of Mary's soul and body highlights the importance of Mary's virginity in giving birth, which is the Catholic doctrine of her *virginitas in partu*. The Catholic Church believes that Mary's physical sign of virginity was miraculously preserved when she gave birth to Jesus. The Lateran Synod of 649 presided over by Pope St. Martin I teaches that Mary gave birth to Jesus "without corruption, her virginity remaining equally inviolate after his birth."[20] Fr. Juan Luis Bastero believes this teaching has the dogmatic value of an *ex cathedra* papal definition because the Synod "was presided over and sanctioned by the Pope, who proposed this doctrine as a condition for being in communion with the Roman See and condemned its denial with an anathema."[21] Vatican II likewise teaches that, in giving birth, Mary's virginity was not diminished but sanctified.[22] In his May 24, 1992 discourse in Capua, in honor of the 16th centenary of the 392 Council of Capua, St. John Paul II draws a parallel between the begetting of Christ *ex intacta*

18. Ibid.

19. Fehlner, "Mary's Virginity: God's Gift and a Pledge of Eternal Glory," 10.

20. D-H, 503.

21. Bastero, *Mary*, 174 n. 41.

22. *Lumen Gentium*, 57. The footnote to this passage cites not only the Lateran Synod of 649 but statements by Pope St. Leo I, the Council of Chalcedon, and St. Ambrose that make it clear that Mary's physical integrity was preserved.

Virgine (from the intact Virgin) and his resurrection *ex intacto sepulcro* (from the intact sepulcher).[23] I have never doubted the truth of Mary's *virginitas in partu.* I did, however, publish an article in 2007 in which I questioned whether the preservation of the physical sign of Mary's virginity requires the assent of faith as a *de fide* dogma.[24] One reason I raised this question was because the Holy See did not condemn Albert Mitterer and others who denied this teaching as heretics. Rather, the Holy Office only issued a warning (*monitum*) about publishing texts that deny the traditional teaching.[25] My reasoning, though, was flawed. The Magisterium need not punish those guilty of heresy with the most severe penalties permitted.[26]

I was also misled by the treatment of Mary's *virginitas in partu* in Father Ludwig Ott's *Fundamentals of Catholic Dogma.*[27] In the 1958 English translation that I was using, Fr. Ott mentions Mitterer's thesis (that injury to Mary's hymen would not destroy her virginity), and he does not label it as heretical.[28] Fr. Ott, though, revised his book in 1969, and he removed any reference to Mitterer. Moreover, he describes Mary's *virginitas in partu* as "De fide on the ground of the universal teaching of the doctrine (*De fide auf Grund der allgemeinen Lehverkündigung*).[29] In his 1969 revised text, Fr. Ott leaves no doubt as to what the Church teaches on this matter: "The dogma asserts that the bodily integrity of Mary was not injured in the act of giving birth. Just as in conception her virginal integrity was preserved."[30]

The preservation of Mary's virginal integrity in both soul and body helps us understand her great role as the virgin Mother of God. Fr. Fehlner sees a direct link between Mary's perpetual virginity and her role as Mother of God:

> The mystery of virginity in Mary, as so many Greek Fathers stress, is intimately linked both to reality of divine being and to the direct knowledge of divinity. In giving birth, Mary's body

23. *AAS* 85 (1993) 665.

24. Fastiggi, "Francisco Suárez," 26–45.

25. See ibid., 44.

26. The case of Hans Küng comes to mind. Even though he denied the dogma of papal infallibility, the Magisterium chose not to excommunicate him as a heretic but only deprive him of his license to represent himself as a Catholic theologian. I am grateful to Msgr. Arthur Calkins, Fr. Frederick Miller, Fr. Donald Libby, and Dr. Lawrence Feingold for their help in convincing me that Mary's *virginitas in partu* is a *de fide* dogma of the Catholic Church.

27. Ott, *Fundamentals of Catholic Dogma*, 205–6.

28. Ibid., 205.

29. Ott, *Grundriss de Dogmatik*, 300.

30. Ibid., my translation.

remained incorrupt and integral, just as the Godhead in the eternal generation of the Son from the Father remained undivided and integral. Thus, the virginal maternity on earth reveals the eternal generation of the Son from the Father, and so makes manifest not only the Son, but the Father as well: "Who sees me, sees the Father also." (Jn 14:9). In enabling us to see the Son, the Virgin Mary also reveals the Father, and therefore the Holy Spirit in whom the Father and the Son are one in love . . . Mary, then, is our teacher of theology. She teaches us about God and the things of God because she is Mother of God. In a word, she is *Mater et Magistra*, and without her no one can learn about God or teach the word of God in truth.[31]

Here we see that Mary's perpetual virginity not only serves her role as Mother of God but also her role as teacher. Being completely "incorrupt and integral" she is able to reflect the communion of love that eternally exists in the most holy Trinity. She is "the teacher of authentic theology"[32] because she knows God's love and communicates this love to us.

Mary as the Immaculate Mother of God

Father Fehlner believes Mary's Immaculate Conception, like her perpetual virginity, is a necessary corollary of her divine maternity. As the Immaculate and ever-virgin Mother of God, Mary's entire being is related to Christ and the work of salvation. Fr. Fehlner offers this explanation:

Mary would not have existed except that the Incarnation was *de facto* decreed as the reason for creation. That means that Mary in her being and in her activity is totally related to Christ and to the work of salvation and redemption. The perfection of human existence and personal freedom is directly proportionate to its assimilation within the totality of Mary's relation to Christ and to his work. This is what it means to be full of grace; so holy that one can contribute to the sanctification of others even if sanctified by the merits of Christ. Mary is in some true manner the maternal Mediatrix of all persons: as Christ's mother bringing him to us; as the Mother of the Church and of believers bringing

---

31. Fehlner, "Fitting Sign of God and Salvation," 9.

32. Pope Francis in his Address to the International Theological Commission on December 5, 2014 referred to the Madonna as the "teacher of authentic theology" (*maestra dell'autentica teologia*).

us to Christ. On this rests the meaning and importance of total consecration to Mary Immaculate.[33]

Mary's Immaculate Conception is directed to the Incarnation. True Marian devotion is supremely incarnational and Eucharistic. Devotion to the sacred humanity of Christ is at the heart of Franciscan piety and Marian piety. As Fr. Fehlner writes:

> The reason for St. Francis' extraordinary devotion to the Virgin Mary and his surrounding her with ineffable praise, according to Thomas of Celano and St. Bonaventure, is to be found in the fact that "she made the Lord of majesty one of us and accessible to us." Out of this devotion to the Incarnation above all for its own sake came the famous celebration of Christmas in Greccio toward the end of his life. . . . He who has not understood Christmas has not understood the decisive element of human existence. It is humility which makes one truly human, one in the love of God. . . . Humble, human, "homo" all derive from the same root: "humus" or earth from which the first man was formed and named "Adam": from the earth. The virgin earth is a type of the Virgin Mother who begot the New Adam for all His members. This is why Marian devotion is inseparable from the devotion of Greccio and the love of the Heart of Jesus in the Eucharistic mystery. Truly, the kindness and humanity-humility of God has appeared in Christ Jesus, Son of the heavenly Father and Son of Mary, shown to us in Bethlehem.[34]

Mary as the Mother of God and Mother of the Church

Vatican II refers to Mary as "our mother in the order of grace (*mater nobis in ordine gratiae*)."[35] As Mother, Mary mediates divine life to the children of her Son. As Mother of Christ, Mary is also the Mother of the Church because the Church is the mystical body of Christ. Fr. Fehlner sees the roles of Mary as Mother of Christ and Mother of the Church as distinct but interrelated. As he explains, both roles flow from a "single maternal vocation":

> [T]he two aspects of this single maternal vocation of Mary in relation to Christ and the Church are distinct. The first is in the

33. Fehlner, "The Virgin Mother's Predestination and Immaculate Conception," 227.

34. Fehlner, "Motherhood in the Order of Grace," 5.

35. *Lumen Gentium*, 61.

order of nature and the second in the order of grace. The first involves the formation of the human body for the God-man, the second reanimates an already existing man with divine life (i.e. all men, in the state of original sin before being baptized). Nevertheless, they both pertain to a single Mother and single motherhood. Divine Maternity and spiritual Maternity are both "real" maternity, not simply metaphorical. . . . In the case of the Word become flesh, that divine filiation is natural. Jesus is not a second, adopted son of God, as Nestorius erroneously proposed. In the case of the members of the Church, Mary's children are truly hers, yet adopted, and so are also adopted children of the Father and brothers and sisters of Jesus. Indeed, adopted and not natural as is Jesus by virtue of His being eternally generated, yet we are really, and not merely legally, children of the Father and coheirs of Christ, temples of the Holy Spirit.[36]

Conclusion

Fr. Fehlner's theology of Mary's divine maternity manifests the richness of his spiritual insight and synthesis. He shows how Mary's divine maternity is intimately connected to her predestination, perpetual virginity, and Immaculate Conception. He also explains how Mary's divine maternity serves the Incarnation and also the life of the Church and the Eucharist. He likewise shows how Mary's divine maternity enables her to be spiritual Mother, teacher, and Mediatrix of grace to the children of her Son who are also her children.

Bibliography

Bastero Juan Luis. *Mary, Mother of the Redeemer*. Translated by Michael Adams and Philip Griffin. Dublin: Four Courts, 2011.

Denzinger, Heinrich, and Peter Hünermann, eds. *Compendium of Creeds, Definitions, and Declarations on Matters of Faith and Morals*. 43rd ed. San Francisco: Ignatius, 2012.

Fastiggi, Robert. "Francisco Suárez, S.J. (1548–1617) on Mary's Virginitas in Partu and Subsequent Doctrinal Development." *Marian Studies* Volume 58 (2007).

Fehlner, Peter M. "The Great Sign (Apoc 12:1)—The Virginal Maternity and Maternal Virginity of Mary: Fitting Sign of God and Salvation, Part 1." *Missio Immaculatae International* 2 (March–April 2009) 8–9.

36. Fehlner, "Motherhood in the Order of Grace," 5.

————. "The Great Sign (Apoc 12:1)—The Virginal Maternity and Maternal Virginity of Mary: Mary's Virginity: God's Gift and a Pledge of Eternal Glory." *Missio Immaculatae International* 3 (May–June 2009) 8–10.

————. "The Great Sign (Apoc 12:1)—The Virginal Maternity and Maternal Virginity of Mary: Motherhood in the Order of Grace." *Missio Immaculatae International* 6 (November–December 2009) 4–5.

————. "The Sense of Marian Coredemption in St. Bonaventure and Bl. John Duns Scotus." In *Mary at the Foot of the Cross: Acts of the International Symposium on Marian Coredemption*, 103–118. New Bedford, MA: Academy of the Immaculate, 2000.

————. "The Virgin Mother's Predestination and Immaculate Conception." In *Mariology: A Guide for Priests, Deacons, Seminarians, and Consecrated Persons*, edited by Mark Miravalle, 213–76. Goleta, CA. Queenship, 2007.

Francis. "Address to the International Theological Commission." December 5, 2014. http://w2.vatican.va/content/francesco/it/speeches/2014/december/documents/papa-francesco_20141205_commissione-teologica-internazionale.html.

Ott, Ludwig. *Fundamentals of Catholic Dogma*. Translated by Patrick Lynch. St. Louis: Herder, 1958.

————. *Grundriss de Dogmatik*. 11th ed. Bonn: Nova et Vetera. 2010.

Pius IX. Bull, *Ineffabilis Deus* (December 8, 1854). http://www.papalencyclicals.net/pius09/p9ineff.htm.

7

Mary and Divinization

*Peter Damian Fehlner on Our Lady
and the Holy Spirit*

JOHN-MARK L. MIRAVALLE

Introduction

BY THE TIME PAUL VI issued *Marialis cultus,* calling on theologians to study
the relationship between Mary and the Holy Spirit, there had already been
scholars at least since Scheeben in the nineteenth century dealing thematically and extensively with the question. Since the Second Vatican Council,
and Congar's alarm that a theology of substitution, with Mary replacing the
Holy Spirit, had threatened Catholic doctrine and piety, an enormous amount
of ink has been spilled by professional Mariologists, some working from
within and some from without the confines of orthodox Catholicism, but all
attempting to elaborate and refine a correct pneumatology-Mariology.

One of these scholars, Fr. Peter Damian Fehlner, sees the key locus for
understanding the profound relationship between Our Lady and the Holy
Spirit not so much in the writings of salaried academicians, but in the meditations of the saints. Fr. Fehlner's presentation of Franciscan Mariology and
Pneumatology, from Francis, through Bonaventure and Scotus and finally
climaxing in St. Maximilian Kolbe, powerfully illustrates the ineffable bond
existing between the divine Advocate and the woman Advocate, the Con-
soler and the Coredemptrix.

It seems to me that perhaps the best way to unpack Fr. Fehlner's insights
on Mariology-pneumatology is to begin rather sensationally by recalling St.
Maximilian's provocative language concerning Mary and the Holy Spirit, and

then discuss how Fr. Fehlner employs all the resources of the Franciscan tradition to contextualize, clarify and confirm the insights of Fr. Kolbe.

We may begin with the title "Spouse of the Holy Spirit," a title to which St. Francis himself ascribed. Though still hotly contested by professional Mariologists for varied and sometimes conflicting reasons, to common sense at least it seems a safe and unobjectionable title. We can then move on to St. Maximilian's assertion that the Holy Spirit is the "Uncreated Immaculate Conception," just as Mary is the created Immaculate Conception. This leads us into less intuitive waters; many of us haven't recovered from Our Lady's self-given title at Lourdes (She *is* the Immaculate Conception? Doesn't she mean that she is immaculately conceived?). To apply the same title to the Holy Spirit seems to be making things, which already appear needlessly difficult, harder still.

Still, though we mop our brow, we brace ourselves and take it in stride. After all, Fr. Kolbe was a saint, and it probably won't be hard to interpret these expressions satisfactorily with a little finesse. Then the bomb drops. We hear to our astonishment that St. Maximilian called Mary the "Complement of the Trinity," a "quasi-part" of the Trinity, the "Quasi-Incarnation of the Holy Spirit," and stated further that Mary is "Transubstantiated into the Holy Spirit." Complement of the Trinity? As though the Trinity isn't enough on its own? Quasi-Incarnation of the Holy Spirit? Quasi-part of the Trinity? Is this finally the Catholic Mariolatry we're always hearing about? Transubstantiated into the Holy Spirit? The Thomists and the ecumenists (who are, by the way, rarely the same people) sink down into deep despair. What can these things mean? What does St. Maximilian Kolbe mean?

Of course St. Maximilian didn't have the opportunity to explain himself systematically; he had to attend to the more pressing business of love greater than which no man has. But Fr. Fehlner has dedicated himself over the decades to providing the rich theological framework for grasping and acknowledging the truth at the heart of Kolbe's luxuriant language.[1] To that framework we now turn.

The Divinization of the Most Holy Mother of God

St. Maximilian's language about Our Lady and the Holy Spirit simply cannot be understood apart from the Catholic doctrine of divinization, especially

---

1. Part of this contextualization consists in showing that much of this terminology is not original to Kolbe (although he is surely original in the significance he assigns to the terms); cf. Fehlner, "Complementum Ss. Trinitatis," 177–204.

as expressed in the Franciscan tradition. Yet, we may begin with the biblical foundations for this astounding reality, starting with Our Lord's words:

> The Jews answered him, "We are not stoning you for a good work but for blasphemy. You, a man, are making yourself God." Jesus answered them, "Is it not written in your law, 'I said, "You are gods"'? If it calls them gods to whom the word of God came, and scripture cannot be set aside, can you say that the one whom the Father has consecrated and sent into the world blasphemes because I said, 'I am the Son of God.'?" (Jn 10:34-36).

Christ shows His detractors that the language of deification is already present in the Old Covenant, and St. Peter irrevocably establishes the same language for the New Covenant when he declares that we are all called to become "partakers of the divine nature" (2 Pet 1:4). Surely this language is not less strong than Kolbe's? St. Athanasius takes up the cry in the patristic era and declares of Our Lord that "He was made man that we might be made God."[2] St. Thomas Aquinas, standing for scholasticism, declares "it was the will of God's only-begotten Son that men should share in his divinity, he assumed our nature in order that by becoming man he might make men gods."[3] We cannot deny it, no matter how many distinctions we draw: the uniform teaching of the Bible and the saints is that divinization or *theosis* is a reality to which the human race is called. We are to become, in some real sense, God—to participate through grace in the divine life.

How does this occur? Through what Fr. Fehlner calls *exemplary* or *personal* causality; a causality which transcends the categories of Aristotelian causality[4] and is likewise irreducible to the Thomistic distinction between physical and moral causality.[5] This *personal causality*, or *dynamic exemplarism* is a causality deriving from the Trinitarian mode God's own being.[6] God leaves the imprint not only of his singular being or nature, but also of his threeness, on creation. Thus, for Fehlner, as for St. Bonaventure, all of reality is hierarchized or ordered in some way. The Trinity leaves its mark on the material order and in the image of the human creature and most of all in the likeness of grace where the human person is admitted into the divine drama of the perichoresis.[7] In other words, by means

---

2. *On the Incarnation of the Word*, 54, 3.

3. *Opusculum 57, in festo Corporis Christi*.

4. Fehlner, *St. Maximilian M. Kolbe*, 86.

5. Fehlner, "De Metaphysica mariana quaedam," 13–42, 29–34.

6. Ibid., 18.

7. Fehlner, *St. Maximilian M. Kolbe*, 61–62: "The created similitude by grace, while entailing a participation of divine perfection in the form of created grace nonetheless

of sanctifying grace, the rational creature is elevated, caught up into the Trinitarian order, and brought into the eternal dynamic of the circumincession, where distinct persons are completely themselves and yet completely possessed by others.

Now according to plain Catholic teaching this participation in the divine life is granted above all to the Mother of God, whose share in the Trinitarian personal exchange is so unique that St. Bonaventure declares Mary a hierarchy in her own right. Due to her unparalleled fullness of Grace, Mary shares in and makes manifest the whole Trinity in a unique way as Daughter of the Father, Mother of the Son and Spouse of the Spirit. This model clarifies "Mary's unique relationship to the Most Holy Trinity, the divine hierarchy," and explains "why it is she who, among creatures, reflects the entire mystery of the Trinity, as a hierarchy in her own right, above all others."[8]

Making Sense of Kolbe's Language

It is precisely within *this* context of divinization effected through exemplary or personal causality, where the Holy Spirit elevates Mary to the supreme creaturely participation in the divine personal processions—a participation, moreover, to which we are all called[9]—that St. Maximilian's language can be unpacked. We are now in a position to appreciate his remarkable expressions, taking them one at a time.

Mary is transubstantiated into the Holy Spirit. Mary is transubstantiated into the Holy Spirit in the sense that she is divinized, made the partaker of a new nature, brought into God's inner life. Here, according to Fr. Fehlner, St. Maximilian is simply continuing the tradition from St. Bonaventure, who holds that "sanctifying grace . . . transforms the substance of the soul to the point of radically altering the mode or order of loving from that of a creature in view of fulfillment to that of a divine person solely in view of the supreme good."[10] Although this description of sanctifying grace differs from the Thomistic tradition (in which sanctifying grace involves an accidental,

---

allows something else for which the created grace is the disposition: viz., a communion of persons not so much sharing as mutually possessing each other."

8. Fehlner, "Metaphysica," 41, translation mine.

9. Of course, it is the whole Trinity which brings about the state of grace, the fellowship of divine life, and yet it is the Holy Spirit to whom we primarily attribute responsibility for this effect. Cf., Leo XIII, *Divinum Illud Munus*, #9: "Now this wonderful union . . . differing only in degree or state from that with which God beatifies the saints in heaven, although it is most certainly produced by the presence of the whole Blessed Trinity . . . nevertheless is attributed in a peculiar manner to the Holy Ghost."

10. Fehlner, *St. Maximilian M. Kolbe*, 64.

not substantial change[11]), it can certainly be harmonized with the Catholic tradition as a whole. If we are all to partake of a new nature, the divine nature; if we are all to "become gods," or even "become God"; if we are to make the transition from operating at the human level to living at the divine level, then we should not be surprised to find this described as a transition from one primary mode of being to another, from one nature to another, from one substance to another. Sanctifying grace is in itself the shift from natural to supernatural (without, of course, any obliteration of our human nature). And if this "transubstantiation" is undergone by each of the baptized, why would we deny it of the immaculately conceived Virgin?

We can approach *Mary as quasi-part of the Trinity* in the same vein; it does not imply the transition from a Trinity to a Quaternity—note the "quasi" at the beginning, which, Fr. Fehlner reminds us, indicates analogy, and therefore a dissimilarity as well as a similarity.[12] Rather it refers to the participation in divine life through grace, enjoyed at the highest levels by the Blessed Virgin: "Such a human person, so united to the divine will, is *eo ipso* a part or *quasi-part* of the Blessed Trinity with unique relations to each of the divine persons, precisely because perfect personality entails a communion of love."[13]

Moreover, since Mary's life of grace is flawless, unmitigated, and supreme in all of creation, she is the most perfect correspondence and expression of the Holy Spirit. She is perfectly synchronized, both at the level of her being and her action, to the Holy Spirit. This is simply what the Dogma of the Immaculate Conception entails—that Mary expresses the Holy Spirit by all that she is and does. That such is the case can further be seen from noticing that *the Holy Spirit is an Uncreated Immaculate Conception*, insofar as he is an eternal person who proceeds from the love of two other persons.[14] Thus, for Mary to call herself the Immaculate Conception at Lourdes, is to affirm that she always, and not merely at one moment, corresponds perfectly to the Holy Spirit.

More than that, for Kolbe, Mary's revealed title at Lourdes expresses her status as *Spouse of the Holy Spirit*, since by calling herself the Immaculate Conception she is essentially accepting the name of her eternal Spouse. Spouses, Kolbe reminds us through Fr. Fehlner,[15] share the same last name,

11. Cf. *Summa Theologiae*, I–II, q. 110, a. 2, ad. 2.

12. Fehlner, *St. Maximilian M. Kolbe*, 49, cf. Fehlner, "Is the Martyr of Charity a Heretic?" 97-103, 101.

13. Fehlner, *St. Maximilian M. Kolbe*, 75.

14. Fr. Fehlner points out that it is Bonaventure who first connects the Holy Spirit's procession to the language of conception, Fehlner, *St. Maximilian M. Kolbe*, 40.

15. Fehlner, *St. Maximilian M. Kolbe*, 94.

and thus the title of St. Francis is vindicated; Mary is the Spirit's perfect, docile, and absolutely faithful spouse.[16]

The two final expressions dealing with Mary and the Holy Spirit are invaluable in illustrating how it is that the Holy Spirit is reflected through the Blessed Mother. Thus, Mary is the *Complement of the Holy Trinity* temporally because the Spirit is the Complement of the Holy Trinity eternally.[17] He is the fullness of the Holy Trinity, the last person who fulfills the eternal processional sequence. In fact, it is the Holy Spirit who is in some way the eternal foundation for all final causality,[18] for in Him the trinitarian processions reach their conclusion, their final point of completion. So too "to call Mary the Complement of the Trinity is to assign her in the economy of salvation (and so in 'economic' theology) a central role which is also that of the Holy Spirit."[19] What the Holy Spirit does he does through Mary: and it is no surprise that His two primary economic acts are themselves conceptions: " . . . through the spiritual Motherhood of Mary we are born of the Holy Spirit, we are purely conceived, just as She, through the work of the Holy Spirit, virginally conceived the Savior of the world, the Incarnate God."[20]

We come then finally to Mary as the *Quasi-Incarnation of the Holy Spirit*. Here again there is no affirmation of anything like a hypostatic union in the case of Our Lady and the Holy Spirit; rather there is the affirmation of something like an Incarnation of the Holy Spirit.[21] The point is quite transparent: just as Our Lord's humanity perfectly expresses the Second Person of the Trinity, so too does Our Lady's humanity perfectly express the third person of the Trinity. The glaring difference, of course, is that in the case of Our Lord there is only one person, while for Our Lady and the Holy Spirit there are two persons, albeit two persons in absolute alignment.

This is expressed in the Franciscan terminology by saying that while the Son possesses Jesus of Nazareth *properly*, such that the one is the other, with the same self, the Holy Spirit possesses Mary *appropriatively*, such that one is not the other, but the two are joined through free mutual possession.[22] Fr. Fehlner insists that according to this terminology, both proper and appropriated relations refer to the objective order—they express the

16. Fr. Fehlner also suggests that not only can "Spouse of the Spirit" be inferred from "Immaculate Conception," but vice versa. Cf. "The Virgin Mother's Predestination and Immaculate Conception," 260–61.

17. Fehlner, *St. Maximilian M. Kolbe*, 33–35.

18. Fehlner, "Metaphysica," 20.

19. Fehlner, *St. Maximilian M. Kolbe*, 103.

20. Fehlner, "Metaphysica," 36, my translation.

21. Fehlner, *St. Maximilian M. Kolbe*, 50.

22. Ibid., 39.

way things are, not just the way we think about them—but he clarifies the distinction by showing that a proper possession is exclusive, while an appropriated possession is inclusive.[23] In other words, while a proper possession can involve only a single self (no one but Jesus can be the Eternal Word), an appropriated possession can involve many selves. Thus, the relationship between Mary and the Holy Spirit not only involves two persons, but it further invites *all* persons to participate in it. It is precisely this which Kolbe has in mind when he says that we must all be "transubstantiated into the Immaculate," as she has been transubstantiated into the Holy Spirit.[24] All humanity is invited into the multi-personal exchange between God and creature which Mary enjoys first and foremost with the Holy Spirit.

Conclusion: Knowing the Holy Spirit through Mary

It scarcely needs to be said that Fr. Fehlner's work on the relationship between Mary and the Holy Spirit has vast implications. Among the most crucial is one that provides yet another answer to the question, "Why do we need Mary?"

This is the perennial question in a post-reformation world, a world in which the law of parsimony, so suited to matters of pure logic or mathematics, is restlessly and repeatedly misapplied to the divine economy. Why have Mary—or, for that matter, why Mary or the saints or the Church herself—when we could just have Jesus? Why clutter up an elegant and immediate spirituality, the spirituality of *Solus Christus,* with a complicated tangle of intermediaries, represented first and foremost by the Mother of God?

The answers of revelation to this question are manifold: because that's how God wants it, because Scripture says so, because the Church teaches that Mary is indispensable to the order of salvation, or simply because without a Mother Christ's family would be tragically incomplete. But with Fr. Fehlner's exposition of the Franciscan tradition, we are given greater confidence in responding with a new answer: *We need Mary because of her relationship to the Holy Spirit.*

It is a remarkable principle of the Trinitarian order that in some mysterious way each divine person requires another person to reveal Him. Thus the Father will only be revealed by the Son, as Our Lord says, "No one knows the Father but the Son, and anyone to whom the Son chooses to reveal Him" (Matt 11:27; Luke 10:22). So too, the Son will only be revealed by the Holy Spirit, "No one can say 'Jesus is Lord' except by the Holy Spirit" (I

23. Fehlner, "Metaphysica," 23 n. 27.
24. Fehlner, *St. Maximilian M. Kolbe,* 146–49.

Cor 12:13). But how then will the Holy Spirit be revealed? The other divine persons have shown an exquisite and infinite modesty in refusing to speak of themselves; will the Holy Spirit be the first to flout these divine decencies? Quite the contrary, he will observe them to such a point that the *Catechism of the Catholic Church* speaks of the Holy Spirit as operating on a principle of "divine self-effacement":

> Now God's Spirit, who reveals God, makes known to us Christ, his Word, his living Utterance, but the Spirit does not speak of himself. The Spirit who "has spoken through the prophets" makes us hear the Father's Word, but we do not hear the Spirit himself. We know him only in the movement by which he reveals the Word to us and disposes us to welcome him in faith. the Spirit of truth who "unveils" Christ to us "will not speak on his own." Such properly divine self-effacement explains why "the world cannot receive (him), because it neither sees him nor knows him," while those who believe in Christ know the Spirit because he dwells with them.[25]

The Spirit is only made manifest through his effects on the human soul. By implication, then, if there is one in whom he achieves his greatest effects, it is there that he most manifests himself, reveals himself, makes himself known. The process of economic unveiling is therefore clear: who manifests the Father? The Son. Who manifests the Son? The Spirit. Who manifests the Spirit? Well, quite simply, Mary does. Everyone who responds to the Spirit's promptings shows the Spirit's personality and power, but Mary responds incomparably better than anyone else. In fact, as we have seen, Mary *is* incarnate responsiveness to the Holy Spirit.

Consequently, Mary (and to a lesser degree the saints and every soul in grace) is not a peripheral figure on the margins of salvation—a side distraction to the Protestants and a fringe benefit to the Catholics—she is the primary way in which the Holy Spirit makes himself and his work concrete in the world. Mary isn't the substitute for the Holy Spirit; she is his human representative, his created personal reflection. She is therefore our primary point of contact with the third person of the Most Holy Trinity. To quote from Fr. Fehlner, "In venerating the Immaculate, we *eo ipso* venerate the Holy Spirit and enter into the dynamism of the order of grace, the sharing in the divine nature of Father, Son and Holy Spirit."[26] It is she who has been divinized first and foremost. For us, looking to her reveals to us the Spirit's power, and such a gaze welcomes us into the divine life which he alone can bestow.

25. CCC #687.
26. Fehlner, "Complementum," 180.

Bibliography

Fehlner, Peter Damian. "Complementum Ss. Trinitatis." *Miles Immaculatae* 21 (1985)
    177–204.

———. "De Metaphysica mariana quaedam." *Immaculata Mediatrix* 1 (2001) 13–42.

———. "Is the Martyr of Charity a Heretic?" In *Kolbe: Saint of the Immaculata*, edited
    by Francis Mary, 97–103. New Bedford, MA: Academy of the Immaculate, 2001.

———. *St. Maximilian M. Kolbe, Martyr of Charity: Pneumatologist.* New Bedford,
    MA: Academy of the Immaculate, 2004.

———. "The Virgin Mother's Predestination and Immaculate Conception." In
    Mariology: A Guide for Priests, Deacons, Seminarians and Consecrated Persons,
    edited by Mark Miravalle, 213–76. Goleta, CA: Seat of Wisdom, 2007.

8

Fr. Peter Damian Fehlner on the Coredemption and Mediation of the Blessed Virgin Mary

GLORIA FALCÃO DODD

Whether Mary's Coredemption and Mediation Are Clearly Understood?

BEFORE AND AFTER THE II Vatican Council, Catholic theologians have vigorously disputed the meaning of Mary's coredemption and mediation. In tribute to Father Fehlner's love for Latin, his scholastic approach, and his sense of humor, some answers to the following speculative question illustrate how Marian concepts can be misunderstood in our modern world: What car would Mary drive if she lived on earth today? A typical Mariologist might take a Scriptural approach to hold that Mary would drive a Fiat (Luke 1:38). With the upcoming Jubilee of Mercy, others could think that Our Lady of Mercy would surely drive a Mercedes.[1] However, a Scotist might note that as the perpetual Virgin, first in the perfect redemption, and the *a priori* condition for creation and redemption, the most fitting car that Mary could drive, should drive, and therefore would drive, is a Prius![2] While these jokes are amusing, they also point to the confusion that exists about what some Marian doctrines actually mean.

---

1. Rev. Francois Rossier, S.M., personal interview on May 4, 2015, provided the answer of a Mercedes.

2. Br. Andrew Kosmowski, S.M., personal interview on May 14, 2015, answered a Prius based on the Marian description as the "*Virgo Prius ac posterioris*" in the hymn, *Alma Mater Redemptoris*, one of the Marian antiphons for Advent, used for Compline. *The Liturgy of the Hours, Vol. 1: Advent Season, Christmas Season,* 1189, gave both the Latin and English versions. Fehlner took this Scotistic approach in Apollonio and Fehlner, "The Concept of Redemption in the Franciscan-Scotistic School," 111.

As just one part of this collaborative series, this paper will set aside the Marian topics covered by others and focus specifically on Fr. Peter Damian Fehlner's contribution to the post-Vatican II discussion of Mary's coredemption and mediation. In 1997, a pontifical theological commission of twenty-three theologians responded to the requests for the dogmatic definition of Mary as Coredemptrix, Mediatrix of All Graces, and Advocate of the People of God with a "Declaration" that called for clarification of these ambiguous terms, a remembrance of history, further study, and ecumenical sensitivity.[3] After this Declaration, Fr. Fehlner helped to organize ten international symposia from 2000 to 2009 to study Marian coredemption, usually chairing the event, presenting papers at these meetings, and then publishing the papers in the series, *Mary at the Foot of the Cross.*[4] While Fr. Fehlner advocated the dogmatic definition of Mary as Coredemptrix, Mediatrix of All Graces, and Advocate of the People of God,[5] he also humbly acknowledged his role as a theologian, not a papal advisor; as he said: "We are not here to pressure the Pope or to tell him how or how not to conduct his affairs. That is for Our Lord and our Lady to do, not for me, nor for you, and I insist not for critics of the

---

3. "Declaration of the Theological Commission of the Pontifical International Marian Academy: Request for the definition of the dogma of Mary as Mediatrix, Coredemptrix and Advocate." *L'Osservatore Romano*, June 4, 1997. The International Marian Research Institute. https://udayton.edu/imri/mary/m/mediatrix-coredemptrix-and-advocate-declaration.php. "1. The titles, as proposed, are ambiguous, as they can be understood in very different ways. Furthermore, the theological direction taken by the Second Vatican Council, which did not wish to define any of these titles, should not be abandoned. The Second Vatican Council did not use the title "Coredemptrix," and uses "Mediatrix" and "Advocate" in a very moderate way (cf. *Lumen Gentium*, 62). In fact, from the time of Pope Pius XII, the term "Coredemptrix" has not been used by the papal Magisterium in its significant documents. There is evidence that Pope Pius XII himself intentionally avoided using it. With respect to the title "Mediatrix," the history of the question should not be forgotten: in the first decades of this century the Holy See entrusted the study of the possibility of its definition to three different commissions, the result of which was that the Holy See decided to set the question aside.

2. Even if the titles were assigned a content which could be accepted as belonging to the deposit of the faith, the definition of these titles, however, in the present situation would be lacking in theological clarity, as such titles and the doctrines inherent in them still require further study in a renewed Trinitarian, ecclesiological and anthropological perspective. Finally, the theologians, especially the non-Catholics, were sensitive to the ecumenical difficulties which would be involved in such a definition."

4. Fehlner was the "Chairperson of the Symposium" in 2001, in *Mary at the Foot of the Cross II: Acts of the Second International Symposium on Marian Coredemption* (New Bedford, MA: Franciscan Friars of the Immaculate, 2002), 458, and "moderator" of the "Round Table Discussion: Common Objections to Marian Coredemption," 441.

5. Fehlner, "Sense of Marian Coredemption in St. Bonaventure and Bl. John Duns Scotus," 118.

coredemption either."[6] Thus, this paper will focus on Fr. Fehlner's understanding of the truth of the Marian doctrines of coredemption and mediation, as given in those ten international conferences. This paper in his honor will use a scholastic style to synthesize the objections Father noted as well as his explanation of the doctrines, before setting forth his responses to the objections. The conclusion will provide some evaluation of his ideas.

Objections: What's Wrong with Calling Mary "Coredemptrix" and "Mediatrix of All Graces"

Fr. Fehlner acknowledged a variety of objections that he liked to describe by quoting G.K. Chesterton's Marian poem, *A Party Question*: "When in the midst of all the din of controversy, with rights and wrongs on all sides, there was heard the mocking and demeaning of the 'Virgin Mother mild,' at that moment one distinctly began 'to hear the little hiss that only comes from hell.'"[7]

These challenges are presented in the chronological order in which Fr. Fehlner first identified them in these ten conferences.

Objection 1 (2000, 2001, 2002, 2003, 2004, 2005, 2006, 2007): Christ alone is the Redeemer and Mediator. Calling Mary "Coredemptrix" and "Mediatrix" confuses the role that belongs to Christ alone with the role that others might have by participating in it.[8]

Objection 2 (2000, 2005): A redeemed person can not also be involved in redeeming.[9]

Objection 3 (2001): "The title Coredemptrix is ambiguous; therefore, it needs to be substituted by another."[10]

6. Fehlner, "Introduction to the Second International Symposium on Marian Coredemption," in *Mary at the Foot of the Cross II*, xii.

7. Short form of the quote: Fehlner. "Opening Address–Symposium 2004," in *Mary at the Foot of the Cross V*), ix. Complete quote: Fehlner, *"Mariae Advocatae Causa*. The Marian Issue in the Church Today," 530, for the long quote, and, 543, for the short form. Fehlner, "Opening Address," in *Mary at the Foot of the Cross*, 2–3.

8. Fehlner, "The Coredemptrix: Key to the Mystery of Christian Life," 363. Fehlner, "Introduction to the Second International Symposium," xvii. Fehlner, *"Mater Unitatis,"* 1, 22. Fehlner, *"Maria Coredemptrix—Mater Viventium (Gen 3, 20),"* 2. Fehlner, "Opening Address—Symposium 2004," vii. Fehlner, *"Mariae Advocatae Causa,"* 530, 535–36. Fehlner, "Opening Address" in *Mary at the Foot of the Cross VII*, 4.

9. Fehlner, "Sense of Marian Coredemption," 110. Fehlner, *"Mariae Advocatae Causa,"* 570. This comes from St. Thomas Aquinas, *Summa Theologica*, III, q. 2, a. 11, "The principle of merit does not fall under merit."

10. Fehlner, "Round Table Discussion," 445.

Objection 4 (2001): "Biblical patristic foundations for the doctrine of the Coredemption are lacking so we should not promote it."[11]

Objection 5 (2001, 2006 and 2009): The ecclesio-typical approach to Mary in Vatican II excluded the terms of "coredemptrix" and "mediatrix of all graces" as theological and semantic anachronisms.[12]

Objection 6 (2002): All ecclesiotypical approaches to Marian coredemption entail Mary's passivity in Christ's action in the redemption on the cross.[13]

Objection 7 (2002): "Mary is neither directly nor immediately actively involved in the dynamism of the sacramental order or of the single sacraments, nor can she be because she is not a priest."

Objection 8 (2003): Mary's mediation is "mere intercession."[14]

Objection 9 (2004): The argument in favor of Mary's coredemption is only abstract, "unrelated to theological reality."[15]

Objection 10 (2009): A modern culture of contentment and self-gratification does not value sacrifice.[16]

Fr. Fehlner's Appeal to Authority

On the contrary, Gen. 3:15 presented the Father's joint predestination of the Redeemer and his Mother in "one and the same decree" (*uno eodemque decreto*).[17] St. Francis called Mary "the Spouse of the Holy Spirit"[18] and the "Virgin made Church."[19] St. Bonaventure taught that "the price of our redemption Mary brought forth into the world, paid, and possesses,[20] and that

11. Ibid., 448.

12. Fehlner, "Introduction to the Second International Symposium," xix. Fehlner, "Opening Address," in *Mary at the Foot of the Cross IX: Mary:Spouse of the Holy Spirit, Coredemptrix and Mother of the Church: Acts of the Ninth International Symposium on Marian Coredemption,* 4. Fehlner, "Concluding Reflections" in *Mary at the Foot of the Cross IX: Mary: Spouse of the Holy Spirit, Coredemptrix and Mother of the Church,* 521.

13. Fehlner, "*Mater Unitatis,*" 2.

14. Fehlner, "*Maria Coredemptrix–Mater Viventium,*" 11.

15. Fehlner. "Opening Address—Symposium 2004," v.

16. Fehlner, "Introduction to the Second International Symposium," xx.

17. Ibid., xvi.

18. Fehlner, "Sense of Marian Coredemption," 108. Fehlner, "Opening Address" in *Mary at the Foot of the Cross IX,* 4, "the Immaculate Coredemptrix because Spouse of the Holy Spirit, the title first given Mary by St. Francis in his *Salute to the Virgin.*

19. Fehlner, "*Maria Coredemptrix—Mater Viventium,*" 1, 3, "*Virgo Ecclesia facta*" from St. Francis' *Salute to the Virgin.*

20. Fehlner, "*Mater Unitatis,*" 14, and "*Maria Coredemptrix—Mater Viventium,*" 10:

Mary is "our Mediatrix with Christ as Christ is our Mediator with the Father."[21] Bl. John Duns Scotus taught that the preservatively redeemed Immaculate Conception "can actively cooperate in the redemption of all" others who are liberated from sin.[22] Cardinal John Henry Newman noted the foundation of theology on the Patristic Eve-Mary typology.[23] St. Maximilian M. Kolbe named Mary to be the 'uncreated Immaculate Conception.'"[24] Pope Paul VI said that "no one is *Christ-like*, except to the degree he is first *Mary-like*."[25] Pope John Paul II taught Mary's maternal mediation in *Redemptoris Mater*.[26] Benedict XVI explained the marian principle of the Church.[27]

Fr. Fehlner's concept of Mary as the Maternal Mediatrix: "I Answer That"

Let us distinguish between salvation and redemption. Salvation from non-existence and for eternal happiness comes from "the absolute primacy of Christ and the Immaculate Conception," meaning that God created the world with the intention of the Son's Incarnation and the creation of Mary for the sake of a loving union with man. However, since the Original Sin was foreseen, the Incarnation also became redemptive, meaning that it freed humanity from sin so that all could be saved.[28]

Let us then distinguish two types of redemption: preservative and liberative. Christ redeemed Mary in "the most perfect way" by preserving her from sin, i.e. as the Immaculate Conception, which is "qualitatively different from liberative redemption," whereby Christ redeemed everyone else by freeing them from sin.[29] Mary's redemption is also qualitatively different from liberative redemption because she was then also preserved from ever commit-

---

"*pretium redemptionis nostrae Maria protulit, persolvit, possidet*," citing *Collationes in septem Donis Sancti Spiritus*, c. 6. Fehlner, "*Mariae Advocatae Causa*," 537.

21. Fehlner, "*Mariae Advocatae Causa*," 538, citing *III Sent.*, d. 3, p. 1, a. 1, q. 2.

22. Fehlner, "Sense of Marian Coredemption," 104-105. Fehlner, "Introduction to the Second International Symposium," xii.

23. Fehlner, "*Maria Coredemptrix—Mater Viventium*," 2. Apollonio and Fehlner, "Concept of Redemption," 117–18.

24. Fehlner, "Opening Address" in *Mary at the Foot of the Cross IX*, 4.

25. Fehlner, "*Maria Coredemptrix—Mater Viventium*," 11.

26. Ibid., 11.

27. Fehlner, "Opening Address," in *Mary at the Foot of the Cross VII*, 1–2, 7-8.

28. Fehlner and Apollonio, "Concept of Redemption," 111-17.

29. Fehlner. "Opening Address—Symposium 2004," vi-vii. Fehlner, "*Mariae Advocatae Causa*," 534. Fehlner and Apollonio, "The Concept of Redemption," the entire article, but especially 113-17, 122-25, 129.

ting a sin.[30] Yet, as a redeemed person, Mary is a member of the Church. [31]As a creature and a human being, Mary is dependent on and subordinate to God, her Creator, and specifically Christ, her Redeemer.[32]

Preservatively redeemed as the Spouse of the Holy Spirit, i.e. the Immaculate Conception, [33] and as the Mother of the Church, Mary's cooperation has been unique has been cooperating actively in the objective, liberative redemption of all others.[34] Her cooperation began by becoming the Virgin Mother of God and continued at the foot of the cross where she sacrificed her maternal rights in Christ's sacrifice that reaches all people in the subjective redemption through each and every Mass that is the re-presentation of the sacrifice on the cross and her spiritual maternity.[35]

The united action of Jesus and Mary in the objective redemption began when the Redeemer took the form of a slave (Phil. 2:4-10) in the womb of the Handmaid, or slave of the Lord.[36] Mary's cooperation was immediate in the Incarnation[37] and established her in "the order of the hypostatic union."[38] Mary's cooperated mediately throughout Christ's life through her help to him throughout His life as shown by her actions at the Annunciation, Nativity, Circumcision, Presentation, flight into Egypt, loss and finding in the temple, Cana, and culminating with her compassion with Christ at Calvary.[39] At the foot of the cross, Mary was Christ's "immediate visible source of support."[40]

Mary's cooperation is unique for several reasons. First, because she alone is the Immaculate Conception, she is the only one so completed united to the Holy Spirit that whenever He acts, she does also, and thus is able to cooperate actively and directly/immediately in the objective redemption.[41] Second, Mary's active cooperation also functions as a "type,"

30. Fehlner. "Opening Address—Symposium 2004," viii.

31. Ibid., vii.

32. Ibid., vi-vii.

33. Fehlner, "Opening Address" in *Mary at the Foot of the Cross IX*, 4.

34. Fehlner, "Sense of Marian Coredemption," 104. Fehlner. "Opening Address—Symposium 2004," vi-vii. Fehlner, "Opening Address" in *Mary at the Foot of the Cross IX*, 5.

35. Fehlner, "Sense of Marian Coredemption," 108.

36. Fehlner, "Introduction to the Second Internation Symposium," xiii-xv.

37. Fehlner, "*Maria Coredemptrix—Mater Viventium*," 2.

38. Ibid., 3.

39. Fehlner, "Introduction to the Second International Symposium," xvi.

40. Fehlner, "*Maria Coredemptrix—Mater Viventium*," 3.

41. Fehlner, "Introduction to the Second International Symposium," x. Fehlner, "*Maria Coredemptrix—Mater Viventium*," 4, defined the "espousal of the Holy Spirit"

i.e. the very form and empowerment for all others to cooperate as well in the subjective redemption.[42] As such, Mary's cooperation is also personal and instrumental.[43]

In summary, the Immaculate Conception/Spouse of the Holy Spirit is the first principle of Mariology.[44] Because she is the Immaculate Conception, then she is also the Maternal Mediatrix that is a general category (Bl. John Duns Scotus) as 'Co-head' of the Church. . . . " [45] Mary's maternal mediation is realized in three moments (St. Bonaventure): 1) as Mother of God (Divine Maternity);[46] 2) as Coredemptrix with a coredemptive offering and being offered, culminating on Calvary (Spiritual Maternity);[47] and 3) as since she possesses all graces, "Distributrix of all graces in the Church,"[48] also known as "Mediatrix of All Graces,"[49] especially in the Eucharist.[50] Each of these three moments are causally related; Coredemption is a consequence of the Divine Maternity, and then Mediatrix of all graces or Mother of the Church is a result of her Divine Maternity and her Coredemption.[51]

---

as "that singular communion of hearts and wills in which two persons, without ceasing to be distinct persons, are totally 'in-existent', as it were 'melted', 'liquefied' like wax, the Virgin being 'transubstantiated into the Holy Spirit'" (St. Maximilian Ma. Kolbe, *SK* 509; *CK*, Nov. 26, 1938.)

42. Fehlner, "Opening Address" in *Mary at the Foot of the Cross IX*, 3, 5.

43. Fehlner, "*Maria Advocatae Causa*," 539.

44. Fehlner, "Opening Address—Symposium 2004," vi, substituted the Immaculate Conception for the Lutheran *sola fides* as "the *articulus stantis vel cadentis Ecclesiae*." Fehlner, "Opening Address" in *Mary at the Foot of the Cross IX*, 4, the Immaculate Conception is the basis for Marian coredemption.

45. Fehlner, "Opening Address" in *Mary at the Foot of the Cross IX*, 8.

46. Fehlner's agreement with St. Bonaventure's three moments was confirmed in a phone interview on May 15, 2015. Peter Damian Fehlner, "Opening Address" in *Mary at the Foot of the Cross VI*, 2. Apollonio and Fehlner, "Concept of Redemption," 119. Fehlner, "Opening Address" in *Mary at the Foot of the Cross IX*, 7, "active Mediatrix as Mother of God."

47. Fehlner, "Sense of Marian Coredemption," 104. Fehlner, "*Mater Unitatis*," 14. Fehlner, "Opening Address," in *Mary at the Foot of the Cross IX*, 1.

48. Fehlner. "Opening Address." In *Mary at the Foot of the Cross IX*, 1-2, and 7. Fehlner, "*Mater Unitatis*," 14. The concept of Mary's maternal mediation as the general category realized in three moments was confirmed in a phone interview with Fehlner on May 15, 2015.

49. Fehlner. "Opening Address." In *Mary at the Foot of the Cross IX*, 1-2

50. Fehlner, "*Maria Coredemptrix—Mater Viventium*," 10. Fehlner, "Opening Address," in *Mary at the Foot of the Cross VI*, 2-9.

51. Fehlner, "*Maria Coredemptrix—Mater Viventium*," 10. Fehlner, "Opening Address" in *Mary at the Foot of the Cross IX*, 8. Fehlner. "Opening Address." In *Mary at the Foot of the Cross IX*, 1-2.

Replies to Objections

Reply to Objection 1 (solus Christus): St. Paul describes Christians as "core-deemers, filling up with is lacking to the passion of Christ in the Church (cf. Col. 1, 24)."[52] Mary's mediation as mother is both chronologically and logically prior as the pre-condition for Christ's existence as the one Mediator.[53] In the reversal of the Fall in which Eve came from Adam alone, Mary is the solitary human parent as the "virgin earth" from which the New Adam was formed, while remaining His helpmate or bride, although not physical wife.[54] Mary's maternal mediation as the New Eve, the Mother of all the Living, is then required for all others to have spiritual life as part of the Body of Christ by being conformed to her obedient reception of Christ, i.e. "marianized" by a total consecration to Mary.[55]

This "Christ alone" objection would be valid if there were only a liberative redemption; however, as the Immaculate Conception, the uniquely preservatively redeemed Mary, can participate in the liberative redemption of all others.[56] Therefore, just as the Mary's Divine maternity manifests the divinity of the Son, "the profession of Faith in the Coredemption does not detract from but enables us to affirm the one mediation of Jesus,"[57] because, it is Christ's perfect mediation that graced her as the Immaculate Daughter of the Father and Spouse of the Holy Spirit, enabling her to become the Virgin Mother of the Son.[58] Thus, the title as "Coredemptrix" expresses her distinction and derivation from the Redeemer/Mediator, a dependence that "neither adds nor subtracts from the dignity of the first in actively contributing."[59]

Cardinal John Henry Newman taught that "chronolotry, the worship of this moment and the satisfaction and gratification that this moment brings" is the underlying basis for this "Christ alone" objection that is linked to "faith alone."[60] Newman noted that excluding Mary results in ignoring Jesus because the refusal to acknowledge Mary's intercession, also rejects the pope's authority, as well as the sacraments, and without these secondary causes, one

52. Fehlner, "The Coredemptrix: Key to the Mystery of Christian Life," 362.

53. Fehlner, "*Maria Coredemptrix—Mater Viventium ,*" 2.

54. Fehlner, "Opening Address—Symposium 2004," xiii–xiv, noting Gen. 1:26–27, 2:4–7 and 18–25. Apollonio and Fehlner, "Concept of Redemption," 123–24.

55. Fehlner, "*Maria Coredemptrix—Mater Viventium,*" 5–6, 9.

56. Fehlner, "Opening Address — Symposium 2004," vii–ix.

57. Fehlner, "Introduction to the Second International Symposium," xx.

58. Fehlner, "*Maria Coredemptrix—Mater Viventium,*" 4.

59. Fehlner, "*Mater Unitatis,*" 22.

60. Fehlner, "Introduction to the Second International Symposium," xviii.

becomes the arbiter of truth and enters into a sea of "doubt and anxiety of conscience."[61] The logical consequence of the "*solus Christus*" premise would exclude the possibility of any creature's free cooperation in redemption, such as the divine Maternity. Therefore, Mary's free cooperation in the Incarnation is sufficient to refute the principle of "*solus Christus*."[62]

Reply to Objection 2 (no one can redeem himself): Mary did not merit her own preservative redemption that came from the merits of Christ alone; however, she did help Christ in the liberative redemption of all others.[63] This Thomistic objection simply needed a further distinction provided by a Scotistic perspective; use both soteriologies since the Thomistic approach provided the idea of a single mystical person of Christ within which Mary's distinctive role is explained by Scotus.[64]

Reply to Objection 3 (ambiguity of "Coredemptrix"): The uneducated find it difficult to understand "any theological term, any philosophical phrase even the most ordinary, even the most fundamental."[65] Our modern culture is also so pragmatic that anything that is not available to the physical senses "does not enter the mind."[66] Thus, rather than change the terminology, teach the audience that, although there have been a multitude of titles to express the truth of the doctrine, "there is no better title to express exactly what this mystery is all about than Coredemptrix."[67] Quite precisely because a mystery is beyond a complete human understanding, "There is no word in our language that can fully express any theological mystery . . . [such] as Trinity, Hypostatic Union, Soteriology."[68] Therefore, since Catholic theology does not hesitate to use these terms, Catholic theologians should not fear using "Coredemptrix."

Reply to Objection 4 (lack of Biblical Patristic foundations for Mary's coredemption): " . . . the Greek fathers of the 5th Century and the 6th Century" teach us that Mary is so far superior to us that "we can compare ourselves to her but not the other way around."[69]

61. Ibid., xviii.

62. Fehlner, "Opening Address" in *Mary at the Foot of the Cross VII*, 3.

63. Fehlner, "Opening Address—Symposium 2004," vii-viii.

64. Fehlner, "Concluding Observations on the Eighth Symposium," 501-2.

65. Fehlner, "Round Table Dicsussion," 445.

66. Ibid., 445–46.

67. Ibid., 446.

68. Ibid.

69. Ibid., 448.

Reply to Objection 5 (pre-Vatican II anachronism): "[O]ur faith . . . is first of all a matter of humble faith in the tradition received, not adjustment to current intellectual or cultural fashion."[70]

Rather than "Mary either related to Christ or to the Church," Fr. Fehlner held a "both/and," just as the title of chapter eight of *Lumen Gentium* indicates: the Blessed Virgin in the Mystery of Christ **and** of the Church, or in Bonaventurian terms: the Blessed Virgin as Mother of the Whole Christ, Head and Body, and this from the first moment of the Incarnation ever after . . . "[71] Thus, to resolve post-Vatican II objections, use an ecclesio-typical approach.[72] For example, the Pauline and patristic concept of "'co-redeemers' in the Church, . . . rests on an interpretation of Mary Coredemptrix as 'type' of the Church primarily as a dynamic Mother rather than static model . . . ."[73] Mary's coredemption and mediation establishes the very possibility of the Church's "spousal union with Christ . . . [and] any possibility of attaining justice and cooperating in the work of sanctification and salvation."[74] Thus, while Vatican II did not make "the solemn definition of the Coredemption and Universal Mediation of Mary, the structure and the presentation of *Lumen Gentium* presupposed precisely that traditional, Franciscan thesis: the mystery of Mary in Christ and in the Church . . . [and] the underlying assumptions pointing to the Coredemption remain in place."[75]

The hermeneutic of continuity between pre and post-Vatican II doctrine is exemplified in Paul VI's *Mater Ecclesiae* and *Marialis Cultus* that support Mary's spiritual maternity in regard to the entire Body of Christ.[76] John Paul II and Benedict XVI's teachings on the "marian principle of the Church" explain Mary's maternal mediation in the distribution of graces.[77]

Reply to Objection 6 (ecclesiotypical approach denies Mary's active role): While "subordinate to Christ" and a "member of the Church," Mary's role is uniquely "preeminent" and active in Christ's redemption because "She alone is Mother of God," and therefore Mother of the Church.[78] Mary's

70. Fehlner, "Introduction to the Second International Symposium," xv.

71. Fehlner, "Concluding Reflections" in *Mary at the Foot of the Cross IX*, 522.

72. Ibid., 521.

73. Fehlner, "Opening Address" in *Mary at the Foot of the Cross IX*, 6.

74. Ibid., 7.

75. Fehlner, "Round Table Discussion," 451. Fehlner, "Opening Address—Symposium 2004," xiv–xvi.

76. Fehlner, "*Mater Unitatis*," 4–11. Fehlner, "Opening Address" in *Mary at the Foot of the Cross VII*, 4, for the hermeneutic of continuity.

77. Fehlner, "Opening Address" in *Mary at the Foot of the Cross VII*, 1–2, 7–8.

78. Fehlner, "*Mater Unitatis*," 2–3. Fehlner, "*Mater Coredemptrix–Mater Viventium*," 1, alluded to *Marialis Cultus* 53, and 11, referred to Paul VI's *Mater Ecclesiae*, as well as *Lumen Gentium* in general.

maternal causality is not physical, but rather meritorious and moral, as a "type" that first forms and then incorporates others in the Church into her form, i.e. into the Body of Christ in a typical causality that perhaps is best called "personal."[79]

Reply to Objection 7 (sacraments): Mary's involvement in the sacraments has been recognized in "the ancient canons of the Mass in all rites." Mary's reception of Holy Communion "is an aspect of her mediation whereby we are able to take advantage of this great Sacrament and achieve full incorporation into the Body which She conceived virginally and first received into Herself at that virginal conception. That mediation therefore is in some way truly sacerdotal."[80]

Reply to Objection 8 (mere intercession): Mary's active and dynamic mediation or presence in the Church is more than just intercession because *she alone* is the Immaculate Conception and the Coredemptrix *jointly predestined with Christ* and *actively involved in* the triumph of the Cross.[81] Her mediation is a moral cause that is voluntary, personal, and dynamic, in its inseparability from Christ's, affecting each and every member of the Church.[82]

Reply to Objection 9 (only abstract): Christ as the Mediator who is "of Mary, with Mary, and for Mary."[83] As mother of the Mediator, Mary is a concrete reality for Jesus. With Jesus, Mary is our spiritual mother and is a practical reality for us.

Reply to Objection 10 (immoral behavior): The life of self-gratification and contentment is a "disguised pantheistic egoism" that is not true happiness. Those who live the doctrine of the Coredemption would "reform our lives and our secular culture in a Marian way so as to become a genuine 'civilization of love'" and find the joy that all desire.[84]

An Evaluation of Fr. Fehlner's Contributions regarding Marian Mediation and Coredemption

In evaluation, since Fr. Fehlner is a human being, there is room for some improvement in his approach. His brilliance lends itself to some academic

79. Fehlner, "*Mater Unitatis*," 8–11. Fehlner, "*Mater Coredemptrix—Mater Viventium*," 8.

80. Fehlner, "*Mater Unitatis*," 18.

81. Fehlner, "*Maria Coredemptrix—Mater Viventium*," 11.

82. Fehlner, "Opening Address" in *Mary at the Foot of the Cross VII*, 9.

83. Fehlner. "Opening Address—Symposium 2004," v–vi.

84. Fehlner, "Introduction to the Second International Symposium," xx–xxi.

problems. Sometimes he referred to something without citing it, perhaps considering it to be common knowledge, when it might not be;[85] occasionally this "common knowledge" might be incorrect.[86] Other times, his succinct statements leaped from premise to conclusion, perhaps because the intervening steps are obvious to him, when they might not be to his reader.[87] It was confusing to find the term "mediation" used for both the overarching category of Mary's three-fold cooperation in redemption, as well as for the third moment of her cooperation. But, even with such flaws that verify his humanity, his contribution to Mariology remains admirable.

Fr. Fehlner consistently used a "hermeneutic of continuity." He rejected the false dichotomy between the past and present doctrine of the Church, a separation that Fr. Fehlner noted was proposed by *avant-garde* theologians who err either by minimalism or a maximalism that strays from *Lumen Gentium* chapter 8.[88] While his critique was aimed at those who rejected the past in their claim to follow Vatican II, his principle of continuity also implied a rejection of those who adhered to the past and refused to accept Vatican II. As a Franciscan, he integrated a scholastic theology from St. Francis, St. Bonaventure, Bl. John Duns Scotus, all the way to St. Maximilian Kolbe theology, presenting the Immaculate Conception as the fundamental principle. He integrated Christ's teachings from Scripture to those given by Christ's current vicar on earth. He found support for Mary's coredemption in unusual Scripture passages such as the "virgin earth" Genesis 1–3 and the "doulos" of Philippians 2:4–10. He used the teachings of Vatican II, Paul VI, and John Paul II to provide ecclesio-typical answers to modern objections. In particular, his insight into the necessity of the anthropological basis for mediation is most helpful: "The model of mediation of not legal, nor social,

85. For example, Fehlner, "*Maria Advocatae Causa*," 543, referred to Paul VI's famous "remark that one can smell the smoke of Satan within the Church," without citing that this was from his homily on June 29, 1972, as reported by *Insegnamenti di Paulo*, 707, according to McClarey, "Pope Paul VI and the Smoke of Satan."

86. For example, Fehlner, "*Maria Advocatae Causa*," 542, stated that there is a "higher divorce rate among Catholics than among non-Catholics," when the opposite is the case at least for U.S. Catholics according to The Catholic News Agency, "Catholics Continue to have Lowest Divorce Rates, Report Finds," October 1, 2013, http://www.catholic-newsagency.com/news/catholics-continue-to-have-lowest-divorce-rates-report-finds/.

87. E.g. Fehlner, "Opening Address," in *Mary at the Foot of the Cross VII*, 3, "Either Mary is Mediatrix of all graces because She is Coredemptrix, or there is no fruitful mediation: magisterial, pastoral, sacramental, charismatic, by anyone in the Church."

88. Fehlner, "Opening Address," in *Mary at the Foot of the Cross VII*, 4–5, 10, rejected the hermeneutic of discontinuity that could be called "Vatican II triumphalism," in the sense of a minimalism. Fehlner, "*Mariae Advocatae Causa*," 565–66, corrected a false maximalism of Mary as a goddess, which this author notes remains an unfortunate error of some post-Vatican theologians.

but a woman, the Spouse of the Holy Spirit."[89] Until that is realized, the theological objections to Mary's mediation cannot be resolved.[90]

As Fehlner noted, "what is needed is a more careful and exact terminology to describe the divine action involved in the infusion of grace and in the process of sanctification within the economy of salvation."[91] In a Thomistic tradition, Christ's mediation has been distinguished from Mary's because Christ's is principal, perfect, sufficient, independent, absolutely necessary, and completely universal because His is ontological as the God-man, and moral by His will, while Mary's mediation is secondary/subordinate to Christ's, dependent on Christ's, not strictly necessary, but chosen by God to be necessary ministerially or instrumentally as the Mother of God, not just physically but formally by her consent, and as a cooperator associated with Christ in the redemption for all others.[92] Many theologians made this distinction between two types of redemption: 1) Christ's redemption of all, including Mary; and 2) Mary's cooperation in the redemption of all others. [93] As proposed by Bl. John Duns Scotus, the unique redemption by Christ of Mary has been called preservative.[94] In contrast, what should the redemption of everyone else by Christ with Mary's cooperation be called? As early as 1957, Juniper Carol, described the second type of redemption "liberative."[95] However, although Roschini also used this terminology in 1969, this description of the "liberative redemption" did not become popular.[96] Fehlner's 2004 and 2005 presentations may have influenced Calkins who had attended the 2004 symposium to highlight in his 2007 presentation Roschini's use of the term, as well as perhaps prompting its adoption by Cardinal Vithayathil, CSsR, in 2008, after having heard Fehlner at the

89. Fehlner, phone interview, May 15, 2015.

90. Ibid.

91. Fehlner, "Opening Address," in Mary at the Foot of the Cross VII, 9.

92. Naulaerts, "Responsa ad quaestiones," 263–68. See St. Thomas Aquinas, Summa Theologica, III, q. 26, a. 2, corpus.

93. Roschini, Mariologia, 2:395. Bittremieux, De Mediatione universali B.M. Virginis, 44–45; Bittremieux, "De Congruo promeruit nobis B. Virgo," 427–33. Lebon, "Comment je conçois," 709.

94. Later repeated in the very title of the article, Carol, "Reflections on the Problem of Mary's Preservative Redemption," 19–88.

95. Carol, "Our Lady's Coredemption," in Mariology, 2:418; Carol's citation pointed to a F. Tummers, Het mede-verdienen van de h. Maagd in het verlossingswerk, in Bijdragen van de philosophische en theologische Faculteiten der Nederlandsche Jesuiten 1 (1938) 81–103, especially 93, but it was not clear that this terminology came from that article.

96. Calkins, "Mary Co-Redemptrix," 383–84, mistakenly credited Gabriele Roschini for this term in his 1969 book, Maria Santissima nella Storia della Salvezza.

2005 Fatima symposium.[97] Whether or not Fehlner was influential in these cases, his use of the term in his writings sets an example worth following. The description of a "liberative redemption" is simple, clear, and precise in distinguishing how the redemption of everyone else is different than Mary's preservative redemption. Fehlner's use of the term showed the value of this term that is worth becoming standard. His use also suggests perhaps an application of the adjective to mediation as well so that Mary's "liberative" mediation for all others would be distinguished from Christ's salvific mediation of all, including Mary.

Hopefully this brief overview is sufficient to inspire the audience to read more of Fehlner's Marian writings. There is a rich treasure of many ideas, some more developed than others. It is this author's hope that a scholar might be prompted to do further research to identify the origin of the description of liberative redemption.

But equally important to Fehlner's theological insights, is his confidence in Mary; as he wrote, perhaps as a confession, "The believer may well be initially irked by this kind of slick anti-marianism circulated by Catholics, but on second thought we may smile. It is the hiss of desperation directed against the impregnable 'Tower of David' about to crush still again with her heel the head of the serpent-liar lying in wait for the blow . . . . "[98] Thus, in the spirit that Fr. Fehlner inspires, it is appropriate to conclude by invoking her, "O Mary conceived without sin, pray for us who have recourse to you."

Bibliography

Bittremieux, Joseph. "De congruo promeruit nobis B. Virgo quae Christus de condigno promeruit." *Ephemerides Theologicae Lovanienses* 8 (1931) 422–36.

———. *De Mediatione universali B.M. Virginis quoad gratias.* Brugge: Beyaert, 1926.

Calkins, Arthur Burton. "Mary Co-Redemptrix: The Beloved Associate of Christ." In *Mariology: A Guide for Priests, Deacons, Seminarians, and Consecrated Persons,* edited by Mark Miravalle, 349–409. Goleta, CA: Queenship, 2007.

Carol, Juniper B. "Our Lady's Coredemption." In *Mariology,* 2:377–425. Milwaukee: Bruce, 1957.

———."Reflections on the Problem of Mary's Preservative Redemption." *Marian Studies* 30 (1979) 19–88.

"Catholics Continue to have Lowest Divorce Rates, Report Finds." *Catholic News Agency,* October 1, 2013. http://www.catholicnewsagency.com/news/catholics-continue-to-have-lowest-divorce-rates-report-finds/.

"Declaration of the Theological Commission of the Pontifical International Marian Academy: Request for the Definition of the Dogma of Mary as Mediatrix,

97. Vithayathil, "Blessed Virgin Mary," Fifth Marian Dogma.

98. Fehlner, "Opening Address—Symposium 2004," ix.

Coredemptrix and Advocate." *L'Osservatore Romano*, June 4, 1997. https://udayton.edu/imri/mary/m/mediatrix-coredemptrix-and-advocate-declaration.php.

Fehlner, Peter Damian. "Concluding Reflections." In *Mary at the Foot of the Cross VIII: Coredemption as Key to a Correct Understanding of Redemption, and Recent Attempts to Redefine Redemption Contrary to the Belief of the Church: Acts of the Eighth International Symposium on Marian Coredemption*, 497–503. New Bedford, MA: Academy of the Immaculate, 2008.

———. "Concluding Reflections." In *Mary at the Foot of the Cross IX: Mary: Spouse of the Holy Spirit, Coredemptrix and Mother of the Church: Acts of the Ninth International Symposium on Marian Coredemption: Fatima, Portugal, July 15–17, 2009*, 521–25. New Bedford, MA: Academy of the Immaculate, 2010.

———. "The Coredemptrix: Key to the Mystery of Christian Life." In *Mary at the Foot of the Cross: Acts of the International Symposium on Marian Coredemption*, 361–85. New Bedford, MA: Franciscans of the Immaculate, 2001.

———. "Introduction to the Second International Symposium on Marian Coredemption." In *Mary at the Foot of the Cross II: Acts of the Second International Symposium on Marian Coredemption*, viii-xxiii. New Bedford, MA: Franciscan Friars of the Immaculate, 2002.

———. "*Mariae Advocatae Causa.* The Marian Issue in the Church Today." In *Mary: "Unique Cooperator in the Redemption": Atti del Simposio sul Mistero della Corredenzione Mariana, Fatima, Portogallo, 3–7 Maggio 2005*, 529–77. New Bedford, MA: Academy of the Immaculate, 2005.

———. "*Maria Coredemptrix–Mater Viventium* (Gen 3, 20)." In *Mary at the Foot of the Cross IV*: Mater Viventium *(Gen 3, 20): Acts of the Fourth International Symposium on Marian Coredemption*, 1–16. New Bedford, MA: Academy of the Immaculate, 2004.

———. "*Mater Unitatis.*" In *Mary at the Foot of the Cross III*: Mater Unitatis: *Acts of the Third International Symposium on Marian Coredemption*, 1–24. New Bedford, MA: Academy of the Immaculate, 2003.

———. "Opening Address—Symposium 2004." In *Mary at the Foot of the Cross V: Redemption and Coredemption under the Sign of the Immaculate Conception: Acts of the Fifth International Symposium on Marian Coredemption*, 1–9. New Bedford, MA: Academy of the Immaculate, 2005.

———. "Opening Address." In *Mary at the Foot of the Cross VI: Marian Coredemption in the Eucharistic Mystery: Acts of the Sixth International Symposium on Marian Coredemption*, 1–9. New Bedford, MA: Academy of the Immaculate, 2007.

———. "Opening Address." In *Mary at the Foot of the Cross VII: Coredemptrix, therefore Mediatrix of All Graces: Acts of the Seventh International Symposium on Marian Coredemption*, 1–14. New Bedford, MA: Academy of the Immaculate, 2008.

———. "Opening Address." In *Mary at the Foot of the Cross VIII: Coredemption as Key to a Correct Understanding of Redemption, and Recent Attempts to Redefine Redemption Contrary to the Belief of the Church: Acts of the Eighth International Symposium on Marian Coredemption*, 1–8. New Bedford, MA: Academy of the Immaculate, 2008.

———. "Opening Address." In *Mary at the Foot of the Cross IX: Mary: Spouse of the Holy Spirit, Coredemptrix and Mother of the Church: Acts of the Ninth International*

Symposium on Marian Coredemption: Fatima, Portugal, July 15-17, 2009, 1–8. New Bedford, MA: Academy of the Immaculate, 2010.

———. "Round Table Discussion: Common Objections to Marian Coredemption." In *Mary at the Foot of the Cross II: Acts of the Second International Symposium on Marian Coredemption*, 441–56. New Bedford, MA: Franciscan Friars of the Immaculate, 2002.

———. "The Sense of Marian Coredemption in St. Bonaventure and Bl. John Duns Scotus." In *Mary at the Foot of the Cross: Acts of the International Symposium on Marian Coredemption*, 103–18. New Bedford, MA: Franciscans of the Immaculate, 2001.

Fehlner, Peter Damian, and Alessandro M. Apollonio. "The Concept of Redemption in the Fransciscan-Scotistic School: Salvation, Redemption, and the Primary of Christ." In *Mary at the Foot of the Cross VIII: Coredemption as Key to a Correct Understanding of Redemption, and Recent Attempts to Redefine Redemption Contrary to the Belief of the Church: Acts of the Eighth International Symposium on Marian Coredemption*, 111–56. New Bedford, MA: Academy of the Immaculate, 2008.

Lebon, Joseph. "Comment je conçois, j'établis et je defends la doctrine de la mediation mariale." *Ephemerides Theologicae Lovanienses* 16 (1939) 655–744.

The Liturgy of the Hours. Vol. 1: *Advent Season, Christmas Season*. Translated by the International Commission on English in the Liturgy. New York: Catholic Book, 1975.

McClarey, Donald R. "Pope Paul VI and the Smoke of Satan." *Catholic Stand*, January 29, 2013. http://www.catholicstand.com/109/.

Naulaerts, J. "Responsa ad quaestiones conferentiarum ecclesiasticarum mensis Februarii 1922." *La Vie Diocésaine* 11 (1922) 261–71, 431–45.

Roschini, Gabriele. *Mariologia*. Vol. 2: *Summa Mariologiae. Pars Prima. De Beata Maria Virgine considerate in sua singulari missione*. 2nd ed. Rome: Angelus Belardetti, 1947.

Vithayathil, Varkey. "Blessed Virgin Mary: Unique Cooperator in the Redemption." *Fifth Marian Dogma*, July 29, 2008. http://www.fifthmariandogma.com/witnesses/cardinals-and-bishops/blessed-virgin-mary-unique-cooperator-in-the-redemption/.

9

Themes and Sounding in the Marian Metaphysics of Peter Damian Fehlner

J. Isaac Goff

This paper takes its point of departure from several seminal essays of Fr. Peter Damian Fehlner on the topic of what he terms "Marian Metaphysics." All told, these essays comprise over four hundred pages throughout which Fehlner systematically expounds and applies the fruits of over fifty years of prayerful reflection upon the central place and role the Blessed Virgin Mary in the eternal plan of God, as manifested and accomplished throughout salvation history. I will offer some reflections upon two axiomatic Fehlnerian positions: (1) the primacy of charity in God and (2) the order of the hypostatic union in economy/ies of creation and salvation. It is my hope that the following will serve as motivation to look directly into Fehlner's work on Marian Metaphysics.[1]

1. These include: "Mater et Magistra apostolorum" (Mother and Teacher of the Apostles), 15–54; "De Metaphysica Mariana Quaedam" (Some Considerations on Marian Metaphysics), 13–42; "Scientia et Pietas" (Knowledge and Piety), 11–48; "'Io sono l'Immacolata Concezione': Adhuc Quaedam de Metaphysica Mariana" ("I am the Immaculate Conception": Some Further Considerations on Marian Metaphysics), 15–41; "'I am the Immaculate Conception': Redemption and Coredemption, Recirculation and Recapitulation in the Light of Metaphysics: Bonaventurian Exemplarism and Scotistic Univocity," 2005, *Unpublished Manuscript* (hereafter cited as "Redemption and Coredemption"); "Mater et Magistra Theologorum: The Immaculate Conception and the Notion and Method of 'Our Theology' According to Bl. John Duns Scotus," 2004, *Unpublished Manuscript* (hereafter cited as "Magistra Theologorum"); "Mary and Theology: Scotus Revisited," 111–72 (New Bedford, MA: Academy of the Immaculate, 2015). The above texts are currently in preparation for collection and republication as a part of the *Collected Works of Peter Damian Fehlner*. This author, as editor of the *Collected Works*, has in his possession the original typescripts of each of these essays. Because of this, coupled with the that fact that some of these essays exists only in manuscript for and the difficulty of obtaining those studies, which were published, some of the essays of Fehlner listed in this note will be cited in this essay according to their typescript

Metaphysics and the Charity of God?

Talk of *metaphysics* evokes several questions: what is metaphysics all about? its scope and methodology? its realm of discourse and inquiry? Are we talking philosophy, theology, both and more?

Fr. Peter Fehlner's overall approach to metaphysics might be summed up in the following manner: "Christ is "our" Metaphysics and its Mode is Marian in the one economy of salvation." Elsewhere Fehlner unpacks the meaning of these two assertions:

> Metaphysics . . . is rightly designated as exemplaristic, i.e., the thought form which enables us not only to compare finite *exemplatum* with infinite *exemplar* (the *ars aeterna, rationes aeternae*), but eventually to recognize in the Son of Mary the Son of God, the divine person not compared to, but on a par with the Father, *fontalis plenitudo bonitatis*, whose Incarnation is not only the primary basis for the possibility of creation, but for its eventual recapitulation and integration with the circle of divinity, viz. the unity of infinite and finite, divine being and human, in the substantial unity of one person without confusion of natures.[2]

With respect to the epistemic, critical question of gaining access to the metaphysical knowledge, Fehlner is quite traditional. He writes:

> Exemplarism, or typology [as exemplarism applied to Scripture] is not only the starting point of all theological method . . . it also underlies all reasoning as rooted in the power to compare, assess, judge in terms of a standard. The univocal concept of being [the translation of the metaphor of divine illumination shining upon the soul translated into logical form][3] is but a neat way of summing up exemplarism at the level of reason, a foreshadowing of what will be the dogmatic formula at the heart of all biblical exemplarism [or typology]: one person in two natures, hypostatically united yet really distinct, adumbrated in the notion of being containing its intrinsic modes, the *prima diversa*, unconfused, yet perfectly integrated in a certain order, permitting us to reason "typologically" or significantly.[4]

---

editions. The reader will alerted when typescripts versions of Fehlner's essays are cited.

2. "Redemption and Coredemption," unpublished manuscript.

3. Ibid.

4. Ibid.

Fehlner's explicit framing of metaphysics in a Christo-Marian, exemplarist key, designating it as "OUR" metaphysics, pinpoints the distinctiveness of his Franciscan approach and outlook: an understanding that *metaphysics*, although supposing "brute" logical possibility, scientific analysis and categorization, is not ultimately based upon natural, impersonal forces or causes, but upon the order between persons, who by essence are rational agents, manifesting their rationality, or lack thereof, in terms of their judgments about and love of Wisdom.

Fehlner, therefore, articulates a vision of creation, in the light of the priority of personal agency acting in terms of exemplarism and recapitulation in a manner that situates the rationality and purpose of material creation within this order of persons as well, justifying secondary causality on the part of material forces on the supposition of the teleological priority of synergy between created will and Divine will in the transformation of the *Imago Dei* into the *Similitudo Dei*. He explains that the divine intention in creating

> [I]ncludes not only a passive role for creation in its recapitulation, but also its cooperation in the accomplishment of this stupendous work, the recirculation of the original "circulation" from the Creator and secondly the "recirculation" after the tragic "misdirection" represented by original sin. Thus, what St. Bonaventure call the Marian mode of the Incarnation is nothing but a technical term for the cooperation of the entire creation centered in "our tainted nature's solitary boast," the person of the Immaculate, or pre-redeemed. Here is the mystery, the apparent impossibility, nonetheless real, which must with Scotus be unraveled not merely at the empirical level of chronological succession or of a series "accidentally ordered," but at the metaphysical level of a series "essentially ordered" in the mind an heart of the Creator-Savior . . . if we are to understand redemptive Incarnation: how the created in Mary can at once be redeemed, yet active participant in effecting the order of the hypostatic union and redemption.[5]

For Fehlner, then, the reasonability of the created order, exemplified most fully in human beings as the mediatory *Imago Dei*, a composition of soul and body, explains the originating-exemplary-final causal circle nested in the heart of the Father whose infinite loves flourishes in the eternal perichoretic love of the Trinity: a love, so Fehlner following Bonaventure and Scotus, that, in the light of revelation, is able to be clearly understood to be

5. Ibid.

the ground of the possibility (*potuit*) of a created order. Infinite goodness and charity, as best characterizing the *Deum esse et trinum*, in its being and relations of origin, is the basis of the *ordered* love of God as manifested in the actual economy of redemption and salvation (the *fecit* and *decuit*).

On this point Fehlner writes: " . . . The antecedent unity of power of the three divine persons in creating has as its premise the dual processions of Son from the Father and Spirit from Father and Son, a duality reflected in creation."[6] Fehlner, in seeing the root of God's infinite power in the processions of the Persons of the Trinity and, thus, the primacy of divine circumincession, implies two foundational truths about God and his activity. First, perfect being is rational by nature and therefore personal, originating from the person of the Father and *in actu primo* acts as a person. Second, in perfect, i.e., infinite being, personal being is necessarily tripersonal and free, accenting the complement of divine knowledge, appropriated to the Son-Word in the spiration of the Spirit *through* the Son (middle and mediating Person),[7] which affects a return to the Father. This infinite flourishing in the Trinity is personal and free, rooted and fulfilled in charity: loving acceptance of the infinite good for its own sake. Fehlner, following Bonaventure and Scotus, explains that this charity originates in and from the Father-Memory, in a natural mode of activity that terminates in the Son-Word-Intellect, and is simultaneously "perfected" in the voluntary mode of activity in the spiration of the Spirit-Gift-Bond-Love.[8] Although we cannot here give an adequate summary of Fehlner's Bonaventurian account of the mystery of *Deum esse et trinum*, the central point is that charity holds a certain primacy and the voluntary mode of action is most perfectly personal because free, and, as personal, rational.

Flowing out of the above considerations, Fehlner contends that a "pure metaphysics" that systematically or merely *de facto* fails to consider the priority of divine charity, is not only incomplete, but false in its implication and application. According to Fehlner, metaphysics, like philosophy in general,[9] is in the final analysis a consideration of an order of persons in

6. Fehlner, "Redemption, Metaphysics and the Immaculate Conception," 215. In "De Metaphysica Mariana Quaedam," Fehlner makes the point, following Bonaventure, that the Son in the "middle person" of the Trinity.

7. Cf. "De Metaphysica Mariana."

8. Cf. Fehlner, "DE DEO UNO ET TRINO ad mentem Caroli Rahner," 73–161.

9. Cf. Fehlner, "Scientia et Pietas." Fehlner insists both upon the autonomy of or distinction between philosophical and theological modes of inquiry and reasoning as well as upon the balanced, mutual relation and con-penetration of reason and faith in the life of the human person whose thought is truly balanced. For Fehlner, the failure to attain such a balance eventually becomes plain in the form of skepticism and/or cynicism.

charity. When the economy of salvation is seen in terms of the priority of divine charity extended to creation, metaphysics becomes fundamentally dogmatic theology as revealed in faith in the trinity and the economy of salvation rooted in the fittingness and priority of the Order of the Hypostatic Union: the incarnation and divine maternity.[10]

According to Fehlner, the purpose or teleology of the created person, bearing upon the relation and resolution of nature to supernature in general, and knowledge and judgment, specifically, is bound up in how one understands the place of Mary as *Panagia Theotokos* in the eternal counsels of God[11] and as realized in history. For Fehlner, the resolution of the purpose of human rationality is bound up with the perfect created personhood of mary as both condition of the Word's assumption of our humanity as well as the realization of the Incarnate Word's perfect work of redemption and salvation. As Fehlner puts it:

> The issue [of created rationality as perfected in Mary] concerns the relations between philosophy and theology, reason and faith. How one understands Mary relates directly to any answer offered to the question: "What difference does the light of faith working through charity make in the use of reason (*in fieri*) and its outcome: knowledge (*in facto esse*) of being?"[12]

The iconic and mediating nature of the *Imago Dei*, uniting both matter and spirit, perfectly personified in the hypostatic union and perfectly personalized in Mary, then, serves, for Fehlner, as the presupposition for understanding the purpose and end of creation willed by God. Mary as a created perfection also locates the concrete realization and actualizing of this purpose in time as fulfillment and supernatural eschatological call for all humanity. Thus, creation's meaning is bound up with anthropology understood metaphysically in terms of the divine will and its created rational complement and fulfillment in the persons of Incarnate Word and his mother.

Mary as all holy, virgin mother of God, posits a unique relation to the Incarnate Word. She is the perfect term or concrete archetype of creation, who by virtue of her purity from sin and fullness of grace, manifests creaturely perfection as a mirror of Christ as he mirrors and mediates divine perfection. In her created perfection, Mary receives the fullness of the Spirit from

---

10. This is a theme found throughout Fehlner's writings. In addition to the essays listed in note 1, *supra*, cf. Fehlner, Introduction and Appendix I to Bonaventure, *The Triple Way*, 51–85, 215–21; idem, "Sources of Scotus' Mariology in Tradition," 249.

11. For Fehlner's most complete presentation of this theme see, "The Predestination of the Virgin Mother," 213–76.

12. "Scientia et Pietas."

the beginning of her existence on account of her unique relation to Christ, allowing her to bring forth Christ from her own substance as well as within her heart. Mary as mother and *perfect* disciple of Jesus, uniquely—i.e., with perfect freedom because all holy, can cooperate in every aspect of Christ's life and ministry in the Spirit. Mary then also becomes the exemplar of the typological-antitypological pattern of biblical revelation as well as in her personal agency bringing to bear upon those God has chosen to love a dynamic influence upon all who, in the words of Paul,[13] would also bring forth Christ in their hearts in the hope of the resurrection.

Fehlner notes that "In the present order of creation actually willed by the Creator in view of the Incarnation and redemption (absolute primacy of Christ . . .) each of these points [concerning Christian philosophy and metaphysics] reveals a profoundly Marian mode . . . . "[14] The Franciscan school of theology and spirituality reasons first from the *single real* order of creation as revealed in Christ, which, in turn, encompasses every aspect of life and reality, including the purpose of creation. This indicates that while speculation about *possibles* and *counter factuals* has a place, on the one hand, and theology, philosophy and other humane and scientific pursuits have an integrity and distinctness of their own, on the other, the economy of salvation founded upon the absolute primacy of Jesus Christ in a Marian mode or coefficient reveals the reason (*ratio*) of finite reality. For Fehlner, this primacy of the hypostatic order is mediatory both ontologically and epistemically in revealing the priority of the charity in the Godhead, rooted in the originative plenitude of the Father *ad intra* as well as the primacy of Divine Charity, manifest *ad extra* in the fitting order (the *decuit* rather than *potuit*), deriving from the free act of loving and willing creation in and for the sake of Jesus and Mary. Thus, for Fehlner, the absolute primacy of Jesus and Mary implies a both metaphysical theology as well as a theological metaphysics revealing and articulating the good pleasure of God as well as the modes of activity and purposes of creation as such.

The Divine Image for the Sake of Divine Likeness and Mary as Perfect Likeness of God

Fehlner's development of Franciscan theological anthropology in the light of his convictions about the interrelation and interaction between God and human persons is extensive, nuanced and complex. Above I discussed how metaphysics and theology neither derive from nor ultimately concern

13. Cf. Galatians 4:19.

14. "Scientia et Pietas."

notions of essence, idea or end, considered in abstraction apart from Christ and Mary. For Fehlner metaphysics pertains to concrete reality rooted in the charity of the Father: The Trinity *ad intra* and The Whole Christ in a Marian Mode *ad extra*. This insight, when systematically applied to theology and metaphysics carries profound implications for several theological (and philosophical) topics. Here I mention a few:

1. Relation and resolution between intellect and will;

2. Natural and voluntary powers and manners of activity;

3. Human beings as created in the image and likeness of the Trinity;

4. The relation and order between nature and supernature, especially as it pertains to the natural desire for God and the final cause of created rational agents;

5. Finally, the resolution and retracing of created reason and natural faith into supernatural faith and charity.

Each topic just mentioned is deeply affected by how one understands the primacy of Jesus and Mary. If charity, personal action and, thus, persons are the most real and therefore structure the purpose of creation, then what God actually prefers and actually accomplished should never (and cannot reasonably) be excluded from theological and philosophical discourse, however, distinction must remain.

For Fehlner the pivotal fact, which is a mystery in itself, is human nature as the divinely illumined image of God perfectly realized in the person of Mary. Because Mary from the first moment of her existence is filled with every virtue and perfection, making her qualitatively, in the perfection of her humanity, a perfect similitude to the man-God Jesus in his perfect humanity, she reveals the full potential of human persons to freely correspond and synergistically act with the Spirit to shape and govern the created order in its recapitulation in Christ and return to the Father. It is in and through Mary, then, that we discover the only *real* purpose of being a rational, personal creature.

Analogy of Emphasis and Manifestation in the Soul as Image and Similitude

It is important at this point to realize that the pairs I just noted are not in relations of exclusion, considered static contraries. Rather, for Fehlner, in Mary's perfect humanity each is ordered, yet in-existent; and their relation is a question of emphasis, mode and degree, implying a certain front-loading of the end or purpose into the beginning, realized, however, not in a closed and imperative monergism, but in spontaneous and perfectly free (because of a divine quality) synergy between creator and creature. For Fehlner, then, it seems questions of nature-supernature, reason-faith, and the like should not be in theory or in fact separated, even if distinguished.[15] Any analysis, then, of these seemingly contrary disjuncts, must be approached according to what one could term an "analogy of emphasis," with the prior understanding that in Mary nature and person, though distinct cannot be separated, and the concrete divine purpose of the created image in Mary is to become a likeness of God.

In the light of the revelation of the economy of salvation in Christ, for each pair, the foundation requires its complement and the complement its foundation. Put in a different manner, what is ultimately at issue for Fehlner is a question of mode of activity and degree of activation rather than an aggregation of accidental powers and/or habits. In each pair there is (1) participation-concursus; which (2) is dynamically oriented towards its complement, (3) which is realized also in a (a) specifically different mode (not object or agent), (b) an interrelation and interaction [extensively and intensively] between personal agency, in (c) a specific mode of concursus.[16]

Thus, by dint of the nature of being the image of God, intellect is always ordered towards voluntary act (practical not pragmatic) as well as disposed towards similitude. Moreover, voluntary act is never totally devoid of knowledge (natural/faith/infused/beatific) and natural knowledge is perfected in and through the grace of charity: formally identical in *via et it patria*, though differing in degree and thus intensity and stability. In this account, then, the created image of God can have certainty about God's infinite perfection on the basis of a kind natural faith applying reason, which is rooted in the illuminating concept of being, a concept in its purity that distinguishes on the epistemic and noetic level the image from the vestige, the rational being from the brute. When *being* is seen to transcend categorization and in itself admit of no circumscription, a knowledge of pure, perfect or infinite being is possible. In knowledge of creation—being and thus infinite being—however, the reality of the transcendence and goodness infinite being is always, whether acknowledged or not, present to the soul and thus calling the person to take a personal stance with respect to this source of truth and goodness. For Fehlner knowledge itself is a call to the person to

15. This also touches upon why it is possible (conceivable) to separate these realities in theory, even if (a) such a separation is only ever partial, incomplete, unstable and ultimately false and (b) can only be resolved in the light of faith.

16. Fehlner deals with these topics in his lengthy unpublished manuscript, "Transcendental Thomism and Bl. John Duns Scotus," 2003.

humble adoration of infinite truth, beauty and goodness, which the person, through the powers of judgment and choice, can accept or reject. However, knowledge of infinite being in the natural mode is only ever indirect, and inferential, proceeding from finite effect to infinite cause. Although the will is bound up in such knowledge, again because the whole person is acting in and through each of its powers, the accent is upon intellect in "objectifying" being through an inner "word" or concept. Such natural knowledge, rooted in a kind of natural faith in the light of reason cannot fully satisfy or realize the purpose of created rationality, which is to directly love infinite goodness in its truth and beauty in a manner characterized by perfect peace and rest. This is because perfect charity is not yet activated. Faith is needed to provide clear knowledge of God's salvific purpose and charity for direct contact with the object of our faith and love. If human persons, considered under the aspect of knowledge and the image, more clearly manifest intellect without separating such activity from the will, the life of charity in faith accents the will without severing it from knowledge. As charity perfects voluntary action, so is knowledge perfected in love as it forms faith, contemplation and, ultimately, the vision of God face to face.

On this account of theological anthropology, clarified in the person of Mary, sin takes on its proper character as a virtually unintelligible mystery. However, from the vantage point of the finitude of the image, and the formal distinction between the soul's powers, it becomes possible to describe the possibility of a kind of short-circuiting of the resolution of intellect into affection as both commonly flow from memory. For Fehlner, it is the irrational incomplete resolution of the divine light of being that illumines the soul to its divine source that lies at the heart of the critical question, sin and the will to autonomy. As finite, it is possible that human nature, not achieve perfect similitude to God. God's creative freedom is in no way forced. However, the perfection of God's work in working in, with and through creation in the persons of Jesus and Mary, declares with ringing clarity that God wills and has in fact accomplished what is most fitting and loving. God calls all created images of God, that is created persons to find their true selves, their eternal well being in likeness to Christ through Mary.

Conclusion

I shall close my paper with Fehlner's own words:

> The absolute primacy of Christ reduced to its radical practical implications, no longer familiar to most, was taken for granted by the great Franciscan scholars of the past. Hence the difficulty

at present of appreciating the Marian character of all genuine philosophy or love of wisdom, the subconscious inclination to think it odd to call Mary "the philosophy of Christians," and the refusal by so many to accept that Christian metaphysics is not primarily about efficient and final causality, but literally is Christ, viz., to use the Bonaventurian term, is a metaphysics of exemplarism and divine illumination. Precisely because the Virgin Mary pertains to the "order of the hypostatic union" and so is uniquely associated with the theandric actions of Her Son and Savior, She is uniquely the teacher of the Apostles and faithful.[17]

Bibliography

Fehlner, Peter Damian. "DE DEO UNO ET TRINO ad mentem Caroli Rahner." In *Karl Rahner. Un'analisi critica: Le figure, l'opera e la recensione: Teologia di Karl Rahner (1904–1984)*, edited by Serafino Lanzetta, 73–161. Siena: Cantagalli, 2009.

———. "De Metaphysica Mariana Quaedam" (Some Considerations on Marian Metaphysics). *Immaculata Mediatrix* 1/2 (2001) 13–42.

———. "'I am the Immaculate Conception': Redemption and Coredemption, Recirculation and Recapitulation in the Light of Metaphysics: Bonaventurian Exemplarism and Scotistic Univocity." Unpublished Manuscript, Collected Papers of Peter Damian Fehlner. 2005.

———. "'Io sono l'Immacolata Concezione': Adhuc Quaedam de Metaphysica Mariana" ("I am the Immaculate Conception": Some Further Considerations on Marian Metaphysics). *Immaculata mediatrix* 2 (2002) 15–41.

———. Introduction and Appendix I to Bonaventure, *The Triple Way*. Translated by Peter Damian Fehlner. New Bedford, MA, Academy of the Immaculate, 2012.

———. "Mary and Theology: Scotus Revisited." In *The Newman-Scotus Reader: Contexts and Commonalities*, edited by Edward J. Ondrako, 111–72. New Bedford, MA: Academy of the Immaculate, 2015.

———. "Mater et Magistra apostolorum" (Mother and Teacher of the Apostles). *Immaculata Mediatrix* 1/1 (2001) 15–54.

———. "Mater et Magistra Theologorum: The Immaculate Conception and the Notion and Method of 'Our Theology' According to Bl. John Duns Scotus." Unpublished Manuscript, Collected Papers of Peter Damian Fehlner. 2004.

———. "The Predestination of the Virgin Mother and Her Immaculate Conception." In *Mariology: A Guide for Priests, Deacons, Seminarians and Consecrated Persons*, edited by Mark I. Miravalle, 213–76. Goleta, CA: Queenship, 2008.

———. "Redemption, Metaphysics and the Immaculate Conception." In *Mary at the Foot of the Cross*, edited by Peter Damian Fehlner, 5:186–262. New Bedford, MA: Academy of the Immaculate, 2005.

———. "Scientia et Pietas" (Knowledge and Piety). *Immaculata mediatrix* 1/3 (2001) 11–48.

17. "De Metaphysica Mariana Quaedam."

————. "Sources of Scotus' Mariology in Tradition." In *Blessed John Duns Scotus and His Mariology: Commemoration of the Seventh Centenary of His Death*, edited by Peter Damian Fehlner, 235–96. New Bedford, MA: Academy of the Immaculate, 2009.

————. "Transcendental Thomism and Bl. John Duns Scotus." Unpublished Manuscript, Collected Papers of Peter Damian Fehlner. 2003.

Part 3

Scholarly Explorations in the Spirit of Peter Damian Fehlner

10

John Duns Scotus on the Existence of God

JEREMY DAGGETT

Preliminary Dedicatory Remarks

IT IS HARD TO state, without failing to give due laud, the great impact on and depth of contribution to Franciscan thought and development made by Father Peter Damian Fehlner. I must confess my deep gratitude at being able to contribute to this volume honoring Father Peter. As a convert to Roman Catholicism, I was introduced first to St. Thomas, knowing little to nothing of Bl. John Duns Scotus and Franciscan thought in general. But through Fr. Peter's influences, not least of whom is Dr. J. Isaac Goff, I have come to know and love the Franciscan tradition and, in particular, the Blessed Subtle Scot. It is with a sense of great appreciation and thanksgiving that I offer this paper on Scotus's argument for the existence of God.

Introduction

It was common for Medieval thinkers to bring forth various arguments, or "ways," for the existence of God—from motion, from efficient, formal and final causality, eminence, and others—and conclude each distinct "way" with a rather unsatisfying (for some) "and this everyone calls God." Scotus does not attempt to show that God exists by a series of arguments that can be used in a cumulative case, but by a single argument that contains several steps, each concluding to something that some might have added the tag, "and this we call God."[1]

1. As Wolter says in his discussion about Scotus's Triple Primacy argument:
What is interesting to note is that Scotus, unlike Henry of Ghent, or for that matter St. Thomas, does not pause here to tell us that this first cause, or this ultimate end, or this supreme nature is God. In fact, he almost seems loath to use this term until he believes he has established the existence of a being so different and unique among

Scotus does something a little different, pressing into service an argument from metaphysical (rather than physical) efficient causality as he begins his single (and rather long) proof for the actual existence of an infinite being. In the *Lectura*, Scotus explains why he intends to take the metaphysical route.

> Now efficiency can be considered either as a metaphysical or as a physical property. The metaphysical property is more extensive than the physical for "to give existence to another" is of broader scope than "to give existence by way of movement or change." And even if all existence were given in the latter fashion, the notion of the one is still not that of the other. It is not efficiency as a physical attribute, however, but efficiency as the metaphysician considers it that provides a more effective way of proving God's existence, for there are more attributes in metaphysics than in physics whereby the existence of God can be established. It can be shown, for example, from "composition and simplicity," from "act and potency," from "one and many," from those features which are properties of being. Wherefore, if you find one extreme of the disjunction imperfectly realized in a creature, you conclude that the alternate, the perfect extreme exists in God.

> Averroës, therefore, in attacking Avicenna at the end of Bk. I of the *Physics*, is incorrect when he claims that to prove that God exists is the job of the physicist alone, because this can be established only by way of motion, and in no other way—as if metaphysics began with a conclusion which was not evident in itself, but needed to be proved in physics (For [*sic*] Averroës asserts this falsehood at the end of the first book of the *Physics*). In point of fact, however, [God's existence] can be shown more truly and in a greater variety of ways by means of those metaphysical attributes which characterize being. The proof lies in this that the first efficient cause imparts not merely this fluid existence [called motion] but existence in an unqualified sense, which is still more perfect and widespread.[2]

---

existing things that we can attribute this name to it in a meaningful fashion. (Wolter, "Duns Scotus and the Existence and Nature of God," 100).

2. Scotus, *Lectura*, I, d. 2, p. 1, q. 2, n. 40, in *Medieval Philosophy*, 403.

Efficientia autem potest considerari vel ut est passio metaphysica vel passio physica, et in plus est ut est passio metaphysica quam physica, quia in plus est dare esse alteri quam dare esse per motum et mutationem, licet non haberet aliquid esse nisi per motum et mutationem; tamen una non est intentio alterius. Et via efficientiae, ut pertinet ad metaphysicum, est via efficacior ad concludendum esse de

We should note now that Scotus has a problem with the argument from motion; i.e., the *ergo* of that particular argument. What is that thing to which we conclude? We can agree that the "this everyone calls God" is most assuredly the first and unmoved mover, the God of the philosophers. But even more sure are we that "what everyone calls God" is much more than prime mover. That among movers, the first mover is the most noble or perfect mover is granted. But this does not entail that the first mover is therefore the most noble being. Scotus argues thus by way of example.[3] We may find a donkey which is the most noble (even maximally noble) donkey. But this only proves that among donkeys there exists one which is most noble. But one can hardly infer from this that, therefore, the most noble animal exists. It is plain to see that additional arguments are necessary to establish more than the existence of a prime mover. Scotus is not content to arrive at a being which is merely the *ergo* of a particular argument, He is after something greater. Scotus desires to arrive at a concept of a first being that cries out for what Christianity has to offer in its conception of God. For we must admit that the first mover is a being. But by what means can one argue that the most perfect mover is also the most perfect being? Even more exactly, how is it infinite being? Again, as Scotus says of metaphysical efficiency vs. physical efficiency, the notion of one is not that of the other.

Let us briefly outline Scotus's argument. He begins the *Ordinatio* proof (which we will follow in this paper, except where otherwise stated[4]) by ex-

---

Deo quam ut est passio physica, quia plures passiones sunt in metaphysica quibus potest ostendi esse Dei quam in physica, ut per compositionem et simplicitatem, per actum et potentiam, et per unum et multa, et per illa quae consequuntur ens. Unde quorum extrema dividentia ens imperfecte inveniuntur in creatura, eorum opposita concludunt extrema perfecta in Deo. Et ideo male dixit Averroes in fine I *Physicorum*—contra Avicennam—quod solum ad physicum pertinet ostendere Deum esse quia hoc solum potest ostendi per motum et non alio medio, ac si metaphysica inciperet a conclusione probata a physica et indigeret ea, quasi non exsistens certa in se (falsum enim dixit ibi in fine I Physicorum); immo verius et multiplicius potest ostendi per passiones metaphysicas, quae consequuntur ens. Cuius probatio est: primum efficiens non solum dat hoc esse fluens, sed dat esse simpliciter, quod est communius et perfectius . . . .

Scotus, *Opera omnia*, 14:125–26. All Latin citations are from the Vatican Edition of the *Ordinatio* and *Lectura*. Latin citations from *De Primo Principio* are those found in the work cited.

3. *Lectura*, I, d. 2, p. 1, q. 2, n. 40., 126. " . . . nunc autem ex primitate inferioris non sequitur primitas superioris nisi illud inferius sit nobilissimum (unde non sequitur 'est asinus nobilissimus, igitur est animal nobilissimum', sed sequitur 'est homo nobilissimus, igitur est animal nobilissimum'); et ideo ex proprietate entis nobilissimi magis potest argui primitas entis quam ex primitate moventis primi."

4. *Ordinatio*, I, d. 2, p. 1, q. 2. in Scotus, *Opera omnia*, 2:150–244.

plaining that there are two angles we must take in arguing for the existence of an actually infinite being. First, we must approach from the view of the relative properties of God; second, from the absolute properties of God. Relative properties are those which are predicable of God in relation to creation; absolute properties are those which belong to God whether or not the cosmos exists. Under the first heading of relative properties, Scotus argues for a triple primacy of efficiency, finality and eminence. From there he shows that one primacy implies the others, and finally there can only be one nature that is the first efficient cause, ultimate end, and the most perfect nature. The Subtle Doctor then discusses the absolute properties of God. The first being is intellectual *and* volitional, and the intellect and will are identical with the essence of this supreme nature. The first being is also infinite being. While discussing the infinity of God, Scotus resurrects Anselm's *That Than Which* argument and responds to the criticism that Anselm makes an illicit leap from concept to reality. Finally, he gives a definite answer of "yes" to the question of whether there exists an actually infinite being.

The very next question of the *Ordinatio*[5] deals with the unicity of the nature thus proved to exist. However, the *De Primo Principio* (4.87-4.93) version concludes with this argument.[6] This key question will be included in our overview. The reason is this: We worship not merely a nature or a multiplicity of gods, but one personal God who has a name—I AM—who spoke with Adam, Noah, Abraham and Moses. This sublime truth is not lost on Scotus as he begins his *De Primo Principio* (1.2) proof with a prayer to the I AM who revealed his NAME.[7]

Part 1: The Relative Properties of God

I. The Primacy of Efficient Causality

A. There exists a first efficient cause

Beginning with the God's relative properties, Scotus argues for a triple primacy of efficiency, finality and eminence. He spends the bulk of time establishing the primacy of efficient causality. The first conclusion he argues for is this: "some efficient cause is simply first such that neither can it be an

---

5. The *Lectura* and *Reportatio* also treat unicity separately in the immediately following question.

6. Scotus, *De Primo Principio*, 146–51.

7. Ibid., 2-3. For excellent insight into the Anselmian and Bonaventurian flavor of Scotus's reasoning, especially as it relates to the *coloratio Anselmi*, see Fehlner, Appendix I to *The Triple Way*, 195–221.

effect nor can it, by virtue of something other than itself, cause an effect."[8]
The proof for the conclusion runs like this:

1. Something can be produced.

2. It is produced either by itself, nothing, or another.

3. Not by nothing, for nothing causes nothing.

4. Not by itself, for an effect never causes itself.

5. Therefore, by another; call it *A*.

6. If *A* is first, then we have reached the conclusion.

7. If *A* is not first, but is either an effect or it is only able to exercise its causal powers in producing the effect because of dependence on another cause, we argue as before.

8. Thus, we say *A* is dependent on another, *B*. The ascending series will either continue infinitely or we finally reach something which has nothing prior to it.

9. An infinite ascending series is impossible.

10. Therefore, etc.[9]

Scotus anticipates two objections to his argument. First, that he begs the question in 9); second, that the argument cannot be a demonstration since it begins with contingent propositions. He responds in order.

Objection 1. Assuming the impossibility of
infinite ascending series begs the question

The force of the first objection is established by the fact that philosophers have always admitted the possibility of infinite regress in an ascending

8. Scotus, *Ordinatio I, dist. 1–2*, 105. "Quod aliquod effectivum sit simpliciter primum, ita quod nec sit effectibile nec virtute alterius a se effectivum" (*Ordinatio*, I, d. 2, p.1, q. 2, 151 n. 43).

9. Ibid., 151–52: "Probatio, quia aliquod ens est effectibile. Aut ergo a se, aut a nihilo vel ab aliquo alio. Non a nihilo, quia nullius est causa illud quod nihil est, nec a se, quia nulla res est quae se ipsam faciat vel gignat, I De Trinitate l; ergo ab alio. Illud aliud sit a. Si est a primum, hoc modo exposito, propositum habeo; si non est primum, ergo est posterius effectivum, quia effectibile ab alio vel a virtute alterius effectivum, quia si negetur negatio ponitur affirmatio. Detur illud alterum et sit b, de quo arguitur sicut de a argutum est, et ita aut proceditur in infinitum, quorum quodlibet respectu prioris erit secundum, aut statur in aliquo non habente prius; infinitas autem impossibilis est in ascendendo, ergo primitas necessaria, quia non habens prius nullo posteriore se est posterius, nam circulum in causis esse est inconveniens."

series, as in the case of generation. It also begs the question. However, Scotus notes that although philosophers admit the possibility of infinite regress in an accidentally ordered ascending series, they do not do so when it comes to an essentially ordered ascending series. He is not assuming (neither does he argue for) a beginning in time and therefore a Creation that requires a Creator.

Wolter notes that Scotus is careful to distinguish between accidental/essential causes and accidentally/essentially *ordered* causes:

> This is not the classical distinction between *per se* and *per accidens* causes, for the parents or parent is a *per se* cause of the child. The distinction regards not primarily the being but the act of causation itself. Any cause that needs the co-causality of a second cause in the act of exercising its causality, depends upon that second cause essentially and not accidentally. Such a relationship would obtain between the four classical causes of Aristotle. A material cause can not "matter" unless a formal cause "forms" and vice versa. These intrinsic causes in turn depend essentially on extrinsic causes and according to the Aristotelian and medieval conceptions a hierarchy of efficient causes essentially ordered also existed. In the Christian notion of the relationship of God to the world, all secondary causes are related to the First Cause by an essential order of efficiency, for God must cooperate with them or at least conserve them and their powers in being.[10]

We see, therefore, that Scotus is not arguing that each cause in the series is produced by a prior[11] cause, but rather, as the second option in premise (7) makes clear, it depends on the "co-causality" (as Wolter puts it above) of another cause. In the quote above, Wolter offers the Aristotelian four causes as examples of essentially ordered causes. In the production of a given effect, the intrinsic (formal and material) causes depend essentially on the extrinsic (efficient and final) causes.[12]

Scotus explains the differences between a series of essentially ordered causes (EOC) and a series of accidentally ordered causes (AOC). He recognizes three key differences which proceed from the nature of each kind.

---

10. Wolter, "Duns Scotus," 106.

11. In the sense of temporally prior, although that may be true. Rather, the priority is an order of essential dependence, as will be explained below.

12. Cf. *De Primo Principio*, 24–29. Paras. 2.26–2.33.

First, in EOC, the second cause depends upon the first in its very act of causation. [13] In AOC, the second cause can act independently of the first cause in the series. Bob senior begets (causes) Bob junior. However, Bob senior may die and afterward Bob junior may still beget (cause) Bob III.

Second, in EOC, the causality is of a higher order. In AOC, there is no necessary hierarchy of order. Scotus explains that this follows from the first difference because in AOC, a cause does not essentially require another cause of the same nature in order for it to exercise it causal power. However, this dependence upon another cause is precisely what is required for EOC, per the first difference. It follows that the higher cause in the chain is of a different nature and more perfect than the lower cause which is dependent upon the higher cause; or we must admit the absurd conclusion that a cause is essentially dependent upon another cause of the same nature for its own causation.[14] Lastly, while in EOC all causes are simultaneously required, the causes can be successive in AOC (as in the case of the begetting Bobs

13. Richard Cross believes he has found a fatal flaw in Scotus's argument here and claims the *Doctor Subtilis* begs the question. He writes in his book on Scotus (aptly titled "Duns Scotus"):

Scotus's suggestions here [in this first conclusion, i.e., *the second cause depends upon the first in its very act of causation*] are rather puzzling and seem to me to be inconclusive. [From this conclusion], it follows straightforwardly that there must be a first member of an [EOC]. But the premise is question-begging, and I can see no reason for wanting to accept it. It requires that a first cause is necessary as well as sufficient for any effect in an [EOC].

(Cross, *Duns Scotus*, 18–19). This objection assumes that Scotus is using *first* either in the sense of *absolutely first in the series* or *simply first* as defined in the first major conclusion ("some efficient cause is simply first such that neither can it be an effect nor can it, by virtue of something other than itself, cause an effect") rather than *first* in the sense of *prior*. Does he also reject the remaining two differences which proceed from the first difference? I assume he must. Curiously, he does reformulate Scotus's proposition so as to make explicit the reading of *first* as *prior*. But he goes on to assert that even if we give the broader and weaker sense to *first*, then there still seems to be no reason to deny infinite regress in EOC. All this he says without even the slightest discussion of the five "proofs" Scotus offers for A (an infinity of EOC is impossible), which follows these three differences. Assuming the weaker sense of *first*, Scotus explains how an infinity of EOC is impossible. A rebuttal of these proofs would be necessary for Cross to sustain his accusation that Scotus has failed to show the impossibility of an infinity of EOC. It seems, at least absent any consideration from Cross of these five proofs, that Scotus is not guilty of either begging the question or failing to prove that an infinity of EOC is impossible.

14. Wolter points out in his commentary on *De Primo Principio* that Scotus is referring here to degrees of perfection in the qualitative sense. While instances of the same nature may vary in their degree of perfection as it relates to quantity, they will enjoy the same degree of qualitative perfection since they possess the same nature. In Scotus, *De primo Principio*, 229.

above). So it is evident that AOC is diachronic causation while EOC is synchronic, and this is very important for the defense of premise (9). These three important differences lead to three propositions: A, an infinity of EOC is impossible; B, an infinity of AOC is impossible unless we admit the EOC is finite; C, even if the existence of any EOC series is denied, an infinite series of causes is still impossible.

Scotus offers five proofs in favor of proposition A (an infinity of EOC is impossible). First, certain curiosities follow from an infinite series of EOC. For every cause in the series is dependent upon a prior cause (per the first difference between EOC and AOC). This cause, the first efficient cause, cannot be part of the series, for then it would be the cause of itself, which is absurd. And even if there were an infinite number of caused things, it would still require the existence of a cause outside the group. Second, nobody thinks that an infinite number of essentially ordered causes could act simultaneously to produce a certain effect. Third, if a cause is essentially prior to another, it must be in closer proximity to the beginning.[15] But if there is no beginning, there are no essentially prior causes. Fourth, the second difference shows us that there is a hierarchy in the causal chain and whatever is higher in the series is more perfect. If the series were infinite, it would be in the unfortunate position of being at once infinitely perfect and imperfect, since the causes of the series cause because of another cause and are dependent upon other causes. Fifth, imperfection is not a necessary entailment of being able to produce an effect.[16] But if the series were infinite, then there could never be an instance of perfect efficient causality. But it is possible for such a nature to exist which is simply first and able to produce without imperfection.[17]

The argument for B (an infinity of AOC is impossible unless we admit the EOC is finite) runs thus. The causes in an accidentally ordered series are successive and not simultaneous. Each successive cause is independent of its proximate cause in its own causal action. But the AOC series cannot exist without the existence of some other thing which is itself of infinite duration, and upon which every part of the succession (indeed, the series itself) depends. This series of perishing causes (AOC) is therefore essentially dependent on EOC. The argument depends on the fact that

15. Here Scotus notes that he is following Aristotle in *Metaphysics*, V, 11.

16. In the *De Primo* version (3.13), Scotus refers back to the second chapter of the treatise (2.26–28) where he explains that extrinsic causes (in this case, efficient causes) do not necessarily entail imperfection. *De primo Principio*, 24, 46, 48.

17. "Simply first" is explained above as "some efficient cause is simply first such that neither can it be an effect nor can it, by virtue of something other than itself, cause an effect."

contingent things are dependent on other things for existence and continued existence; more directly, existence at any one moment. Since nothing is
the cause of its own existence or continued existence, we arrive at an EOC
which explains that existence.

Finally, C is proved (even if the existence of any EOC series is denied,
an infinite series of causes is still impossible). Nothing causes nothing.
Therefore, something is capable of efficient causality. This cause either is
dependent on a first cause or it is a first cause. If it is dependent, then it
relies on a prior cause in order to exercise its causality (as in EOC), or for its
existence. It cannot be the first, for a finite series is what is denied! Therefore, it relies on another for its existence. But B proved that an infinite series
accidentally ordered causes is impossible unless you admit EOC. Therefore,
we reach a first efficient cause, or we admit EOC, which also entails the
existence of the first efficient cause.

Objection 2. The argument is not a demonstration

The objector points to the fact that the argument begins with a contingent
proposition: that is, *something can be produced*. But effects are not necessary.
Rather, they exist contingently. Therefore, the argument is not a demonstration. Scotus responds that the premises may not be necessary, but they are
manifest. No one denies that there is in fact something really existing which
has been produced or is an effect. Since nothing is the cause of itself, there
must be an efficient cause which produced the effect. But Scotus, in order
to respond more forcefully to the objection, proposes that the premises
can be reformulated so that they are in fact necessary and, thus, defang the
complaint. It is possible[18] for something to exist which can be changed. This
is a necessary proposition because there is nothing contradictory about
it. Therefore, it is possible that some nature exists that can cause an effect.
Therefore, it is possible that some nature exists that is a first efficient cause.
This alters the propositions for the existence of a first efficient cause somewhat. He explains in the *Lectura* proof:

> Although beings different from God are actually contingent with
> respect to their factual existence, nevertheless, they are not with
> respect to their possible existence. Hence, those entities which

18. Scotus defines "possible" here as being distinguished from "necessary."
"Potest tamen sic argui, probando primam conclusionem sic: haec est vera 'aliqua
natura est effectibilis, ergo aliqua est effectiva'. Antecedens probatur, quia aliquod subi-
ectum est mutabile, quia aliquod entium est possibile distinguendo possibile contra
necessarium, et sic procedendo ex necessariis" (*Ordinatio*, I, d. 2, p. 1, q. 2, n. 56, 161).

are called contingent with respect to their factual existence are
necessary with respect to their possible existence—for instance,
although "There exists a man" is contingent, nevertheless "It is
possible that he exists" is necessary, because his existence does
not include any contradiction. Therefore, "Something—different from God—is possible" is necessary, because being is divided
into the contingent and the necessary. Just as necessity belongs
to a necessary being in virtue of its condition or its quiddity, so
possibility belongs to a possible being in virtue of its quiddity.
If the first argument is alternatively qualified with the notion
of ontological possibility, then we have necessary propositions
as follows: It is possible that there is something different from
God—it is not of itself (because then it would not be the case
that it were possible), nor from nothing. Therefore, it is possible
that it is from something else. Either it is possible that the other
agent acts by virtue of itself—and not by virtue of something
else, not being from something else—or it is not possible. If so,
then it is possible that there is a first agent, and if it [is] possible that it exists, then it exists, just as we have proved before. If
not and if there is no infinite regress, then the argument at once
comes to a standstill.[19]

In *De Primo Principio*, Scotus argues this way from the very beginning:

3.4   (First Conclusion) Some nature among beings can produce an effect.

      . . .

3.6   In this conclusion, as in some of those which follow, I could argue
      in terms of the actual thus. Some nature is producing since some
      nature is produced, because some nature begins to exist, for some
      nature is contingent and the result of motion. But I prefer to propose

---

19. Scotus, *Lectura* I, 2.57, in Vos, *The Philosophy of John Duns Scotus*, 470—71:
"Item, dico quod licet entia alia a Deo actualiter sint contingentia respectu esse actualis, non tamen respectu esse potentialis. Unde illa quae dicuntur contingentia respectu
actualis exsistentiae, respectu potentialis sunt necessaria, ut licet hominem esse sit
contingens, tamen ipsum esse 'possibile esse' est necessarium, quia non includit contradictionem ad esse; aliquid igitur 'possibile esse', aliud a Deo, est necessarium, quia
ens dividitur in possibile et necessarium, et sicut enti necessario ex sua habitudine sive
quiditate est necessitas, ita enti possibili ex sua quiditate est possibilitas. Fiat igitur ratio,
quae prior, cum possibilitate essendi, et erunt propositiones necessariae sic: 'Possibile
est aliquid aliud a Deo esse, et non a se (quia tunc non esset possibile esse) nec a nihilo;
igitur ab alio potest esse. Illud aliud aut potest agere in virtute sui, et non alterius, et esse
non ab alio, - aut non. Si sic, igitur potest esse primum; et si potest, igitur est, sicut prius
probatur. Si non, et non est processus in infinitum, igitur aliquando stabitur'" (Scotus,
Lectura, I, d.2, p.1, q.2, n. 57. 131-132).

conclusions and premises about the possible. For once those about the actual are granted, those about the possible are also conceded, but the reverse is not the case. Also those about the actual are contingent, though evident enough, whereas those about the possible are necessary. The former concern the being as existing whereas the latter can pertain properly to a being considered even in terms of its essentials. The existence of this essence, of which efficiency is now established, will be proved later.[20]

Returning to the *Ordinatio* version, Scotus assures us that the third conclusion below will establish the actual existence of the first efficient cause.

B. This possible first efficient cause is simply first (it cannot be caused)

It was shown above that the possible first efficient cause is by nature uncaused since there would be either infinite regress of causes or a circle of causes. It is also clear that this being acts such that it is causally independent of any other being, else it could not be considered first. That it lacks an efficient cause means that it also has no final, formal, or material causes. This is obvious since if it cannot be produced, it neither exists for the sake of anything else, nor does it have extrinsic or intrinsic causes. As Scotus says,

> . . . what does not have an extrinsic cause does not have an intrinsic cause either, because the causality of an extrinsic cause implies perfection without any imperfection, but the causality of an intrinsic cause necessarily implies some imperfection annexed to it, because an intrinsic cause is part of the caused thing. . . [21]

20. Scotus, *De Primo Principio*, 42–44: 3.4 Prima Conclusio. "Aliqua est natura in entibus effective. . . . 3.6 In hac conclusione et quibusdam sequentibus possem proponere actum sic: Aliqua natura est efficiens, quia aliqua est effecta, quia aliqua incipit esse, quia aliqua est terminus motus et contingens. Sed malo de possibili proponere conclusiones et praemissas. Illis quippe de actu concessis, istae de possibili conceduntur; non e converso. Illae etiam de actu sunt contingents, licet satis manifestae; istae de possibili sunt necessariae, Illae ad ens existens,istae ad ens etiam quidditative sumptum possunt proprie pertinere. Et existentia illius quidditatis inferius ostendetur, de qua nunc ostenditur efficientia."

21. Scotus, *Ordinatio*, I, d. 2, p. 1, q. 2, n. 57, 163. ". . . quia cuius non est causa extrinseca, nec intrinseca, quia causalitas causae extrinsecae dicit perfectionem sine imperfectione, causalitas vero causae intrinsecae necessario dicit imperfectionem annexam, quia causa intrinseca est pars causati . . ."

C. "The first effective thing is actually existing and some nature is truly actually existent in the way it is effective"[22]

Scotus says this third conclusion is implied by the second conclusion. The nature of the first efficient cause is to exist of itself, since it cannot be caused to exist by anything else. It was proved earlier that it is possible that this first being exists and must be absolutely first. Here, Scotus makes a fascinating move. Scotus states:

> But the other proofs for that very [proposition A, namely, an infinity of essentially ordered causes is impossible] can be brought to bear on the existence which this third conclusion proposes, and they are about contingents, though manifest ones; or let them be taken of the nature and quiddity and possibility of a, and they proceed from necessities. Therefore a simply first effective thing can be from itself. But what is not from itself cannot be from itself, because then a non-being would bring something into being, which is impossible, and further it would then cause itself and so would not be altogether un-causable.[23]

Here he recalls the second objection that the argument begins with contingent propositions and is therefore not a true demonstration. He refutes the objection by starting, yes, with a contingent proposition, but he draws from this manifest proposition a necessary proposition, namely, that it is possible that something exists. From there, we can move through all the steps of the argument and arrive at an actually existing first efficient cause. Scotus concludes:

> [T]he first [efficient cause] is not only prior to other things but, because a contradiction is involved in something else's being prior, thus, to the extent it is first, it exists. The proof is as in the preceding; for un-causability is most included in the idea of such a first, as is proved from the second; for if it can be (because this does not contradict its being, as proved from the first), it follows that it can be of itself, and so it is of itself.[24]

---

22. Ibid., 112. *Ordinatio*, I, d. 2, p. 1, q. 2, n. 58, 164: "[P]rimum effectivum est in actu exsistens et aliqua natura vere exsistens actualiter sicut est effectiva."

23. Scotus, *Ordinatio*, I, d. 2, p. 1, q. 2, n. 58, 164: "Aliae autem probationes ipsius a possunt tractari de exsistentia quam proponit haec tertia conclusio, et sunt de contingentibus, tamen manifestis; vel accipiantur a de natura et quiditate et possibilitate, et sunt ex necessariis. Ergo effectivum simpliciter primum potest esse ex se. Quod non est a se non potest esse a se, quia tunc non ens produceret aliquid ad esse, quod est impossibile, et adhuc, tunc illud causaret se et ita non esset incausabile omnino."

24. Ibid., 166 n. 59: "... primum effectivum non tantum est prius aliis, sed quo prius

What Scotus is saying here is that if it is possible for an uncausable nature to exist, then it must exist. For if it is possible for it to exist, and it does not exist now, then it can never exist. Nay, more, it is impossible for it to exist if it does not exist. But the possibility of such existence has been shown. Therefore, a Simply First Efficient Cause exists.

Again, Scotus is not content to end here with an "And this we all call God." He is looking for something more than a first cause. He now argues for two more primacies.

II. The Primacies of Finality and Eminence

In these final two arguments for primacy of finality and eminence, Scotus argues in a similar manner as for the first primacy. It seems that if the line of reasoning holds for the primacy of efficient causality, a similar proof will work for the other two primacies. The three conclusions are: first, the first efficient cause is also the ultimate end; second, this ultimate end is uncaused; third, it actually exists and some nature actually existing possesses this primacy. In the interest of space, we will let this suffice and move on to the unity of the divine nature.[25]

There is only one Divine Nature

Before moving to the absolute properties of God, the Subtle Scot intends to prove that there can only be one divine nature, which follows from the fact that the first efficient cause is also the ultimate end and the most perfect nature. He offers two conclusions, one "preliminary" and one "principle."[26] While the principle conclusion simply states there is only one divine nature, the preliminary conclusion states that the first efficient cause exists necessarily. It is wholly unimaginable that the first efficient cause (which primacy implies the other primacies, "for that in which one primacy is the others are too"[27]) should be second in existence, finality or eminence to anything. It is simply impossible that it could be the effect of some other

---

aliud esse includit contradictionem, sic in quantum primum exsistit. Probatur ut praecedens; nam in ratione talis primi maxime includitur incausabile, probatur ex secunda; ergo si potest esse (quia non contradicit entitati, ut probatur ex prima), sequitur quod potest esse a se, et ita est a se."

25. For the full argument see Scotus, *Ordinatio*, I, d. 2, p. 1, q. 2, nn. 68–73, 168–173.

26. Scotus, *Ordinatio*, I, d. 2, p. 1, q. 2, n. 70, 170.

27. See http://aristotelophile.com/Books/Translations/Scotus%20Ordinatio%20 I%20dd.1-2.pdf (115). Ibid., 169–170 n. 70: ". . . quia cui inest una insunt et aliae . . ."

cause. It is incompatible with the very nature of the first efficient cause. This is proved by the fact that there is no incompatibility of existence between the first being and any other being. This is because the supreme nature exists of itself. But it could only lack existence if something else were incompatible with its existence which could cause it to not exist or prevent its possible existence from becoming actual existence. This has already been shown to be impossible. Therefore, etc.

There are three reasons given to support the principle conclusion (that there is but one divine nature). First, Scotus makes his point by appealing to the nature of necessary existence. If there were, in fact, two natures which existed necessarily there would be some essential property peculiar to each which would serve to distinguish them from one another. If these differences are formally necessary to each nature, then both natures would necessarily possess these essential properties. But this is impossible, since if one of the differences were removed, the nature would still exist as necessarily as before since it retains the other essential property formally necessary to the nature. However, if we assume that these natures are not necessary because of the distinguishing properties, then it follows that these differences play no role in the necessary existence of the nature. In fact, these properties could not even be included in the necessary natures, "because whatever is not necessarily existent is of itself possible, but nothing possible is included in necessary existence."[28]

The second reason is this: since two eminent natures cannot coexist, neither can two first efficient causes. This is rather obvious, and Scotus refers only to Aristotle's point that since species are like numbers and there is never an instance of two numbers being the same number, likewise there cannot be two first efficient causes (or eminent natures).

Finally, the third reason takes the angle of the primacy of finality. Supposing there were two ultimate ends, we note that something can be ordered to only one end, not two (or more), for only one thing can be the total cause of another (and thus possess the triple primacy). Furthermore, if one of the ultimate ends should cease to exist, the effect which is the result of another ultimate end would be in no way altered since it does not depend on any other ultimate end. But the ceasing ultimate end would not possess the primacy of finality then since it is not that on which all things depend. And, again, where one primacy is, the other two necessarily are present. It

28. Ibid., 117. Ibid., 172 n. 71: "... quia quaecumque entitas non est necesse esse, est de se possibilis, sed nihil possibile includitur in necesse esse." This is not to argue yet for there being only one God, but that only one nature of this kind could exist. He argues for that in the following question of the *Ordinatio*, but includes the argument for only one God in the *De Primo Principio*.

is thus proved that only one nature can be considered to possess the triple primacies of efficiency, finality and eminence.

Part 2: The Absolute Properties of God

Scotus intends to prove that the being described in the first article (on the relative properties of God) is infinite being. In the first part, the Subtle Scot shows that the first being possesses both intellect and will; this is proved and expounded upon with four conclusions. Finally, in the second part, he offers proofs for the infinity of the first being. Let us elide past the very interesting and fruitful discussion about infinite intellect and will, and consider his argument for the infinity of the first being.

The infinity of the First Being

Scotus offers four ways of proving that the first being is infinite being. Taking from the attributes found in the triple primacy of God, Scotus proposes two ways from efficient causality, one from finality, and one from eminence. He lastly attacks what he calls an ineffective proof, taking special aim at Aquinas. We set forth here the fourth proof.

Proof from eminence

It is repugnant to the notion of perfection that anything should be more perfect than the most perfect, which is, in the case, the infinitely perfect. But one finite being having greater perfection (or less) than another is neither odd nor unnatural. And since the infinite is compatible with being, and being infinite is obviously greater than being finite, it follows that the first being is an infinite being. He gives another version of the argument: if something can be infinite, it is not perfect unless it is infinite. Since "being" and "infinity" are not repugnant to one another, the most perfect being possible would be infinite. Now, Scotus readily admits that the minor (positively stated, infinity and being are compatible with one another) is not easily argued for in a strict demonstrative sense, and most certainly is not proved *a priori*. But there is nothing in the notions that would cause them to be incompatible or contradictory. The Subtle Scot then shifts the burden to the objector. Prove that the two are incompatible, says he. Unless it can be seen that the combining of two notions is impossible, we always acknowledge that it is possible. In fact, being seems to admit of finitude or infinitude, and neither is coextensive with being. Scotus gives other arguments, but we shall move to his retouching of Anselm's famous argument.

The ontological argument has not a few detractors; many dismiss it as a sort of philosophical pipe dream, obviously flawed, and it is parodied and mocked.[29] But, as Bertrand Russell wisely remarked, "it is much easier to be persuaded that ontological arguments are no good than it is to say exactly what is wrong with them."[30] One of the criticisms leveled against St. Anselm by St. Thomas is that he moved illicitly from an idea existing in the mind to asserting its actual existence in reality.[31] In the *Lectura*, Scotus argues that this objection really misses the point:

> As for the other [argument/objection], where it is argued that according to Anselm the existence of a thing is self-evident, if it is impossible to think of anything greater, I reply that such is not the case. Hence Anselm's intention there is not to show that the existence of God is self-evident, but that it is true. And he make two syllogisms, of which the first is: "Something is greater than anything which does not exist; but nothing is greater than the highest; therefore the highest is not non-being." There is another syllogism: "What is not a non-being, exists; but the highest is not a non-being, therefore the highest exists."[32]

However, that being said, Scotus does intend to do some "touching up" or "coloring" of the argument. He says that we need to insert the phrase "without contradiction" (*sine contradictione*)[33] into the description of God so that what is only implicit in the argument becomes explicit. For what is

---

29. Graham Oppy, "Ontological Arguments," *The Stanford Encyclopedia of Philosophy*.

30. Ibid. At least, he is reported to have said something like that in the entry at SEP.

31. Aquinas, *Summa theologiae*, III, q. 2, a. 1. This is the question on whether God's existence is self-evident. Scotus thinks this is missing the point and also mischaracterizes the argument. We note that it may be that St. Thomas is attacking St. Bonaventure here more directly than St. Anselm, but the criticism stands and applies either way.

32. Scotus, *Lectura*, I, d. 2, p. 1, q. 2, 471-72 n. 35; *Lectura*, I. d. 2, p. 1, q. 2, 123 n. 35: "Ad aliud, quando arguitur de Anselmo 'illud quo maius cogitari non potest esse, est per se notum', dico quod non. Unde intentio Anselmi ibi non est ostendere quod Deum esse sit per se notum, sed quod hoc sit verum. Et facit duos syllogismos, quorum primus est: 'omni eo quod non est, aliquid est maius; sed summo nihil est maius; igitur summum non est non ens. Est alius syllogismus: 'quod non est non ens, est; sed summum non est non ens; igitur summum est.'"

33. *Ordinatio*, I, d. 2, p. 1, q. 2, 208-9 n. 137: "Per illud potest colorari illa ratio Anselmi de summo bono cogitabili, Proslogion, et intelligenda est eius descriptio sic: Deus est quo cognito sine contradictione maius cogitari non potest sine contradictione. Et quod addendum sit 'sine contradictione' patet, nam in cuius cognitione vel cogitatione includitur contradictio, illud dicitur non cogitabile, quia sunt tunc duo cogitabilia opposita nullo modo faciendo unum cogitabile, quia neutrum determinat alterum."

conceivable is that which is without contradiction. Anything which includes a contradiction is necessarily inconceivable, even if we can speak of something (or *no* thing) like a square circle or irrational man. Because there is no contradiction between *God* and *exists*, we can safely conclude that the being which is the greatest conceivable without contradiction could possibly exist. But this being cannot only exist in virtue of the mind of the one conceiving it, for then it would be caused, in which case there would be a contradiction since the First Cause is uncaused.

Here is where the touch up to Anselm becomes more interesting. Scotus inserts it not as an argument all on its own, but as a final touch, as it were, to the whole argument for the existence of God. It is less desirable to begin with Anselm and would seem to be much more convincing to start with efficiency, finality and eminence. Scotus sees Anselm's ontological argument as a corollary for showing the infinity of God's perfect being. Rather than proving the existence of God, it presupposes that what has been said up to this point in Scotus's argumentation has been accepted.

The conclusion reached at the end of the section on the primacy of efficiency has already established the existence of some being. The other primacies and the absolute properties of God work out what else we can know about the first being once we have established its existence. Again, Anselm is helpful for showing that the first being (which we already know exists) is that than which nothing greater can be conceived without contradiction, viz. the most perfect being.

Final statement of solution to the question of
whether an infinite thing really exists.

Scotus gives a general outline of the argument, that he established the triple primacy of the first being, that it is absolutely first, that it is infinite. He concludes:

[S]ome real being triply first among beings actually exists; and that triply first thing is infinite; therefore some infinite real being actually exists. And it is the most perfect conceivable, and the most perfect, absolute conceived, that we can naturally have about God . . . And thus it has been proved that God exists as to his concept or existence, the most perfect conceivable or possible to be had by us of God. [34]

34. See http://aristotelophile.com/Books/Translations/Scotus%20Ordinatio%20I%20 dd.1-2.pdf> (145); *Ordinatio*, I, d. 2, p. 1, q. 2, n. 147, 214–215: " . . . aliquod ens tripliciter primum in entibus exsistit in actu; et illud tripliciter primum est infinitum; ergo aliquod infinitum ens exsistit in actu. Et istud est perfectissimum conceptibile et conceptus

Part 3: The Unicity of God

Now we noted in the beginning that Scotus argues for the unicity of God in *De Primo Principio*, leaving this issue for the next question in the *Ordinatio* and *Lectura* treatments. We have asserted that the Blessed Subtle Doctor is concerned with more than a general proof of a mere first cause, or prime mover, or necessary existent, an impersonal (or worse yet, non-personal) force. This is on full display in his exposition in *De Primo Principio*. Opening and closing chapters and arguments with beautiful prayers to the Almighty, we see that he is arguing not for some*thing*, but some*one*. He argues for the existence of an infinite person as far as reason can possibly take us down this path. Up to this point, Scotus has only argued for the existence of an infinite nature. But it is necessary to show that there can be only one existent with this nature, and, against objections that only faith can reveal this truth, he sets out to show that it is logically demanded by everything that has been proved thus far.

Arguments Proving the Unicity of God [35]

While Scotus offers seven arguments for the unicity of God, given space restrictions, we shall only examine the argument from necessary being. It runs thus. If a necessary being can exist, it must exist. Therefore, any possible necessary being must actually exist. And if it is possible that more than one necessary being exist, then a potentially infinite number of necessary beings could exist. Therefore, an infinite number of necessary beings actually exist, unless it can be shown that it is impossible for more than one to actually exist. But it is impossible. Therefore, etc. This may seem obvious enough, but Scotus provides a second argument in the *Ordinatio* which gives a reason as to why it is impossible for there to be more than one necessary being.

The impossibility of such a reality is proved thus. Consider two necessary beings, 1 and 2, respectively. Each must possess a distinguishing pure perfection which serves as an identifier. (If both were exactly the same in every respect, they would be identical, and therefore not two, but one.) Say 1 possesses perfection A, while 2 possesses perfection B. Either gods 1 and 2 are necessary in virtue of these perfections which they possess, such that

---

perfectissimus, absolutus, quem possumus habere de Deo naturaliter, quod sit infinitus . . . Et sic probatum est Deum esse quantum ad conceptum vel esse eius, perfectissimum conceptibilem vel possibilem haberi a nobis de Deo."

35. The *Ordinatio* (I, d. 2, p. 1, q. 3, nn. 157–190) version presents seven ways, while five ways are offered in the *De Primo* (4.87–4.93) which coincide with same proofs in the *Ordinatio* version, complementing where appropriate.

without A, 1 could not be necessary, and the same with respect to 2, or they are not. If A and B are not necessary for the necessity of 1 and 2, but are accidental perfections (as it were), then it must be admitted that neither 1 nor 2 are necessary beings. This is because the perfections A and B are neither necessary in themselves or are required for the necessity of 1 and 2. Still more absurd is the alternative, wherein 1 lacks B and 2 lacks A, yet both are still necessary. The irrationality of this position is the fact that 1 could have B (and thus be formally necessary in virtue of B), then lose B and still be necessary (thanks to A). Likewise with 2 and perfection A. Therefore B (or A) is and is not at the same time, with respect to the same being, that in virtue of which 1 (or 2) is necessary.

Concluding Remarks

The First Cause, is One being, Intellectual, Volitional, and Infinite in every way. It is not thought thinking itself, apparently unaware of the cosmos it sustains by its very existence. It is not a necessary Will, somehow fatalistically determined by its nature to create this world in only this way, the events being eternally set in the divine nature itself.

The first being wills to sustain everything in existence in virtue of its Primacy of Efficiency. This Being is infinitely Good, knows all other beings, and knows that it is the supreme Good which satisfies all other beings in virtue of its Primacy of Finality. It is that for which all other things are made and exist. And the first being is the one, supreme infinite being, which none other can equal or surpass in virtue of its Primacy of Eminence. With the Subtle Doctor, we glorify God:

> O Lord our God! You are one in nature. You are one in number. Truly have you said that besides you there is no God. For though many may be called gods or thought to be gods, you alone are by nature God. You are true God for whom, in whom and through whom all things are; you are blessed forever. Amen.[36]

---

36. Scotus, *De Primo Principio*, 4.94, 150: "Domine Deus noster! Tu es unus naturaliter Tu es unus numeraliter. Vere dixisti quod extra te non est Deus. Nam etsi sint dii multi nuncupative vel putative, sed tu es unicus naturaliter. Deus verus, ex quo omnia, in quo omnia, per quem omnia, qui es benedictus in saecula. Amen."

Bibliography

Aquinas, Thomas. *Summa theologica: Complete English Edition in Five Volumes*. Vol. 1. Translated by the Fathers of the English Dominican Province. New York: Cosimo Classics, 2007.

Cross, Richard. *Duns Scotus on God*. Burlington, VT: Ashgate, 2005.

Scotus, John Duns. *De Primo Principio*. Edited and translated by Allan Wolter. Chicago: Franciscan Herald, 1966.

————. *Lectura*. In *Medieval Philosophy*, edited by John Wippel and Allan Wolter, 392–419. New York: The Free Press, 1969.

————. *Ordinatio I, dist. 1–2*. Translated by Peter Simpson. http://aristotelophile.com/ Books/Translations/Scotus%20Ordinatio%20I%20dd.1-2.pdf.

————. *Opera omnia studio et cura Commissionis Scotisticae ad fidem codicum edita praeside Carolo Balić*. Vol. 14. Edited by C. Balić, et al. Vatican City: Typis Polyglottis Vaticanis, 1960.

————. *Opera omnia studio et cura Commissionis Scotisticae ad fidem codicum edita praeside Carolo Balić*. Vol. 2. Edited by C. Balić, et al. Vatican City: Typis Polyglottis Vaticanis, 1950.

Vos, Antonie. *The Philosophy of John Duns Scotus*. Edinburgh: Edinburgh University Press, 2006.

Wolter, Allan B. "Duns Scotus and the Existence and Nature of God." *Proceedings of the American Catholic Philosophical Association* 28 (1954) 94–121.

11

Gregory Nazianzen's Prepurified Virgin in Ecumenical and Patristic Tradition

A Reappraisal of Original Sin, Guilt, and Immaculate Conception

CHRISTIAAN W. KAPPES

Introduction

THIS STUDY ATTEMPTS A tour de force of the Greek East and Latin West in the first millennium to uncover the patristic components of Mary's all-holiness (nowadays popularly equated to the Immaculate Conception) leading to the Lateran Synod of 649. Thereafter, owing to intricacies involved in the vocabulary surrounding the *terminus technicus* "(pre-)purification" (*prokatharsis*) in the Greek East, Latin authors of the Middle Ages managed only to embrace this Greek mode of describing Mary's privilege of grace in select instances. All the same, some Latin works imitate Nazianzen's uniquely Greek phraseology and his interpretation of the Annunciation sufficiently to argue for the limited impact of his doctrine on Latin Fathers up to the Carolingian period. Ultimately, this study finds that Paschasius Radbertus' Mariology in dialogue with Augustinian theology of original sin was synthesized at the culmination of this tradition. My study outlines and augments already published findings on the doctrine of the prepurification of Mary in the Greek East. Thereafter, it supplements this narrative with material demonstrating ecclesiastical reception of prepurification of Mary into the coeval Latin West. My conclusions provide the first assessment of this primordial and patristic mode of approximating what Latin Schoolmen were accustomed to call the "Immaculate Conception."

The Prepurified Virgin: Gregory Nazianzen

Nazianzen grappled with making sense of Jesus' (and Mary's) purifications in the New Testament; namely, their conjoint purification in the Temple and Christ's personal purification at his baptism. In my view, Nazianzen suggested a "Copernican revolution" in his theological worldview. In the olden familiar view, (pre-)purification's primary meaning concerned *fallen* humans who underwent cleansing from sin in baptism, as signified in ceremonial washing. Being soiled persons as they are, post-lapsarian humans need to be *purified in soul and body:*

> [Theology] is not for all people but for those who have been tested and have found a sound footing in study, and, more importantly, they *have been purified,* or at very least *are being purified (kathairomenon), in both soul and body (kai psychen kai soma kekatharmenon).* For one who is not pure to lay hold of pure things is dangerous . . . (emphasis mine)[1]

Elsewhere, below, we will see a revolution in theological semantics, where Nazianzen subalternated the natural and primary lexical meaning of purification (cleansing from impurity) to a definition descriptive of Christ's sinless experiences of being purified.[2] Whether considering Jesus' hallowing in the Temple, or his sanctification during his baptism, Nazianzen prioritized a veritable dove's-eye-view of purification, i.e., the Spirit's perspective. The Spirit did not descend at these Christological and Mariological events to take away sin, but rather to add grace and testify to glory. Nazianzen's version of the Greek New Testament recorded that Jesus and Mary were conjointly purified within the Temple. This led Nazianzen to theologize about each respective human nature as having experienced a univocal kind of grace and manifestation of glory.[3]

Nazianzen unquestionably defined purification in theology as a purely positive term whenever utilized within two modern subsets of theology;

---

1. All English translations without citation are my own. Gregory Nazianzen, *Adversus Eunomianos: Oration 27,* sec. 3 (= Gregory Nazianzen, *Oration 27,* in *On God and Christ,* 27).

2. Luke 2:22: "When the days of their [viz., Jesus' and Mary's] purification (*katharismou auton*) were fulfilled according to the Law of Moses . . ."; Luke 3:3, 21; 4:1: "[John] was preaching a baptism of repentance unto the remission of sins . . . And after Jesus was baptized . . . Jesus, full of the Holy Spirit, returned back from the Jordan." NB, Biblicists have argued purification to be that of Mary and Joseph in Hatch, "The Text of Luke 2:22," 378.

3. For nuances behind Gregory's supposed anticipation of Chalcedonian Christology, see Beeley, "The Early Christological Controversy," 400–402.

namely, Christology and Mariology. Nevertheless, this unusual term in Christology becomes equivocal when applied to someone in need cleansing from sin (in that physical or moral filth are in the nature of the subject being cleansed). So clearly did Nazianzen's Christocentric and Mariological sense of purification impact his readers, that the entire Byzantine reception of this doctrine faithfully fell within the pale of Nazianzen's all-positive definition until the fall of Constantinople (1453). In addition to the pioneering study of Candal that first demonstrated this point, a recent monograph has expanded this thesis, cataloguing every known Father and ecclesiastical writer who commented on this subject in Greek.[4] It suffices to mention that—of fourteen Greek Fathers and ecclesiastical writers known to mention explicitly Mary's prepurification—not a single author mistook Mary's purification at the Annunciation to signify remedying of a moral (let alone a physical) defect, but only to convey a special privilege of grace.[5] More complex is Gregory's associated notion of "purity in soul and body." Among Christians, the pre-Nicene Father, Dionysius of Alexandria (d. 264), first employed the phrase in ecclesiastical jargon. Dionysian legislation meant to imply that feminine menstruation somehow sullied the female body and therefore prevented her from fulfilling prescriptions of purity in order to receive Holy Communion. Similar to Nazianzen, *menses* rendered a woman "not pure to lay hold of pure things":

> Regarding menstruous women, whether it belongs to them, who are in such a state, to enter the Temple of God? I think it too much even to seek to answer the question. For, I don't even think that they themselves, who are faithful and pious, who are in this state, would dare such wise, either to approach the holy table, or to touch the body and blood of Christ . . . Someone not entirely *clean both in soul and in body* (*katharos kai psychei kai somati*) will be prevented from coming up to the holy gifts and unto the Holy of Holies.[6]

4. Candal, "La Virgen Santísima 'prepurificada' en su Anunciación," 241–76.

5. Kappes, *Immaculate Conception*, 29–137, uncovered the following witnesses: Alexander the Monk (?), Emperor Justinian I, Sophronius of Jerusalem, Emperor Constantine IV, John Damascene, Nicephorus of Constantinople, Basil the Lesser of Caesarea, Andrew Libadenus, Gregory Palamas, Philotheos Kokkinos, Theophanes of Nicaea, Nicholas Cabasilas, Joseph Bryennius, and Mark Eugenicus.

6. NB, Dionysius likely betrayed remnants of Hellenistic Jewish evaluation of impurity, as mentioned multiply in Philo of Alexandria, *De vita Mosis*, in *Philonis Alexandrini opera quae supersunt*, 4.2.68. Herein, cleansing of soul and body is a requirement for liturgical worship to be acceptable to God. See also Philo of Alexandria, *De specialibus legibus*, in *Philonis Alexandrini opera quae supersunt*, 5.1.257–258. Herein, purity of body refers to following prescriptions of purity in the Law. See also Philo, *Questiones in*

Above, the indefinite reference to "someone not . . . clean both in soul and in *body*" acts as a genus under which women (who are pious and clean in mind but unclean in body) fall, constituting a species within the wider genus of either physical, or moral, uncleanness. The Dionysian canon gained wide acceptance in later Byzantine canon law due to the fame and antiquity of the legislator.[7] Nevertheless, Dionysius' ostensible Judaizing enjoyed no noteworthy popularity among the works of coeval and immediately posterior Fathers.[8] The Alexandrian first to affirm clearly that feminine *menses* is objectively impure turns out to be Origen.[9] I consider it obvious that we need only hearken back to Origen's positive references to Jewish teachers and to literary influence of Philo of Alexandria in order to uncover Origen's sources for this quasi-Jewish reflection. For his part, Nazianzen adopted, too, this very same Dionysian phraseology. However, if Origen had hypothetically employed it prior, it is not to be found in his extant Greek works and fragments. It seems that Nazianzen was either exposed to Dionysius, or (perhaps through coeval Gregory Nyssa) to Philo of Alexandria. The original notion of "purity in soul and body" smacks of Philonic teaching, whereby physico-ritual impurity somehow diminishes one's status as an otherwise clean or pure member of the elect. The key to decoding the language of "purity in body" lies in Philo's association of *miaino* with bodily impurity. This is most specifically related to unsanctioned blood polluting the Temple in the LXX.[10] If unlawful blood automatically pollutes (*miainein*) the Temple according to the Law, then one application of this principle naturally led Jewish leaders to permit only a bloodless woman (*amiantos*) or virgin to sew the instruments for cultic worship.[11] On another score, God himself enjoyed the attribute of being without stain (*amiantos*).[12] With this in mind, we turn to Nazianzen's principal texts and his conception of this Jewish originate mode of expressing ritual purity. To

---

Exodum, in *Quaestiones in Genesim et in Exodum: Fragmenta Graeca*, frag. 14. Herein, the ritual washings make one pure in soul and body.

7. Ohme, "Sources of the Greek Canon Law," 89–90.

8. Larin, "What Is 'Ritual Im/Purity' and Why?," 279–82.

9. Ibid., 282.

10. Ibid., 277–78.

11. Nutzman, "Mary in the *Protevangelium of James*," 569–570. "*Hai amiantai parthenoi*" designates virgins chosen for pre-menstrual youth to make the Temple accouterments.

12. Lampe, *A Patristic Lexicon*, 89, notes the primary definition as "morally pure." Alexandrian Clement is earliest to refer to the effect of baptism, then to the moral status of saints and virgins. Lastly, the term refers to Jesus as creator. Cf. Liddell and Scott, *Greek-English Lexicon*, 83, where Greek literature generally associated it with water, light, ether, and the opposite of ungodliness.

begin with, let us turn to Nazianzen's idea (*scripsit* c. 380–381) that Jesus himself was capable of purification:

> So, shortly, you will see Jesus purified (*kathairomenon*) in the Jordan for my purification; or rather, he is cleansed for the purification of the waters, for he indeed did not need purification, who takes away the sin of the world (*Patrologia Graeca*, 36:325B).[13]

Above, Nazianzen clearly takes into account a double definition of purification: *both* a cleansing from sin for ordinary humans *and* an equivocal experience of grace for Jesus. The primary meaning of purification, centered upon Jesus, ranks as something typifying our subsequently inferior holiness that was obtained by Jesus' prior participation in sacramental rites. Somehow, Jesus had an experience that was substitutionary for and productive of grace for humanity. This delimitation supplied the figure for a concentric meaning of purification shared among aforementioned Greek Fathers who applied (pre-)purification to Mary's experience of mysteries (such as the Annunciation). Earlier, in the same oration, Nazianzen had already remarked of the *Theotokos*:

> And in all things he becomes human, except sin. He was conceived by the Virgin, who was prepurified (*prokathartheises*) in both soul and *flesh* by the Holy Spirit, for it was necessary that procreation be honored and that virginity be honored more. (*Patrologia Graeca*, 36:633C)[14] (emphasis mine).

First of all, I note that the use of "soul and flesh" with respect to Mary is contrasted to sinful humans cleansed at baptism in "soul and *body*." Nazianzen associated Mary's "purity in soul and *flesh*" with a mystery that was not totally dissimilar from humans' and Christ's baptisms. For Nazianzen, human baptism was linked to two essential dualities; whereby, firstly, water cleansed the *body* and, thence, the Spirit cleansed the soul. With Jesus, for Nazianzen, he himself was cleansed in *flesh* by water in the Spirit, who added another graceful experience to his soul and to the very ritual by its descent upon him in the water. With sinful humans, a proportional analogy is applied to their passive (versus Jesus' active) human natures, who do not supply something to baptismal water, but only receive something from it. In the case of the *Theotokos*, her purification is quite equivocal to that of customarily human baptism and, therefore, appropriately falls outside the

---

13. Gregory Nazianzen, *On Theophany: Oration 38*, 74.

14. This passage in an act of self-plagiarism. Cf. Gregory Nazianzen, *On Easter: Oration 45*, 169. Likely dated to 383, per McGuckin, *St Gregory of Nazianzus*, 386.

analogy applied to sinful humans. Instead, Mary's experience approached closer to the all-pure definition of purifying in Nazianzen, exemplified by Moses (*Oration* 38.7)[15] seeing a sea of infinite substance or God, whereby Moses underwent the purifying operation of desire only. If water and Spirit act together as "cleansers" in normal humans, the Spirit alone performs a singular cleansing activity on the *flesh*-soul duality in Mary.[16] Ordinarily, the cleansing of *body* should occur through baptismal water, while the Spirit should perform the cleansing of soul. For Nazianzen, the Spirit did double duty in Mary in anticipation of the prototypical sacrament of the Incarnation. In this vein of exegesis, Rufinus translated correctly, if dynamically, Nazianzen's Marian doctrine into Latin as follows:

> In every way, he also became man, save sin. He was brought forth from a virgin, herself too immaculate (*immaculata*) in soul and *body*, for it was necessary indeed that the birth of a human creation be honored, yet it was necessary that the glory of virginity be more highly honored (*Oration* 38, emphasis mine).[17]

Finally, to extinguish any doubt about parallelism or the univocal definition of purification by the Spirit in respect to Jesus' and Mary's human natures, Nazianzen paired the duo as follows:

15. See another self-plagiarism in Nazianzen, *On Easter: Oration 45*, 163.

16. These two senses of purification appear at the beginning of Nazianzen, *On Easter: Oration 45*, 165. First baptism is styled a purifying *sine qua non* for humans in order to see God (who is a sea of infinite substance), as Moses saw on the mountain. Secondly, vision of God is styled *in se* as purifying experience: "One wonders at the ungraspable, and one desires more intensely the object of wonder, *and being desired it purifies, and purifying it makes deiform.*" The entire context of the Theophany and Paschal orations falls within the angelomorphic descriptions as in Bucur, "Sinai, Zion, and Tabor," 33–52. Accordingly, Nazianzen utilized angelomorphic or theophanic themes of Jewish inspiration typical of early Christian reception thereof. Particularly significant is Moses and Sinai (according to LXX), where Moses had seen God's glory on Sinai, the full meaning of which was revealed on Tabor by Moses contemplating Jesus. Clearly, Origen, as noted in Bucur, is the likely source for Nazianzen. Additionally, Origen connected the Tabor (and, thus, Sinai) experience to Mary, in that she had been the prototype for overshadowing (Luke 1:35) experienced by Peter, James, and John (if less intensely) at the Transfiguration (Mark 9:7). Ingeniously, this nebulous overshadowing (*nefele episkiazousa*) of persons at the Transfiguration occasions Christians a chance to participate in Mary's prototypical experience. See Origen, *Commentarium in evangelium Matthaei*, frag. 12.42.

17. Rufinus, *De Epiphaniis*, 38.13.4: "*et fit per omnia homo absque peccato editus ex virgine etiam ipas anima et corpore [sic] inmaculata; oportebat enim honorari quidem nativitatem humane conditionis, gloriam tamen virginitatis praeferri.*" See also ibid., 38.16.1: "*Et paulo quidem post videbis etiam fluento Iordanis purificari Iesum, sed purificationem meam, immo potius sui purificatione sanctificantem aquas –non enim ipse purificatione indigebat qui tollit peccatum mundi.*"

> Nor was he mortal fashioned by the flow of mortal seed, but came from human *flesh*, which the Spirit had previously hallowed (*hegnise prosthen*), that of a noble mother, unwedded, and a self-formed mortal, he came and he was purified (*katherato*) for my sake (emphasis mine).[18]

Above, Marian prepurifying is substituted by the alternative vocabulary of "previously hallowing." Nonetheless, Nazianzen jolted his reader when theologizing about "the purified Jesus" in full force. In poetic verse, Nazianzen saw both of these sanctifications as décor of grace, without slightest hint of impurity. This tradition was so acutely perceived in Byzantium that Damascene (d. 753) posteriorly, yet accurately, reflected this one-to-one proportionality of elevating grace in all-pure natures of both Jesus and Mary. Damascene grafted Nazianzen's Christological explanation of baptism, where Jesus actively touched and purified the waters of the Jordan, onto Mary's flesh acting as an agent of the same kind:

> The air, the fiery ether, the sky would have been hallowed by the ascent of her spirit, as earth was hallowed by the deposition of her body. Even water had its share in the blessing: For [water] washes, not so much by pure water cleansing her, but by [water itself] being purified [through her] in the highest degree.[19]

The Prepurified Virgin: Latin Reception in Augustine

Augustine serves as our point of departure for a Greco-Latin Mariology related to the initial theme under investigation. Augustine's acknowledgement of Mary's actual sinlessness has long been a focal point of discussion. On the one hand, it is universally accepted that Augustine bowed in reverent silence, refraining from any affirmation of ethical sinfulness in Mary's person. On the other hand –even if not stated as clearly as one would like– Augustine all but determined that Mary was somehow caught up into the sinful inheritance of Adam. This was the inevitable result of his *ex professo* and a priori commitment to traducianism. For Augustine, traducianism ostensibly provided an explanation for how natural or physical conception

---

18. Gregory Nazianzen, *De Testamentis et adventu Christi*, 45 (*Patrologia Graeca* 37:455–462).

19. John Damascene, *Sermo de dormitione beatae virginis Mariae* 2, 11.14–16 (= John Damascene, *Second Oration on the Dormition*, 215). Damascene potentially cited a source attested only one other place; namely, Maximus Confessor (?), *The Life of the Virgin*, 75.

acted as the carrier of physico-ethical original sin.[20] Yet, despite Augustine's growing fascination with the Greek Fathers during the Pelagian crisis, scholars have never asked: "Did Augustine know about the Greek doctrine of a prepurified Virgin?"

Reynolds' excellent introduction to history of Marian doctrine and devotion traces some general outlines of the prepurified Virgin's western migration.[21] Though Reynolds does not identify Augustine as specifically struggling with the Greek notion of Greco-Marian purification, his research correctly confronts a most relevant passage to the discussion, where Augustine wrote (411/2):[22]

> He is therefore the only one who, remaining God after he made himself a man, never had any sin and did not assume "flesh of sin," although he took on flesh from maternal "flesh of sin." As to the flesh, which he certainly took up from his Mother: [a.] He either actually purified it, needing [it] to be taken up, or [b.] he purified [it] by virtue of taking [it] up. Therefore, she—whom he was choosing—created; from her, whom he elected, was he creating the Virgin-Mother. She did not conceive through the law of sin (i.e., not through the movement of carnal concupiscence) but she continuously merited a holy seed to be brought about in herself through pious faith. Therefore, how much more has "flesh of sin" been baptized due to [divine] judgment that must be avoided, if "flesh without sin" has been baptized serving for imitation's exemplar?[23]

Three categories are commonly employed by specialists to speak of Augustine's sources: (1.) impressionistic, (2.) census-based, and (3.) textual methods.[24] The first two, though not definitive, nonetheless contribute to my upcoming narrative. All three methods taken together suggest probably, if not definitively, that the puzzle of Nazianzen's prepurified Virgin undergirded Augustine's own reflection on the Annunciation.

Impressionistically, Nazianzen first developed his notion of prepurification at Mary's Annunciation. No earlier Greek source is extant, which advocates this theme. The closest contender appears to be a fifth-century

20. See Congourdeau, L'embryon et son âme dans les sources grecques, 269–70, for evidence of the fact and for Augustinian loci on the aforesaid.

21. Reynolds, Gateway to Heaven, 345–32.

22. Ibid., 346.

23. Augustine, De peccatorum meritis et remissione et de patismo parvulorum, 2.24.38.

24. Leinhard, "Augustine of Hippo," 83–87.

homily attributed to Pseudo-Ephrem the Syrian. I designate him "Ephraem" *graecus*, who showed himself directly dependent upon Nazianzen's motif and vocabulary. Below, I will discuss the surprising and fundamental importance of Ephraem *graecus* for Latin reception of prepurification. In the census method, Scholars have already catalogued the multiple instances where Augustine invoked the authority of Gregory Nazianzen, whom Augustine claimed to read profusely.[25] Textually, a satisfactory proof derives from Augustine's verifiable citations of Rufinus (*scripsit* c. 398–399).[26] Therein, I imagine that Augustine saw a key passage in Rufinus, which I compare to the original Nazianzen *graecus*: "He was brought forth from a virgin, herself too immaculate (*immaculata*) in soul and *body* [*omisit*: "by the Holy Spirit"]."[27] Comparing, again, the original Greek to Rufinus, we notice the total lack of literalism between *immaculata* and the Greek term: "He was conceived by the Virgin, who was prepurified (*prokathartheises*) in both soul and *flesh* by the Holy Spirit."[28]

Though Rufinus' translation of *prokathartheisa* is accurate *ad sensum*, it managed to convey nothing of Nazianzen's Mariological terminology (viz., purification as the activity of a pure nature participating in the divinity through divine grace). Still, the Latin text perfectly conveyed Nazianzen's theological point that Mary's whole flesh and soul were immaculate at the Annunciation. Did Augustine read Rufinus' translation of *Oration 38* before composing his aforementioned anti-Pelagian treatise? It seems to me that his knowledge of some kind of purification of Mary's flesh at the Annunciation strongly argues for his reliance upon Nazianzen's Greek oration. Rufinus might have been subsequently consulted for Augustine to understand this difficult passage, but he would have rejected Rufinus' summary attribution of purity to Mary due to his traducian commitments in relation to *caro peccati*.[29]

Might yet another circumstance, too, account for Augustine's minimization of Mary's all-holiness of her flesh at the Annunciation, besides traducianism and a misunderstanding of Nazianzen *graecus*? In answer, not much ingenuity is required: Augustine was at the beginning of the Pelagian controversy so that his ethico-physical convictions about sinful

25. Ibid.

26. Surveying recent Augustinian scholarship highlights progress in uncovering Augustine's Greek sources since the turn of the century, whereupon Augustine's use of Rufinus was adjudged inconclusive in Cavadini et al., *Augustine through the Ages*, 224–27.

27. Rufinus, *De Epiphaniis*, 13.4.

28. Gregory Nazianzen, *Oration*, 38.13.

29. Keech, *The Anti-Pelagian Christology of Augustine of Hippo*, 204.

human flesh and inherited concupiscence, coupled with preoccupations about Pelagian emphasis of humanity's collectively sinless nature, tempted Augustine to exclude unqualified purity from Mary at the moment her physical conception. Above, Augustine affirmed that a portion of Mary's *flesh* that was employed by Christ at the Annunciation was indeed purified. This is uncannily in tandem with Nazianzen's Greek vocabulary. If Augustine was unable to decide whether or not Mary's flesh was purified just prior to being taken up, or by the act of being taken up, might this easily reflect the inherent ambiguity of Nazianzen's lexical term: *prokathartheisa*? Augustine clearly used the Tertullianic and Origenistic formula "*caro peccati*" to imply (underlying traducian commitments) that Mary participated in Adamite flesh, stemming from her natural mode of conception.[30] Both of Augustine's *ad hoc* and confused proposals (glossing prior Greek tradition of Mary's purification at the Annunciation) could be readily explained by familiarity with Nazianzen's purifying-language in relation to her putatively infected flesh (as Augustine would have read into Nazianzen's anthropology). Any possible comparison of Nazianzen to Rufinus would have only puzzled Augustine, providing no help for explaining how prepurification signifies that Mary's *flesh* and soul were simply immaculate. The *doctor gratiae* likely felt justified in implicating Mary in conception from her parents' concupiscence, resulting in her receiving Origenistic "flesh of sin." Plausibly misinterpreting this passage from Nazianzen's *Oration* 38, Augustine supposed a moment of ethico-physical cleansing in Mary's flesh, allowing Jesus to avoid the taint of Mary's Adamite inheritance. Be that as it may, only a few years later, Augustine affirmed (c. 415):

> [A Pelagian] also adjoins women [without sin], asserting of them. . . . "Even the very Mother of our Savior and Lord, of whom is it necessary to confess in piety she was without sin." Since the Holy Virgin Mary had also been excluded in just this manner, I wish absolutely (*prorsus*) nothing at all to be related to her when treating the question of sins. Hence, due to the honor of the Lord, regarding her: We certainly know what abundance of grace in every mode was conferred upon her for the sake of sin to be conquered. She merited (*meruit*) to conceive and to bear him, who most certainly had no sin.[31]

---

30. Augustine's source, besides Ambrose, is convincingly argued to have been Origen *latinus*, who had been translated by Jerome. See Keech, *The Anti-Pelagian Christology of Augustine*, 83, 102–4, 116–22, 142, 204.

31. Augustine, *De natura et gratia*, 36.42.

If we attempt to harmonize this passage with the aforementioned *De pec-catorum meritis*, Mary formerly had the capacity to merit at the Incarnation by some prevenient grace. The rationale for Mary's all-holiness seemed to derive from the fact that she had possessed pious faith and *was not herself a victim of concupiscence*.[32] Now, in the passage above, Mary is defended as someone in whom total sinlessness is more than just a possibility. Augustine's view of the all-holiness of Mary appears to be incommensurate with the mechanism and explanatory power of traducianism, whereby both sexual lust and the natural production of the human soul axiomatically result in the infection of concupiscence transmitted to offspring in every passionate act of coitus.[33] Augustine's posterior *Contra Julianum* (*scripsit* 422) and his *Opus Imperfectum contra Julianum* (*scripsit* 428) bear greatest witness to Augustine's Greek sources that influence his theology of original sin.[34] Referencing the Greco-patristic tradition, Augustine claimed never to assert anything other than his Greek predecessors.[35] Indeed, investigation into passionate sexual relations and inherited sinfulness in utero therefrom justify Augustine's claim to be following a Greek (if only North African orig-inate) tradition. Augustine acted as a synthesizer of primitive Greco-Roman tradition of "nightly pleasure" or coitus as the mechanism for transmitting sin to a child in utero.[36] Augustine's claims stand on a firm foundation when his approach is compared to ecclesiastical writers and African Fathers who comment on LXX Ps 50:5: "My mother conceived me in sins."[37]

32. See Buonaiuti and La Piana, "The Genesis," 168–13, for a convincing narrative and primary sources showing that meriting in original sin and/or concupiscence is impossible for Augustine in the period of the Pelagian crisis.

33. This unresolved tension is best illustrated in Augustine's *Contra Julianum* (*opus imperfectum*), 4.122: "*Non transcribimus diabolo Mariam conditione nascendi; sed ideo, quia ipsa conditione solvitur gratia renascendi*."

34. Buonaiuti and La Piana, "The Genesis," 170, 174. NB, Augustine youthfully misidentified Ambrosiaster as "Hilary," when appealing also to Nazianzen and Am-brose for his doctrine on original sin. Augustine discovered his error of attribution and somewhat distanced himself from Ambrosiaster thereafter.

35. Leinhard, "Augustine of Hippo," 86, and Lukken, *Original Sin*, 275.

36. Though parents are cleansed by original sin, their concupiscence in coitus propagates sin, as shown in Lukken, *Original Sin*, 274–275.

37. The source for Greco-Latin N. Africans is Origen, *Homilia in Psalmum L*, 9:88–90. Athanasius of Alexandria, *In Psalmum L* (*Patrologia Graeca*, 27:240), taught that man was not meant initially to reproduce in carnal marriage. Sexual production stems from the trespass (*parabasis*) of the commandment. Adam's sin brought about reproduction. So, all people from Adam are conceived in iniquities, falling under the condemnation (*katadikei*) of the forefather. "My mother conceived me in sins" refers to Eve. Basil, *De baptismo libri duo* (*Patrologia Graeca*, 31:1536), virtually reproduced themes and vocabulary of Origen's commentary on Luke, where baptism is a correction

Given the fact that Augustine struggled to understand the Latin and Greek meaning of Gregory's original and polyvalent sense of purification, his solution made little impact on discussion about Mary until well into the Middle Ages. Augustine's notion of original sin was built on the foundation of a North African tradition of sexual concupiscence to explain the transmission of sin from the maternal womb.[38] The tradition of original sin was subsequently, if imperfectly, synthesized with Ambrose of Milan's theology of original sin (though Ambrose is diversely employing the notion of *culpa*), along with Augustine's own traducian commitments.[39] The synthesis of these sources—albeit not always consistent—produced a construct that proved to be an attractive theory for theological successors. However, I insist that it is mistaken that Augustine had held for intrinsically and personal "guilt" (*culpa*) in the transmission of parental liability for Adam's sin to children.[40] The literary and contextual evidence make it only demonstrable that Augustine held for a child to be designated a *reatus*. It seems clear that Augustine was far too conscious of Roman law to analogize the status of a fetus to someone bound under contract "liability" (*culpa*). Legal liability implied at least minimal personal and moral negligence (*culpa levissima*) by

---

(*epanorthosin*) of "prior birth" in sordidness (*rhyparai*) of sins. As Origen, Basil cited Job: "nobody is clean of sin, not even one day of life." LXX Ps 50 is also cited as in Origen. Cyril of Alexandria, *De adoratione e cultu in spiritu et veritate* (*Patrologia Graeca*, 68:1008), wrote that devilish deceit brought death into the world. Satan defiles (*katamolynei*) human nature through destruction. Death has its root in sin. Death defiles (*katamiainei*) in another way; namely, through the act of human seminal production in carnal pleasure (*to hos en philedoniai sarkikei speiresthai ta gennomena*). Cyril of Alexandria, *In Psalmum L* (*Patrologia Graeca*, 69:1089), explained David's LXX Ps 50 on conception. Human nature is unclean (*akathartos*), subject to destruction from trespass and curse (*eks aras*). Though "conceived in iniquities," the activity of sin is not natural (*physike he tes hamartias energeia*) but is rather an inherited unsteadiness in nature (*to euolisthon tei physei sygkeklerotai*).

38. Beatrice, *The Transmission of Sin*, 233–35.

39. Ibid., 147. See Ambrose of Milan, *Exposition on the Gospel according to Luke*, 178 (4.67), citing the *Vetus Latina* Rom 5:12. Cf. Augustine, *Contra Julianum*, 1.3.10 (*Patrologia Latina*, 44:646). Ambrose (citing Rom 5:12) interpreted Paul to mean: "*culpa mors omnium est.*" Augustine knew Ambrose's prior work. See also Ambrose referring again to Rom 5:12 in Ambrose, *Apologia David altera*, 12.17: "*omnes in primo homine peccavimus, per naturae successionem culpae quoque ab uno in omnes transfuse successio est.*" Augustine's self-styled faithfulness to Ambrose needs no explanation, but rather his departure from Ambrose's guilt-laden language when speaking of infants (implied by Ambrose). My objection was long ago argued in Buonaiuti and La Piana, "The Genesis," 160–61.

40. Beatrice, *The Transmission of Sin*, 49, 177, 259, still holds for Augustine promoting the controversial: "hereditary guilt" in some sort of non-legal (non-Roman juristic) sense. The author admits that "culpa" is lacking in Augustine, but attempts (wrongly) to press the phrase "*originalis reatus*" into service to mean exactly the same idea.

the time that Augustine began to learn and adjudicate Roman law.[41] Instead, Augustine adopted idiosyncratically non-culpable language and descriptions of the status of embryos in utero, just at a time when he was embroiled in adjudicating disputes about property and inheritance law, along with slavery law, and while he was receiving, as if a dilettante lawyer, instruction on Roman law.[42] Unsurprisingly, this was precisely the time when Augustine imputed guilt only to adults for committing delicts, for which they were held responsible, whether these stemmed from malice or neglect.[43]

On the question of Augustine's peculiar vocabulary for infants, Roman law does not appear very promising to provide insight, for it mainly prescribed punishments on persons of criminal status or *in reatu* (such as treason). One application of Roman law seems to apply to infants in respect to Augustine's sense of *reatus*.[44] Recent studies do point to a possible solution in that Augustine's doctrinal source for his notion of *massa* (as in

41. Buckland, *The Main Institution of Roman Private Law*, 556–59. *Culpa* originally signified "active conduct": *culpa in faciendo* and was extended to imprudent negligence: *culpa in non faciendo*. A variety of distinctions gradually came into play.

42. Dodaro, "Between the Two Cities," 100–111. Some of his legal actions date c. 400. Augustine, for example, exercised a recently instituted kind of legal action: *episcopalis audientia,* ranking as arbiter of his Christian people on concrete questions of property and inheritance. See Humfress, "Patristic Sources," 97–118.

43. Guilt could be parsed into *culpa* (legal liability of the least [*culpa levissima*] personal fault) and *dolus* (malice). For example, destructive slaves created situations of liability (*culpa*) obligating their owners as in Aubert, "Commerce," 226. In another example of liability, a boy kicks a ball and it hits a barber shaving a slave (thus killing the slave). The liability is completely put upon the boy since *causation* of the liable action properly belongs to the boy. However liability might be shared if the barber were trying to shave at a ball game! See Sirks, "Delicts," 259–61. In another case, whenever a paterfamilias incurs debt, he hands on the entirety to his heir. It requires little theologizing to see the ready application of this day-to-day state of affairs to original sin, as if it were an inheritance. See Berger, *Encyclopedic Dictionary of Roman Law*, 485, where "a damned inheritance" constitutes a legal term in Roman law (per Gaius) regarding someone's heredity, where debt (versus wealth) passes from a father to his son. In this sense, being the patrilineal offspring makes one legally "liable" to debt versus the beneficiary of assets. Augustine described the debt of liability (too large for humans to pay) as if liable (*reatus*) to incur an original debt that now consumes the olden inheritance of the paterfamilias (Adam). Each heir still owes for his father's, as yet, unpaid debt. Debtor terminology occurs in Augustine as affirmed in Cavadini et al., *Augustine through the Ages*, 224–27.

44. The term in Christian Latin is entirely ambiguous (though with juristic undertones), meaning essentially: "state of accusation." The accused need not actually be "guilty" of any crime, but is somehow implicated in the same (in this case, by God). See Lukken, *Original Sin*, 282–283.

massa damnata[45]) *assuredly hails from Ambrosiaster.*[46] *Augustine associated his vocabulary of reatus with Adam (in place of Ambrosiaster's Eve*[47]), *who sinned for and in the entirety of the posterior human race, whom he begot after his own* quasi-legal transgression *of a divine precept.*[48] Ambrosiaster laid out the anthropological principle that: *"infirmum esse hominem ad praecepta legis servanda."*[49] Ambrosiaster equated this infirmity to the state of humanity, *qua* composite body and soul, being "yoked to delict" (*delicto*) with a "corrupted body." Using a clever wordplay, Ambrosiaster contrasted the law that is "firm" (*firma*) and devoid of *culpa* (that is, it is not faulty) to each "sick" (*infirmum*) human who is always joined to the delict of Adam. Ambrosiaster was commenting on Paul's concept of law in his *Epistle to the Romans.*[50] Given Augustine's adoption of the Ambrosian sense of devilish infection causing infirmity, every human—from inception—is rendered incapable of observing the precepts of law in virtue of the criminal heritage of Adam.[51] Each fetus might be styled a violator *in fieri* of divine precepts (at

45. A recorded instance of Pseudo-Ambrose (Ambrosiaster) associates his vocabulary word *cumulus* (= *massa*) with both the devil and *reatus*. See Souter and Armitage, *A Study of Ambrosiaster*, 98. On another occasion, Eve's transgression is styled "origin of guilt" (*originem reatus*). See Lunn-Rockliffe, *Ambrosiaster's Political Theology*, 119. Might this be propitious for Augustine categorizing a fetus as a *reatus* in relation to the lineage of Eve?

46. Pereira, *Augustine of Hippo*, 49.

47. See Lukken, *Original Sin*, 77–78, for Ambrosiaster's word-play, where each human is at conception *infirmus*, while the law is *firma* without *culpa*, meshes quite well with the Roman liturgy's (*Sacramentarium Veronense*) coeval designation of woman (in the image of Eve) as "infirma mundi," whose nature participates in *feminea infirmitas*, but nonetheless women overcome by grace their *feminea condicio* (which is derived from Eve).

48. Herein, lies the question of the chicken or the egg: The earliest Roman liturgy (*Sacramentarium Veronensis*) speaks of "we humans" as having fallen in nature because of the violation of a precept. Does the liturgical language pre- or post-date late fourth-century Fathers?

49. For this discovery, see Buonaiuti and La Piana, "The Genesis," 160–61, 168. Pereira, *Augustine of Hippo*, 49, affirms the same, as if a discovery, though bibliographically unaware of the aforementioned a century prior. Pereira compares Ambrosiaster's language and arguments to Augustine's *Contra Julianum*. NB, the author conflates *culpa* with *reatus* without embarking on a similar *ressourcement* into Augustine's thought and vocabulary.

50. It is from Ambrosiaster that Augustine appears to have taken his interpretation of Rom 5:12: "*in quo omnes peccaverunt.*" See Lukken, *Original Sin*, 271–72.

51. Augustine, *Sancti Aurelii Augustini De trinitate libri xv*, 13.18.23. This notion concurs with Ambrose, *Explanatio Psalmorum XI*, n. 5:

facta enim erat fraude et veneno infusa serpentis caro nostra, caro peccati. Postquam est obnoxia facta peccato, facta erat caro mortis; quia erat morti debita. Huius

the very least being persons unable to merit) and, thus, liable to the pain of loss (according to Roman inheritance law) or hell.

In comparison to Augustine *ad litteram*, Augustinian theology in posterior papal decretals turns out to be unconsciously non-Augustinian in vocabulary. For example, shortly after Augustine's death, Pope Anastasius II (*scripsit* 498) found it necessary to condemn putatively Augustinian traducianism, while yet affirming that parents pass on to their children punishment and "guilt" (*poena culpaque peccati*) of Adam.[52] While the former doctrine represents authentic Augustinianism, the latter is simply not Augustine's mode of expression. If perchance legal guilt (legal liability or fault according to Roman law) also influenced Ambrose of Milan's terminology, it in nowise constitutes a feature of sin in Augustine's fetal lexicon. Later, when we take a look at ecclesiastical writers who interpreted Augustine's Latin, such writers historically had limited acquaintance with the existence and practice of Roman law (along with its legal institutions), which had long ceased to condition legal discussions on the matters of liability.

At this point, I introduce the important figure of Pope Leo I. He was committed to the idea of human flesh being encumbered by the *culpa* (guilt/liability/fault) of Adam. Incontestably Augustinian in his theological proclivities, Leo's teaching on original sin was enshrined at Chalcedon with the famous *Tome of Leo* (*scripsit* 449). When speaking of Christ's assumption of Mary's human flesh, he wrote:

> All this [i.e., the devil causing humans to lose the gifts of God and to die] called for the realization of a secret plan whereby the unalterable God, whose will (*voluntas*) is indistinguishable from his goodness, might bring the original realization of his kindness towards us to completion by means of a more hidden mystery, and whereby humanity, which had been led into guilt (*in culpam*) by the craftiness of the devil, might not perish contrary to the purpose of God. . . . Nature was taken from the mother of the Lord, not guilt (*non culpa*[53]). And the fact that the birth was

---

carnis iam reae, iam praeiudicatae similitudinem Christus in sua carne suscepti. Quia etsi naturalem substantiam huius susceperat carnis, non tamen contagia ulla susceperat nec "in iniquitatibus conceptus et natus est in delictis" [Ps 50:5] . . . *sed de Spiritu Sancto natus ac virgine est.*

52. Anastasius II, *Bonum atque iucundum* (= *Enchiridion symbolorum definitionum et declarationum de rebus fidei et morum*, *Compendium of Creeds, Definitions, and Declarations on Matters of Faith and Morals*, 129 n. 361). Anastasius merely recapitulated: Leo I, *In Nativitate Domini: Sermo 2*, in *Léon le Grand: Sermons*, sec. 4: "*dum vitiatae originis praeiudicium generale persequitur, chirographum quo nitebatur excedit, ab illo iniquitatis exigens poenam, in quo nullam reperit culpam.*"

53. This phrase cryptically reworks Leo I, *In Nativitate Domini: Sermo 2*, sec. 3: "*Et*

miraculous does not imply that in the Lord Jesus Christ, born from the virgin's womb, the nature is different from our own.[54]

The post-Augustinian tendency to cover Augustine's language with the umbrella of some or other definition of *culpa* was hardly peculiar to Leo. However, despite the strong Latin tradition of using *culpa* in both Ambrose and the Roman liturgy, the Greek Fathers of Chalcedon adopted a translation-interpretation of Leo's key phrase as follows: [55] "Humanity was seized by devilish wickedness with respect to sin (*pros hamartian*) . . . Nature, not sin (*ouch hamartia*), was taken from the mother of the Lord."[56] Some as-

---

cum in omnibus matribus non fiat sine peccati sorde conceptio, haec inde purgationem traxit, unde concepit." If we take this to mean: "And since among all mothers conception does not happen without filth of sin, then –in consequence– this conception drew forth purification, whence she conceived." The passage does not fit well with Augustine, *Opus Imperfectum contra Julianum*, 4.22 (*Patrologia Latina*, 45:1417), as cited earlier. Notice that mothers conceive because of some filth, which Leo immediately identifies as: "*Quo enim paterni seminis transfusio non pervenit, peccati se illic origo non miscuit.*" Clearly original sin rides on the vehicle of seminal transfusion. However, if Leo were really Augustinian, we would expect him to affirm that Mary's flesh needs to be purified "when taken up" or "in the act of taking it up" since Mary is naturally conceived. Notice the very next line: "*Inviolata virginitas concupiscentiam nescivit, substantiam ministravit. Assumpta est de matre Domini, natura, non culpa.*" As Lukken, *Original Sin*, 279–81, proves via primary texts: "*nescius peccati*" expresses the biblical, Latino-patristic, and liturgical modality for designating Christ's very identity. Here, we have Mary: "*nescivit concupiscentiam*"! Perpetual virginity (herein, always including with Mary's virginal modes of conception and birth) is treated as the natural symbol of unqualified moral purity. Consequently, the *Tome of Leo* ought to be interpreted as saying: "Mary's non-concupiscential and virginal nature was assumed, not soiled nature with original sin." So, what is this "purgation" of which Leo speaks? I simply consider him to refer obliquely to the Greco-Latin and Augustinian patristic reception of Mary's purification at the Annunciation. Clearly, Mary did not lust (typically an alleged condition for fecundity) like other women, so she needed the purification of the Spirit to make her fertile and to galvanize her against sin.

54. Leo I, *Tome of Leo*, in *Chalcedon 451*, in *Decrees of the Ecumenical Councils*, 1:79a.10–18 [For the English trans., see ibid., 1:79*]:

> *Opus fuit secreti dispensatione consilii, ut incommutabilis deus, cuius voluntas non potest sua benignitate privari, prima erga nos pietatis suae dispensationem sacramento occultiore conpleret et homo diabolicae iniquitatis versutia actus in culpam contra dei propositum non periret . . . Adsumpta est de matre domini natura, non culpa, nec in domino Iesu Christo ex utero virginis genito, quia nativitas est mirabilis, ideo nostri est natura dissimilis.*

55. Lukken, *Original Sin*, 11. The vocabulary of the collects-orations stems mainly from Tertullian, Ambrose, Augustine, Leo, and Gregory the Great. The ancient sacramentary tradition in question extends from c. 350–700.

56. Leo I, *Tome of Leo*, in *Concilium universal Chalcedonense anno 451*, 2.1.1:14.10–11, 20–21: "*Ho anthropos ho te kakourgia tes diabolikes kakias pros hamartian synelatheis . . . proselephthe ek tes metros tou despotou physis, ouch hamartia.*" This translation is quite

pects of Augustine's doctrine on original sin were indeed affirmed in the *Tome of Leo* (*graecus*). As my footnote to the Greek text of the *Tome of Leo* explains, Chalcedon correctly translated Leo's sense, though I was required to look at both the Roman liturgy and Leo's Christmas sermon to understand clearly that Leo was actually asserting a sort of anticipatory doctrine to what medieval immaculatists termed: "the Immaculate Conception."

Be that as it may, Leo imitated theological terminology akin to Ambrose of Milan by interpreting some notion of "guilt" as the human inheritance (what Augustine sees more ambiguously as a status meriting legal liability coupled with proneness toward moral defect versus an actual delict). In relation to this, Leo invented the term "*natura rea*" in league with the notion that human nature was in a sort of prison for Adam's crime. This was obliquely enshrined in the Roman liturgy as "*reatus naturae*."[57] Leo's relevant discussion of "guilty flesh" in the *Tome of Leo* summarized Augustine's *De trinitate*, but decidedly ignored any notion of Mary being infected as a product of sexual concupiscence.[58] Otherwise, Leo embraced a sort of *Augustinian reception*, for the notion of ancestral or original "culpa'" was simply not from Augustine *ad litteram*.[59] Despite the fact that traducianism was

---

defensible, for Lukken, *Original Sin*, 279–81, explores the language of transmission of sin in the *Sacramentarium Veronense* and so-called *Gelasianum*, so as to discover 1 Cor 5:21: "*ton me gnonta hamartian*" (= *nesciam peccati*) as the relevant formulaic expression. Pope Gelasius himself utilized this by now traditional expression for Christ, i.e., "*nescius peccati*," in reference to original sin. Most importantly, Lukken, *Original Sin*, 391–92, correctly draws attention to the Ambrosian-inspired *Exultet* or *praeconium paschale*, where the *Gelasianum* poetically forms an apposition between "*felix culpa*" and "*necessarium peccatum*"! The Chalcedonian translator of Leo's *Tome* appears to be familiar with these associations. Collects expressing sinful propagation: "*de obnoxia generatione*," and the like, are convincingly traced back to Leo as their literary source.

57. Lukken, *Original Sin*, 283.

58. Bernard Green, *The Soteriology of Leo the Great*, 148–50, demonstrates Augustine's influence on the relevant section concerning humanity subjection to the devil and original sin. See ibid., 189–208, for arguments supporting Leo's true authorship and his literary sources. Importantly, the *Tome of Leo* reproduced above, in Latin and Greek, at times repeats verbatim Leo I, *In Nativitate Domini: Sermo 2*, sec. 1–2. Leo's Christmas sermon (*scripsit* 441) will be investigated, below, for it vies with Augustine for being the source of the Greek dictum-become-dogma concerning Mary's triple virginity (albeit a pithy version of the axiom, in both Latin and Greek, is absent from the *Tome of Leo*).

59. Though Leo relied on Augustine's *De trinitate* in his Christmas sermon and *Tome of Leo*, he introduced *culpa* in relation to Mary's triple virginity; whereas Augustine never did so in his *De trinitate*. Instead, Augustine's *Sermon 231*, chap. 2, as discovered by Aldama, *Virgo Mater*, 229, is clearly Leo's source of triple virginity mixed with *culpa*: "*Non enim legibus mortis venit obstrictus . . . quem sine concupiscentia virgo concepit, quem et virgo peperit, et virgo permansit; qui vixit sine culpa, qui non est mortuus propter culpam*." NB, Aldama, *Virgo Mater*, too, tries to make "culpa" apply to Jesus' conception without concupiscence, but Augustine systematically avoided *culpa*

eventually condemned by a pope a few generations later, subsequent ecclesiastical writers continued to use Augustine's language and images of reproduction but coupled with the additions of non-Augustinian associations of "culpa" with infants (e.g., in the Pseudo-Augustinian works of Fulgentius of Ruspe). Consequently, the attraction of Augustine's traducian metaphors of infected flesh and a received doctrine of fetal guilt gained popularity among Latin authors of the Middle Ages. Consequently, Leo the Great seemingly departed from Augustinian original sin in relation to Mary's particle of flesh (likely opting for John Cassian's notion, *infra*, of Mary's total sanctification at the Annunciation). Thereafter, this question seemed to peak little interest in the West, until well after the fall of the Roman Empire.

The Prepurified Virgin:
Sophronius and Lateran Council 649

A veil of silence appeared to fall on prepurification during the next centuries until the period of Christological controversies involving Maximus Confessor (d. 666). Even if Maximus did not know Latin, he lived in North Africa for years and, thus, specialists are convinced that Augustine's writings were available to him.[60] Scholars continue to debate whether or not Maximus partially adopted Augustine's doctrine of original sin.[61] The most recent evidence leads us to believe that Maximus derived considerable inspiration for his thought on original sin from Augustinian extracts present in *florilegia*

---

in relation to the fetus. In the same vein, Augustine's *Sermon 231* says that Jesus "lived" without fault/guilt, dying for humans' fault/guilt. Guilt is applied to Adam's and Jesus' moral mode of living. Proof: Paschal *Sermon 231*, chap. 1, falls in the context of an explanation of how Jesus can die. In chap. 2, the principle is espoused: "the parent of death is sin." The discussion is of death. The "origin" of death is real sin. Adam accepted the law and precept that death is conditioned on obedience. Effects of sin listed herein are only: death, mortality, toil, misery, and loss of heaven. All people are subject to these, save Christ. Jesus shares in our punishment (*poena*), but not in Adamite *peccatum* or *culpa*, for "the death of guilt is punishment." Jesus came to die, not to sin (*peccare*). Finally, Jesus dissolved both sin-guilt/fault and punishment. Really, the only punishment dissolved is eternal loss of souls. Then, Augustine cited Rom 4:25, where Jesus died for humans' *actual* sins. Leo (and posterity) read "culpa" here generically, instead of Augustine's strictly moral sense of the term with regard to original sin! Cf. *Patrologia Latina* 38:1104, col. b–1105, col. a.

60. The proof for this assertion, along with a list of theological similarities between the two, is argued in Johannes Börjesson, "Maximus the Confessor's Knowledge of Augustine," 325–26.

61. Larchet, "Ancestral Guilt," 42–43; Louth, *Maximus the Confessor*, 58, 201; Daley, "Making a Human Will Divine," 101–26.

at Lateran 649,[62] which Maximus certainly had in possession during his doctrinal disputes with the Monothelites in the East in the second half of the seventh century.[63]

I suggest another point of literary dependency of Maximus on Augustinian Mariology. Augustine best accounts for Sophronius of Jerusalem's solidly datable witness in Greek to this North African tradition, as it had pithily been summarized in Augustine, who had argued Mary's thrice-integral virginity.[64] Augustine wrote of Mary: "She conceived him as a virgin, she gave birth as a virgin, she remained a virgin."[65] This, again, occurs in a Christmas sermon (as elsewhere): "The virgin conceived . . . the virgin gave birth . . . after giving birth she still remained a virgin."[66] Recent studies of Augustine's works have exhaustively catalogued coeval and posterior Latin authors' use and variations of this formula.[67] Maximus' spiritual Father, Sophronius of Jerusalem (*scripsit* 634–638), bequeathed a similar phraseology to the Greek East, per his *Synodical Letter*, which was ecumenically approved at Constantinople III.[68] Furthermore, in a biography of Mary,

62. Börjesson, "Maximus the Confessor's Knowledge of Augustine," 327, 331. The Lateran *acta*, which (perhaps were composed and) were undoubtedly inspired by Maximus' writings, contain Greek citations from the following: *Epistle 140, In Johannis evangelium tractatus, Enarrationes in Psalmos, De civitate dei, Contra sermonem Arianorum,* and *Contra Julianum opus imperfectum.*

63. Börjesson, "Maximus the Confessor's Knowledge of Augustine," 327–28. Maximus used Lateran 649 in a dispute in the year 656.

64. Augustine carried on what may be a North African tradition from Zeno of Verona (c. 300-371/80), who also spent time in Italy. See Zeno, *Tractatus Sancti Zenonis Veronensis episcopi,* 1.54.11: "*virgo incorrupta concepit, post conceptum virgo peperit, post partum virgo permansit.*" NB, Zeno might contrast Mary's virginity as the sign that she did not suffer original lust, or the putative crime of Adam and Eve that initiated the fall. Again, Zeno points to North African theology supposing Adam's and Eve's unlawful coitus as origin and vehicle of ancestral sin. See Lukken, *Original Sin,* 56.

65. Augustine, *Sermo 51,* in *Sermones de novo testamento,* 28.525: "*Illa enim virgo concepit, virgo peperit, virgo permansit.*"

66. See also Augustine, *Sermo ad catechumenos de symbolo,* 6.143: "*virgo concepit, virgo peperit, et post partum virgo permansit.*" For other sermons, whose phraseology is virtually the same, see Augustine, *Augustinus,* 190; *Sermon 21,* 13.401; *Sermo 170.3* (*Patrologia Latina,* 38:928); *Sermo 363b,* sec. 2.3.

67. See Aldama, *Virgo Mater,* 213–47, and Weidman, introduction to Augustine, *Augustinus,* 190, who supplements Aldama, *Virgo Mater,* 213–216, who locates additional variants of Augustine's dictum in numerous other works.

68. Considering Augustine's biographer, Possidius, this Augustinian phrase in the Greek is potentially explicable through the existence of Augustinian (and perhaps Ps.-Augustinian?) sermons in Greek translation. Apropos, the no longer extant Greek translations of Augustine's works (save fragments/excerpts) were partly selected to confute Nestorius. See Dekkers, "Les traduction grecques," 207–12.

attributed to Maximus Confessor and estimated to date between the 620s–630s, the author steadfastly claimed: "There is no . . . pain of childbirth, for truly she alone is a virgin exalted above all virgins, a virgin ever immaculate: before birth, in birth, and after birth."[69] Because a recent study has called into question Maximian authorship of *The Life of the Virgin*, I refrain from basing my arguments on this disputed work.[70] Nonetheless, upon comparing Sophronius' *Synodical Epistle* and *The Life of the Virgin* to a relevant canon of Lateran 649, we find that the Greek (original) text of the latter, like many of the canons of the synod, safely derives its statement on Marian virginity from the pages, if not the very pen, of Maximus:

> Canon 3: If anyone does not acknowledge in accordance with the holy Fathers, properly and truly, the holy, ever-virgin and immaculate (*ten hagian aeiparthenon achranton*) Mary to be *Theotokos*, as having properly and truly at the end of the ages conceived from the Holy Spirit . . . born from God the Father before all ages in a manner without [physical] injury (*aphthoros*), while her unimpaired virginity remained intact even after birth (*alytou meinases autes kai meta tokon tes parthenias*), let him stand condemned.[71]

Börjesson has already shown that reference to "the holy Fathers" repeated a formulaic expression of a list of approved Greco-Latin Fathers from

---

69. Maximus, *The Life of the Virgin*, 51.

70. I refrain addressing Booth's arguments contra Shoemaker, who authenticates *The Life* by arguing that George of Nicomedia et al. used it a source. See Shoemaker, "The Mother's Passion," 53–68. NB, Booth's "A New Date-List," 149–203, accepted Shoemaker's general invitation to proffer scholarly arguments against Maximian attribution to *The Life*. Yet, Booth passed over paramount liturgical data. *The Life* shows no substantial interest in the Conception of Mary (that is, by Ann)! Booth's hypothetical and post-tenth century date ignores the universal pull of Andrew of Crete et al. (on Mary's Conception) in the mid-eighth century, the structural finalization of the *Typicon* of the Great Church in the ninth century (celebrating Mary's Conception), and the international popularity of the feast already attested by 850 in Southern Italy. See Calabuig, "The Liturgical Cult of Mary," 5:270–22. *The Life* creates a narrative from the Byzantine cycle of Marian feasts in harmony with dominical feasts and salient events in the life of Jesus. If Booth's arguments exploit Shoemaker's weak evidence, *The Life* is nonetheless liturgically primitive and lacks fascination with Mary's conception in the wake of Andrew of Crete and others. See Cunningham, "The Use of the *Protevangelion of James*," 167, 175–78. For his part, George of Nicomedia argued only for a greater *rank* of the feast (adjudging it ancient), so that it might enjoy a pre- and post- festive day. See Krausmüller, "Making the Most of Mary," 235–45. *The Life* so ignores Mary's conception that its composition assuredly predates the mid-eighth-century fad to speculate on Mary's conception by recourse to the *Protevangelium of James*.

71. Maximus Confessor (?) et al., *Concilium Lateranense a. 649 celebratum*, 1:370.

Constantinople II (553).[72] Maximus knew this list. Clearly, Sophronius cannot be Maximus' aforementioned "Father," in the relevant sense.

Only three other candidates, besides Augustine, can currently be considered for transmitting this doctrine to the East. First there is Zeno of Verona, but he must be immediately excluded, for neither was he listed among "approved" Fathers, nor was he known in a Greek translation. However, as the earliest witnesses to our axiom, Zeno is singular for associating *incorrupta* with the triple virginity formula. The *enkritos* or approved Ambrose left us with no extant writings wherein he penned the triple virginity formula, although such a doctrine can be gathered piecemeal from his mature works (c. 393) within his corpus (a modest portion of which was available in Greek).[73] Our best evidence is provided by John Cassian who testified: "That famous priest of God, Ambrose . . . in his book that is to virgins [wrote] . . . 'Likewise, [be mindful] upon the birthday of the Lord himself: See the miracle of the Lord's mother: A virgin conceived (*concepit*), a virgin bore (*peperit*) as the virgin gave birth (*parturiit*), a virgin was pregnant, she a virgin post partum.'"[74] Clearly this cannot explain the pithy Greek phrase, but probably reflects Ambrose expanding on Zeno of Verona's phraseology. After all, Zeno was known to Ambrose and in proximity to Milan. Cassian's witness is propitious, for Leo the Great commissioned Cassian to write (429/430) against Nestorius.[75] Aldama has found that, in one instance, Zeno accounts verbatim for Augustine's doctrine,[76] but Ambrose's phraseology and attributed quote cannot account for the pithy Greek version of the phrase: "before birth, in birthing, and after birth."[77]

Lastly, in Leo's case, we do encounter an approved Father who learned about Mary by reading Ambrose, Cyril, Augustine, and John Cassian. Leo, upon exploring Cassian's treatment of the Annunciation, seemed faintly to echo the Greek tradition of prepurification,[78] where Cassian interpreted

72. Börjesson, "Maximus the Confessor's Knowledge of Augustine," 329.

73. Aldama, *Virgo Mater*, 228, and Corsaro, "La mariologia," 309–36. Cf. Dekkers, "Les traduction," 193–233.

74. John Cassian, *De Incarnatione Domini contra Nestorium*, 7.25.23–26.

75. Green, *The Soteriology of Leo the Great* , 25, 28–29.

76. Aldama, *Virgo Mater*, 222.

77. The phrase "virgin in birthing" (*virgo in partu*) does not appear in any securely dated homily of the fifth century. Aldama, *Virgo Mater*, 234–35, lucidly explains it as development of Augustine's phraseology that, at its earliest, reflects North African Mariology at the opening of the sixth century.

78. John Cassian, *De Incarnatione*, 7.27, provided an extensive quote from a translation of Nazianzen's *Oration 38*. Cassian also cited Athanasius ambiguously, concerning Christ and Mary as parallel examples of Jeremiah's and the Baptist's sanctification in the womb. However, this might refer only to Christ in utero. See John Cassian, *De Incarnatione*, 7.39.

Luke 1:35 as the moment of "sanctification" of the whole subject Mary (versus Augustine's interpretation of purifying a sordid part of her flesh).[79] We will see this theme again in Leo's posterior Christmas sermon, below. Before looking at Leo's discussion of the purification of Mary at the Annunciation, we might note that Leo preached the following in his sermon on Christmas of 441: "She was devoid of the normative and the usual . . . in that a virgin conceived, a virgin bore, and yet remained a virgin."[80] A respectable portion of Leo's epistolary was in fact translated into Greek. Still, there is no evidence that the aforementioned sermon was ever translated into Greek. Contrariwise, in Augustine's case, Greek translations of his sermons (along with other works) were selected for anti-Nestorian purposes.[81] These could have easily contained the virginal aphorism in question. Nonetheless, Leo merits exploration as a possible source for the pithy Greek aphorism, due to the fact that sections of Leo's Christmas sermon, above, were later self-plagiarized nearly verbatim in the posterior *Tome of Leo*.[82]

Problematically, if we suppose the virginal Greek dictum to have been a translation from some work of Leo, as with the *Tome of Leo* itself (though dependent on his Christmas sermon), Still Leo only affirms Mary's triple virginity in its opening section in a relatively verbose manner devoid of pithy content. Afterwards, openly commending Leo and his writings,

---

79. Ibid., 2.2:

spiritus enim sanctus virginis interiora sanctificans et in his potentiam divinitatis suae spirans humanae se inseruit miscuitque naturae atque id, quod alienum a se fuerat, suum fecit, virtute id sua scilicet ac maiestate praesumens. Ac ne ad introitum divinitatis humana fortasse infirmitas non subsisteret, venerandam omnibus virginem virtus altissimi roboravit, ut corpoream inbecillitatem circumfuse umbrae suae protectione firmaret et ad consummandum conceptus sacri inenarrabile sacramentum humana infirmitas non deficeret, quam divina obumbratio sustineret. (underline mine)

80. Leo I, *In Nativitate Domini: Sermo 2*, sec. 2: "*humano usu et consuetudine caret . . . quod virgo conceperit, quod virgo pepererit et virgo permanserit.*"

81. From the evidence, the *florilegia* at or in the *acta* of Chalcedon, Constantinople II & III, and Lateran 649 included no sermon, among those of Augustine, containing Augustine's Marian maxim. See Alexander Alexakis, *Codex Parisinus Graecus 1115 and Its Archetype*, Dumbarton Oaks Studies 34, 8–21.

82. Leo I, *In Nativitate Domini: Sermo 2*, sec. 1:

Deus enim omnipotens et clemens . . . statim ut nos diabolica malignitas veneno suae mortificavit invidiae . . . praesignavit . . . denuntians serpenti futurum semen mulieris quod noxii capitis elationem sua virtute contereret . . . Opus fuit, dilectissimi, secreti dispensatione consilii, ut incommutabilis Deus, cuius voluntas non potest sua benignitate privari, primam pietatis suae dispositionem sacramento occultiore compleret, et homo diabolice iniquitatis versutia actus in culpam, contra Dei propositum non periret.

Constantinople III (553) next affirmed Mary as "ever-virgin," leaving us to guess as to whether Leo's Augustinian axiom within his Christmas sermon lurked somewhere behind the Constantinopolitan scenes with its recent ecumenical emphasis on Mary's perpetual virginity. Parsimoniously, the inspiration for the Greek axiom is best attributed to one of the many Greek sermons (no longer extant) of Augustine, rather than to anyone of Leo. One remaining problem calls into question our capacity to attribute the Greek axiom directly to Augustine since we must account for the transition from three Latin verbs, where a virgin "conceived, birthed, and remained" into the pithier Greek, where a virgin continued "before, during, and after birth." Aldama's thorough study located Pseudo-Augustinians of the fifth century that account, verbatim, for the Greek triple virginity formula. As for the Greek axiom, it can, at its earliest, be confidently dated only to the period following Sophronius' sojourn in N. Africa (634). Because no ostensible reason exists to hypothesize a translation of Leo's Christmas sermon, which would have lain dormant for centuries, only to be rediscovered and quoted in the 630s by Sophronius, parsimony forces me to conclude that Augustine must have been early imitated as the Latin source for the fifth-century Latin expression using a triplex of prepositional phrases. This Pseudo-Augustinian tradition (the sermons of which transitioned from the authentic Augustine's three verbs to three prepositional phrases) enjoys the most logical claim to parentage of the Greek formulaic confession of Mary's triple virginity in the seventh century.[83]

83. Booth, "A New Date-List," 159, seems unaware of any source for this phrase that chronologically pre-dates either Sophronius, or *The Life*. Only two Greek sermons, falsely attributed to Athanasius, might prima facie pose a threat to Sophronio-Maximinian temporal priority. See Pseudo-Athanasius, *In occursum Domini* (*Patrologia Graeca*, 28:996): "She is stainless on [the matter of] purity (*amolynton tes hagneias*), in no way to suffer the natural law and maternal consequence in birthing (*en tokoi*), through which [birthing] (*dia tou*), just as both before birth (*pro tokou*) as well as after the birth (*met tokon*), she was in a like manner a virgin and so she remained in an absolutely real manner." Sophronius' *Synodical Letter* (*infra*), not to mention Maximus' *The Life*, pre-dates this and another sermon, employing vocabulary presuming post-monoenergistic issues (cf., *supra*, *Patrologia Graeca*, 28:976). The sermon also betrays itself by: "For by means of both [natures] shall Christ be preached; he will be known as both God and very man, too, who himself wills and operates on his own volition (*auteksousios theolon kai energon*), on one hand [willing and doing] the former items by means of divinity and, on the other hand, the latter items by humanity" (*Patrologia Graeca*, 28:997C). This public sermon is combatively dyothelite, presupposing outbreaks of the ultimate controversy (post-634). NB, George of Nicomedia (c. 860) is contested as its author per Constas, *Proclus of Constantinople*, 380, and Shoemaker, *The Life of the Virgin*, 35. See a second homily, also too late for candidacy, in Pseudo-Athanasius, *Quaestiones aliae* (*Patrologia Graeca*, 28:773–796). This equally post-Chalcedonian author states: "The unseen divinity was not apparent and the divinity operates (*energei*) through

Let us recall, however, that Mary's perpetual virginity marked the end term of theological development reliant on Origen's original exegesis of Mary's purification in the Temple after childbirth.[84] After her miraculous process of birth, she avoided the penalty of impurity laws (Ex. 13:2, Lev. 12:6). Jesus and Mary were even scripturally paired in this ritual purification of body (Luke 2:22). Origen exempted both of them from the Law because there was: (1.) absence of human seed in conception, (2.) absence of a male phallus opening Mary's womb, (3.) and preservation from shedding blood in the birthing process. These demonstrate Mary's and Jesus' technical exemption from the law commemorated in the Purification in the Temple and the Circumcision of the Lord. The former rite "purifies" a mother, while the latter "sanctifies" her first-born who opens her womb.

What bearing, besides Pseudo-Augustinian influence on Sophronius' and Maximus' triple virginity formulas, does all the aforementioned have with respect to the term: *prokathartheisa*? The key lies in the adjectives associated with the virginal axiom. Both Sophronius and the (Maximian) Lateran 649 introduced Mary's triple virginity formula by calling her: *achrantos*. This denotes an embellishment of the axiom in comparison to Zeno, Augustine, and Leo (not to mention Peudo-Augustinians). Sophronius wrote (*scripsit* 634–638) in his *Synodical Letter*:

> [God accomplished] the conception without seed . . . the uncorruptive birth (*ho tokos ho aphthoros*), the undefiled/immaculate virginity (*he parthenia he achrantos*), which was intact before the birth and during the birth and after the birth (*he pro tou tokou kai en toi tokoi kai meta ton tokon alobetos*).[85]

Maximus and his companions (perhaps monks of Eucratas in general)[86] likely adopted an already popular practice of substituting and/or interchanging

---

the visible humanity' (*Parologia Graeca*, 28:793). The sources of operation for the two perfect natures are the "humanity and divinity" in abstract; whereas only one divine operation is supposed. This bespeaks a pro-monothelite theology after the beginning of the outbreak of controversy.

84. Origen, *Homily on Luke*, 9:88–90. Cf. Maximus, *The Life*, 75 (4.46), which derives two entire paragraphs of its exegesis of Mary's purification from Origen.

85. Sophronius of Jerusalem, *Synodical Letter*, 2.3.14.

86. Booth, *Crisis of Empire*, 147–49. Maximus can safely be counted among the companions of John Moschos and Sophronius of Jerusalem, the latter of whom taught Maximus. Moschos, as an ecclesiastical writer, ranks among the earliest to combine Mary's title of "immaculate" (*achrantos*) with "ever-virgin" (*aei parthenos/aeiparthenos*). See Moschos, *Pratum Spirituale*, chap. 180 (*Patrologia Graeca*, 87.3:3052). Moschos lifted this phrase from a combatively anti-Nestorian passage of a Palestinian episcopal and synodical *libellus* addressed to Justinian. See Palestinian bishops et al., *Libellos episkopon toi basilei Ioustianoi*, in *Synodus Constantinopolitana et Hierosolymitana anno*

the title "immaculate" for the more traditional term "prepurified" around the beginnings of monoenergism.[87] One can suspect that canon three of Lateran 649 actually addressed Nestorian heretics, who allegedly denied Mary's integral virginity *during and after birth*;[88] perhaps exploiting ambiguities surrounding Mary's "prepurification" (which only concerned Mary's virginal purity before and during the Incarnation) and/or her purification in the New Testament. As Chadwick notes, there was "a nest of Nestorian monks" that managed to hold out in Rome until 677.[89]

Antithetically, Hurley argues that Monothelites are the target of canon three. When Honorius openly confessed one will (*hen thelema homologoumen*) in Christ,[90] Hurley correctly interprets the pope as attempting to protect Christ from possessing a voluble and changeable will through *not* being born of either cursed or sinful flesh in Mary.[91] Hurley draws attention

---

536, ed. E. Schwartz, Acta Conciliorum Oecumenicorum, 3:31.5–6: "*anthropolatrou Nestoriou ten diairesin apopheugontes homologoumen hoper ekeinos ernesato, ten hagian achranton and aeiparthenon metera tou kyriou kai theou hemon Iesou Christou theotokon*." Importantly, this synod repeated no triple virginity axiom, though its doctrine is concentric. This means that, posterior to Moschos, Sophronius and Maximus might have only encountered their shared dictum on Marian virginity in Africa. When surveying pre-sixth century writers, one can suspect that *achrantos*, which was formerly applied to the ever-Virgin's *act of giving birth* to Jesus, was transferred to the agent of "immaculate birth," namely, Mary.

87. Booth, *Crisis of Empire*, 188–89, records this movement occurring after compromises on a local level in 620s, lasting until the 630s, whereupon Heraclius was emboldened to adopt the doctrine as officially imperial policy. Later, because of disputes, Patriarch Sergius drafted prohibition decree: *Ekthesis* (*scripsit* 636). This took effect in 638 as per Alexakis, "Before the Lateran Council of 649," 93–95.

88. Per Aldama, *Virgo Mater*, 104, my interpretation might be thought too restrictive, for Augustine had argued Zeno's doctrine of Mary's *incorruptibility* in birthing against Jovinian. Still, we must locate similar heretics opposed to Augustinian teaching, who were somehow known to Greeks writing canon three. Historically, Greek dogmatic preoccupations with original sin and heresy can be focused on the unique condemnation of Nestorius together with Celestius and other Pelagians within the *Acta* and canons of the Council of Ephesus (431).

89. Chadwick, "Theodore," 94. Almada, *Virgo Mater*, 118–19, adds that some "Nestorian" statements of Theodore of Mopsuetia on Mary were sufficiently ambiguous to demand the dogma contra Antiochene Mariology."

90. Honorius I, *antigraphos epistole Honoriou papa Rhomes*, 2:550.16.

91. Hurley, "Born Incorruptibly," 229–30. Contra Hurley, see Aldama, *Virgo Mater*, 110–16. Aldama convincingly shows that Hurley's argument lacks force, since the formula of canon three adopts its phraseology and vocabulary surrounding *incorruptibiliter* from Pope Hormisdas, who predated Monothelitism. To explain Greek familiarity with Hormisdas' doctrine and mode of expression, see Hormisdas, *Inter ea quae* [to Emperor Justinian], in *Enchiridion*, 132–133 (no. 368): "*ut servaret partum sine corruptione, qui conceptum fecit esse sine semine*."

to Honorius' focus on Jesus taking up a nature "without sin" from Mary. Additionally, Hurley supposes that canon three on Mary's "uncorrupted virginity" addresses the issue of Jesus gestating in such a manner as to have a will that was unable to fall. However, when contextualizing canon three philologically and exegetically, Hurley proves to be unaware of Zeno to be first to coin the formula of triple virginity (traditional by Lateran 649) along with *incorrupta* and supposes that canon three contained inventive vocabulary to address a Monothelite theology.[92]

In response, Hurley failed to notice the source of Honorius' statement: "Whence, we confess one will of our Lord Jesus Christ, since clearly our nature, not our sin in that nature, was taken up (*proselephthe he hemetera physis, ouch hamartia en ekeinei*) from the divinity; namely, nature that was created before sin, not what was corrupted after sin (*meta ten parabasin ephthare*)."[93] Honorius was simply citing the *Tome of Leo* and interpreting it by means of Leo's prior Christmas sermon. Granted the existence of one-will terminology in the Fathers prior to Sophronius, Honorius was still suspicious for using a more doctrinally forthright one-will expression.[94]

Honorius may have been tempted to embrace this one-will expression *because of* Leo's I (orthodox) Christmas sermon, for it had primitively considered the entire Incarnation and work of Christ exclusively under the umbrella of the Trinitarian *voluntas*. Therein, Leo made no mention of something like Jesus' human will cooperating in the plan. Honorius might have simply added *una* to Leo's divine *voluntas* (going beyond the bounds of Leo *ad litteram*) with heresiarchal effect. Otherwise, Honorius' aforementioned citation correctly interpreted the *Tome of Leo*; namely, Mary's hypostasized nature (versus Augustine's piece of sordid flesh) was precisely of the sort of Adam and Eve before sin. Honorius and the Monothelites are entirely exempted from canon three; for, in a virtual plagiarism, Honorius mimicked the *Tome of Leo* while yet adding the newfangled dyothelite term

92. Still, while I agree with critiques of Aldama, *Virgo Mater*, 101–27, he fails to discover that Leo's Christmas sermon and *Tome of Leo* are the very sources for Honorius' epistle and statement on Mary. Hence, Hurley happens to be partially correct that the theme of human will's volatility is central to Honorius per his source Leo (and Leo's own source from Augustine, *De trinitate*, 13.18.23). Honorius exaggerated Jesus possessing the divine will *alone*, likely exploiting the exclusive mention of the *divina voluntas* within Leo's Christmas sermon.

93. Honorius I, *Antigraphos epistole Honoriou papa Rhomes*, 2:550.16–19. Cf. The (possibly original) Latin version in Honorius, *Scripta fraternitatis*, 167 n. 487: "*Unde et unam voluntatem fatemur Domini nostri Iesu Christi, quia profecto a divinitate assumpta est nostra natura, non culpa; illa profecto, quae ante peccatum creata est, non quae post praevaricationem vitiata.*"

94. Allen, "The Life and Times," 12–15.

immaculata: "for since [humanity] was conceived 'without sin'[95] from the Holy Spirit, for this reason is the birth from the holy *immaculate* virgin and *Theotokos*, whose conception in no way partook of concupiscence of nature, which had sinned."[96]

Herein, Honorius did nothing less than restate the *Tome of Leo* in clearer language: Mary's nature was never touched by original sin.[97] Mono-

---

95. Hurley, "Born Incorruptibly," 231, errs, thinking that Honorius' or Lateran 649's "*choris hamartias*" (*sine peccato*) is strictly equivalent to "sine semine" as in the Symbol of the Council of Toledo (400). Really, this expression is a variation in Greek of Honorius' Latin citation of the Chalcedonian *Tome of Leo* (*non culpa* [= *ouch hamartia*]). Naturally, Hurley is correct that the systematic theology behind canon three of Lateran 649 presumes "sine semine" as a prerequisite for Leo's, Chalcedon's, and Honorius' Marian "non culpa," "*ouch hamartia*," and the above "*choris hamartias*." Therein, *culpa/hamartia* denotes human conception in a non-concupiscential Mary and by the Holy Spirit. This likely addresses an Augustinian notion of the transmission of original sin (per *Opus Imperfectum contra Julianum* that was read among the Lateran Fathers) through coitus (Leo's *perfusio seminis*). Significantly, the originally Greek Maximus, *The Life*, 57 (2.26), fully addresses this North African doctrine: "'Blessed are you among women, and blessed is the fruit of your womb' [Luke 1:41–42] For the fruits of other women were under the curse from the original sin of Adam and Eve, and by carnal marriage and the corruption of sin they entered the world." This smacks of Zeno of Verona's theory that premature sex caused the fall, as summarized in Lukken, *Original Sin*, 56, as well as the corruption mentioned by Honorius in plagiarizing Leo. Later, a viscerally Augustinian notion of carnal transmission of sin occurs in Maximus, *The Life*, 75 (4.46): "'Behold, I was conceived in lawlessness, and in sin my mother brought me forth' [LXX Ps 50:7], for not only birth but also conception is accomplished according to the order and form of sin." The only Greek theologian of the first or second millennium (until Planudes' translation of Augustine's *De trinitate*), who thought thusly about original sin, is Maximus Confessor. Booth, "On the *Life of the Virgin*," 149–203, passed over this point, likely due to concentrating on refuting *Shoemaker's* arguments.

96. Honorius I, *Antigraphos epistole Honoriou papa Rhomes*, 2:550.22–24: "*epeide gar choris hamartia synelephthe ek pneumatow hagiou, dia touto kai choris hamartias estin ho tokos hagias achrantou parthenou kai theotokou [oudemias] metaskon peiras tes harmatesases physeos.*" Cf. Honorius, *Scripta fraternitatis*, 167 n. 487: "*Christus enim . . . since peccato conceptus de Spiritu sancto etiam absque peccato est partus de sancta et immaculata Virgine Dei genitrice, nullum experiens contagium vitiatae naturae.*"

97. Importantly, both Leo and Honorius also developed the theme of their common source, Augustine, *Sancti Aurelii Augustini De trinitate libri xv (libri xiii–xv)*, 13.18.23. Hurley, "Born Incorruptibly," 231, (without recognizing Leo's *Tome* as source [not to mention Leo's use of Augustine's *De trinitate* therein]) supposed canon three of Lateran 649 and Honorius to be debating the human will of Jesus without sin. Propitiously, Augustine affirmed that Mary conceived without seed of concupiscence (and without its infective genitalia), but her virginity functioned as a sign of her flesh conceiving in opposition to Adam and Eve. Furthermore, Augustine asserted that the human will produced in such a conception, either had no concupiscence, or diverted its natural movements in some sinless manner as first in paradise. Nonetheless, for Augustine, Mary's flesh had to be purified from *caro peccati* at the moment of being taken up by Jesus in Augustine, *De peccatorum meritis*, 2.24.38.

thelites could not have been the object of canon three of Lateran 649, for Honorius merely reworked Leo's Christmas sermon for glossing the *Tome of Leo* and its notion of *culpa*, while explicitly affirming Mary immaculate (in line with Maximus) as source of pure human nature with a perfectly graced will to provide Jesus in utero with a nature mirroring her own.[98] Given the state of scholarly research, Honorius likely committed an error not unlike that with which posterior popes saddled him:[99] Honorius failed to make a sentential judgment on behalf of *au courant* O/orthodoxy (favoring instead sloppy language and formulas common among some dyophysites prior to the 620s–630s).[100] Whatever the case, Like Honorius, both Sophronius and (Maximian) Lateran 649 coevally added the *achrantos* (while employing too the N. African *aphthoros*) to their dictum concerning Mary's triple virginity. This common Marian vocabulary, shared between Maximus and Sophronius, is hardly coincidental. Did elder Sophronius learn Augustine's doctrine from youthful Maximus, or vice versa?

98. Honorius I, *Antigraphos epistole Honoriou papa Rhomes*, 2:552.10–19:

So "sinful nature (*he amartesasa physis*) was not assumed (*ou proselephthe*)," as we said, from the same, which was "embattled by the law of the mind" (*he anti-strateuomene toi nomoi tou noos* [Rom 7:23]), rather "he came to seek and save the what was lost" (Luke 19:10), i.e., the sinful nature of humankind. For "there is another law in my members" (Rom 7:23), or a different will or something contrary that did not happen in the Savior (*thelema diaphoron e enantion ou gegonen en toi soteri*), since he was also conceived above the law of human nature. Now if it has been written: "I did not come to do my will by that of the Father who sent me" (John 6:38), and: "Not as I will, but exactly as you will, Father" (Matt 26:39) . . . the aforementioned do not belong to some other will, but because economy, i.e., what is human, was additionally understood. For these things were said for our sake, for whom it seemed good as a paradigm. (translation mine)

Honorius's first citation is from the *Tome of Leo* (*contradicting* the express phrase of Augustine), where there is exemption of Mary's nature from the least bit of taint of Augustinian concupiscence at the Annunciation. Importantly, neither Leo, nor Honorius, referred to Mary's need of her *flesh* to be purified as had Augustine. Notably, Venerable Bede later witnessed an epistle of Honorius who embraced Augustine's doctrine of original sin. Above, Honorius's principal citation is of the Augustinian *Tome of Leo* and Leo's Christmas sermon, but without the Augustinian sense of purification of Mary's "flesh" at the Annunciation. Honorius's heresy lies in his dismissal of Jesus's phrase "not as I will but as you will," as if speaking "according to economy." Honorius correctly rejected Jesus' will as susceptible to concupiscence, but bungles how human will might never even hypothetically be in conflict with divine will.

99. Price, "Monotheletism," 232.

100. See John IV, *Dominus qui dixit* [to Emperor Constantine III], in *Enchiridion*, 171 nn. 496—98; Leo II, *Regi regum* [to Emperor Constantine IV], in *Enchiridion*, 195 nn. 561–63.

Importantly, *achrantos* was never associated with triple virginity in any recorded Latin witness to North African tradition, suggesting a Greek addition (or interpretation). In the decade prior to Lateran 649, Sophronius (*scripsit* 634) promoted Mary's prepurification *ad mentem Nazianzeni*: "Nobody is blessed as you, nobody is sanctified as you; nobody is magnified as you, nobody is prepurified (*prokekathartai*) as you; nobody is beaming as you, nobody is brilliant as you!"[101] Sophronius elucidated his meaning later in the same sermon: "The Holy Spirit comes down upon you, the stainless woman (*ten amolynton*) . . . [The Spirit] is going to make you more pure (*katharoteran*) and is going to provide for you a fructiferous power."[102] Sophronius explicitly lauded Mary's purification at the Annunciation as the moment when a totally spotless nature was made somehow holier. Nevertheless, Sophronius sometimes replaced prepurification with the term "immaculate," as in his *Synodical Letter*.[103] I take this abandonment of the more traditional terminology to be significant (i.e., to extend Marian virginity beyond just the Incarnation). In favor of my hypothesis, following Maximus' death, the Sixth Ecumenical Council of Constantinople III (680–681) canonized Maximian theology and ratified Sophronius' *Synodical Letter*. Therein, Emperor Constantine IV ostensibly mixed the archaically traditional Nazianzeno-Justinian tradition of prepurification with the recent innovation (shared by Maximus and Sophronius) in his profession of faith:

> We confess . . . the only-begotten Son . . . Who emptied himself in willful humility in the womb of the spotless (*achrantou*) virgin and *Theotokos* Mary, after she was prepurified (*prokathartheises*) in *body* (*soma*) and soul. He made his dwelling via the Holy Spirit and from her holy and blameless (*amomou*) flesh (emphasis mine).[104]

Why are both terms used if *achrantos* came into fashion as an elaboration on *prokathartheisa*? We should notice—in addition to Nazianzen's unrivalled authority in the East—that Emperor Constantine IV was quite aware of history and his privilege to call ecumenical assembly. His public profession of faith was somewhat reminiscent of his illustrious imperial

101. Sophronius of Jerusalem, *In Sanctissimae Deiparae Annuntiationem* (*Patrologia Graeca,* 87.3:3248A 24).

102. Ibid. (*Patrologia Graeca,* 87.3:3273D).

103. Judging from canon three of Lateran 649 and Constantine IV's profession (not to mention Maximus, *The Life*), *achrantos* functions as the condition for being prepurified, formerly only implied by Nazianzen.

104. Constantine IV, *Antigraphos . . . pros ten hagian synodon tou apostolikou thronou . . .* , in *Concilium universale Constantinopolitanum tertium (680-681): Concilii actiones I-XVIII,* ed. R. Reidenger, Acta Conciliorum Oecumenicorum: Pars 2, 2:838.

predecessor, Justinian I, who had penned an anti-Nestorian letter of profession, appealing to Nazianzen's *Oration 38*. I note that Constantine IV shifted from Nazianzen's and Justinian's "prepurified in soul and *flesh*" to "prepurified in soul and *body*." Hence, subsequent references to "body" betrays a Justinianic variant of the formula prior attested only by Rufinus. Again, this had contained a primordial appellation of Mary as *prokathartheisa*.[105] If Justinian had never paired *achrantos* with Mary's virginity, Constantine added it, as if a gloss, to explain that—even before her elevation in grace (prepurification)—Mary had already been without stain. This is exactly one of the points made by Sophronius and Maximus in their anti-Antiochene glorification of Mary.[106] Constantine combined a more archaic participle to the *au courant* adjective of reverence. Although the archaic *prokathartheisa* continued to survive in the witnesses of Damascene and Nicephorus of Constantinople, the triple purity formula joined to *achrantos* likely sounded better to pious ears in a culture of ever-increasing Marian devotion. Subsequently, during the Palamite school's *ressourcement* into the Fathers, early synods, and ancient liturgies, Philotheus Kokkinos bore witness to a possible recovery of the older form of penning a profession of faith. As Arampatzis discovered, Kokkinos profoundly engaged materials from the Fifth and Sixth Ecumenical Council.[107] Hence, it is no surprise that his profession of faith imitates an antique model:

> The *Theotokos* ineffably conceived the Son of God . . . not through the laws of nature, but only after she was prepurified

105. Justinian I, *A Letter on the Three Chapters*, 120.

106. Hurley, "Born Incorruptibly," 226–30, explains well how original sin was at the basis of the Monothelite objection of an integral and total humanity. If human will were "changeable," then Christ's would voluble from conception. *The Life* also repeats Nazianzen's phraseology of "the purified Jesus" in Maximus, *The Life*, 93 (5.64). Using the same language, if Esbroeck's translation of this passage in *The Life* is correct, the author of *The Life* transferred Nazianzen's description of "the purified Jesus" to Mary. See Maximus (?), *Maxime le Confesseur*, 38 (4.46). Mary acts as if she were somehow making clean (sacraments). Cf. Maximus, *The Life*, 75 (4.46): "And on the fortieth day after the Nativity they went up to Jerusalem to present him before the Lord, as is the ordinance of the Law, which says that every child that opens the womb shall be called holy to the Lord (Luke 2:22–23). Now it is understood by all that *s/he* is purifying and also is purified." NB, the ancient Georgian *ad litteram* is ambiguous, for it literally translates: "It is purifying and is purified (or pure)," or "s/he is purifying and is purified" (ibid., 186 n. 1). If Esbroeck's translation is correct, then Damascene, *Sermo de dormitione beatae virginis Mariae* 2, 11.14–16–claiming that Mary sanctified the waters by touching them at baptism– is alone known by me to repeat this tradition of Mary purifying (instead of being purified by) sacraments. This fact still does not prove an early date for *The Life*, but suggests shared sources from Palestine.

107. Arampatzis, "I omologia pistis," 6–9.

and hallowed (*prokathartheisan te kai hagiastheisan*)[108] in soul
and *body* (*ten psychen kai to soma*) by the power and operation
of the all-holy Spirit [and because] a Virgin continued supernaturally incorrupt before birth and during birth and after birth,
did he become man (emphasis mine).[109]

Kokkinos appears to uncover and imitate an ancient model for his profession, or at least to have combined formulaic elements typical of post-
Justinian and Constantinian periods (NB, "body" and not "flesh"). We
should notice, while there is present the traditional North African dictum,
Kokkinos perhaps omits *achrantos*. Instead, he employed the participle
prokathartheisa. In harmony with Arampatzis' identification of the ancient
sources for this profession of faith, Kokkinos conceivably came across a
profession of faith that post-dated Justinian, but also predated the dictum
as revised by Sophronius and Maximus. I set out this plausible narrative as
the foundation upon which I plan to build a case for the existence of the
term and concept of "prepurified" among Greek monks within the environs of Rome prior to and during Lateran 649. The dispersion of Justinian's
writings and his conciliar *acta* of Constantinople II easily explains how the
doctrine of Mary's prepurification first spread into Byzantine Spain (if not
uniquely owing to Lateran 649).[110] However, for the purposes of this study,

108. The pairing of these to terms is traceable to Damascene's re-elaboration of
Mary's prepurification in his poetic hymnody. See John Damascene, *In S. Basilium, Ode
IV: Theotokion* (*Patrologia Graeca*, 96:1373C): "*ten psychen hagiastheisa, kai to soma
prokathartheisa, semne, elthontos tou hagiou epi se, panamome, Pneumatos, ten tou Yp-
sistou apeiron dynamin soi episkiasasa kathypodekso.*"

109. Philotheus Kokkinos, "I omologia pistis tou patriarchi Konstantinopouleos
Philotheou Kokkinou," 20 (lines 130–136).

110. Evidence of Pope Martin's epistolary provides no hint of a letter and *acta* of
Lateran 649 sent particularly into Spanish environs, though such were sent into many
regions, suggesting Spanish familiarity of its contents. See Hurley, "Born Incorruptibly,"
220. This is confirmed in the early post-Byzantine (viz., post–625 *quoad Iberiam*) witness of Ildephonse of Toledo, *Liber de virginitate perpetua S. Mariae*, sec. 2 (*Patrologia
Latina*, 96:61D–62A):

As he was entering, not into a house of [sexual] shame, did he take spoils. Yet,
when exiting, he enriched [the house] with integrity. Indeed, she was purified
(*erat mundata*) by the Lord. After the angel was heralding, she knew the advent
of her own founder and she marvels at the arrival of a new kind of congress. She
knows that the dweller is in herself, and in what manner he works in her depths,
though she does not completely penetrate [the reasons]. Nonetheless, though she
proves virtues of mind for her duties of service, she carries the legal penalties of
the [human] condition (*debita jura conditionis*) before the Lord; namely, what
that one presiding had ordained from heaven; she ministered in herself to the one
received [in utero]. While showing herself to her creator that she had prepared
a clean flesh and soul (*approbans se Conditori suo mundam carnem simulque*

we concentrate on the prepurified Virgin's decisive influence on exegesis of the Annunciation in England and Gaul, both of which benefitted from the writings of Venerable Bede.

The Prepurified Virgin: Theodore of Tarsus and Venerable Bede

Auspiciously, both Maximus Confessor and his disciple, Theodore of Tarsus (or Theodore of Canterbury), were present at the proceedings of Lateran 649.[111] There is no doubt that Maximus served as the theological template (if not the author) for the doctrines of the synod.[112] Circumstantially, Theodore was poised to be the conveyer of piety surrounding the prepurified Virgin in her spread into England in succeeding decades. Following Maximus' return to the East, Theodore of Tarsus remained in Rome. We can safely suppose that Theodore would have cited Maximus in his theological writings in England.[113] As we shall see, Theodore—or his Greek-speaking companions—possessed not only Maximus' Lateran Mariology, but also a Nazianzeno-Mariological source that was employed in an English biblical commentary (associated with Theodore) of the late-seventh century. Theodore undoubtedly incubated Maximus' Marian piety in the hotbed of theological activity within orthodox Rome;[114] namely, in Greek or Syrian monasteries filled with political and religious refugees from the East.[115] Maximus would have handed on Nazianzen's doctrine that Jesus, too, was

---

animam praeparasse), which were both, too, spiritual offerings carried to her fleshly son (*quae et spiritualia obsequia carnali filio detulit*). She also vested the Lord with the incorruptible and unchangeable truth of her own flesh (*Dominum suae carnis incorrupta et incommutabili veritate vestivit*).

Justinian's writings were available to Ildephonse's master, Isidore of Seville, but the citation above refers to the recent canonization of Mary's integral "incorrupt" virginity in birthing along with her "purification" at the Annunciation of "soul and *flesh*." Nevertheless, the term "*caro*" was typical of Nazianzen and Justinian, but had been changed by the time of Constantine IV (and Sophronius and Maximus?). One can suspect both Isidore passed on Justinian phraseology, though Ildephonse's own knowledge of Lateran 649 are in play. Both thematically signify that Mary was somehow the representative of Adam's cursed flesh, but yet unaffected in her all-pure nature.

111. Lapidge, "The Career of Archbishop Theodore," 22. Theodore was likely a *peritus* of Lateran 649, judging from the *acta*.

112. Ibid., 21.

113. Ibid., 24.

114. For arguments that he was a theological *peritus* at Lateran 649, see ibid., 24–25.

115. Noble, "Rome in the Seventh Century," 68–87.

purified,[116] albeit free from sin.[117] Studies on Theodore's sources—uncovering dependencies on Maximus—have provided tantalizing reasons for supposing that Theodore also knew Nazianzen's *Oration 38*.[118] Nonetheless, evidence for Theodore's dependence on the *Maximinian* doctrine of a purified Jesus and Mary remains circumstantial.

Be that as it may, Theodore (or his monastic team) brought with him a work of Pseudo-Ephraem the Syrian or "Ephrem" *graecus* to seventh century England. Ephraem's *Adversus haereticos* completely vindicates my claim that the prepurified virgin was known as a source for theological reflection in Medieval English Christianity.[119] Upon investigating the sermon, the theme of Nazianzen's purified Virgin occurs in relation to the Annunciation. Within the context of the sermon, Mary's status is one of all-holiness in line with Nazianzen. Even so, the author uniquely struggled—among relevant Greek authors—to combine the idea of Mary's "purification" at the Annunciation with unconditioned holiness, as if seeking to associate Adamite flesh with Mary for the sake of connecting Christ to Adam:

116. See Maximus, *Maximi Confessoris Quaestiones ad Thalassium*, 2:357, for a citation of Nazianzen's *Oration 38*. This theology is explicitly upheld in Maximus, *The Life*, 75 (4.46) and, again, verbatim in ibid., 93 (5.65).

117. Maximus explicitly associated (an alternate reading of) the Our Father (Luke 11:2): "*eltheto to pneuma sou to hagion eph'hemas kai katharisato hemas.*" with "purification." This activity is univocal to the epiclesis-action: "let the Spirit come" in liturgical prayer. This is significant, for Luke 1:35 serves as a clear point of intersection in Greek for coming and cleansing of the Spirit at the Annunciation. Later, Eucharistic epicleses mimic the Incarnation in language and modality of making Jesus present. For these early associations, see Leaney,"The Lucan Text of the Lord's Prayer," 103, 108–9. See Maximus, *Our Father*, 41 (lines 242–45): "Indeed, what Matthew here calls kingdom another evangelist elsewhere calls Holy Spirit: 'May your Holy Spirit come and purify us (*Eltheto sou to Pneuma to hagion kai katharisato hemas*).'" The English edition correctly locates Maximus' source in a rare, ancient MSS, as mediated through Gregory Nyssa, *The Lord's Prayer*, chap. 3 (*Patrologia Graeca*, 44:1157C; 44:1160). See Maximus, *Commentary on the The Our Father*, 122.

118. See Sevenson, "Theodore and the *Laterculus Malalianus*," 208, where she notes that this Canterbury biblical commentary explicitly appeals to Nazianzen.

119. The sermon has been dated to the fifth century. We should place its *terminus post quem* at 428, because of the following evidence: (1.) There is no known Syriac original for the sermon, though it seems based upon Ephrem the Syrian's authentic works, (2.) Initial references are reminiscent of pagan opposition to the term "Theotokos," (unknown in Ephrem's Syriac). The sermon quickly transcends Hellenistico-Christian concerns (Julian the Apostate and Diadore of Tarsus [c. 363]) and advances a Mariology of one subsistence in Jesus, (3.) The sermon is combatively anti-Nestorian and explicitly rejects Antiochene designation of Mary as a "conduit," (4.) and vigorously opposes the terminology the Antiochene school.

Now, to learn that animals in the sea are water, read the Law and hear God, who bears witness, that he ordered—along with all creatures—to produce shellfish, for these are the creeping creatures in the waters. The pearl is from among unclean (*aka-tharton*) animals: seeing that too Christ was a begotten nature, which had been befouled (*ek physeos tes rhpoueises*) and eager for purification (*katharseos*) through the visitation of God. Just as lightning to everything, so God, and just as that lightning en-lightens hidden things, in this way does Christ purify (*kathairei*) too the hidden things of nature. For this reason he also purified (*ekathere*) the Virgin and in this manner was he begotten; in or-der to show that, wherever Christ is, all purity operates (*kathar-otes energei*). He, having made a preparation, purified her in the Holy Spirit, and in this manner does the womb, having become pure (*he metra genomene kathara*), conceive. He purified her in her purity (*en hagneiai*), wherefore was he also begotten, having left her a virgin. Muscles showed that the Virgin did not con-ceive through the female member, for she unfolded the entire body via two folds, and was not producing in a fleshly manner. Muscles are accustomed to have a carelessly unformed body, and suddenly become filled with lightning. Thus, the Virgin took for herself the Word of God—with simplicity of nature—along with a whole body and not through the meddling of nature . . . She was made full of the divinity.[120]

The author initially affirmed, in abstract, tainted "human nature." Mary provided a connection between Jesus to fallen humanity. However, Ephrem qualified Mary's purification of the Annunciation-Incarnation event similar to his Byzantine confreres; namely, Mary was purified as one already in a holy state (*en hagneiai*). The author placed the motif (at least philologically) of virginity to the fore in his mind. Now, I have already shown that the entire tradition of Greek prepurification, assuming virginity as a co-natural symbol of all-holiness, leaves little doubt as to the author's intentions. The author asserted that virginal flesh—ambiguously connected to the lineage of fallen nature—is otherworldly in its peculiar disposition to bear the Incarnate Word. Hence, Mary possessed flesh that was contradictorily (or poetically) both prelapsarian and postlapsarian. Ephrem's more metaphori-cal approach differs from other Greek writers only in his mode of conveying their shared theological dictum. Significantly, this very sermon was cited in an English biblical commentary attributed to Theodore:

120. Ephrem, *Sermo adversus haereticos*, 6:153–154. NB, the purification of "body" tradition differs from the Greek of Nazianzen and Justinian but agrees with the age of Maximus Confessor. Might this homily account for the varied use of "body" and "soul"?

> Pearl (*margarita*) [Mt 13:46] in Greek, in Latin "a gem."
> Ephrem says that in the Red Sea there are pearl-oysters
> (*conc[h]ae*) swimming up from the depths on top of the sur-
> face which, when there is a thunderstorm and lightening and
> they are struck and entered by the lightning, they close up and
> conceive and produce a pearl. Thus did Mary conceive the
> Word (*sermonem*) of God.[121]

This excerpt, referencing the famous pearl, immediately demonstrates that
the Latin editor, or translator, had access to the whole sermon. I note that
the opening lines of this homily *Adversus haereticos* explicitly claims to gloss
Jesus' pearl-parable (Mt 13:46). Solving a related puzzle, the Anglo-Saxon
commentary elsewhere in the same work exegetes a variant reading of *Luke*
common to both the *Vetus Latina* and *Vulgate*.[122] Augustine would himself
have run into this problem with respect to Mary's "purifying" (*mundare*).
Employing a citation smacking of Augustine's virginal axiom, the exegete
rejected any attribution of taint to Mary, for her virginity was perpetual:

> Days of her purification (*purgationis eius*) [Luke 2:22],[123] that is
> according to the precepts of the law. Of course, she had no need
> of purification (*purificatione*), since she was a virgin before giv-
> ing birth and remained a virgin afterwards (*quae erat virgo ante
> et post partum virgo permansit*).[124]

Even if the author correctly affirmed traditional Mariology, whereby Mary
had been exempt from the Mosaic Law, the passage also employs a negative notion of "purification" (*purgatio*). We should also note that the author
utilized a reading different from the Syriac Bible available to Theodore.[125]
Both Jesus and Mary were together purified persons in the Greek and Syriac
traditions of this passage.[126] The textual difference in Latin naturally serves
to prevent this instance of purification to envelop *both* Jesus *and* Mary, since
the Latin comment makes purification uniquely feminine. Contrariwise,
the Greco-patristic tradition was tasked with explaining how *both* Jesus *and*

---

121. Theodore of Canterbury (?), *Second Commentary on the Gospels*, 402 (no. 29).
Cf. Ephrem, *Sermo adversus haereticos*, 6:153–154.

122. Hatch, "The Text of Luke 2:22," 378.

123. For history of the verse in various languages and versions, see Greenstein,
Mantegna and Painting, 125–26. In summary, the following is the case: *Vulgate: "purifi-
catio eius"*; *Vetus latina: "eius."* Cf. Greek: *"eorum"*; Syriac: *"eorum."*

124. Theodore of Canterbury (?), *Second Commentary on the Gospels*, 412 (no. 92).

125. Cf. *Syriac NT and Psalms*.

126. Hatch, "The Text of Luke 2:22," 377–78.

Mary can be univocally purified. This strikes a biblical note of discord between the Oriental and Occidental traditions of biblical purification.

The Prepurified Virgin: Anglo-Saxon England

What evidence have we for Byzantine and Syriac traditions of Mary's purification enjoying a revered place in Anglo-Saxon theology? Under the aegis of Theodore of Tarsus/Canterbury, a satisfactory instance exists: Venerable Bede (673–735) was not merely aware of Theodore, his school, and his theology, but he also explicitly incorporated the tradition of Mary's purification at the Annunciation into his works.[127] Bishop John Beverly, himself a probable trainee of Theodore, was Bede's ordaining bishop for diaconate and priesthood; a propitious connection.[128] Per Beverly (*inter alia*), Bede would have been aware of living Greek scholarship among his fellow Anglo-Saxon clergy and religious.[129] A full-fledged Greco-Latin school of theology and arts existed at this time.[130] Bede himself not only knew Latin but was also versed in Greek, among his other literate languages.[131] Finally, as if a *praeparatio synodica* to Constantinople III, Pope Agatho—in characteristically Roman fashion—promoted synodical affirmation of Lateran 649 outside the environs of Rome (as a prelude to Constantinople III).[132] In fact, a papal legate (John the Archchanter), in England at the time, promoted this papal policy leading to the Synod of Hatfield (679) to affirm Maximian theology of Lateran 649.[133] As Holder points out, Bede provided accounts of both Lateran 649 and Constantinople III (680–681)[134] in his *Greater Chronicle* at the end of his treatise *On the Reckoning of Time*.[135] These circumstances alone portend Oriental

127. Bede's liturgical calendar certainly observed the new feasts of the Annunciation and the Purification. See Clayton, *The Cult of the Virgin*, 36–37.

128. Ward, *The Venerable Bede*, 7.

129. Ibid. For Bede's references to the oral tradition of handing down Theodore's teaching see Tsorbatzoglou, "St Theodore, Archbishop of Canterbury," 82.

130. Ward, *The Venerable Bede*, 8.

131. Ibid., 15.

132. Agatho's letters citing from Lateran 649 were approved at Constantinople III as explained in Hurley, "Born Incorruptibly," 219, 222–23.

133. Hurley, "Born Incorruptibly," 222; Brett, "Theodore and Latin Canon Law," 128–29.

134. Bede called this Constantinople *II*, following the *Liber Pontificalis* in execrating Justinian and his Council for violence against the papacy. Bede's designation of Justinian as a heretic is chronicled by Brunet 2011, 20.

135. Holder, "Bede and the Christological Controversies."

influence on Bede.[136] From several of Bede's discussions on the matter of Monothelitism, as cited by Holder, it becomes abundantly clear that Bede was adequately informed about the two natures and their respective operations.[137] Bede applied dyothelitism to his scriptural exegesis.[138] Not only did Bede testify to the fact that a papal legate had left a copy of Lateran 649 at the Wearmoth-Jarrow library, but Bede even cited it in the 720s.

Going against the grain of Bede's life circumstances and education in Christology and Mariology, a curious passage in Bede seems, at first glance, to lean toward some sense of Mary's outright sinful behavior:[139]

> [Luke 1:35 Commentary:][140] The Holy Spirit, while descending into the Virgin in two modes, manifests in her the efficaciousness of his divine power, for he certainly purified (*castificavit*) the mind of that famous maiden from every uncleanness (*sorde*) of vice—as much as human fragility allowed it—so that she would be worthy for heavenly birth. Also, he created a holy and venerable *body* of our Redeemer, through his operation alone, in the womb of that maiden (i.e., there was no intervention of manly touch). He formed his own flesh from the sacrosanct, inviolate flesh of the Virgin . . . Now, the power of the Most High overshadowed the blessed Mother of God. Because the Holy Spirit, when he filled her heart, he tempered it from every ardor of carnal concupiscence, he cleansed (*emundavit*) it from temporal desires, and he *simultaneously consecrated her mind and her body* with heavenly gifts (emaphasis mine).[141]

As both Clayton and Reynolds observe, Bede's comments on the Annunciation might appear to echo Augustine, nearly implying Mary's cleansing

136. For other sources, see Siemens, "Another Book for Jarrow's Library?," 15–34.

137. See also Siemens, "A Survey of the Christology," 213–25.

138. Ibid., 215–16, argues for Bede incorporating the Syrian method of exegesis per Theodore.

139. Clayton, *The Cult of the Virgin*, 15–16:

The view that the Virgin had been purified at the Incarnation necessarily entails the belief that she had, until then, been subject to sin. As her perfection and freedom from actual sin were generally accepted from about the fourth century onwards, her purification at the Incarnation could only be from original sin. The question . . . had been explicitly raised by Augustine in the Pelagian controversy. For Augustine, original sin was indissolubly bound up with the *concupiscentia carnalis* accompanying all human generation and it is clear that he believed Mary to have been born in it, although protected by grace against its consequences.

140. Holder, "Bede and the Christological Controversies," suspects that Bede, *Homily 1 in Adventu*, 3.97, reflected dyothelite theology from Lateran 649.

141. Bede, *Homily 1 in Adventu*, 3.144–46, 151–55.

(*mundare*)[142] of sinfulness at the Annunciation.[143] Bede was explicitly aware of Pelagian controversies surrounding Augustine and original sin, for he knew of an official Epistle from Pope Honorius to the Irish, and his successor John IV, who presumably continued Honorius' policy of requiring the observance of Roman Easter and the doctrine of original sin. Pope John employed Psalm 50 as a proof text for transmission of original sin to a fetus.[144] After the lines above, Bede immediately cites Psalm 50 with respect to Jesus' seedless conception underlining the traditional formula that Jesus alone "*sine iniquitate conceptus est.*"

In response, Bede's overall theological context—as we saw above—need not make this exegesis a case of dependence on Augustine. The critical edition of Bede's *homiletica* indeed contains citations of Augustine's *Contra Julianum* and *De trinitate*, making Clayton's and Reynolds' suspicions plausible. Oppositely, we should note that the beginning of the homily, in support of Holder, smacks eerily of Lateran 649 by referring to Mary the virgin as "*incorrupta genetrix.*"[145] Secondly, albeit a peripheral reading of the singular citation above might suggest Mary as lustful, the beginning of the very same sermon claims that she was devoid of the normal feminine "condition" and Mary had (prior to the Annunciation) already flown from terrestrial things and dedicated herself to celestial things and to virginity.[146] If we take the prima facie interpretation of the passage, Bede looks to be cutting and pasting irreconcilable traditions into sermoncinal pabulum. As a prelude to his exegesis of Luke 1:35 in the citation above, Bede began this sermon asserting Mary's virtue and the angelic salutation and prophecy as something to strengthen human fragility for her mission. Thus, Mary's

---

142. Cf. Bede, *In Lucae Evangelium Expositio*, 1.2.1 (*Patrologia Latina*, 92:341A–D). Bede understood this verb in relation to the purification of Mary in the Temple. In league with Origen (to whom Bede had access) and the Anglo-Saxon biblical commentaries, Bede noted that Mary had nothing to be cleansed (*mundanda*), for she had been spared seed, blood, and opening of the womb in birthing.

143. Reynolds, *Gateway to Heaven*, 348.

144. Bede, *The Ecclesiastical History*, 2.19:

Pope Honorius also wrote to the Irish, whom he learned to be in error about the observance of Easter, as I mentioned earlier . . . Similarly John [IV] . . . successor to Honorius [writes:] "We learn also that the pernicious Pelagian heresy has once again revived among you . . . No one can be sinless save the one mediator between God and man . . . who was conceived and born without sin. All other men are born in original sin and bear unmistakable evidence of Adam's fall, even when they are innocent of actual sin. For, as the prophet says, 'Behold, I was shapen in iniquity, and in sin did my mother conceive me.'"

145. Bede, *Homily 1 in Adventu*, 3.37.

146. Ibid., 3.66–69.

holy life receives only a boost at the Annunciation.[147] This initial part of the sermon is followed by a Chalcedonian confession of Jesus as *in duobus naturis persona*.[148] More importantly, when discussing the Annunciation in the above citation, nearly every theme (e.g., human fragility) reflects the prior thematic exegesis of John Cassian.[149] Though Cassian's Mary is more clearly sinless upon a prima facie reading than that of Bede, Cassian more forcefully refers to human *infirmitas* in both fallen and neutral senses. Christ supplied grace to both kinds of human infirmity; namely, to sinful humanity and to humanity, *qua* limited in power. Although Cassian's exegesis parallels Bede in propitious ways, I am forced to admit that their overlap of vocabulary is minimal. This causes me to wonder if Cassian may have been mediated through another Latin Father. Whatever the case, there is one happy coincidence between Cassian and Bede in that they refer to the Annunciation moment as a double action of spirit sanctifying *body* and soul.[150] Cassian departed from the Greek the notion of "prepurification in soul and *body*," or Damascene's "purification in soul and sanctification in body," opting for "*sanctificans interiora*" and "*spirans potentiam . . . humanae . . . naturae*." Bede's clear preference for a classically Greek mode of expressing Mary's experience of double sanctification of mind and *body* (not Augustine's *caro*). This strongly argues for him mixing (1.) Augustinian theology with (2.) Cassian's and Ephrem's notion of weak human nature, and (3.) the Greek notion of prepurification at the Annunciation. When we combine this explanation with strong circumstantial evidence linking England and Bede to Ephrem *graecus* and to the prepurified virgin mentioned thereby, then I consider my exegesis capable of saving Bede's homily from being an amalgamation of contradictory statements, while able to exegete it with relative ease. After all, Bedan Mariology is otherwise entirely devoid of attribution of sin and taint to Mary.

Additionally, as Holder has satisfactorily demonstrated, Bede was disproportionately interested in Monotheletism for someone who had never even known a Monothelite. Bede made efforts to include the teaching of Lateran 649 into his biblical exegesis. In these circumstances, why would he be tempted assume that Bede proffers a more lusty interpretation of Luke 1:35 than even Augustine, especially in a sermon that already asserted dyothelite themes (likely from Lateran 649)? What is more, how could Bede dare to pen such an exegesis, when he had come across the canon and anathema

147. Ibid., 3.72–78.
148. Ibid., 3.97.
149. Cassian, *De Incarnatione*, 2.2.
150. Ibid.

declaring Mary *"immaculate"* within the Latin version of Lateran 649? Even Bede's discussion of original sin in England is colored with the mention of the Monothelite personality of Honorius. Strangely, though a staunch dyothelite, Bede portrayed the Pope Honorius (a factual and canonically condemned Monothelite) as if he were of a noble and honorable character.[151] Bede's putatively orthodox Honorius coincides neatly with Maximus Confessor's own propaganda on behalf of Honorius, excusing him from heresy.[152] Theodore of Tarsus surely absorbed this narrative and, thereafter, propagated it in England until Bede's day. Bede promoted this pro-papal account of Honorius in England (720s), well after Honorius' condemnation at Constantinople III (680–681) and Trullo (691).[153]

Next, in his treatment of the Annunciation, Bede harmonized with Byzantine medical literature—a distinct feature of Theodore of Tarsus' contribution to England—so that the purification involved the Virgin's mind (not her flesh as in Augustine).[154] Also, Bede emphasized that prepurification served to elevate Mary as a subject to birth worthily, not to cleanse sinful flesh as in Augustine. As in Byzantine literature, carnal desire was presumably causative of fecundity (as with coeval Damascene).[155] Bede provided an alternative explanation, in that the Holy Spirit substituted for the physical passions that normally lead to fertility and conception. If the Holy Spirit had not filled her mind at conception, Mary would have required passionate thoughts to pursue a natural modality of conception.[156]

---

151. This should be applied with due caution, as in Price "Monotheletism," 221–32.

152. Maximus was equally promoting a narrative of the O/orthodoxy of Heraclius, as plausibly explained in Alexakis, "Before the Lateran Council of 649," 99–101.

153. Bede accepted and accurately (albeit briefly) described Pope Agatho and his dyotheletism at Constantinople III, but Bede rejected Trullo and named Justininian II as a heretic in the image of Justinian I. For Bede's knowledge of the Council, see Brunet, *La ricezione del Concilio Quinisesto*, 21–23, 26.

154. Brock, "St Theodore of Canterbury," 431–38; Siemens, "A Survey of the Christology," 215–16, 220–22.

155. See John Damascene, *Ekdosis akribes tes orthodoksou pisteos*, 46.19–25. A virgin's fertility could only be affirmed on the basis of her first menses, which was considered a blessing *insofar as* it was a sign of childbearing potency (in Byzantine gynecology). See George, *Bodies of Knowledge*, 91–92. Mary had just passed the traditional legal age of marriage for girls in Byzantine legislation (i.e., twelve years old). See Prinzing, "Observations on the Legal Status of Children," 34. Byzantine medical prejudice often supposed any woman who did not have emotional desires for a man to be less fecund. For this reason, feminine aphrodisiacs became a practical necessity for ensuring conception. Mary's lack of concupiscence would commonly be taken to decrease her fecundity. It necessitated divine intervention. For these popular and professional medical beliefs, see Congourdeau, "Les variations," 51; George, *Bodies of Knowledge*, 87–91.

156. Cf. Augustine, *De trinitate*, 13.18.23. Augustine was familiar with the lust

Lastly, the highly traditional Bede used a word to signify Mary's purification atypical of Augustinian exegesis on the Annunciation.[157] *Castificare* specifically regards the passions associated with sexual reproduction.[158] This is the same motif in Greek reception of Nazianzen's *Oration 38*, as elaborated upon by Bede's contemporary, Damascene.[159] Significantly, patristico-Byzantine creedal formulas refer to Mary's purification as happening "in soul and body." This entirely Greek mode of expression auspiciously upholds a peculiarly Greek patristic tradition, not excluding Ephrem *graecus*. Bede knew Greek and had access to the wisdom of Theodore's school. Plausibly, Bede might have synthesized Augustinian *mundare* and Byzantine *castificare* in deference to the Nazianzeno-originate exegesis of Mary's purification at the Annunciation. For his part, Augustine never parsed Mary's purification into "soul and body." Contrariwise, Bede parallels Damascene in bifurcating the purification of body and soul to an action of the Spirit. Bede's exegesis in nowise declared Mary's purification to be "from uncleanness" and "from temporal desires," but plausibly to elevate human nature *qua* fragile and limited in its capacity.

Contrariwise, if we try to make a purely Augustinian read of Bede's somewhat cryptic exegesis, then Mary underwent a kind of cleansing from recurrent mental lust of the flesh; a bizarre position for Bede's time and place and wholly beyond Augustine's view. Did Bede really mean to say that Mary was ethically unclean and, thereafter, cleansed of lustful thought . . . especially given the fact that Mary was distraught by the Angel Gabriel, for she "did not know man" (Luke 1:34)? No, more plausibly, she was protectively fortified in virtue for the realization of her vocation, undergoing none of the passions associated with conception and sexual intercourse.

tradition here (and elsewhere), but his solution is that "she conceives by faith," not by purification. Whatever the complementarity, two traditions sources are at work. Ambrose also proposed faith in league with Mary's "desire" as the central them of the Annunciation per Corsato, "La mariologia," 296–301.

157. Bede had access to Isidore of Seville. The Visigothic tradition might have adopted the (pre-)purified Virgin either in Byzantine Spain (*terminus ante quem* c. 625), or Lateran 649. NB, Bede's Mariology has been studied in-depth and found conservatively traditional in form and content. See Gambero, *Mary in the Middle Ages*, 36.

158. Now, Holder, "Bede and the Christological Controversies," argues for the more likely influence of Lateran 649 on Bede's *Homily 1 in Adventu*. Happy to agree with Holder, I also emphasize that Holder produces evidence of Bede knowing, to whatever extent, the content of the *Tome of Leo*, though not Leo I's *In Nativitate Domini: Sermo 2*, sec. 3. Nonetheless, Bede's interpretation fits perfectly with my reference to Leo's reception of the medical notion of fecund passion as a condition for conception in women.

159. Damascene likely built upon the foundation of Sophronius and Maximus, both of whom manifested interest in medicine. See Booth, *Crisis of Empire*, 62–66; Lapidge, "The Career of Archbishop Theodore," 17–18.

Still, the forceful objection remains, as noted above, that Bede cited Ps 50 to speak of Jesus' conception at the Annunciation as a case of the only person born without iniquity and delict.[160] In response, Bede merely lifted this exegesis wholesale from Pope John IV, whom he cited in his *Ecclesiastical History*. The object of this statement is not Mary in particular, but Pelagians in Ireland. Still, if we were systematically to apply this exegesis of Ps 50 to Mary we do run into a contradiction between Augustinian original sin theory and the prepurified Mary of the Annunciation. I don't think that Bede provided a systematic solution to *how* Mary could have been exempt from this law of sin, he only cited Theodore's tradition that she could have no taint of sin whatsoever. In fact, coeval Damascene similarly found himself explicitly struggling with Mary's prepurification, the North African tradition of sexually transmitted sin (mediated through Maximus et al.) and Mary' conception. Joachim and Anna's coitus ought ordinarily to have subjected Mary's conception to passion and infuse sin.[161] Damascene's solution (at the onset of Byzantine preoccupations surrounding the conception of Mary) was to suppose that Joachim had "all-pure sperm" and that Anna (similar to Mary) possessed a womb "wider than heaven" (implying the capacity to receive some measure of the Spirit in utero as did Mary at Luke 1:35). In Bede's case, liturgical and popular interest in Mary's conception had not yet arisen. Only in the next century did the feast of Mary's conception appear in Western Europe. In my interpretation, Bede simply juxtaposed the traditional N. African theory of sexual transmission in concupiscence with Theodore's and his school's doctrine of Mary's inexplicable exemption from taint of sin and lust.

The Prepurified Virgin: Paschasius Radbertus

In general, Bede exercised literary influence upon Paschasius Radbertus (c. 790–865), who was finally able to solve the riddle of how to speak about Mary's flesh in a postlapsarian world. As Clayton chronicles, Paschasius puzzles scholars: He explicitly exempted Mary in utero from Augustinian

---

160. Bede, *Homily 1 in Adventu*, 3.160–65:

Omnes quippe homines in iniquitatibus concipimus et in delictis nascimur [Ps 50:7]; quotquot autem donante Deo ad vitam praeordinati sumus aeternam ex aqua et spiritu sancto renascimur. Solus vero redemptor noster pro nobis incarnari dignatus est mox sanctus natus est quia sine iniquitate conceptus est.

161. John Damascene, *Sermo in Nativitatem BVM*, sec. 2.11–14: "*Hypochreos humin esti pas he physis, di'humon gar prosegage doron toi ktistei doron apanton hyperpheresteron . . . O osphys tou Ioakeim pammakariste, eks hes kateblethe sperma panamomon.*"

original sin, while simultaneously holding the doctrine of Mary's purification at the Annunciation.[162] How do these two doctrines make the slightest bit of sense whatsoever when placed side-by-side in the life of Mary?
Scholars have attempted to solve Paschasius' unseemly inconsistency by
supposing (with a dearth of options) that the purification of the Annunciation has to do with the otherwise "unclean" birthing process and ritual
impurity of Mary in Luke 2:22. Yet, Clayton is wisely cautious and suggests
that Paschasius was simply unconcerned with this apparent inconsistency
between being born without original sin and purification at the Annunciation. In reality, Paschasius simply built on the theological foundations
undergirding the Byzantine (along with Bede's) notion of purification at
the Annunciation to their logical conclusion contra Augustine. Paschasius'
use of purification at the Annunciation, as Reynolds judiciously describes,
might readily be taken to mean 'that her flesh had not been infused with
the extraordinary grace necessary to conceive a divine son.'[163] However, per
our prevenient investigation of prepurification, Paschasius' witness to the
feast of Mary's conception simply brings us full circle, back to Augustine's
handling of Nazianzen's Mary at the Annunciation. Paschasius additionally
had to confront exaggeratedly Augustinian claims that *Jesus' and* Mary's
flesh had been tainted:

> I beseech, let these infamous men cease to speak in such a way
> that [Jesus] was born as other infants are born, since the Virgin,
> Mother of God, did not bear him out of the origin of the first
> prevarication, in order to be reborn, but from the Holy Spirit . . .
> without pain and groaning, without annoyance and bitterness,
> without sorrow and affliction, since all these are most justly the
> damned and vindictive retributions of flesh in the first origin.
> What is more, blessed Mary—although she was born and pro-
> created *from* "flesh of sin" (*caro peccati*)—as much as you wish
> her to be "flesh of sin," she—from that point and [conceptive]
> moment—was not when she is called "blessed" by the angel
> (since there was a prevenient grace of the Holy Spirit, forgone
> by all other women). [Luke] says: "The Holy Spirit will come
> upon you, and the power of the Most High will overshadow
> you" (Luke 1:35). If she was not sanctified (*sanctificata*) and
> cleansed (*emundata*) in some other way through the same Holy
> Spirit, in what way is his flesh not "flesh of sin"? If, too, his flesh
> comes from the mass of the first prevarication, in what manner

162. Clayton, *The Cult of the Virgin*, 20–22.
163. Reynolds, *Gateway to Heaven*, 349 n. 85.

was Christ, the Word, flesh without sin? Did he assume flesh from "flesh of sin"?

Unless first the Word overshadowed her (because he was made flesh), whom did the Holy Spirit overcome and the power of the Most High totally possess? Wherefore, truly, the flesh was not at that same instant "flesh of sin," in her whom God completely diffused himself and the Word (who was made flesh without sin) came to us. By right, not alone, did he retain neither the law of vitiated nature in birthing, nor the law of first origin (which women possessed), if indeed his mother had conserved the commandment of all things, [as if] an Eve in paradise. Sometime prior, in a manner unlike the Holy Spirit filling her [at the Annunciation], she was without original sin, whose glorious birth is especially lauded . . . in every Church.[164] Yet, indeed, if she were not blessed and glorious, her feast would not be celebrated everywhere by all. Yet, because it is observed so solemnly, it is established from the authority of the Church that in no ways, at the time when she was born, did she come under transgressions, and neither –when she was sanctified in utero– did she contract (*contraxit*) original sin.[165]

Paschasius skillfully exploited the ambiguities behind Augustine's modes of expression, when he had referred to sin in reference to Mary. Whereas Augustine left his reader in doubt as to whether Mary's flesh was explicitly the product of concupiscence *and* mired in concupiscence, Paschasius adroitly developed a *lectio difficilior* without doing violence either to Augustine's *verba* or to Byzantine tradition of prepurification of Mary at the Annunciation. Paschasius reproduced the vocabulary and theology of the *Contra Julianum*, but he also exploited the fact that elsewhere Augustine had inconsistently supposed Mary to have never suffered actual sin (a natural product of flesh subjected to concupiscence). As we already saw in Augustine, so had Paschasius seen; namely, that Augustine designated Mary as one conceiving by faith and in meritorious obedience. How was any assertion of Mary's merit possible, if she had been produced from an act of concupiscence? If Paschasius' *mundata* might, at first, be reminiscent of Augustine, Paschasius immediately clarified it to mean that Mary should have been *sanctificata*. His use of this term is propitious. After all, Paschasius cited Cassian's *De Incarnatione* multiply in this very same work. Of course, we immediately recall that Cassian's version of the Annunciation, where he

164. This feast was known in England at this time per Clayton, *The Cult of the Virgin*, 39–40.

165. Paschasius Radbertus, *Paschasii Radberti De partu virginis*, 1.156–84.

seems to interpret Greek prepurification to mean "*sanctificans interiora.*" Consequently, the Paschasian synthesis marked the culmination of doctrine on Mary's prepurification in the West before its mysterious disappearance from Latindom thereafter. Using his understanding of Mary's purification in relation to the Annunciation, Paschasius concluded the section of his sermon, above, by theologically asserting that: "She was immune from all original sin."[166] Mary's sanctification at her conception, as asserted above, must have only differed in mode (*qua* fetus) but not in kind (viz., a species of Spirit's *mundare* or *sanctificare*).

Conclusions

In the first section of our disquisition we exhausted Gregory Nazianzen's doctrine of prepurification. We saw that, among possible meanings, it clearly designated a privilege of grace and glory occurring at Mary's Annunciation. Furthermore, we saw that Christ's human nature underwent a similar process of purification. Lastly we saw that Gregory associated Marian prepurification with an entirely Greek mode of expression; namely, "being prepurified in soul and flesh." We also saw strong arguments for supposing that Augustine had some familiarity with Nazianzen's doctrine. Still, for a possible variety of reasons, Nazianzen's distinctions did not make the necessary impact on Augustine to dissuade him from associating Mary with "*caro peccati.*" Although Augustine's illustrious successor, Leo the Great, ignored Augustinian references to the purification of a parcel of *sordid* flesh at the Annunciation, he nonetheless held a robust notion of original sin that was partly dependent on Augustine, albeit widening the use of *culpa* beyond Augustine's restrictive language. Leo also benefitted from Cassian's *De Incarnatione*, in that Leo's Christmas sermon and *Tome of Leo* propitiously refer to Mary's Annunciation in terms that suppose the entire person of Mary (versus Augustine's parcel of Mary's flesh in utero) to transmit to Christ nothing of the fault of Adam. Later, the Roman See returned to both Augustine's and Leo's notions of original sin, as well as Leo's description of Mary's flesh, in the works of the Monothelite Pope Honorius. On one hand, Sophronius of Jerusalem, Maximus the Confessor, and Lateran 649 all affirmed Honorius' title for Mary. On the other hand, they rejected his explicit confession of one will in the dyophysite Christ. Canon three of Lateran 649 embraced a traditional N. African mode of referring to Mary's triple virginity, but augmented this expression with Mary's new title: "immaculate," replacing the more traditional and restrictive term: "prepurified."

166. Ibid., 1.200.

Mary's prepurification was consistently taken to signify in the East that Mary's personhood was devoid of the effects of normal sexual reproduction in the postlapsarian world, but never directly addressed her moment of conception so as to clarify the modality of her absolute purity. Only in the time of John Damascene had reflection on Mary's conception reached a point where Byzantines needed to explain Mary's privilege in terms of the quality of sperm and the kind of womb that produced Mary's all-pure flesh. Contrariwise, in the West, Mary's prepurification was handed on in a Latin translation of Ephrem *graecus* and by other means, but the interplay between Mary's privilege and the robust western doctrine of original sin failed to become a subject of systematic reflection until—like the East (c. 750)—the feast of Mary's conception was introduced into the West (c. 850). Paschasius's solution addressed entirely Augustinian concerns, instead of more modest N. African and Greek descriptions of passionate coitus as the vehicle for passing on original sin in utero in order to justify Ps 50. The fact is that both East and West nonetheless addressed their respective notions of sin in utero and managed to work out entirely separate solutions within a century of one another in favor of Mary's all-holiness. From this, we can infer that, by then, there was universal interest in finding a modality by which Mary's privilege of prepurification or absolute holiness could be justified in two loose theological systems which were equally concerned with sexuality as a conduit of sin. In effect, I would propose, centuries prior to the maculist and immaculatist debates in the Latin West, a Medieval Latin and Greek proposal for justifying Mary's immaculate conception had already proffered solutions to the puzzle.

Bibliography

Aldama, J. A. *Virgo Mater: Estudios de telogia patristica*. Biblioteca Teologica Granadina 7. Madris: Heroes, S.A., 1963.

Alexakis, Alexander. "Before the Lateran Council of 649: The Last Days of Herakleios the Emperor and Monotheletism." *Annuarium Historiae Conciliorum* 27/28 (1995–96) 93–101.

———. *Codex Parisinus Graecus 1115 and Its Archetype*. Dumbarton Oaks Studies 34. Washington, DC: Dumbarton Oaks, 1996.

Allen, Pauline. "The Life and Times of Maximus the Confessor." In *The Oxford Handbook of Maximus the Confessor*, edited by Pauline Allen and Neil Bronwen, 3–18. New York: Oxford University Press, 2002.

Ambrose. *Apologia David altera*. Edited by Carolus Schenkl. Corpus Scriptorum Ecclesiastorum Latinorum 32.2. Vienna: F. Tempsky, 1897.

———. *Explanatio Psalmorum XI: Explanatio psalmi 37*. Edited by Michael Petschenig. Corpus Scriptorum Ecclesiasticorum Latinorum 64. Vienna, F. Tempsky, 1897.

————. *Exposition on the Gospel according to Luke.* Edited by Gabriel Tissot. Sources Chrétiennes 45.1. Paris: Cerf, 1956.

Arampatzis, Christos. "I omologia pistis tou patriarchi Konstantinopouleos Philotheou Kokkinou." *Epistimoniki Epetirida Theologikis Scholis* 10 (2000) 1–33.

Athanasius of Alexandria. *Expositio In Psalmos.* In *Patrologia Graeca,* edited by J.-P. Migne, 27:295–373. Paris: Migne, 1857.

Aubert, Jean-Jacques. "Commerce." In *The Cambridge Companion to Roman Law,* edited by David Johnston, 213–45. Cambridge: Cambridge University Press, 2015.

Augustine. *Augustinus: Sermones Selecti.* Edited by Clemens Weidman. Corpus Scriptorum Ecclesiasticorum Latinorum 101. Berlin: Gruyter, 2015.

————. *Contra Julianum, Haeresis Pelagianae defensorem, libri sex.* In *Patrologiae Latina,* edited by Jacques-Paul Migne, 44:641–874. Cols. Paris: Migne, 1866.

————. *Opus Imperfectum contra Julianum,* 4.22. In *Patrologiae Latina,* 45:1417. Paris: Migne, 1866.

————. *De natura et gratia.* Vol. 1. In *Sancti Aureli Augustini opera* 8. Edited by Carolus Urba and Ioseph Zycha. Corpus Scriptorum Ecclesiasticorum Latinorum 60. Vienna: F. Tempsky, 1913.

————. *De peccatorum meritis et remissione et de patismo parvulorum ad marcellinum libri tres.* In *Sancti Aurelii Augustini opera* 1. Edited by Carlus Urba and Ioseph Zycha. Corpus Scriptorum Ecclesiastorum Latinorum 60.8. Vienna: F. Tempsky, 1913.

————. *Sancti Aurelii Augustini De trinitate libri xv (libri xiii–xv).* Corpus Christianorum 50. Aurelii Augustini Opera 16.2. Edited by William Mountain. Turhout: Brepols, 1968.

————. *Sermo ad catechumenos de symbolo.* Edited by R. Vander Plaetse. Corpus Christianorum: Series Latina 46. Turnhout: Brepols, 1969.

————. *Sermones de novo testament.* Edited by Pierre-Patrick Verbraken et al. Corpus Christianorum: Series Latina 41A.a. Turnhout: Brepols, 2008.

Basil, *De baptismo libri duo.* In *Patrologia Graeca,* 31:1536.

Beatrice, Pier Franco. *The Transmission of Sin: Augustine and the Pre-Augustinian Sources.* Oxford: Oxford University Press, 2013.

Bede. *Bedae Venerabilis Opera: Pars 3.* Vol. 4. Edited by D. Hurst. Corpus Christianorum: Series Latina 122. Turhout: Brepols, 1955.

————. *The Ecclesiastical History of the English People.* Translated by E. McClure and R. Collins. Oxford World Classics. New York: Oxford University Press, 1969.

Beeley, Christopher. "The Early Christological Controversy: Apollinarius, Diodore, and Gregory Nazianzen." *Vigiliae Christianae* 65 (2011) 1–32.

Berger, Adolf. *Encyclopedic Dictionary of Roman Law.* Transactions of the American Philosophical Society Held at Philadelphia For Promoting Useful Knowledge: New Series 43.2. Philadelphia: The American Philosophical Society, 1953.

Bischoff, Bernhard, and Michael Lapidge, eds. *Biblical Commentaries from the School of Theodore and Hadrian.* Cambridge Studies in Anglo-Saxon England 10. New York: Cambridge University Press, 1994.

Bonaiuti, Ernesto, and Giorgio La Piana. "The Genesis of St Augustine's idea of Original Sin." *The Harvard Theological Review* 10 (1917) 159–75.

Booth, Phil. *Crisis of Empire: Doctrine and Dissent at the End of Late Antiquity.* Los Angeles: University of California Press, 2014.

———. "A New Date-List of the Works of Maximus the Confessor." In *The Oxford Handbook of Maximus the Confessor*, edited by Marek Jankowiak and Phil Booth, 149–203. Oxford: Oxford University Press, 2015.

———. "On the *Life of the Virgin* Attributed to Maximus Confessor." *The Journal of Theological Studies* 66 (2015) 149–203.

Börjesson, Johannes. "Maximus the Confessor's Knowledge of Augustine: An Exploration of Evidence Derived from the *Acta* of the Lateran Council of 649." *Studia Patristica* 68 (2013) 325–36.

Brett, Martin. "Theodore and Latin Canon Law." In *Archbishop Theodore: Commemorative Studies on His Life and Influence*, edited by Michael Lapidge, 120–40. Cambridge: Cambridge University Press, 1995.

Brock, Sebastian. "St Theodore of Canterbury, the Canterbury School and the Christian East." *The Heythrop Journal* 36 (1995) 431–38.

Brunet, Ester. *La ricezione del Concilio Quinisesto (691–692) nelle fonti occidentali (VII–IX sec.): diritto–arte–teologia*. Autour de Byzance 2. Paris: Centre d'Études Byzantines, Néo-Helléniques et Sud-Est Européennes, 2011.

Buckland, William. *The Main Institution of Roman Private Law*. New York: Cambridge University Press, 1931.

Buckland, William, and Peter Stein. *A Text-Book of Roman Law from Augustus to Justinian*. 3rd ed. Cambridge: Cambridge University Press, 1968.

Bucur, Bogdan. "Sinai, Zion, and Tabor: An Entry into the Christian Bible." *Journal of Theological Interpretation* 4 (2010) 33–52.

Calabuig, Ignazio. "The Liturgical Cult of Mary in the East and West." In *Handbook for Liturgical Studies*, edited by A. Chapungco, 5:219–98. Collegeville, MN: Pueblo, 2000.

Candal, Manuel. "La Virgen Santísima 'prepurificada' en su Anunciación." *Orientalia Christiana Periodica* 31 (1965) 241–76.

Cavadini, John, Marianne Djuth, et al. *Augustine through the Ages: An Encyclopedia*. Grand Rapids: Eerdmans, 1999.

Chadwick, Henry. "Theodore, the English Church and the Monothelete Controversy." In *Archbishop Theodore: Commemorative Studies on His Life and Influence*, edited by Michael Lapidge, 88–95. Cambridge: Cambridge University Press, 1995.

Clayton, Mary. *The Cult of the Virgin in Anglo-Saxon England*. Cambridge Studies in Anglo-Saxon England 2. New York: Cambridge University Press, 2002.

Congourdeau, Marie-Hélène. *L'embryon et son âme dans les sources grecques (vie siècle av. J.-C.-ve siècle apr. J.-C.)*. Collège de France—Centre de Recherche d'Histoire et Civilisation de Byzance. Monographies 26. Paris: Association des amis du Centre d'histoire et civilisation de Byzance, 2007.

———. "Les variations du désir d'enfant à Byzance." In *Becoming Byzantine: Children and Childhood in Byzantium*, edited by Papaconstantinou, Arietta and Alice-Mary Talbot, 35–64. Washington, DC: Dumbarton Oaks Research Library, 2009.

Constas, Nicholas. *Proclus of Constantinople and the Cult of the Virgin in Late Antiquity: Homilies 1–5*. Leiden: Brill, 2003.

Corsaro, Celestino. "La mariologia in Ambrogio di Milano." *Theotokos* 11 (2003) 291–336.

Cunningham, Mary. "'The Use of the *Protevangelion of James* in Eighth-Century Homilies on the Mother of God." In *The Cult of the Mother of God in Byzantium:*

Texts and Images, edited by Leslie Brubaker and Mary Cunningham, 163–78. Burlington, VT: Ashgate, 2011.

Cyril of Alexandria. *De adoratione e cultu in spiritu et veritate.* In *Patrologia Graeca*, 68:1008.

———. *In Psalmum L.* In *Patrologia Graeca*, 69:1089.

Daley, Brian. "Making a Human Will Divine." In *Orthodox Readings of Augustine*, ed.ited by Aristotle Papanikolaou and George Demacopoulos, 101–26. Crestwood, NY: St. Vladimir's Seminary Press, 2008.

Denzinger, Heinrich, Peter Hünermann, and Robert Fastiggi, eds. *Enchiridion symbolorum definitionum et declarationum de rebus fidei et morum (Compendium of Creeds, Definitions, and Declarations on Matters of Faith and Morals: Latin-English).* Translated by Robert Fastiggi. 43rd ed. San Francisco: Ignatius, 2012.

Dekkers, Eligius. "Les traduction grecques des éscrits patristiques latins." *Sacris Erudiri* 5 (1953) 207–12.

Dodaro, Robert. "Between the Two Cities: Political Action in Augustine of Hippo." In *Augustine and Politics*, edited by John Doody et al., 99–116. New York: Lexington, 2005.

D'Onofrio, Giulio. *History of Theology in the Middle Ages.* Edited by Angelo Di Berardino and Basil Studer. Translated by Matthew O'Connell. Collegeville, MN: Liturgical, 2008.

Ephrem. *Hosiou Ephraim tou Syrou erga.* Vol. 6. Edited by Konstantinos Phrantzoles. Thessaloniki: To Perivoli tis Panagias, 1995.

Fehlner, Peter. "The Predestination of the Virgin Mother and Her Immaculate Conception." In *Mariology: A Guide for Priests, Deacons, Seminarians, and Consecrated Persons*, edited by Mark Miravalle, 213–76. Goleta, CA: Queenship, 2007.

Frier, Bruce. *Landlords and Tenants in Imperial Rome.* Princeton: Princeton University Press, 1980.

Gambero, Luigi. *Mary in the Middle Ages.* Translated by Thomas Buffer. San Francisco: Ignatius, 2005.

George, Eugenia. *Bodies of Knowledge: the Medicalization of Reproduction in Greece.* Nashville: Vanderbilt University Press, 2008.

Giuseppe Alberigo, and Norman Tanner, eds. *Decrees of the Ecumenical Councils.* Vol. 1. Washington, DC: Sheed & Ward, 1990.

Greenstein, Jack. *Mantegna and Painting as Historical* Narrative. Chicago: University of Chicago Press, 1992.

Gregory Nazianzen. *De Testamentis et adventu Christi.* In *Patrologia Graeca* 37:455–62.

———. *The Festal Orations: Saint Gregory Nazianzenus.* Translated by Brian Daley. Popular Patristics Series 36. Crestwood, NY: St. Vladimir's Seminary Press, 2008.

———. *Gregor von Nazianz: Die fünf theologischen Reden.* Edited by Joseph Barbel. Düsseldorf: Verlag, 1963.

———. *On God and Christ: The Five Theological Orations and the Two Letters to Cledonius.* In *On God and Christ: The Five Theological Orations and Two Letters to Cledonius.* Translated by Frederick Williams. Popular Patristics Series 22. Crestwood, NY: St. Vladimir's Seminary Press, 2002.

Gregory Nyssa. *The Lord's Prayer*, chap. 3. In *Patrologia Graeca*, 44:1157C; 44:1160.

Hatch, J. Hugh. "The Text of Luke 2:22." *The Harvard Theological Review* 14 (1921) 377–81

Holder, Arthur. "Bede and the Christological Controversies." 50th International Congress on Medieval Studies, May 14–17, 2015. Kalamazoo, MI: Medieval Institute. Forthcoming.

Humfress, Caroline. "Patristic Sources." In *The Cambridge Companion to Roman Law*, edited by D. Johnston, 97–118. Cambridge: Cambridge University Press, 2015.

Ildephonse of Toledo. *Liber de virginitate perpetua S. Mariae*, sec. 2. In *Patrologia Latina*, 96:61D–62A.

John Cassian. *De Incarnatione Domini contra Nestorium*. In *Iohannis Cassiani Opera* 1. Edited by Michaelis Petschineg. Corpus Scriptorum Ecclesiasticorum Latinorum 17. Vienna: F. Tempsky, 1888.

John Damascene. *In S. Basilium, Ode IV: Theotokion*. In *Patrologia Graeca*, 96:1373C.

———. *Sermo de dormitione beatae virginis Mariae* 2. Edited by Bonifatius Kotter. Die Schriften des Johannes von Damaskos: Patristische Texte und Studien 29. Berlin: Gruyter, 1988.

———. *Sermo in Nativitatem BVM*. In *Die Schriften des Johannes von Damaskos* 5 Edited by B. Kotter. Patristische Texte und Studien 29. Berlin: Gruyter, 1988.

Justinian I. *A Letter on the Three Chapters*. In *The Person of Christ: The Christology of Emperor Justinian*, translated by Kenneth Wesche, 115–58. Crestwood, NY: St. Vladimir's Seminary Press, 1991.

Kappes, Christiaan. *Immaculate Conception: Why Thomas Aquinas Denied, While John Duns Scotus, Gregory Palamas, and Mark Eugenicus Professed the Absolute Immaculate Existence of Mary*. New Bedford, MA: Academy of the Immaculate, 2014.

Keech, Dominic. *The Anti-Pelagian Christology of Augustine of Hippo, 396–430*. Oxford: Oxford University Press, 2012.

Krausmüller, Dirk. "Making the Most of Mary: The Cult of the Virgin in the Chalkoprateia from Late Antiquity to the Tenth Century." In *The Cult of the Mother of God in Byzantium: Texts and Images*, edited by Leslie Brubaker and Mary Cunningham, 219–46. Burlington, VT: Ashgate, 2011.

Lampe, George, ed. *A Patristic Lexicon*. Oxford: Clarendon, 1996.

Lapidge, Michael. "The Career of Archbishop Theodore." In *Archbishop Theodore*, edited by Michael Lapidge, 1–29. Cambridge Studies in Anglo-Saxon England 11. Cambridge: Cambridge University Press, 1995.

Larchet, Jean-Claude. "Ancestral Guilt according to St. Maximus the Confessor: A Bridge between Eastern and Western Conception." *Sobornost* 20 (1998) 26–48.

Larin, Vassa. "What Is 'Ritual Im/Purity' and Why?" *St. Vladimir's Theological Quarterly* 52 (2008) 275–92.

Leaney, Robert. "The Lucan Text of the Lord's Prayer (Lk 11:2–4)." *Novum Testamentum* 1 (1956) 103–11.

Leo I. *Léon le Grand: Sermons*. Edited by René Dolle. Sources Chrétiennes 22.2. Paris: Les Éditions du Cerf, 1964.

Liddell, Henry, and Robert Scott. *Greek-English Lexicon with a Revised Supplement*. Oxford: Clarendon, 1996.

Leinhard, Joseph. "Augustine of Hippo, Basil of Caesarea, and Gregory Nazianzen." In *Orthodox Readings of Augustine*, edited by Aristotle Papanikolaou and George Demacopoulos, 81–100. Crestwood, NY: St. Vladimir's Seminary Press, 2008.

Louth, Andrew. *Maximus the Confessor*. New York: Routledge, 1996.

Lukken, Gerard. *Original Sin in the Roman Liturgy: Research into the Theology of Original Sin in the Roman Sacramentaria and the Early Baptismal Liturgy.* Leiden: Brill, 1973.

Lunn-Rockliffe, Sophie. *Ambrosiaster's Political Theology.* Oxford Early Christian Studies. Oxford: Oxford University Press, 2007.

Maximus. *Commentary on the The Our Father.* Edited and translated by G. Berthhold. Christian Classics. Mahwah, NJ: Paulist, 1985.

——— (?). *Maxime le Confesseur: Vie de la vierge.* Edited by Michael Esbroeck. Corpus Scriptorum Christianorum Orientalium: Scriptores Iberici 22. Louvain: Peeters, 1986.

———. *Maximi Confessoris Quaestiones ad Thalassium.* Vol. 2. Edited by C. Laga and C. Steel. Corpus Christianorum: Series Graeca 22. Turnhout: Brepols, 1990.

——— (?). *The Life of the Virgin.* Edited and translated by Stephen Shoemaker. New Haven: Yale University Press, 2012.

McGuckin, John. *St Gregory of Nazianzus: An Intellectual Biography.* Crestwood, NY: St. Vladimir's Seminary Press, 2001.

Migne, Jean-Paul. *Patrologiae cursus completes, Series graeca: Patrologia Graeca [PG].* 160 vols. Paris: J.-P. Migne, 1844–1868.

———. *Patrologiae cursus completus, series latina: Patrologia Latina [PL].* 225 vols. Paris: J.-P. Migne, 1815–1875.

Noble, Thomas. "Rome in the Seventh Century." In *Archbishop Theodore*, edited by Michael Lapidge, 68–87. Cambridge Studies in Anglo-Saxon England 11. Cambridge: Cambridge University Press, 1995.

Nutzman, Megan. "Mary in the *Protevangelium of James*: A Jewish Woman in the Temple?" *Greek, Roman, and Byzantine Studies* 53 (2013) 551–78.

Ohme, Heinz. "Sources of the Greek Canon Law to the Quinisext Council (691/2): Councils and Church Fathers." In *The History of Byzantine and Eastern Canon Law to 1500*, edited by Wilfried Hartmann and Kenneth Pennington, 24–114. Washington, DC: Catholic University of America, 2012.

Origen. *Commentarium in evangelium Matthaei. Origenes Werke.* Vol. 10.2. Edited by Erich Klostermann. Die griechischen christlichen Schriftsteller 40.1. Leipzig: Teubner, 1937.

———. *Homiliae in Psalmos.* Edited by Max Rauer. Origenes Werke 13. Die griechischen christlichen Schriftsteller 49. Berlin: Akademie, 1959.

———. *Homily on Luke.* Edited by M. Rauer. Origenes Werke: Die griechischen christlichen Schriftsteller 49. Berlin: Akademie, 1959.

Paschasius Radbertus. *Paschasii Radberti De partu virginis, De assumptione sanctae Mariae virginis.* Edited by E. Ann Matter and A. Ripberger. Corpus Christianorum Continuatio Mediaevalis 160. Brepols: Turnhout, 1985.

Pereira, Jairzinho Lopes. *Augustine of Hippo and Martin Luther on Original Sin and Justification of the Sinner.* Göttingen: Vandenhoeck and Ruprecht, 2013.

Philo. *Quaestiones in Genesim et in Exodum: Fragmenta Graeca.* Edited by François Petit. Les Oeuvres de Philon d'Alexandrie 33. Paris: Éditions du Cerf, 1978.

———. *Philonis Alexandrini opera quae supersunt.* Vols. 4–5. Edited by Leopold Cohn. Berlin: De Gruyter, 1962.

Price, Richard. "Monotheletism: A Heresy or a Form of Words?" *Studia Patristica* 48 (2010) 221–32.

Prinzing, Günter. "Observations on the Legal Status of Children and the Stages of Childhood in Byzantium." In *Becoming Byzantine: Children and Childhood in Byzantium*, edited by Arietta Papaconstantinou and Alice-Mary Talbot, 15–34. Washington, DC: Dumbarton Oaks Research Library, 2009.

Reynolds, Brian. *Gateway to Heaven: Marian Doctrine and Devotion, Image and Typology, in the Patristic and Medieval Periods.* Hyde Park, NY: New City, 2012.

Rufinus. *Tyranii Rufini opera 1: Orationum Gregorii Nazianzeni novem interpretio.* Edited by Augustus Engelbrecht. Corpus Scriptorum Ecclesiasticorum Latinorum 46.2. Vienna: F. Tempsky, 1910.

Sevenson, Jane. "Theodore and the *Laterculus Malalianus.*" In *Archbishop Theodore,* edited by Michael Lapidge, 204–21. Cambridge Studies in Anglo-Saxon England 11. Cambridge: Cambridge University Press, 1995.

Shoemaker, Stephen. "The Mother's Passion: Mary at the Crucifixion and Resurrection in the Earliest *Life of the Virgin* and Its Influence." In *The Cult of the Mother of God in Byzantium: Texts and Images,* edited by Leslie Brubaker and Mary Cunningham, 53–68. Burlington, VT: Ashgate, 2011.

Schwartz, Edward, et al., eds. *Acta Conciliorum Oecumenicorum: Series 1–2.* Berlin: Gruyter, 1914–2013.

Siemens, James. "Another Book for Jarrow's Library? Coincidences in Exegesis between Bede and the *Laterculus Malalianus.*" *The Downside Review* 131 (2013) 15–34.

———. "A Survey of the Christology of Theodore of Tarsus in the *Laterculus Malalianus.*" *Scottish Journal of Theology* 60 (2007) 213–25.

Sirks, A. J. B. "Delicts." In *The Cambridge Companion to Roman Law,* edited by David Johnston, 246–71. Cambridge: Cambridge University Press, 2015.

Sophronius of Jerusalem. *Synodical Letter.* In *Sophronius of Jerusalem and Seventh-Century Heresy: The Synodical Letter and Other Documents,* edited and translated by Paul Allen, 67–160. New York: Oxford University Press, 2009.

Souter, Alexander, and Robinso Armitage. *A Study of Ambrosiaster.* Contribution to Biblical and Patristic Literature: Texts and Studies 7.4. Cambridge: The Cambridge Press, 1905.

Syriac NT and Psalms. Edited by G. Gwilliam et al. Istanbul: Bible Society in Turkey, 1991.

Theodore of Canterbury (?). *Second Commentary on the Gospels.* In *Biblical Commentaries from the Canterbury School of Theodore and Handrian,* edited by B. Bischoff and Michael Lapidge. Cambridge Studies in Anglo-Saxon England 10. Cambridge: Cambridge University Press, 1994.

Tsorbatzoglou, Panteleimon. "St Theodore, Archbishop of Canterbury (668–690): A Greek from Tarsus of Cilicia in England: Some Aspects of his Life." *Mediterreanean Chronicle* 2 (2012) 79–104.

Ward, Benedicta. *The Venerable Bede.* Outstanding Christian Thinkers. London: Geoffrey Chapman, 1990.

Zimmerman, Reinhard. "Roman Law in the Modern World." In *The Cambridge Companion to Roman Law,* edited by David Johnston, 452–81. Cambridge: Cambridge University Press, 2015.

Zeno. *Tractatus Sancti Zenonis Veronensis episcopi.* Edited by Bengt Löfstedt. Corpus Christianorum: Series Latina 22. Turnhout: Brepols, 1971.

12

The Center Holds

Echoes of Eriugena in the Christo-cosmic Exemplarism of Bonaventure

T. ALEXANDER GILTNER

IN THIS PAPER, I do not intend to prove anything. That the parallels of thought and systems between two thinkers separated by centuries could represent an intellectual reception is always questionable, at least from a historical perspective, especially without concrete material evidence to substantiate it—which I have no intention of providing here. Rather, this paper is meant to serve as a sort of "think-piece" on the possible influence of John Scottus Eriugena—the Irish-born Carolingian thinker—on the cosmic exemplarism of our Seraphic Doctor, Saint Bonaventure. *Proving* such a relation would require nothing less than a monographic study and said material evidence that I have not yet located. Yet showcasing the plausibility of such a relation by exhibiting said parallels should, I think, give impetus for further investigation.

Scholars have long-assumed Greek influence on Bonaventure's thought, namely Dionysius and the Damascene. This "think-piece" will show the need to investigate an untapped resource for Bonaventurean and Franciscan theology: the Maximian cosmology as it was transmitted through Eriugena. Of course, I am not the first to suspect the possible connection between Bonaventure and Eriugena. Guy Bougerol, in his seminal introduction to Bonaventure studies, noted without qualification the line of influence, though held that it was mitigated by the Victorines—specifically Hugh and Richard—who removed the "fanciful elements," or more colloquially: the crazy bits.[1] Hans Urs von Balthasar, too, speculated on such a connection.[2] And

---

1. Bougerol, *Introduction to the Works of Bonaventure*, 41.
2. As noted by Nichols, *Say It Is Pentecost*, 97.

yet, we have not had much more than hints. Furthermore, speculation has generally stopped short of Dionysian apophaticism.[3] However, when looking at the basic architecture of the cosmos in the systems of these two figures, and especially the prized place of Christ in this structure, one can see striking parallels that suggest more than just a passing influence. By the end, it should be clear that this inquiry is not only warranted, but vital if we are to fully understand the cosmology and metaphysics of Bonaventure.

Word and Creation, Exemplarism and Theophany

Bonaventure writes:

> The Word therefore expresses the Father and [all] things, which were made through him, and leads us principally to the unity of the gathering Father. And accordingly he is the Tree of Life, because through this Center we return and are vivified in the very font of life . . . this is the reducing metaphysical Center, and this is our whole metaphysics: concerning emanation, exemplarity, consummation—namely to be illuminated through the spiritual rays and reduced to the highest. And so you will be a true metaphysician.[4]

This passage is one of the most famous from Bonaventure, and justifiably so, for it represents the heart of Bonaventure's philosophy and theology. It stands as one of the starkest expressions of the core concept at the center of his basic framework: Christocentric exemplarism.[5] It rests very near the center of the first conference of the *Hexaëmeron*, Bonaventure's final and

---

3. The influence of Dionysius on Bonaventure, while not ignored, is also woefully underdeveloped. For example, even basic concepts like illumination and hierarchy, both of which for Bonaventure are crucially Dionysian, have garnered little to no attention in the lore.

4. *Collationes in Hexaëmeron* (hereafter *Hex*) 1.17: Verbum ergo exprimit Patrem et res, quae per ipsum factae sunt, et principaliter ducit nos ad Patris congregantis unitatem; et secundum hoc est *lignum vitae*, quia per hoc medium redimus et vivificamur in ipso fonte vitae . . . hoc est medium metaphysicum reducens, et haec est tota nostra metaphysica: de emanatione, de exemplaritate, de consummatione, scilicet illuminari per radios spirituales et reduci ad summum. Et sic eris verus metaphysicus.

All references and quotes from Bonaventure's corpus are from the standard Quaracchi critical edition, *Doctoris seraphici S. Bonaventurae opera omnia*, vols. 1–10, edited by the Fathers of the Collegium S. Bonaventurae (Ad Claras Aquas (Quaracchi): Collegium S. Bonaventurae, 1882–1902). All translations are my own.

5. This is also called "cosmic exemplarism," e.g., Bowman, "The Cosmic Exemplarism of Bonaventure," 181–98. I find either appellation appropriate, but here I wish to highlight the centrality of Christ in Bonaventure's exemplarist framework.

putatively most mature work. In this first conference, Bonaventure contends Christ is the *medium*, the center of all things—not only of metaphysics, but of every locus of knowledge and reality, and even the center of the divine life *ad intra*, the Trinity itself. To be a *true* metaphysician is to recognize the basic triadic expression of the Word in all things: from the Father as transcendental communicability, the agent through which all of Creation comes into being, and through which all of Creation is brought back into perfect union with the Father.

So for Bonaventure, theology begins with two interrelated points of reference: the Trinity and the Person of Christ. These two points form a sort of double-helix from which all of theology—and ultimately all of reality—flows and finds its end. According to Bonaventure:

> And because in [the Father] the conceptive power conceives a similitude, encompassing all things under one regard or aspect, he conceives or generates one Word, which is the imitative similitude of the Father and the exemplative and operative similitude of things, and so holds as the center [*medium*]. And the Father is said to operate through the Word.[6]

The Word is thus the expression of the Father to every and all other things: "Because the Word expresses both the Father and himself and the Holy Spirit as well as all other things."[7] The Word is center both *ad intra* and *ad extra*, in the Word's mediatory role within the Trinity, in Christ's mediatory role between Creator and creation, *and* between creatures. Christ holds the middle (*medium*) in all positions:

> The key of contemplation, therefore, is the triple understanding [*intellectus*; ff.], namely: the understanding of the uncreated Word, through which all things are produced; the understanding of the incarnate Word, through which all things are repaired; [and] the understanding of the inspired Word, through which all things are revealed. Unless one is able to consider concerning things—how they are originated, how they are reduced into the end, and how God shines in them—one is not able to have understanding [*intelligentiam*].[8]

6. *I Sent* d. 27, p. 2, a. 1, q. 2, concl.: Et quia in ipso vis conceptiva concipit similitudinem, omnia circumplectentem sub intuitu uno sive aspectu, concipit sive generat unum Verbum, quod est similitudo Patris imitativa et similitudo rerum exemplativa et similitudo operativa; ita tenet quasi medium, et dicitur Pater operari per Verbum.

7. *Hex* 9.2: Quia Verbum et Patrem et se ipsum et Spiritum Sanctum exprimit et omnia alia.

8. *Hex* 3.2: Clavis ergo contemplationis est intellectus triplex, scilicet intellectus Verbi increati, per quod omnia producuntur; intellectus Verbi incarnati, per quod

Eriugena too connects the Word's generation to Creation's procession:

> Before, then, this visible world proceeded through generation in genus and species and all sensible numbers, God the Father begot his Word before all worldly times, in which and through which he created the most perfect primordial causes of all natures, which divine providence, by administering in a certain wondrous harmony this visible world in its procession through the generation in numbers of places and of times and in multiple distinctions of genus and species from the moment it begins to the very end.[9]

Or as Eriugena writes in his *Homilia* on the Prologue to the Gospel of John:

> By his being born before all things from the Father, were not all things made with him and through him? Now this generation of this one from the Father is the creation [*conditio*] of all causes and the operation and effect of all that proceeds from the causes in genus and species. Naturally, all things were made through the generation of the Word of God from God the Beginning. Hear the divine and ineffable paradox, the unlockable secret, the invisible depth, the incomprehensible mystery: Through he who was not made but begotten, all things were made but not begotten.[10]

---

omnia reparantur; intellectus Verbi inspirati, per quod omnia revelantur. Nisi enim quis possit considerare de rebus, qualiter originantur, qualiter in finem reducuntur, et qualiter in eis refulgent Deus; intelligentiam habere non potest.

9. *Periphyseon* (hereafter *PP*) II 560A–B: Prius igitur quam mundus iste uisibilis in genera et species omnesque numeros sensibilies per generationem procederet ante tempora saecularia deus pater uerbum suum genuit in quo et per quem omnium naturarum primordiales causas perfectissimas creauit quae diuina prouidentia administrante mirabili quadam armonia processionibus suis per generationem numeris locorum et temporum generum quoque ac specierum multiplicibus differentiis hunc mundum uisibilem ab initio quo coepit usque ad finem.

All quotes from the *Periphyseon* are from critical edition of the Corpus Christianorum; however, I have utilized *Periphyseon (De diuisione naturae)*, vols. 1–4, edited by I. P. Sheldon-Williams and Édouard A. Jeauneau, Scriptores Latini Hiberiae 13, which contains the same text. All translations are my own.

10. *Homilia* 7: Eo nascente ante omnia ex patre, omnia cum ipso et per ipsum facta sunt? Nam ipsius ex patre generatio ipsa est causarum omnium conditio omniumque quae ex causis in genera et species procedunt operatio et effectus. Per generationem quippe dei uerbi ex deo principio facta sunt omnia. Audi diuinum et ineffabile paradoxum, irreserabile secretum, inuisible profundum, incomprehensibile mysterium. Per non factum, sed genitum, omnia facta, sed non genita.

All quotes for the *Homilia* text are from Jeauneau's critical edition *Iohannis Scotti seu Eriugena: Homilia super 'in principio erat verbum' et Commentarius in evangelium Iohnnannis*, in Corpus Christianorum 166. All translations are my own.

Now, there are of course notable differences between the two thinkers on this point. For example, Eriugena believes that the "primordial causes," or the divine ideas, while coeternal with the divine essence, are nonetheless created,[11] while Bonaventure holds that the ideas are essentially identical to God's being—and thus uncreated—though they are rationally distinct.[12] However, like Bonaventure, Eriugena intimates that the causes are "principal exemplars"[13] that especially subsist in the Word, indicative of the Word's mediatory role both in the divine life and between Creator and creature. So, for both Eriugena and Bonaventure, the life of God *ad intra* orders God's work *ad extra*, and that work is specifically mediated through the exemplars, or ideas, from the Exemplar, or the Word.[14] Further, the divine and created orders are both centered in emanation, and attest to the basic circularity of all things, revolving around the second Person of the Trinity.

Bonaventure uses this exemplary logic to elucidate Creation. The world *is*—that is, it exists and is known and knowable—through the emanatory exemplarity of the eternal Art.[15] From this Art, the ideas causally emanate out into creation in similar fashion as the Word emanated from the Father.[16] In all real, knowable things that emanate from the Word, Bonaventure says "we can see the eternal generation of the Word, the Image, and the Son eternally emanating from God the Father."[17] This is why Bonaventure says

11. *Homilia* 10. However, it is worth noting that there are pericopes in which Eriugena appears to vacillate on this question, e.g. *PP* I 448B, where he considers the possibility that the ideas are in fact the Divine Essence itself, which he navigates through his theology of theophany. This could imply that Eriugena had more nuanced thoughts on this question.

12. *De scientia Christi*, q. 3, *in toto*, but particularly the conclusion.

13. *PP* I 446C: "principalia exempla."

14. Eriugena too speaks of God as the "Principal Exemplar." See for example *PP* II 585C–586C, where Eriugena speaks of the soul as the "image" of the Exemplar, and the body as "the image of the soul." This is reminiscent of the vestige/image/similitude distinction found in Bonaventure's corpus, such as the *Itinerarium mentis in Deum*. It is perhaps significant to note that this passage from Eriugena directly precedes one of the "triple infinity formulation" passage, which I discuss below as a possible material link between the Irishman and the Seraphic Doctor.

15. A common name for the Word in Bonaventure and Eriugena.

16. Bonaventure distinguishes three modes in which the ideas subsist: 1) seminally, where they act as the principle causes of material realities; 2) intellectually, the mode in which they inhabit the created, rational mind; and 3) ideally, their essential but rationally distinct inhabitance of the divine essence. See *De reductione artium ad theologiam* (hereafter *DR* 20).

17. *Itinerarium mentis ad Deum* (hereafter *Itin*) II.8: Si ergo omnia cognoscibilia habent sui speciem generare, manifeste proclamant, quod in illis tanquam in speculis videri potest aeterna generatio Verbi, Imaginis et Filii a Deo Patre aeternaliter emanantis.

later in the *Itinerarium* that the conditions of truth come "from exemplarity in the eternal Art, according to which things have a mutual fittingness and relation [*aptitudinem et habitudinem ad invicem*] according to the representation of them from the eternal Art."[18] Thus, exemplarity grounds not only the knowledge of things in certitude (and without which there can be no certitude), but also the certainty of real things, ontologically rooted in the Art himself. Those things that are emanated are the *ontos* of all reality, the basis of every creaturely being.

For Eriugena, these exemplars are found in the theophanies, the "manifestations of the divine:" "the divine nature . . . in its theophanies consents [*accipit*] to appear from the most hidden recesses of its nature . . . "[19] Like Bonaventure, this is how we encounter God and come to know the Creator in things created. Eriugena writes that "from the primordial causes, ideas [*cognitiones*] which are accustomed to be called 'theophanies' by the Greeks, and apparitions of the divine by the Latins, [the soul] fastens to itself and through these perceives a certain notion [*notitiam*] from God, through the first causes."[20] Furthermore, as theophanies function as manifestations or apparitions of the divine, they provide a connection between the procession of ideas and creatures themselves:

> And truly [the divine nature] is said to proceed, beginning to appear in its theophanies as from nothing into something, and which properly is considered [*existimatur*] beyond every essence and also properly is known [*cognoscitur*] in every essence. And therefore every visible and invisible creature can be called theophany."[21]

In this way, Eriugena's theophanic and Christocentric cosmology operates in a remarkably similar vein as Bonaventure Christo-cosmic exemplarism.

18. Ibid., III.3: Huiusmodi igitur illationis necessitas non venit ab existentia rei in materia, quia est contingens, nec ab existentia rei in anima, quia tunc esset fictio, si non esset in re: venit igitur ab exemplaritate in arte aeterna, secundum quam res habent aptitudinem et habitudinem ad invicem secundum illius aeternae artis repraesentationem.

19. *PP* III 689B: Diuina natura . . . in suis theophaniis accipit apparere ex occultissimis naturae suae sinibus . . .

20. *PP* II 576D–577A: Ut enim ex inferioribus sensibilium rerum imagines quas Greci PHANTACIAC uocant anima recipit ita ex superioribus, hoc est primordialibus causis, cognitiones quae a Grecis THEOPHANIAI, a Latinis diuinae apparitiones solent appellari sibi ipsi infigit et per ipsas quandam de deo notitiam percipit, per primas causas dico.

21. *PP* III 681A: At uero in suis theophaniis incipiens apparere ueluti ex nihilo in aliquid dicitur procedere, et quae proprie super omnem essentiam existimatur proprie quoque in omni essentia cognoscitur ideoque omnis uisibilis et inuisibilis creatura theophania, id est diuina apparitio, potest appellari.

Just as for Bonaventure, every creature is an example of the Exemplar, for Eriugena every creature is a theophany of the divine nature, all creatures flowing from the causal principle located in the Word.

Cosmic Word and the Word-Made-Flesh

These two parallel approaches to how God creates and lies hidden in Creation give both Eriugena and Bonaventure a robust ontological foundation for all of reality. God is known and is in the world through the ideas that have emanated or proceeded from the Word, as the Word has emanated from the Father. Christ is the *medium* and expression[22] of both the divine and created order, holding the center place in the Trinity and in all things. The true metaphysician recognizes this basic reality: Christ *is* the center in which all things hold, representing the role of communication in the *vita divinitatis* both *ad intra* and *ad extra*, communicating the innascible, incommunicable *primum principium* as both cosmic Word and, even more crucially for us, Word-Made-Flesh.

Indeed, it is his Incarnation that draws all the aspects of the cosmos together, being the perfect mediation of their origin to their end. Bonaventure writes: "Just as a beginning is conjoined to an end in a circle, so in the Incarnation the lowest is conjoined to the highest, so that God [is conjoined] to the dust, and the first to the final."[23] This extends even to the divine ideas in their various modes:

> Through a similar reason it can be argued that the highest and most noble perfection in the universe cannot be, unless by nature, in which are the seminal reasons, and by nature, in which are the intellectual reasons, and by nature, in which the ideal reasons, simultaneously concur [*concurrant*] in a unity of person, which is made in the Incarnation of the Son of God. Therefore, the whole natural philosophy bespeaks [*praedicat*] through the condition of proportion the Word of God born and incarnated, so that he may be *alpha and omega*, born namely in the beginning and before temporality, incarnated within the bounds of the ages [*in fine saeculorum*].[24]

22. "Expression" is a technical term for Bonaventure in particular; see *DSC* qq. 2 and 3.

23. *Commentaria Sententiarum Liber I* (hereafter *I Sent*) prol. I, 2a: Sicut in circulo ultimum coniungitur principio, sic in incarnatione supremum coniungitur imo, ut Deus limo, et primum postremo.

24. *DR* 20: Per similem igitur rationem potest argui, quod summa perfectio et nobilissima in universo esse non possit, nisi natura, in qua sunt rationes seminales,

The Incarnation of the Word is the fulfillment and perfection of all reality.

But why? Why does this drama turn upon the Incarnation? In one sense, it concerns sin and the Fall, but there is a more fundamental reason: it is because of us—where we stand in the drama of Creation as humans. Humans are the middle creatures, formed from the dust of the earth (*de limo terrae*) but also the celestial nature (*natura caelesti*).[25] As Bonaventure writes in the *Breviloquium*:

> Therefore, so that the Power might be manifested, according to the praise, glory, and honor of its own self, it produced all things from nothing, making something near to nothing, namely corporal material, and near to itself, namely spiritual substance, and it simultaneously joins these in one human in a unity of nature and person, namely a rational soul and body.[26]

The Incarnated Christ is mediator because the *human* is the mediator within Creation all and sundry and between Creation and God.[27] Humanity mediates the entire cosmos as the middle point of all things, the microcosm in which the whole of the macrocosm subsists, though which the cosmos was created. At the most basic level, humankind contains both the sensible nature (of rocks, plants, and animals) and the intelligible nature (of the angels and incorporeal beings) within itself. Like Christ, indeed modeled after Christ, the human being is also a medium.

Eriugena agrees, drawing specifically on Maximus's conception of humanity as the "workshop" of all of Creation.[28] Human nature is the "universal nature," because "all things were created in man."[29] Humanity is the crown of all creation, the apex of the cosmos, and through which all things should return. Eriugena writes:

---

et natura, in qua sunt rationes intellectuales, et natura, in qua rationes ideales, simul concurrant in unitatem personae, quod factum est in Filii Dei incarnatione. Praedicat igitur tota naturalis philosophia per habitudinem proportionis Dei Verbum natum et incarnatum, ut idem sit *alpha et omega*, natum scilicet in principio et ante tempora, incarnatum vero in fine saeculorum.

25. *II Sent* d. 17, a. 2, q. 1, concl.

26. *Brev* VII.7.2: Ut ergo manifestaretur potentia, ad sui ipsius laudem, gloriam et honorem omnia produxit de nihilo, faciens aliquid prope nihil, scilicet materiam corporalem, et aliquid prope se, scilicet substantiam spiritualem, et simul haec iungens in uno homine in unitate naturae et personae, scilicet rationalem animam et corporalem. Cf. *De perfectione evangelica* q.1, a.1, concl.

27. Cf. *III Sent* d. 19, a. 2, q. 2, concl. Though it should be noted that the inverse could just as properly—and perhaps *more* properly—stated, that the human is the mediator of Creation because the Incarnated Christ is the Mediator.

28. See Maximus, *Ambiguum* 41, especially 2–3.

29. *PP* IV 749A: nam in homine omnia facta sunt.

> Therefore with respect to this, it is given to be understood from the words of the aforementioned master:[30] the Human was made among the primordial causes of things according to the Image of God so that in [the Human] every creature, from things both intelligible and sensible as diverse extremes, might be made one inseparable composition, so that [the Human] may be the center and union of all creatures.[31]

This agreement between the two theologians is even seen in their read of the first chapter of Genesis. According to Bonaventure, God creates the human soul (*anima humana*) last "as the end and consummation of all things."[32] So too for Eriugena, though he takes a much less literal reading of Genesis: "So then after the narration of the visible world, the honored human is introduced, as the conclusion of all, so that it might be understood that all created things which are narrated before him ought to be universally comprehended in him."[33]

So the first and final purpose of the Incarnation is that all should become, through humankind, what they were intended to be—as they were intended to be—through God's intended means, mediated through the Exemplar who emanates and draws all *exempla* back to himself through himself to participate fully in the divine life. This is the final *reditus* or *consummatio*. This is why Christ *is* our metaphysic. The interpenetrating power of humanity, as the crown of creation, is taken up in the Word, and through the Word-Made-Flesh, all things are brought along the path of return into God.

And so, finally, we are brought back through the Incarnate Word to the ultimate and first plentitudinal fount of all being. Eriugena writes: "The Word was not made flesh on account of his own self, but on account of us, who could not be transmuted into sons of God except through the flesh of the Word. He descended alone, he ascends with many. He who made the human from God makes gods from humans . . . that is, he possessed our nature, so that he might make us participants in his nature."[34] And so the cosmos is

30. That is, Maximus.

31. *PP* II 536A–B: Ad hoc igitur quantum ex praedicti magistri sermonibus datur intelligi inter primodiales rerum causas homo ad imaginem dei factus est ut in eo omnis creatura et intelligibilis et sensibilis ex quibus ueluti diuresis extremittibus compositus unum inseparabile fieret est ut esset medietas atque adunatio omnium creaturarum.

32. *II Sent* d. 17, a. 1, q. 3, ad 6: Et post omnia producta est anima humana tanquam finis omnium et consummatio.

33. *PP* IV 782C-D: Proinde post mundi uisibilis ornatus narrationem introducitur homo, ueluti omnium conclusio, ut intelligeretur quod omnia quae ante ipsum condita narrantur, in ipso uniuersaliter comprehenduntur.

34. *Homilia* 21: Non propter se ipsum uerbum caro factum est, sed propter nos, qui non nisi per uerbi carnem potuissemus in dei filios transmutari. Solus descendit,

consummated. Christ is all in all, the center of all things and the mediator of all things in the Trinity and in Creation. It should come as no surprise by now that Bonaventure presents a similar theologic: "So the desire [*appetitus*] of the entire human nature was completed, when the noblest fitness, which was in human nature, according to which it was able to be united to the divine, is reduced to the perfect act through the work of the Incarnation."[35] As it is in the divine life, so it was intended in creation *ad extra*, lost but then regained through the Incarnation, which itself is the transcendent point of motion back to the Creator, where all things are brought back through the ideas, causes, or exemplars that form the basis of their ontology to the primal source, the *primum principium*. Bonaventure declares, nearly narrating his entire cosmos: "And because God the Father is the principle of the Son, and the Son the principle of all things, so then the Son is produced and produces," and so "all things are reduced through the Son to and in [the Father]. And therefore reduction[36] is aptly appropriated to the Son."[37]

What is as striking as the parallels themselves is how particularly they are situated within a peculiar, nuanced logic of the divine being, Christ, and Creation. No doubt Bonaventure and Eriugena shared sources, as is evidenced for example by their plain Neoplatonism. And considering each parallel *in solo*, one could perhaps conceive of some shared source or even coincidence. But it is not only the corresponding concepts; it is how they fit together. Connecting theophanic or exemplaristic Creation precisely to its culmination in the Incarnation, through which all things are brought

---

cum multis ascendit. De hominibus facit deos qui de deo fecit hominem . . . hoc est, naturam nostram possedit, ut suae naturae nos participes faceret.

35. III Sent d. 1, a. 2, q. 2, concl.: Completus etiam est totius humanae naturae appetitus, dum per opus incarnationis nobilissima idoneitas, quae erat in humana natura, secundum quam unibilis erat divinae, ad actum perfectum reducitur.

36. Guy H. Allard is an excellent resource for understanding the technical meaning of *reductio* in Bonaventure's thought. *Reductio* is not a diminution but rather the intensification and expatiation of a thing by drawing it deeper into its ontological source. As Allard explains: "Une première observation s'impose qui surprendra certes plus d'un logicien moderne: la *reductio* conduit toujours d'un pole negative à un pole positif. Cette loi génerale revêt une double forme: 1) la *reductio* reconduit de ce qui est imparfait à ce qui est parfait, 2) de ce qui est incomplet à ce qui est complet. C'est pourquoi elle est une montée, une ascension; loin d'être un processus de déperdition de raréfaction ou d'anéantissement, la *reductio* assure au contraire une amplification de l'intelligibilité et une ouverture de plus en plus grande du champ épistémologique" (Allard, "La technique de la <Reductio> chez Bonaventure," 395–416).

37. 1 Sent d. 31, p.2, dub. 7: Et quoniam Deus Pater est principium Filii, et Filius principium omium, ita quod Filius prodicitur et producit . . . sed Pater . . . cum sit innascibilis . . . ideo dicitur fontale principium, a quo omnia et in quem omnia per Filium reducuntur . . . et propterea Filio appropriatur reductio.

back to their final end in God, bespeaks not only an Eastern but a uniquely Maximian influence that Bonaventure would be hard-pressed to encounter simply through the Damascene or Dionysius. It is their theological method and content considered as a whole that most tightly weaves the thread of reception from Eriugena to Bonaventure. There is represented in the theologic of these two thinkers a sort of dialectic that holds their respective universes together. It is not by any means a Hegelian dialectic. Rather, it is a way of thinking-with-the-universe to isolate its moving parts conceptually but not rend them from the whole. As Bonaventure himself contends, we must see the parts, but always with an eye to the totality: "Whence just as no one can see the beauty of a song, unless her vision [*aspectus*] is brought to bear over its entire course [*totum versum*], so no one may see the beauty of the order and governance of the universe, unless she perceives its entirety."[38] Eriugena agrees:

> Now the procession of creatures and their return occur simultaneously in the account inquiring into them, with the result that they seem to be inseparable from each other, and no one can give a worthy and certain explanation concerning one absolutely without the insertion of the other—that is, concerning the procession without the return and collection, and conversely.[39]

This dialectical method, by thinking with the cosmos, illuminates its basic structure and narrative movement. Eriugena writes:

> God, who alone creates all things, alone is ANARCHOS. That is, it is understood to be without beginning, because it alone is the principal cause of all things that are made from itself and through itself. And for this reason, it is also the end of all things that are from itself; all things desire [*appetunt*] it. It is therefore the beginning, the middle and the end [*principium et medium et finis*]: beginning, because all things that participate in essence are from it. It is the middle, because in it and through it they subsist and are moved. It is the end, because they are moved to it, seeking rest from motion to it and the stability of its perfection.[40]

38. *Brev*, prol. 2: Unde sicut nullus potest videre pulcritudinem carminis, nisi aspectus eius feratur super totum versum, sic nullus videt pulcritudinem ordinis et regiminis universi, nisi eam totam speculetur.

39. *PP* II 529A: Processio nanque creaturarum earundemque reditus ita simul rationi occurrunt eas inquirenti ut a se inuicem inseparabiles esse uideantur, et nemo de una absolute sine alterius insertione, hoc est de processione sine reditu et collectione et couersim, dignum quid ratumque potest explanare.

40. *PP* I 451C–D: Praedicatarum itaque naturae divisionum prima differentia nobis

This narratival movement, Bonaventure says, the metaphysician can deduce from the structure of being itself, but only so far without revelation:

> The metaphysician however—even though she rises to the consideration of the principles of a created and particular substance to the universal and uncreated [substance], and to that very Being, so that she possesses the logic of beginning, middle, and final end—nevertheless [does not possess] the logic of the Father and Son and Holy Spirit.[41]

This is because the middle, the center [*medium*], is not just a principle: it is a person. It is Christ "holding the center in all things," in whom "are hidden all the treasures of God's wisdom and knowledge."[42]

So all things that are and can be known, the entire metaphysics of the universe, are rooted radically in the very special role and person of Christ, who is at the center of all things. As Eriugena says in one of his *carminis*, "all things will perceive in the sharp clarity of reason places and times filled within by God the Word, the whole world bearing the symbols of the birth of Christ."[43] So Bonaventure concludes: "The divine Word is every creature, because God is speaking."[44]

A Possible Material Connection

This is just a taste, really. While there remains much more to explore, these parallels and the theologic undergirding them are certainly enough to incite interest in a possibly crucial link of intellectual reception. The lack of a

---

visa est in eam quae creat et non creatur. Nec immerito, quia talis naturae species de deo solo recte praedicatur, qui solus omnia creans ANARXOC, hoc est sine principio, intelligitur esse, quia principalis causa omnium quae ex ipso et per ipsum facta sunt solus est, ac per hoc et omnium quae ex se sunt finis est; ipsum enim omnia appetunt. Est igitur principium et medium et finis: principium quidem, quia ex se sunt omnia quae essentiam participant; medium autem, quia in ipso et per ipsum subsistent atque mouentur; finis uero, quia ad ipsum mouentur quietem motus sui suaeque perfectionis stabilitatem quaerentia.

41. *Hex* 1.13: Metaphysicus autem, licet assurgat ex consideratione principiorum substantiae creatae et patricularis ad universalem et increatem et ad illud esse, ut habet rationem principii, medii, et finis ultimi, non tamen in ratione Patris et Filii et Spiritus sancti.

42. *Hex* 1.10; cf. Colossians 2:3.

43. John Scottus Eriugena, *Carmina*, 25: Intrans armoniam rerum, ducente sophia// omnia perspiciet rationis acumine claro//intus farta deo verbo loca tempora, totum// mundum gestantem nascentis symbola Christi.

44. *Commentarius in librum Ecclesiastes* 1, 11, q. 2, concl.: Verbum divinum est omnis creatura, quia deum loquitur.

material connection, of course, does linger. Some might even wonder about the availability of Eriugena's texts, given the *Periphyseon*'s condemnation in 1225 at the council at Sens. However, this condemnation, rather than propose a paucity of availability of Eriugenian sources, may suggest just the opposite: to be condemned, thinkers must have been reading him (this was certainly the case with the Aristotelian corpus). In fact, we know they were. There resided in the library at the University of Paris a Dionysian textbook compiled in the second quarter of the 13th century.[45] Known as the *Opus maius*, this text included among its five translations of the Dionysius's *Mystical Theology* Eriugena's own. Further, Eriugena's writing makes up a good percentage of the marginalia, including quotes from the *Periphyseon*.[46] What is crucial to note is that this was *the* Dionysian textbook at Paris, which Bonaventure himself certainly used. That the Seraphic Doctor read Eriugena seems incontrovertible.[47]

Yet there is a further connection that suggests the likelihood of the Irishman's contribution to Bonaventure's philosophy and theology. In the *De mysterio Trinitatis* and the *De scientia Christi*, Bonaventure utilizes a peculiar triple predication of infinity concerning the divine being (*pro eo quod infinitum, eo quod infinitum divinum esse est infinitissime infinitum*).[48] J. Isaac Goff has pointed out that this triple formula is found in neither the Damascene nor the Cappadocians, but is present in Maximus. Further, it does not show up in any Latin sources preceding Bonaventure except one: Eriugena, who not only translates the formula from Maximus's *Ad Thalassium*,[49] but employs it three times in the *Periphyseon*.[50] Moreover, the section contain-

45. Paris, BnF Lat. 17341.

46. A partial translation and notes on the marginalia, with introductory material, can be found in L. Michael Harrington's edition *A Thirteenth-Century Textbook of Mystical Theology at the University of Paris*. See also McEvoy, "John Scottus Eriugena and Thomas Gallus, Commentators on the *Mystical Theology*," 193–202.

47. Luke V. Togni, currently dissertating at Marquette University, is specifically analyzing Bonaventure's reception of the medieval Dionysian tradition, and highlights in particular the way in which Eriugena's identification of the Trinity as hierarchy and even as proto-cult anticipates Bonaventure's fully realized doctrine of hierarchy. Togni and I concur that the availability of Eriugena's *Celestial Commentary* in the compilation of texts known as the *Opus maius* (BnF Lat. 17341) in Paris offers an explanation for Bonaventure's unique description of God as the *sui pius cultor* (*Hex* 21.7-8).

Bougerol shows that Bonaventure did tend to favor Eriugena's translation of Dionysius, along with that of John Sarrazin, which he speculates came from "hybrid source . . . a worked-over transcription of Scotus-Sarrazin" (Bougerol, *Introduction*, 39–48). The presence of BnF Lat. 17341 makes this speculation less likely.

48. *De mysterio Trinitatis* q. 3, a. 1, ad 13. See Goff, *Caritas in Primo*, 248–50.

49. Qs 56, 60, and 63.

50. *PP* I 517B; II 525A and 586C.

ing the third use of the formula appears in the marginalia. Unfortunately for this study, the quote of the section begins ten lines below the actual triple predication, thus not providing an actual material connection. Even so, as James McEvoy has commented, this textbook facilitated Eriugena's considerable influence "silent but real, upon the second Latin reception of the *Mystical Theology*."[51] This textbook also enjoyed a commodious dissemination, being the urtext of at least thirteen further manuscripts.

Conclusion

That the Irishman exercised some influence on the Seraphic Doctor's philosophy and theology is to my mind indubitable. The parallels do not just represent a few corresponding concepts, but rather a shared theologic between these thinkers. The very anchors of cosmological and theological thought for these theologians both work and relate within their grand systems in strikingly similar, if not at times identical, ways. Many have spilled ink on the unique thought patterns and systemizations of Bonaventure and Eriugena respectively; perhaps more ink, precious though it may be, is worth spilling on whether Eriugena does not just echo in Bonaventure, but resound in him, and so by extension, the Franciscan intellectual tradition.

51. McEvoy, "Eriugena and Thomas Gallus," 201.

Bibliography

Allard, Guy H. "La technique de la <Reductio> chez Bonaventure." In *S. Bonaventura 1274–1974*, edited by Jacques Guy Bougerol, 2:395–416. Rome: Collegio S. Bonaventura Grottaferrata, 1974.

Bonaventure. *Doctoris seraphici S. Bonaventurae opera omnia*. Edited by the Fathers of the Collegium S. Bonaventurae. Ad Claras Aquas (Quaracchi). 10 vols. Rome: Collegium S. Bonaventurae, 1882–1902.

Bougerol, J. Guy. *Introduction to the Works of Bonaventure*. Translated by José de Vinck. Paterson, NJ: St. Anthony Guild, 1963.

Bowman, Leonard. "The Cosmic Exemplarism of Bonaventure." *The Journal of Religion* 55/2 (1975) 181–98.

Goff, J. Isaac. *Caritas in Primo: A Study of Bonaventure's* Disputed Questions on the Mystery of the Trinity. New Bedford, MA: Academy of the Immaculate, 2015.

Harrington, L. Michael. *A Thirteenth-Century Textbook of Mystical Theology at the University of Paris: The* Mystical Theology *of Dionysius the Areopagite in Eriugena's Latin Translation with the Scholia translated by Anastasius the Librarian and Excerpts from Eriugena's Periphyseon*. Dallas Medieval Texts and Translations 4. Paris: Peeters, 2004.

John Scottus Eriugena. *Carmina*. Edited and translated by Michael Herren. Scriptores Latini Hiberniae 12. Dublin: Dublin Institute for Advanced Studies, 1993.

———. *Homilia super 'in principio erat verbum' et Commentarius in evangelius Iohnannis*. Edited by Édouard A. Jeauneau. Corpus Christianorum 166. Turnhout: Brepols, 2008.

———. *Periphyseon (De diuisione naturae)*. Edited by I. P. Sheldon-Williams and Édouard A. Jeauneau. Vols. 1–4. Scriptores Latini Hiberiae 13. Dublin: School of Celtic Studies, 1999–2009.

McEvoy, James. "John Scottus Eriugena and Thomas Gallus, Commentators on the Mystical Theology." In *History and Eschatology in John Scottus Eriugena and His Time: Proceedings of the Tenth International Conference of the Society for the Promotion of Eriugenian Studies, Maynooth and Dublin, August 16–20, 2000*, edited by James McEvoy and Michael Dunne, 193–202. Leuven: Leuven University Press, 2002.

Nichols, Aidan. *Say It Is Pentecost: A Guide through Balthasar's Logic*. Washington, DC: Catholic University of America Press, 2001.

13

The Problem of María de Ágreda's Scotism

Trent Pomplun

ALTHOUGH LITTLE KNOWN OUTSIDE of Franciscan circles, the visionary and missionary to Texas, Sor María de Jesús de Ágreda (†1665) was once among the most controversial figures in the Church.[1] Although Sor María died in the odor of sanctity and was declared Venerable by Pope Clement X in 1673, her posthumously published *Mística ciudad de Dios* served as the touchstone for several long-ranging theological controversies during the eighteenth and nineteenth centuries, including—but not limited to—debates about the status of private revelations in the Church, the nature of theology as a science, and the definability of the dogma of the Immaculate Conception.[2] The *Mística ciudad de Dios* continues to provoke controversy. As recently as 1998, the theological commission chosen by the Congregation for the Doctrine of the Faith opined—quite wrongly in the judgment of many— that Sor María's presentation of Mary, while containing nothing that was doctrinally suspect, was incompatible with the Mariology developed by the Second Vatican Council and the picture of the Blessed Virgin found in Holy

---

1. Fedewa, *María of Ágreda, Mystical Lady in Blue*; Colahan, *The Visions of Sor María of Ágreda*.

2. María de Jesús de Ágreda, *Mística ciudad de Dios* [=MCD] *Vida de María milagro de su omnipotencia y abismo de la gracia. Historia divina y vida de la Virgen Madre de Dios, Reina y Señora nuestra, María Santíssima, Restauradora de la Culpa de Eva y Medianera de la Gracia, dictada y manifestada en estos últimos siglos por la misma Señora a su esclava Sor María de Jesús, abadesa indigna de este convento de la Inmaculada Concepción de la villa de Ágreda para nueva luz del mundo, alegría de la Iglesia Católica y confianza de los mortales.* The standard English translation of the *Mística ciudad de Dios* is Blatter, *City of God: The Divine History and Life of the Virgin Mother of God manifested to Mary of Agreda for the Encouragement of Men.* The English translation, beloved by many who support Sor María's canonization, must be checked against Father Solaguren's edition, which has added certain details from her autographs.

Scripture.[3] The theologians appointed by Cardinal Ratzinger were not of course the first to see scandal in Sor María's depiction of the Blessed Virgin Mary. The Dominicans and Jansenists who first censured the *Mística ciudad de Dios* in the late-seventeenth and early-eighteenth centuries accused her of being a pawn in a larger Franciscan scheme to advance the dogma of the Immaculate Conception.[4] Some even went so far as to suggest that one of her confessors wrote the *Mística ciudad de Dios*. Everyone acknowledges, of course, that Sor María was an autodidact. She was after all forbidden to study theology professionally, and her learning would have been limited as a result. Most scholars, in their desire to defend the authenticity of the *Mística ciudad de Dios*, resist the temptation to identify possible influences upon it altogether. They content themselves with a noncommittal comparison of the *Mística ciudad de Dios* to the Mariologies of Sor María's contemporaries, or they discuss the influence of the *Mística ciudad de Dios* upon later theologians without addressing any prior influences upon it. This reticence—while understandable given the nature of the charges made against Sor María—risks creating the impression that she was too simple to have followed theologians' arguments or to have read their works. What is more important, such reticence risks a genuine failure to recognize Sor María's contributions to the larger theological tradition.

3. The response is quoted in Calvo Moralejo, "La Purísima Concepción de María," 85–117, here 87: "En su sesión ordinaria de octubre pasado, ha llegado a la conclusión de que no se puede afirmar que se hallen presentes verdaderos errores doctrinales y herejías en el citado libro. Y, sorprendentemente, añade sobre su mariología. La presentación que se hace en dicha obra de la figura de la Madre de Dios, contrasta con la que nos ofrece la Sagrada Escritura, y no es compatible con la mariología desarrollada por el Vaticano II, aunque reconociendo las adquisiciones realizadas, la Congregación para la Doctrina de la fe, ha decidido no conceder el 'nihil obstat' para la prosecución de la causa de beatificación, teniendo en cuenta que una eventual aprobación de la causa comportaría la aprobación del libro en cuestión y una indirecta promoción suya." Father Enrique Llamas, OCD, has challenged this opinion in a small book that has been translated by Father Peter Damian Fehlner and published by the Academy of the Immaculate. Llamas, *Venerable Mother Agreda and the Mariology of Vatican II*, trans. Peter Damian Fehlner, FI. For the original, see Llamas, *La Madre Ágreda y la Mariología del Vaticano II*.

4. Mendía Lasa, and Artola Arbiza, *La Ven. M. María de Jesús de Ágreda y la Inmaculada Concepción*. Compare Campos, *Agredistas y Antiagredistas, estudio histórico-apologético*.

I. ON THE AUTHENTICITY OF
THE *MÍSTICA CIUDAD DE DIOS*

Father Benito Mendía Lasa, who has written the definitive history of the ecclesiastical process against Sor María, outlines the questions that have surrounded her writing. At first sight, he admits, there seems to be solid reasons to question its authenticity. Sor María was, after all, a simple nun with only elementary education.[5] One might, he reasons, admit that Sor María had a hand in the work, but judge it to be fraudulent. One might affirm that Sor María was responsible for the work's general sentiments, but not its formal composition. Of course, one might also simply assume that Sor María's confessors dictated the work to her, in whole or in part. All three of these opinions, however, agree upon one point according to Father Mendía Lasa: that the person principally responsible for the work was a Scotist who supported the dogmatic definition of the doctrine of the Immaculate Conception. In fact, neither supporters nor critics doubted that the author of the *Mística ciudad de Dios* was familiar with the finer points of Scotist Christology. Sor María's first critics, however, adopted the third strategy. Theological science, they reasoned, is either acquired or infused. Sor María never studied theological science, and so could not have had an acquired knowledge of it. Consequently, if the theological science of the *Mística ciudad de Dios* is acquired, then Sor María cannot be its author. But neither can the theological science of the *Mística ciudad de Dios* be infused, the Dominicans reasoned, because then God himself might support the Immaculate Conception or—worse—be himself a Scotist. Therefore, they

---

5. Mendía Lasa, "En torno al problema," 391–430, here 391: "Parece a primera vista que hay sólidas razones para negar que sea Sor María de Jesús la autora de esta obra. ¿Cómo es posible que una simple monja sin más estudios que los elementales y sin ninguna formación filosófico-teológica, ni escriturística, ni científica haya podido escribir una obra como la 'Mística Cuidad de Dios' en que todos los misterios de la revelación cristiana aparecen tan coherente y armónicamente sistematizados en torno a los dos misterios fundamentales de la encarnación y de redención; una obra en que con tanta lógica y tan estrecha consecuencia aparecen concatenados todos los privilegios, gracias y dones concedidos por el Altísimo a María santísima; una obra en que con tanta profusión y tan acomodadamente son aducidos y empleados los textos sagrados, y en que abundan tanto los datos y detalles de orden cronológico, geográfico, científico, etc.? Y todo ello expuesto con admirable orden, claridad y precisión y gran elevación de estilo. Esto explica el hecho de que inmediatamente que apareció impresa fueran muchos los que aseguraban que no podía ser de Sor María de Jesús, sino que debía de ser de algún teólogo franciscano, escotista por añadidura, quien amparándose bajo el nombre y la autoridad de una religiosa famosa por sus visiones y revelaciones, publicaba como reveladas del cielo las doctrinas propias de la escuela."

concluded, the *Mística ciudad de Dios* was written not by Sor María, but by some unknown Scotist.[6]

Although defenders of Sor María, rightly anxious to affirm the authenticity of her work, have hardly attempted to trace its influences, they have done a great deal to explain the context of its writing. In a series of articles in the late 1950s and the early 1960s, Julio Campos outlined the general background of Sor María's writing and provided a great deal of documentary evidence from the various minister generals of the Franciscans (Pedro Manero, Alonso Salizanes, José Ximénez Samaniego), the commissioner general of Spain (Juan de Palma), and the various provincial ministers of Burgos (Francisco Andrés de la Torre, Miguel Gutiérrez, Andrés de Fuenmayor).[7] Campos identifies several theologians who worked in near proximity to Sor María, such as the Mercedarian Pedro Arriola, who examined the *Mística ciudad de Dios*, and—perhaps more suggestively—the Carmelite Raimundo Lumbier y Ángel (†1684) and the great Jesuit Juan Martínez de Ripalda (†1648). Campos also lists a large number of theologians, Franciscan and otherwise, who appear to have been influenced by Sor María or who defended her during the controversies that followed upon her death. He does not, however, compare Sor María's *Mística ciudad de Dios* to other Mariological works of the seventeenth century.

6. Mendía Lasa, "En torno al problema," 394: "Contra las afirmaciones de la Madre Agreda de que ella había escrito la MCD por mandato divino, y para narrar las revelaciones que había recibido de Dios y de su Madre santísima, acerca de los misterios y sacramentos de la Vida y de la Historia de María los adversarios de su origen sobrenatural y divino sostuvieron que se trataba de una obra cuyos verdaderos autores eran los hombres, más concretamente sus confesores o directores espirituales . . . .Todas estas diversas opiniones convenían en un punto: que el autor o inspirador de la MCD era algún teólogo franciscano, seguidor fiel de las doctrinas escotistas, especialmente de la doctrina de la Inmaculada Concepción. El fundamento en que se basaba la negación de la autenticidad de la MCD podríamos resumirlo en el razonamiento que sigue: la 'Mística Cuidad de Dios' encierra un gran caudal de teología escolástica, pero como Sor María no cursó jamás los estudios teológicos, la ciencia que encierra la MCD no es ciencia adquirida. Tampoco puede ser ciencia infundida por Dios, porque en la MCD hay mucha doctrina escotista y es absolutamente inadmisible que Dios no sepa otra teología que la escotista. Y de las premisas de que la MCD no es fruto de ciencia adquirida por la Venerable Madre, ni fruto de ciencia infundida o revelada por Dios, concluían que las doctrinas escotistas de la MCD probaban que el autor de esta obra era algún teólogo franciscano, seguidor y fiel discípulo de la escuela escotista"

7. Campos, "Para la historia interna de la 'Mística Ciudad de Dios.' Fray Andres de Fuenmayor, director espiritual de la M. Agreda," 210–36; idem, "Para la historia externa de la 'Mística Ciudad de Dios.' Fray José de Falces, procurador de los libros de la M. Ágreda," 159–85; idem, "La Venerable Madre Ágreda y su obra en Navarra," 305–93; idem, "Los Padres Juan de Palma, Pedro Manero y Pedro de Arriola y la 'Mística Ciudad de Dios,'" 227–52.

Father Ángel Martínez Moñux did just this in two articles from 1964 and 1968. In the first, he places Sor María in the larger context provided by the debates about the *debitum peccati* that swept Spain in the first quarter of the seventeenth century.[8] In the second, he expands his analysis to discuss Sor María's teachings in light of debates about the definability of the dogma of the Immaculate Conception during the 1630s and 1640s.[9] Father Martínez Moñux addresses the works of Sor María's contemporaries Gil da Presentação (†1626), Juan Serrano (†1637), Francisco Quaresmio (†1650), Luke Wadding (†1657), Francisco Guerra (†1658), Angelo Volpi (†1676), Juan Sendín Calderón (†1676), and Tomás Francés Urrutigoyti (†1682)—as well as the theologians who followed or defended her, such as Carlos del Moral (†1731), Diego González Mateo (†1741), and Dalmatius Kick (†1769). Despite his impressive bibliographical research, Father Martínez Moñux makes little attempt to trace any influences upon Sor María and contents himself with a doctrinal synthesis of her Mariology in light of the aforementioned theologians.[10] As a result, he prefers to speculate less about the influence of Sor María's contemporaries upon her and more about Sor María's influence upon later writers.[11] He does, however, add the tantalizing suggestion that Urrutigoyti might have influenced Sor María's work.

Father Celestino Solaguren continued this line of speculation, with the assistance of Father Martínez Moñux, in his critical edition of the *Mística ciudad de Dios*.[12] Father Solaguren notes, with genuine historical and theological sensitivity, that questions about the work's authenticity help us but little to understand its content.[13] Of course, Father Solaguren does not be-

8. Martínez Moñux, "La Inmaculada Concepción en la 'Mística Ciudad de Dios' de la Madre Ágreda," 645-65.

9. Martínez Moñux, "María signo de la creación,'" 135-78.

10. Martínez Moñux, "La Inmaculada Concepción," 645-46: "Teólogos de renombre y universidades de primer orden militaron, por una y otra parte en la controversia. Unos, condenan implacablemente la obra; otros, hablan de ella como de un quinto evangelico. De este modo seda en ella el caso antitético de ser incluida en el Indice de libros prohibidos y al mismo tiempo ser considerada como algo cuasi inspirado. Falta aún, creemos, una síntesis doctrinal, escrita sin prejuicios y al margen de todo apasionamiento."

11. Ibid., 646: "Esto nos facilitara el camino para comprender después la misma discusión y nos pondrá de relieve el por que del influjo de su obra en los teólogos de su tiempo y en teólogos inmediatamente posteriores."

12. Solaguren, "La doctrina mariológica de la 'Mística Ciudad de Dios' y la teología de su tiempo," lix–xc.

13. Solaguren, "La doctrina mariológica," xxvi: "Pero todo esto, con ser importante, no basta para resolver el problema; antes, en parte, lo complica más, porque puestos a fingir engaños o hipótesis posibles, ¿no pudo todo ello ser hecho de propósito para encubrir fraudes? ¿No pudo Sor María copiar o escribir con su mano una obra de la

lieve the *Mística cuidad de Dios* to be copied in its entirety or in part. He readily acknowledges Franciscan theologians and Sor María's confessors to be the sources of the scholastic theology found in her work, but he does not speculate about how she might have come by that knowledge, except in the most general terms. According to Father Solaguren, Sor María does not use the Scotist theology that her critics saw as evidence of plagiarism or fraud with the technicality of the theologian, but with the personal stamp of the artist.[14] Like Father Martínez Moñux, Father Solaguren presents Sor María's teachings against the backdrop of other Franciscan theologians, but he shies away from addressing any direct literary dependence. In fact, given the personal nature of her conversations with her confessors and theologians, Father Solaguren believes it impossible to trace any direct literary dependence upon the *Mística ciudad de Dios*.[15]

Fathers Martínez Moñux and Solaguren are content to place Mother Ágreda in larger theological contexts, even the great Franciscan theologians of the twentieth century—Parthenius Minges, Carolus Balić, and Pedro Alcántara especially—but hesitant to speculate about any scholastic sources she might have read. Both are confident, however, that Sor María read pious works such as Diego Murillo's *Vida y excelencias de la Madre de Dios* (Zaragoza 1614). Recent scholars, such as Andrés Molina Prieto, Enrique Llamas, and Gaspar Calvo Moralejo, follow their lead in this respect: they minimize the direct impact of Scotist sources on María of Ágreda and emphasize the indirect influence of pious writings on her writing. Prieto, for example, judges the *Mística ciudad de Dio* to be personal and largely autodidactic. Its sources, he thinks, were oral and non-literary, except for the books of prayer and other devotional works suitable for a convent.[16]

---

que en realidad no era ella la verdadera autora, tomando precauciones para que esto no se descubriese? Fuerza es confesar que, poniéndonos a imaginar hipótesis posibles, por poco probables que ellas sean, no se puede descartar ésta."

14. Ibid., xxxvi: "Las mismas doctrinas propiamente teológicas, tanto las comunes como las de escuela estas últimas debidas sin duda a los teólogos y directores franciscanos aparecen en la obra expuestas con un matiz completamente personal, como algo, digámoslo así, digerido, vivido y personalizado por quien escribe la obra. Aun en los casos en que utiliza términos e ideas propios de los teólogos, su utilización y exposición nunca tiene el tecnicismo propio de un teólogo, sino e mismo sello personal de las restantes páginas."

15. Ibid., lv: "Dado este género de información no es posible consignar una dependencia literaria directa. Por esta razón damos en el siguiente capítulo de esta introducción un amplio resumen de las ideas teológico-marianas de la autora confrontándolas con los autores de su época. Creemos hacer así un servicio útil para estudios comparativos ulteriores."

16. Molina Prieto, "El culto mariano de imitación en la 'Mística Ciudad de Dios' de la venerable Sor María de Jesús de Ágreda," 223–50, here 224: "Es un producto literario

Of course, as Ismael Bengoechea has shown, such works are the natural literary context of Sor María's *Mística ciudad de Dios*, which he identifies as one of the four most influential *Vidas* of the Blessed Virgin in seventeenth-century Spain.[17] Father Bengoechea notes Pedro de la Vega's *Dei genitricis semperque Virginis Mariae vita* (Zaragoza 1533), Pedro Alfonso de Burgos's *De vita et laudibus Mariae Virginis* (Barcelona 1562), and Diego Velázquez's *Regina Coeli* (Medina de Campo 1580) as important precursors in the genre, before describing forty-five *Vidas* from the seventeenth century, with extended analysis of Sor María *Mística ciudad de Dios*, Diego Murillo's aforementioned *Vida y excelencias de la Madre de Dios*, Cristobal de Castro's *Historia Deiparae Virginis Mariae* (Alcalá 1605), and José de Jesús María Quiroga's *Historia de la Virgen María* (Amberes 1652). Bengoechea's analysis has led Enrique Llamas to wonder whether to classify the *Mística ciudad de Dios* as a *Vida* or as a work of theology.[18]

The all-too-easy placement of Sor María's *Mística ciudad de Dios* in an appropriately "feminine" context has led scholars to minimize the influence of other types of literature upon Sor María. Father Llamas does not deny that she might have read various works, but dismisses the influence of theological works or "manuals" upon her thought.[19] Father Llamas does not hesitate to write, "Today it is generally presupposed that the *Mystical City of God* is the fruit of meditation on the mysteries of the Mother of Jesus and of contemplative prayer, rather than of academic study."[20] Sor María, he explains, "did not have a theological formation of the scholastic type. For that reason, she could not write or compose a work of theological character on the basis of concepts or thematic expositions as this is done in scholastic treatises on Mariology. It would have been extremely difficult for her to follow this method."[21] According to Father Llamas, Sor María rather "had at

---

personal de índole autodidáctica, ya que sólo disponía de la elemental cultura recibida en su familia y villa natal, cuando ingresó a los doce años en la vida monástica. Sus fuentes son orales y no librescas, a excepción de los libros de rezo y de carácter piadoso, propios del convento. Por ello no puede advertirse una dependencia literaria próxima."

17. Bengoechea, "'Vidas de la Virgen María' en la España del siglo XVII," 59–103.

18. Llamas, "'La Mística Ciudad de Dios,'" 159–60.

19. Ibid., 161: "Pero, la Madre Ágreda—tal como se manifiesta en MCD—no recibe precisamente los conocimientos teológicos relativos a la Madre de Dios de la lectura de los libros y manuales al uso. No quiero decir que no los conociera y los leyese. Pero, muchos de los temas que ella trata y explica en su obra, y muchas de sus afirmaciones no están registradas en las páginas de los libros de su tiempo. En su mayor parte ella recibe sus conocimientos por otro camino. Ella se hace eco de ciertas intervenciones extraordinarias de Dios, de la Virgen María y de los Ángeles."

20. Llamas, *Mother Agreda*, 4.

21. Ibid., 8.

her disposition an ample and precise theoretical knowledge in relation to the principal problems of Mariology . . . acquired in various ways: reading, conversations, listening to conferences and sermons, etc."[22] A final—if yet ambiguous—representative of this view is Gaspar Calvo Moralejo. Father Calvo Moralejo does not address the question of where Sor María learned Scotist doctrine, only that she welcomed it with great enthusiasm as an aid to understanding her visions.[23] Calvo Moralejo rightly praises Sor María as one of the great representatives of the Spanish Mariological tradition of the seventeenth century, but he still treats Sor María—instinctually perhaps— more as a source for that tradition and less as a recipient of it. As a result, Sor María's relationship to her predecessors remains, much as it has since the seventeenth century, unexplored.

II. SOR MARÍA'S PRESENTATION
OF THE DIVINE DECREE

We are, I think, back where we started. Sor María's critics, rightly recogniz- ing the technical Scotist vocabulary in the *Mística ciudad de Dios*, accused her Franciscan confessors of writing it for her (at worst) or instructing her to include some highly polemical passages (at best).[24] Sor María's support- ers, while acknowledging the work's technical Scotist vocabulary, explain its presence largely through osmosis. Both critic and supporter alike share the assumption that Sor María did not read—indeed could not have read—the sort of theological treatises in which one normally finds such technical vo- cabulary. I cannot but repeat my conviction that the reticence of Sor María's

---

22. Ibid., 9.

23. Calvo Moralejo, "El Escotismo de la 'Mística Ciudad de Dios," 2:257–78, here 263: "La doctrina escotista, por su parte, encontraba en la concepcionista franciscana, una simpatía particular. La acoge con entusiasmo, como lo manifestará en sus escritos, pues le ofrecía una ayuda fundamental para la comprensión de las iluminaciones que recibe del Espíritu. Así aparece en su obra cumbre: Mística Ciudad de Dios. Por tanto, la M. Ágreda merece que su nombre figure como el de la gran escotista española del barroco y ella sea uno de los principales referentes de la doctrine de Escoto, particular- mente mariana, en el siglo XVII."

24. Mendía Lasa and Artola Arbiza, *La Ven. M. María de Jesús de Ágreda*, 68. The text of the Holy Office, which they quote, says, "Et quod est gravi consideratione dig- num, semper loquitur juxta principia Scoticae Scholae in his, in quibus ab aliis Scholis discrepant, ita ut ex hujus historiae approbatione approbata videretur universa Scoti doctrina tanquam divinitus revelata." The Holy Office reserved its stronger rhetoric for what it judged to be her confessor's influence: "Quare mirum non est, si ejus confes- sarius ex nimio affectu erga Scoti doctrinam impulit hanc mulierem, ut scriberet hanc historiam: immo vero instruxit" (78).

supporters to explore such influence is entirely understandable given the nature of the claims made against her, but I think little harm would be done were it shown that Sor María read a theological treatise or two. It is generally acknowledged, with Pedro Manero and Andrés de Fuenmayor as authorities, that Sor María could read Latin, and Father Martínez Moñux has already suggested, with great caution, that Tomás Francés Urrutigoyti might have influenced Sor María. Of course, such influence could have been "non-literary," picked up willy-nilly from sermons and personal conversations. Everyone from Julio Campos to Enrique Llamas is comfortable with this suggestion, and the fact of such influence is impossible to deny. To make the case even stronger we should adduce as evidence the well documented capacity of early modern people to memorize vast amounts of material. If Sor María had the opportunity to hear or speak with Tomás Francés Urrutigoyti, Raimundo Lumbier y Ángel, or even Juan Martínez de Ripalda, one might reasonably think she would have learned no small amount of scholastic jargon. These influences, as Celestino Solaguren has already noted, are by nature impossible to trace.

How might one establish a genuine, direct, literary influence? Here, too, I think Father Soluguren provides a way forward. Solaguren judges Sor María to have used the technical terms of scholastic theology in an entirely "personal" way. It is central to his argument—circumstantial though it is—that Sor María uses the technical terms of Scotist theology with none of the technical rigor one might find in professional theologians of the seventeenth century. What, though, constitutes the rigor necessary to make this distinction between the personal and professional use of scholastic jargon? One cannot doubt, of course, that Sor María lacked professional theological training or that the *Mística ciudad de Dios* avoids the conventions of seventeenth-century scholasticism. One might also assume on the contrary that it follows the conventions of *Vidas* of the Blessed Virgin. Strictly speaking, however, if it cannot be established conclusively that Sor María read Scotist works, neither can it be established conclusively that she did not. Consequently, any argument that one might make in this respect shall be of necessity circumstantial. Since the arguments of Sor María's critics and supporters alike hang upon her use of the technical vocabulary of Scotist theology, I should like to take a closer look at it, especially in the third and fourth chapters of the first book of the *Mística ciudad de Dios*. If a case can be made—either for Sor María's dependence on another writer or for her theological daring—I think it best made on her use of Scotist vocabulary.

If nothing else, it must be admitted that *Mística ciudad de Dios* is quite *au courant*: it reads like a typical theological treatise *ad mentem Scoti* from the middle of the seventeenth century While its first chapter recounts the two visions that inspired Sor María to compose the work and its second explains her visions with the familiar Augustinian classification of visions found in *De Genesi ad litteram* XII, the remainder of the book is a faithful exposition of several themes discussed in Scotist Christologies, such as the motive of the Incarnation, the difference between its substance and mode, and the *signa rationis* by which we might understand the decree of the Holy Trinity to become man even if Adam had not fallen. In fact, the Scotism for which Sor María was accused by her Thomist and Jansenist critics is nowhere more apparent than in her treatment of the *signa rationis*, a topic singled out by early modern anti-Scotists with some frequency, even when they were experts in the technical use of such distinctions themselves.

Sor María presents the *signa rationis* in *Mística ciudad de Dios*, book one, chapters three and four. After petitioning the Lord to make known to her the place of the Mother of God in the divine decree, she alerts her readers that she will divide the order of God's decree into "moments" or "instants," since it is impossible to accommodate God's knowledge to our limited minds in any other way. Lest one think Sor María to be but a simple nun, we should note at the outset that she is operating with a level of technical sophistication that would scarcely be available to one with only rudimentary education. Even so, she takes care to explain the *signa rationis* first in non-technical language fit for a generally educated, but non-scholastic, audience:

> I knew that the Most High remained in the state of his own being when (according to our understanding) the three Divine Persons decreed to communicate their perfections as gifts. I should note, for greater clarity, that God understands all things in himself with an act that is indivisible, most simple, and non-discursive. He does not proceed from the knowledge of one thing to the knowledge of another like we proceed, distinguishing and knowing first one thing with an act of understanding and later another thing with a subsequent act. God knows all things together in a single moment, with neither prior nor posterior in his infinite understanding, since all are together in the uncreated divine notions and *scientia*, just as they are in God's being, protected and contained as in the First Principle.[25]

25. *MCD*, lib. I, cap. 3, n. 31, 31: "Conocí, pues, que en el estado de su mismo ser estaba el Altísimo, cuando entre las tres divinas personas a nuestro entender se decretó el comunicar sus perfecciones de manera, que hiciesen dones de ellas. Y es de advertir, para mejor declararme, que Dios entiende todas las cosas con un acto en sí mismo indivisible y simplicísimo y sin discurso; y no procede del conocimiento de una cosa a conocer otra, como nosotros procedemos discurriendo, y conociendo primero una con un acto del entendimiento y luego otra con otro; porque Dios todas

With the mention of God's *scientia*, however, Sor María moves quickly into more technical scholastic vocabulary, which she clarifies with a technical distinction that would be heard outside professional theological circles only rarely:

> In this *scientia*, which is called chiefly the science of simple intelligence, according to the natural precedence of the understanding over the will, we must consider in God an order, not of time, but of nature, by which we understand his act of understanding to precede his will, because we consider first the act of understanding in itself before the decree of his desiring to create anything. In this state or instant the Three Divine Persons confirmed through this act of understanding the fittingness of their works *ad extra* and of all creatures which have been and will be in the future.[26]

We will have plenty of time to unpack this. For now, note that Sor María explicitly defines God's *scientia simplicis intelligentiae*, in contrast to what scholastic theologians call God's *scientia visionis*, as that simple act of God's intelligence by which he knows all beings that could be, before he decides by an act of will to create the particular world in which we live, rather than the uncountable things that could have been. Sor María also distinguishes between God's actions *ad intra* and *ad extra*, as well as between logical and temporal orders of precedence. For good measure, she also uses the technical language of *convenientia* without explaining it, assuming at least that her theologically-educated readers would agree that God does not merely know all things in his *scientia simplicis intelligentiae*, but that he knows all of the possible relations that might obtain between them, harmonious or not. The implication, which would not have been lost on her educated readers, is that God creates only the world that is *convenientissimum*. Sor María then describes the *scientia visionis*:

---

las conoce juntamente de una vez, sin que haya en su entendimiento infinito primero ni postrero, que allí todas están juntas en la noticia y ciencia Divina increada, como lo están en el ser de Dios, donde se encierran y contienen, como en primer principio." On the spelling and punctuation of the modern edition, see the remarks of Father Solaguren at *MCD*, lvi-lviii.

26. *MCD*, lib. I, cap. 3, n. 32, 31: "En esta ciencia, que primero se llama de simple inteligencia, según la natural precedencia del entendimiento a la voluntad, se ha de considerar en Dios un orden, no de tiempo, mas de naturaleza, según el cual orden, primero entendemos que tuvo acto de entendimiento, que de voluntad; porque primero consideramos solo el acto de entender, sin decreto del querer criar alguna cosa. Pues en este estado, o instante confirieron las tres divinas personas, con aquel acto de entender, la conveniencia de las obras *ad extra*, y de todas las criaturas que han sido, son, y serán futuras."

And because his Majesty deigned to respond to the request that I, unworthy, proposed to him that I might know the order (as we should understand it) that he had taken in his determination to create all things, I asked him to know the place of our queen the Mother of God in the divine mind. I will recount, if you will, what God said and showed to me of the order of these ideas in God as I understood them, retracing his knowledge in instants, because without this "reduction" we cannot accommodate to our capacity the notion of the divine *scientia*, which is called here the science of vision, which encompasses the ideas or images of those creatures that God holds in his mind and decrees to create, knowing them infinitely better than we see and know them now.[27]

Sor María's "reduction" or "retracing" of these logical instants, by which we might understand the divine works *ad extra*, was the subject of great debate among scholastic theologians from John Duns Scotus to Sor María's day. As we shall see, the ordering of these *signa rationis* was an important part of arguments for and against the absolute predestination of Christ and the Blessed Virgin. Sor María, however, begins by explaining these logical *signa* in non-technical terms:

For although this divine science is one, simple, and indivisible, but the things that it observes are many, and between them there is order, with some that are first and others after, and some having their being or existence for others in dependence upon them, it is necessary therefore to divide God's *scientia* and will into several instants or acts according to the order of their corresponding objects. And thus we say that God first understood and determined that this thing should be for another, and if he did not know or want one thing through the science of vision, he should not want the other.[28]

27. *MCD*, lib. I, cap. 3, n. 33, 31: "Y porque su Majestad quiso dignarse de responderme al deseo que le propuse, indigna, de saber el orden que tuvo, o el que nosotros debemos entender, en la determinación de criar todas las cosas y yo lo pedía para saber el lugar, que en la mente divina tuvo la Madre de Dios y Reina nuestra diré, como pudiere, lo que se me respondió y manifestó y el orden que entendí en estas ideas en Dios, reduciéndolo a instantes; porque sin esto no se puede acomodar a nuestra capacidad la noticia de esta ciencia divina, que ya se llama aquí ciencia de visión, adonde pertenecen las ideas, o imágenes de las criaturas que decretó criar y tiene en su mente ideadas, conociéndolas infinitamente mejor que nosotros las vemos, y conocemos ahora."

28. *MCD*, lib. I, cap. 3, n. 34, 31: "Pues aunque esta divina ciencia es una y simplicísima e indivisible, pero como las cosas que mira son muchas, y entre ellas hay orden, que unas son primero y otras después, unas tienen ser o existencia por otras con dependencia de las unas, a las otras; por esto, es necesario dividir la ciencia de Dios,

Here, Sor María alludes to a common scholastic trope of the *debitum naturae*. Some things, she explains, logically depend upon others. In the common example: just as beings that breathe depend logically upon air to breathe, it would be supremely unfitting to think that God would create the former without also creating the latter. For Scotists of Sor María's generation, however, the same argument can be used in the order of grace; according to the *debitum gratiae*, it would be supremely unfitting if God, selecting from amongst the uncountable possible worlds known via his *scientia simplicis intelligentiae*, would not choose a world, indeed the world, which is most fitting to express his infinite grace and glory.

Sor María has an especially detailed treatment of the *signa rationis* in the fourth chapter of the *Mística ciudad de Dios*. She divides the divine decree into the following logical moments. In the first logical instant, God, knowing his infinite attributes and perfections, understands that it is natural and fitting to communicate the infinite treasures contained in his divinity. Alluding to standard seventeenth-century treatments of moral causality, Sor María notes that for God, being infinite love, it is more natural to bestow gifts and graces than for fire to ascend towards the heavenly spheres, for a stone to fall to the center of the earth, or for the sun to shed its own light.[29] In the second logical instant, God, knowing and loving himself perfectly, desires to communicate his divine perfections *ad extra* in an orderly fashion for the greater glory and exaltation of his Majesty.[30] For Sor María, God's desire to share his love compromises neither the freedom with which he will bestow his gifts nor the liberality of their outpouring. In order to understand Sor María's place in the

---

y lo mismo la voluntad, en muchos instantes o en muchos actos que correspondan a diversos instantes, según el orden de los objetos; y así decimos que Dios entendió y determinó primero esto que aquello y lo uno por lo otra; y si primero no quisiera o conociera con ciencia de visión una cosas, no quisiera la otra."

29. *MCD*, lib. I, cap. 4, n. 35, 32: "El primero es un el que conoció Dios sus divinos atributos y perfecciones, con las propensión e inefable inclinación a comunicarse fuera de sí; y éste fue el primer conocimiento de ser Dios comunicativo ad extra, mirando Su Alteza la condición de sus infinitas perfecciones, la virtud y eficacia que en sí tenían para obrar magníficas obras. Vio que tan suma bondad era convenientísima en su inclinación comunicativa y ejercer su liberalidad y misericordia, distribuyendo fuera de sí con magnificencia la plenitud de sus infinitos tesoros encerrados en la divinidad. Porque, siendo todo infinito, le es mucho más natural hacer dones y gracias, que al fuego subir a su esfera, a la piedra bajar al centro y al sol derramar su luz."

30. *MCD*, lib. I, cap. 4, n. 38, 33: "El segundo instante fue conferir y decretar esta comunicación de la divinidad con la razón y motivos de que fuese para mayor gloria ad extra y exaltación de Su Majestad con la manifestación de su grandeza. Y esta exaltación propia miró Dios en este instante como fin de comunicarse y darse a conocer en la liberalidad de derramar sus atributos y usar de su omnipotencia, para ser conocido, alabado y glorificado."

larger Scotistic tradition, we shall need to take a closer look at her presentation of the third, fourth, fifth, and sixth instants, which she presents with no small amount of creativity and scholastic ingenuity.

In the third logical instant, according to Sor María, God determines as the first object of his will *ad extra*, the Incarnate Word and all of the blessed coeval with him. If, then, in the first instant, God knows and loves himself and in the second logical instant he desires to communicate himself perfectly, in the third he determines that the most perfect way for his graces and gifts to be bestowed upon others is through the hypostatic union, in which he knows and determines the very order of his communication *ad extra*.[31] If I may be allowed a small digression: Twentieth century Scotists such as Juniper Carol and Allan Wolter interpreted the famous *totus Christus* in *Reportatio* III, qu. 7, dist. 4 to mean that had Adam not fallen, Christ would have been glorified totally, soul and body, in the first moment of creation.[32] Sor María, like many Scotists of the seventeenth century, implies the position that I favor, namely, that the whole Christ, Head and members, would have been glorified:

> In this [third] instant, God determined first that the divine Word should assume flesh and become visible, decreed the composition and perfection of the most holy humanity of Christ our Lord, and composed him in the divine mind. And secondly, so that others might imitate him, the divine mind designed in him the harmony and adornments of human nature, body and soul, with the powers to know and enjoy the Creator, to discern between good and evil, and to love the Lord himself with free will.[33]

In a more scholastic vein, Sor María continues: The hypostatic union of the second person of the most holy Trinity with human nature is the first work and object of the divine understanding and will came *ad extra*, the *primum volitum* in scholastic terminology. God, knowing and loving himself in himself,

31. *MCD*, lib. I, cap. 4, n. 39, 33: "El tercer instante fue conocer y determinar el orden y disposición o el modo de esta comunicación en la forma que se consiguiese el más glorioso fin de obrar tan ardua determinación."

32. Carol, *Why Jesus Christ?*, 123; Wolter, "John Duns Scotus," 149.

33. *MCD*, lib. I, cap. 4, n. 39, 33: "En este instante se determinó en primer lugar que el Verbo divino tomase carne y se hiciese visible y se decretó la perfección y compostura de la humanidad santísima de Cristo nuestro Señor y quedó fabricada en la mente divina; y en segundo lugar, para los demás a su imitación, ideando la mente divina la armonía de la humana naturaleza con su adorno y compostura de cuerpo orgánico y alma para él, con sus potencias para conocer y gozar de su Criador, discerniendo entre el bien y el mal, con voluntad libre para amar al mismo Señor."

and desiring to communicate himself *ad extra*, desires to communicate his perfections in the way "most immediate" to his divinity.[34]

If God determines the *totus Christus*, consisting of the Incarnate Word and all of the blessed coeval with him as the *primum volitum* of his actions *ad extra* in the third logical moment, in the fourth he decrees the gifts and graces that he will bestow upon to the humanity of Christ and upon the Blessed Virgin Mary who shall be the Mother of God.[35] Here, as in any typical Scotist rendering of the *signa rationis*, we have Jesus Christ predestined with his Mother, which—as we shall see presently—will be followed by an account of the predestination of the angels and humanity *ante praevisum lapsum*.[36] In Sor María's account of the fourth logical instant, however, God decrees the adornment of Jesus Christ's humanity in the first place and Mary his Mother in the second, but also very world in which they might share their love:

> In this same instant, in the third and last place, God determined to create an abode and place where the Word of God and his Mother might live and converse. So in the first place, for them and by them alone, he created heaven and earth with its stars and elements and all that is contained therein; in the second place, he decreed as vassals of the King, the members of whom he would be the head; and thus with genuine providence, everything that was necessary and fitting for them was foreseen and prepared.[37]

34. *MCD*, lib. I, cap. 4, n. 40, 33: "Y esta unión hipostática de la segunda persona de la santísima Trinidad con la naturaleza humana, entendí que era como forzoso fuese la primera obra y objeto adonde primero saliese el entendimiento y voluntad divina ad extra, por altísimas razones que no podré explicar. Una es porque, después de haberse Dios entendido y amado en sí mismo, el mejor orden era conocer y amar a lo que era más inmediato a su divinidad, cual es la unión hipostática."

35. *MCD*, lib. I, cap. 4, n. 41, 34: "El cuarto instante fue decretar los dones y gracias que se le habían de dar a la humanidad de Cristo Señor nuestro, unida con la divinidad."

36. *MCD*, lib. I, cap. 4, n. 42, 34: "A este mismo instante, consiguientemente y como en segundo lugar, pertenece el decreto y predestinación de la Madre del Verbo humanado; porque aquí entendí fue ordenada esta pura criatura, antes que hubiese otro decreto de criar otra alguna. Y así fue primero que todas concebida en la mente divina, como y cual pertenecía y convenía a la dignidad, excelencia y dones de la humanidad de su Hijo santísimo."

37. *MCD*, lib. I, cap. 4, n. 45, 35: "En este mismo instante, y como en tercero y último lugar, determinó Dios criar lugar y puesto donde habitasen y fuesen conversables el Verbo humanado y su Madre; y en primer lugar, para ellos y por ellos solos crió el cielo y tierra con sus astros y elementos y lo que en ellos se contiene; y el segundo intento y decreto fue para los miembros de que fuese cabeza y vasallos de quien fuese rey; que con providencia real se dispuso y previno de antemano todo lo necesario y conveniente."

This fourth instant, in other words, following Scotus's rigorous application of the logic of final causality, concerns the total glory that redounds to creation on account of the Incarnation—not just the glory of Christ's soul and the Mother of God, but the New Jerusalem, the Holy Mountain, the eternal banquet.

One might wonder if Sor María hasn't repeated herself here in her description of the fourth logical moment. She hasn't. In fact, she's made an astute technical distinction with an important theological ramification. In the third logical instant, according to Sor María, God decrees the *totus Christus* as the end for which He's created the very world; in the fourth, God decrees the entire supernatural order, the immeasurable graces he freely gives, from the adornments of the soul and body of Christ, to the existence of his mother, to the very world and its subjects, as the supernatural means by which he will accomplish the end for which he has created the world. Here we see a presupposition of any notion of the absolute primacy of Christ made quite explicit, namely, that the entirety of creation is not just created for and by Christ and—in dependence upon him—for and by the Blessed Virgin Mary, according to the logic of a universal secondary final causality, but that as a result, all of creation, from the elements to the stars to humanity itself, speaks of them, grace upon grace.

Sor María also divides the fifth logical instant of God's decree with a threefold pattern. God first decrees and determines the creation of the nine choirs and three hierarchies of angels.[38] Secondly, he predestines the good angels to grace and glory in Christ, their head, exemplar, and King, and (through a merely negative act), permits the reprobation of the angels. Thirdly, God prepares heaven and hell for the good and bad angels just as he prepared the world for Christ and Mary.[39] In the sixth logical instant, God determines and decrees to raise up a people and congregation for Christ,

38. *MCD*, lib. I, cap. 4, n. 46, 35–36: "En este quinto, fue determinada la creación de la naturaleza angélica que, por ser más, excelente y correspondiente en ser espiritual a la divinidad, fue primero prevista, y decretada su creación y disposición admirable de los nueve coros y tres jerarquías .... Y en este instante les mereció Cristo Señor nuestro con sus infinitos merecimientos, presentes y previstos, toda la gracia que recibiesen; y fue instituido por su cabeza, ejemplar y supremo Rey, de quien eran vasallos."

39. *MCD*, lib. I, cap. 4, n. 47, 36: "A este instante la predestinación de los buenos y reprobación de los malos ángeles; y en él vio y conoció Dios, con su infinita ciencia, todas las obras de los unos y los otros con el orden debido, para predestinar con su libre voluntad y liberal misericordia a los que le habían de obedecer y reverenciar y para reprobar con su justicia a los que se habían de levantar contra Su Majestad en soberbia e inobediencia por su desordenado amor proprio. Y al mismo instante fue la determinación de criar al cielo empíreo, donde se manifestase su gloria y premiase en ella a los buenos, y la tierra y los demás para otras criaturas, y en el centro o profundo de ella el infierno para castigo de los malos ángeles."

already predetermined in the divine mind and will, and in whose image and likeness he decreed their very creation. At this moment, Sor María notes, the order of the creation of the whole human lineage was determined, starting with Adam and Eve, and from them to the Virgin and her Son. As with God's determination to create and predestine the angels, the creation and predestination of humanity is ordered in its entirety, from the original justice in which they were created to the perseverance by which they shall attain their end, by Christ's merits. Likewise, the fall of Adam was foreseen and permitted just as the sin of the rebel angels. God decrees Christ the mediator as the remedy for sin only after he had predestined Christ's subjects to grace and glory, so in typical Scotist fashion, for Sor María it is fitting to think that the Word would have still become incarnate even had Adam not sinned, and the predestination of the Blessed Virgin, as the predestination of Jesus Christ himself, lies entirely outside the decree by which God permits Adam's sin.[40] It bears noting that, according to Sor María, God does not prepare a separate world for human beings beyond the worlds he has created for Christ, his Mother, and the angels. The elect, of course, are predestined to share the world that God prepares for Christ and his mother.

We will compare Sor María's arrangement of the *signa rationis* to the arrangements of several prominent Scotist theologians in the next section. For now, however, we should note that Sor María herself notes the scholastic nature of her arrangement, if not its actual provenance:

> Of the doctrine and revelations of the two previous chapters, I formed a doubt, occasioned by what I have often heard and understood of learned persons that is disputed in the schools. My doubt was that if the first cause and motive of the divine Word to become human was to make the Word the head and firstborn of all creatures, and through his hypostatic union with human nature, to communicate his attributes and perfections in an ordered way to the predestined by grace and glory; and if the secondary motive and end of the Incarnation was to take

---

40. *MCD*, lib. I, cap. 4, n. 48, 36: "En el sexto instante fue determinado criar pueblo y congregación de hombres para Cristo, ya antes predetermino en la mente y voluntad divina, y a cuya imagen y semejanza se decretó la formación del hombre, para que el Verbo humanado tuviese hermanos semejantes e inferiores y pueblo de su misma naturaleza, de quien fuese cabeza. En este instante se determinó el orden de la creación de todo el linaje humano, que comenzase de uno solo y de una mujer y de ellos se propagase hasta la Virgen y su Hijo por el orden que fue concebido. Ordenóse por los merecimientos de Cristo nuestro bien, la gracia y dones que se les había de dar y la justicia original si querían perseverar en ella; vióse la caída de Adán y de todos en él, fuera de la Reina, que no entró en este decreto; ordenóse el remedio y que fuese pasible la humanidad santísima."

passible flesh and to die for humanity; how then are there such diverse opinions about this in the holy Church?[41]

Sor María not only mentions the controversy of the so-called motive of the Incarnation explicitly, she goes on to outline the main points of the Scotist position over the remainder of the first book of the *Mística ciudad de Dios*. As would be expected, Sor María bolsters her arrangement of the *signa rationis* with mystical interpretations of the eighth chapter of Proverbs, the first three chapters of Genesis, and the twelfth chapter of the Apocalypse, among other common Scotist proof texts. Sor María also deploys all of the standard technical arguments found in Scotist treatises during this time period in support of her ordering of the *signa rationis*. She uses Scotus's famous *ordinate volens* argument, for example, and states the scholastic axiom upon which it is based clearly.[42] When she places her doubt before the Lord, she receives the following answer, which no doubt piqued her Dominican censors:

> Those who say that the Word became incarnate in order to redeem the world, speak well, and those who say that the Word would become incarnate if man had not sinned, also speak well, if the position is understood rightly. For if Adam had not sinned, the Word would have descended from heaven in the form fitting for the state [of glory], but because Adam sinned, I determined by a secondary decree that the Word would come down passible, because, foreseeing sin, it was expedient that it should be repaired the way he has repaired it. And since you desire to know how the mystery of the Incarnation would have taken place if man had preserved the state of innocence, understand that the human form would have been the same in substance, but with the gift of impassibility and immortality,

41. *MCD*, lib. I, cap. 6, n. 72, 44: "Sobre las inteligencias y doctrina de los dos capítulos antecedentes se me ofreció una duda, ocasionada de lo que muchas veces he oído y entendido de personas doctas que se disputa en las escuelas. Y la duda fue: que si la causa y motivo principal para que el Verbo divino se humanase fue hacerla cabeza y primogénito de todas las criaturas y, por medio de la unión hipostática con la humana naturaleza, comunicar sus atributos y perfecciones en el modo conveniente por gracia y gloria a los predestinados, y el tomar carne pasible y morir por el hombre fue decreto como fin secundario; siendo esto así verdad, ¿cómo en la santa Iglesia hay tan diversas opiniones sobre ella?"

42. *MCD*, lib. I, cap. 6, n. 73, 45: "Este decreto se ejecutara sin duda en la encarnación, aunque el primer hombre no hubiera pecado, porque fue decreto expreso y sin condición en lo substancial, y así debía ser eficaz mi voluntad, que en el primer lugar fue comunicarme al alma y humanidad unida al Verbo, y esto era así conveniente a mi equidad y rectitud de mis obras; y aunque esto fue postrero en la ejecución, fue primero en la intención."

> just as my Only Begotten was after he was raised and before
> he ascended into heaven. He would have become incarnate
> to live and to converse with humanity, and the mysteries and
> sacraments would have all been manifested, and many times
> his glory would shine forth as it did once during his mortal life
> [i.e., on Mount Tabor].[43]

Leaving aside for the moment the very real possibility that God himself is a
Scotist, note that Sor María, when she takes the side of Duns Scotus against
Thomas Aquinas and his followers, shows herself familiar with another
technical distinction common in Scotistic treatises, the difference between
the substance and mode of the incarnation. This Scotistic commonplace
received no small amount of attention during the seventeenth century, as
Scotists then as now debated the relative merits of Christ's coming in impassible flesh. For our purposes, it is sufficient to note that Sor María does not
condemn he Thomist position; in fact, many theologians of her day, Scotist
and non-Scotist, resolved the disputation between the two schools in just
this manner, with the Subtle Doctor speaking well of the substance of the
Incarnation, and the Angelic Doctor speaking well of its mode. Indeed, in
the *Mística ciudad de Dios*, God himself—through Sor María—welcomes
the continuation of scholastic disputation and asserts the usefulness of
controversies in the Church, which serve to make all that he has hidden
manifest to the understanding.[44]

It will be readily apparent to anyone familiar with the history of
Scotism that Sor María has presented the basic talking points found in
Scotistic arguments for the absolute predestination of Christ: the distinction between God's *scientia simplicis intelligentiae* and *scientia visionis*, the
ordinate volens argument in support of Christ's absolute predestination,
a typically-Scotist ordering of the *signa rationis*, the distinction between

43. *MCD*, lib. I, cap. 6, n. 74, 45–46: "Los que dicen que encarnó el Verbo para
redimir el mundo, dicen bien; y los que dicen que encarna si el hombre no pecara, tam-
bién hablen bien, si con verdad se entiende; porque, si no pecara Adán, descendiera del
cielo en la forma que para aquel estado conviniera y, porque pecó, tuve aquel decreto
segundo que bajara pasible, porque, visto el pecado, convenía que la reparase en la
forma que lo hizo. Y porque deseas saber cómo se ejecutara este misterio de encarnar el
Verbo, si conservara el hombre el estado de la inocencia, advierte que la forma humana
fuera la misma en la sustancia pero con el don de la impasibilidad e inmortalidad;
cual estuvo mi Unigénito después que resucitó hasta que subió a los cielos, viviere y
conversara con los hombres; y los misterios y sacramentos fueran a todos manifiestos; y
muchas veces hiciera patente su gloria, como la hizo sola una vez cuando vivió mortal."

44. *MCD*, lib. I, cap. 6, n. 77, 47: "Y con esta variedad se variedad se va rastreando
la verdad y luz y se manifiestan más los sacramentos escondidos, porque la duda sirve
de estímulo al entendimiento para investigar la verdad; y en esto tienen honesta y santa
causa las controversias de los maestros."

the so-called substance and mode of the incarnation, and so forth. If we assume that she picked up these notions from sermons and personal conversations with her confessors—an assumption that remains entirely reasonable—I think it difficult at the very least to assert that Sor María could not have followed complex scholastic arguments. I think it impossible, moreover, to rule out the possibility that Sor María might have read some Scotist treatises by arguing that she used these technical terms in a merely "personal" manner. In point of fact, she uses these terms and distinctions precisely, with the exact same meaning and for the exact same ends that scholastic theologians do. If it is as yet impossible to find the smoking gun that shows she read any scholastic works, we might still compare her use of their technical language to that of her contemporaries.

III. THE *SIGNA RATIONIS* IN SEVENTEENTH-CENTURY SCOTISM

As with most arguments for the absolute predestination of Christ and Mary, the foundation of Sor María's argument is Scotus's famous *ordinate volens* argument from *In III Sententiarum*, dist. 7, qu. 3.[45] One who wills rationally, the Subtle Doctor reminds us, wills the end before the means, and so God wills glory before grace, and the one in whom all are predestined before any of those to be predestined in him. A difficulty arises, however, for the one who wishes to argue for the absolute predestination of Christ from this text alone. On the face of things, it very much appears to assert that God wills the hypostatic union as the means by which the glory of humanity, even the glory of the human soul of Christ, shall be brought about. Scotus, however, rejects the idea that the Incarnation is be occasioned by anything foreseen with the science of vision in *In III Sententiarum*, dist. 19, qu. unica, where he arranges the *signa rationis* as follows: in the first logical moment,

45. I shall use the Wadding edition as it was contemporary with Sor María; in fact, it represented the state of the art when she first placed her doubts before the Lord. Cf. Ioannes Duns Scotus, *In Lib. III Sententiarum*, dist. 7, qu. 3, no. 3, 202: "Praedestinatio cuiuscumque ad gloriam praecedat ex parte obiecti naturaliter, praescientiam peccati, vel damnationis cuiuscumque . . . multo magis est verum de praedestinatione illius animae, quae depraedestinabatur ad summum gloriam; universaliter autem ordinate volens prius videtur velle hoc quod est fini propinquius, et ita sicut prius gloriam alicui, quam gratiam, ita etiam inter praedestinatos, quibus vult gloriam ordinate prius videtur velle gloriam illi, quem vult esse proximum fini, et ita huic animae Christi vult gloriam prius, quam alicui alteri velit gloriam, et prius cuilibet alteri vult gratiam, et gloriam, quam praevideat opposite istorum habituum, scilicet gratiae, et gloriae, scilicet peccatum, et damnationem." For the modern critical text, see idem, *Ordinatio* III, dist. 7, qu. 3, no. 61, 287.

God knows himself as the highest good; in the second, God knows all creatures; in the third, God predestines all in the Incarnate Word *ante praevisa merita*; in the fourth, God foresees the Fall of Adam; and in the fifth, God foresees and ordains the Incarnate Word to suffer for the redemption of humankind.[46] *In III Sententiarum,* dist. 32, qu. unica, the Subtle Doctor, arranges the *signa* in a slightly different manner: in the first moment, God wills himself as the ultimate end of creatures; in the second, God wills the predestination of others as the created good most immediate to this end (which is to say, the ultimate good within the order of secondary causes); in the third, God wills grace as the means necessary to attain these ends; and in the fourth, God wills the sensible world as the remote means to accomplish these goals.[47] These three texts serve as the bedrock of any Scotist argument for the absolute predestination of Christ and Mary. To them, though, we should add a fourth: Scotus's treatment of the *signa rationis* in the *In III Sententiarum,* dist. 7, qu. 4, in the so-called *Reportata Parisiensa.* Here, Scotus casts the *signa* in a more devotional light: in the first moment, God loves himself; in the second, God loves himself for others; in the third, God

---

46. Ioannes Duns Scotus, *In Lib. III Sententiarum,* dist. 19, qu. unica, no. 6, tom. 7, pars 1, 415: "Quantum ad primum, dico quod Incarnatio Christi non fuit occasionaliter praevisa, sed sicut finis immediate videatur a Deo ab aeterno, ita Christus in natura humana, cum sit propinquior fini, caeteris prius praedestinabatur, loquendo de his, quae praedestinantur; tunc iste fuit ordo in praevisione divina: primo enim Deus intellexit se sub ratione summi boni; in secundo signo intellexit omnes alias creaturas; in tertio praedestinavit ad gloriam et gratiam, et circa alios habuit actum negativum, non praedestinando; in quarto praevidit illos casuros in Adam; in quinto praeordinavit sive praevidit de remedio quomodo redimerentur per passionem Filii, ita quod Christus in carne, sicut et omnes electi, prius praevidebatur et praedestinabatur ad gratiam et gloriam, quam praevideretur passio Christi, ut medicina contra lapsum, sicut medicus prius vult sanitatem hominis, quam ordinet de medicina ad sanadum." This text, which does not appear in the modern Ordinatio is still of high pedigree: It is based upon what we now call the *supplementum* to *Ordinatio* III, dist. 19, from Assisi Codex 137.

47. Ioannes Duns Scotus, *In Lib. III Sententiarum,* dist. 32, qu. unica, no. 5, tom. 7, pars 2, 692-93: "Nam omnis rationabiliter volens, vult primo finem, et secundo illud, quod immediate attingit finem, et tertio alia, quae remotius sunt ordinata ad attingendum finem. Cum igitur Deus rationabilissime velit, licet non diversis actibus; sed tantum uno, inquantum illo diversimode tendit super obiecta ordinate, primo vult finem, et in hoc est actus suus perfectus, et voluntas eius beata; secundo vult illa, quae immediate ordinantur in ipsum, praedestinando scilicet electos, qui immediate attingunt ipsum, et hoc quasi reflectendo, volendo alios diligere idem obiectum secum . . . . Qui enim amat se primo ordinate, et per consequens non inordinate zelando, vel invidendo isto modo, secundo vult habere alios diligentes, et hoc est velle alios habere amorem suum in se, et hoc est praedestinare eos, si velit eis hoc bonum finaliter. Tertio vult illa, quae sunt necessaria ad attingendum hunc finem, scilicet bona gratiae. Quarto vult propter illos alia, quae sunt remotiora, puta hunc mundum sensibilem, ut serviat eis." For the modern text, which is considerably cleaned up, see idem, *Ordinatio* III, dist. 32, qu. unica, no. 21, 136–37.

desires to be loved with the greatest love; in the fourth, God foresees that the Incarnation of the Word in glory shall be this very love; in the fifth, God foresees that Christ shall suffer so that his people might participate in this love.[48] There is, of course, no unanimity among Scotists in the interpretation and reconciliation of these texts. Instead we find startling diversity. Indeed, arranging the *signa rationis* was something of a sport for seventeenth and early-eighteenth century theologians. We need not delve into the highly technical aspect of these controversies. For our purposes, it suffices to note that the diversity of such arrangements will allow us to narrow the number of possible influences on Sor María.

The abiding concern of seventeenth-century Franciscans was to determine when Christ was predestined absolutely as the impassible *Glorificator Dei* and when he was predestined conditionally as a passible redeemer. They disagreed, however, about how to align God's *scientia simplicis intelligentiae* and *scientia visionis* with the *signa rationis*. We see an early indication of this disagreement in Juan de Rada (†1608), who outlines our three chief texts with a small but telling gloss on *In III Sententiarum*, dist. 19, where he notes that Gods knows all creatures in the second *signum* via his *scientia simplicis intelligentiae*.[49] Scotus' text says only "Deus intellexit," but, since Scotus takes care to indicate the *scientia visionis* with the verb *praevidit* in the fourth and fifth *signa*, one imagines the Subtle Doctor would have done the same in the second *signum* had he intended to claim the God knew all creatures via the *scientia visionis* there. At any rate, several prominent Scotists of the next generation followed Rada in this basic reading of *In III Sententiarum*, dist. 19, not least among them Filippo Fabri (†1630), Maurizio Centini (†1640), and Bonaventura Belluti (†1676). Fabri synthesizes the *signa* as follows: in the first, God knows himself; in the second, God knows all possibles via his *scientiae simplicis intelligentiae*; in the third, God knows all that he shall decree via his *scientia visionis*; in the fourth, God decrees grace and glory first to Christ, then to the angels, then to humanity; in the fifth, God sees the

48. Ioannes Duns Scotus, *Reportata Parisiensia* III, dist. 7, qu. 4, no. 5, tom. 11, pars 1, 451: "Dico ergo sic: Primo Deus diliget se, secundo diligit se aliis, et iste est amor castus; tertio vult se diligi ab illo qui potest eum summe diligere, loquendo de amore alicujus extrinsicae ; et quarto praevidit unionem illius naturae quae debet eum summe diligere etsi nullus cecidisset . . . .in quinto instanti vidit Deus mediatorem venientem passurum, redempturum populum suum; et non venisset ut mediator , ut passurus et redempturus, nisi aliquis prius pecasset, neque fuisset gloria carnis dilata, nisi fuissent redimenti, sed statim fuisset totus Christus glorificatus." Compare Carolus Balić's text of *Reportatio* III, dist. 7, qu. 4, in *Ioannis Duns Scoti doctoris Mariani theologiae marianae elementa*, 14–15.

49. Rada, *Controversiarum theologicarum*, lib. 3, controv. 5, art. 3, nota 3, 210–12, here 210.

fall; in the sixth, God decrees the passion of Christ as the remedy; and in the seventh, God decrees that our salvation shall depend upon our free embrace of Christ's passion.[50] Fabri, then, makes the intra-Scotist controversy explicit, taking care to distinguish God's *scientia simplicis* and *scientia visionis* in two separate *signa*. Fabri also makes clear what was only implied in Scotus's treatment of God's decree of predestination in the third moment, namely, that it concerns the whole Christ, that is, his mystical body comprised of angels, men, and women. One sees finally in Fabri, quite in opposition to the usual caricature of Scotist voluntarism, that our use of free will is logically subsequent to our predestination in Christ. In other words, Fabri gives us an Augustinian defense of free will using wholly Scotist means, such that our free will considered merely as a nature, finds its perfection, indeed the very nature of its freedom, only in light of its greater end, namely, the glorification of God in the hypostatic union.

Now, few follow Fabri in distinguishing God's *scientia* in quite this way. Centini arranges the *signa* as follows: God first knows himself in the first *signum*; in the second, he knows all creatures via the *scientia simplicis intelligentiae*; in the third, he decrees the glory of all, Christ, the Blessed Virgin, the angels, and humanity; in the fourth, he decrees grace as the means necessary to achieve that glory; and in the fifth, he permits the fall.[51] If Centini returns to Rada's interpretation of the *signa rationis* in *In III Sententiarum*, dist. 19, he also incorporates the texts of *In III Sententiarum*, dist. 32, and *Reportata*, dist. 7, qu. 4, by distinguishing as two separate *signa* the predestination of the elect (as the goal) and the grace necessary to achieve that goal (as the means). We might presume, I think, that Centini assumes Redemption in a sixth *signum*, but not all Scotists did so. Belluti also takes a fairly straightforward path in his synthesis. In a sense, he repeats Rada, or—to be more precise—he bolsters Rada's interpretation of the second *signum* by including it in a near quotation of Scotus's text of *In III Sententiarum*, dist. 19. According to Belluti, then, in the first instant, God knows himself as the highest good; in the second, he knows all possible creatures via his *scientia simplicis intelligentiae*; in the third, he wills to manifest his goodness to angels and humanity through the Incarnation of the Word; in the fourth, he foresees that some will fall in Adam; and in the fifth moment he decrees that the Incarnate Word will suffer to redeem fallen humanity.[52]

50. Fabri, *Disputationes Theologicae in Tertium Sententiarum*, dist. 7, qu. 3, disp. 20, nn. 27–28, 109–10, here 110.

51. Centini, *De Incarnatione Dominica disputationes theologicae ad mentem Scoti*, disp. 2, cap. 7, n. 118, 71.

52. Belluti, *Disputationes de Incarnatione Dominica ad mentem Doctoris Subtilis*, disp. 7, qu. 2, n. 40, 108.

A significant number of Scotists disagreed with Rada's interpretation of *In III Sententiarum*, dist. 19, not least among them Hieronymus Gallus (fl. 1644), Francisco Quaresmio (†1650), and Belluti's own colleague, the great Bartolomeo Mastri da Meldola (†1673). Gallus, for example, gives a complex sequence of ten *signa rationis*: in the first moment, God knows himself and all creatures via his *scientia simplicis intelligentiae*; in the second, he knows the result of his decree via his *scientia visionis*; in the third, God decrees the hypostatic union, grace, and glory; in the fourth, all the elect in Adam; in the fifth, he decrees not to impede Adam's free action; in the sixth, he foresees that Adam will Fall; in the seventh, he determines to create some who are not elect; in the eighth, he permits sin; in the ninth, he foresees sin absolutely via his *scientia visionis*; and in the tenth, God decrees that Christ will come as a redeemer.[53] Gallus's arrangement is clearly designed to address concerns of theodicy; for our purposes, we need only note that he disagrees with the tradition stemming from Juan de Rada and Filippo Fabri on the interpretation of *In III Sententiarum*, dist. 19. On Quaresmio's rendering of the *signa*, God knows all possibles in the first moment; in the second, he wills the hypostatic union for the grace and glory and angels and men; in the third, he predestines all in Christ; in the fourth, he decrees the means necessary to persevere to the end; in the fifth, he permits sin; and in the sixth, he wills the wounds of Christ as a fitting remedy for sin.[54] Compare this to Mastri. Although the great commentator's argument is too complicated to summarize in detail, its salient points are as follows: God, in the first logical instant, knows all creatures via his *scientia simplicis intelligentiae* precisely in his understanding of himself *sub ratione summi boni*; in the second, he knows all creatures that he will create via his *scientia visionis*; in the third, he predestines Christ and the elect; in the fourth moment, God decrees the diverse manners in which men and angels will participate in the life of Christ; and in the fifth, he foresees the fall of Adam and the means of redemption.[55] Again, we need not explore Mastri's arrangement of the *signa* in detail; suffice it to say that he is attempting to incorporate Scotus's own complex understanding of God's knowledge of creatures (from the one side) and the best insights of the *de auxiliis* controversy (from the other). Note, though, Mastri's way of incorporating the distinction between grace and glory into the standard reading of *In III Sententiarum*, dist. 19: He separates

53. Gallus, *Tomus prior in Tertium Sententiarum Subtillissimi Doctoris Ioannis Duns Scoti Opus de Ineffabili Incarnationis Mysterio*, qu. 3, dist. 7, contr. 3, cap. 4, n. 129, 174.

54. Quaresmius, *De sacratissimis D. N. Iesu Christi quinque vulneribus*, tom. 1, lib. 1, cap. 3, sect. 1, 19–20.

55. Mastri, *Disputationes Theologicae in Tertium Librum Sententiarum*, disp. 4, qu. 1, art. 1, nn. 7–13, 301–03.

the predestination of the elect from the diverse ways in which others will participate in Christ. This is every bit as clever as Fabri's distinctive move: for Mastri, then, all grace is not only the *gratia Christi*—a typical Scotist position—but also a participation in his glory. One could object—in fact, many did object—to Mastrius's separation of the *scientia visionis* and God's decree of predestination. God's *scientia visionis* is after all *cum decreto* by definition. Without worrying ourselves over the technical details, we should note that Quaresmio chose to close this gap while retaining the distinction between ends and means from *In III Sententiarum*, dist. 32, and *In III Sententiarum*, dist. 7, qu. 4 in the *Reportata*.

Other Scotists avoided the interpretive dilemma occasioned by the first two *signa* by concerning themselves only with the order of God's actions *ad extra*. Angelo Volpi (†1676), a theologian often mentioned in connection with Sor María, adopts a fairly straightforward ordering of God's decree *ad extra*: in the first moment *ad extra*, God predestines Christ absolutely and substantially as the *Glorificator Dei*, Mary is absolutely predestined in the same decree with her Son, and Adam and Eve are predestined *ante preavisa merita*; in the second, God elects to give grace to angels and human beings; in the third, God creates angels and human beings; in the fourth, God permits the fall; and in the fifth, God decrees that Christ will serve as a remedy and sacrifice for sin. [56] We probably cannot yet speak of a controversy about the *signa* as Volpi writes (circa 1646), so we do not know if he has deliberately avoided the issue. Volpi does give evidence of two important trends in Scotism during the middle of the seventeenth century, however. On the one hand, Scotists broadly synthesized Scotus's three presentations of the *signa rationis* into a (relatively stable) whole. On the other, Volpi—like Maurizio Centini before him—places the Blessed Virgin in the *signa rationis*.

This trend is most developed in independent Mariological treatises of the time, especially those written by Juan Serrano (†1637) and Francisco del Castillo Velasco (†1641). Serrano, whom Father Solaguren places in Sor María's ambit, has the first action *ad extra* to be the hypostatic union, the second to be the Blessed Virgin, the third to be the election of angels and men to grace and glory, the fourth the fall of Adam, and the fifth Christ's coming as a redeemer.[57] Serrano is thus an early example of the "explosion"

56. Volpi, *Sacrae Theologiae Summa Ioannis Duns Scoti Doctoris Subtilissimi*, tom. 3, part 4, disp. 71, art. 2, n. 2, 269.

57. Serrano, *De immaculata prorsusque pura sanctissime semperque Virginis Genetricis Dei Marie conceptione*, lib. 4, cap. 4, nn. 5–6, 461. Solaguren points to Serrano's treatment of the *signa rationis* as an illustration of a contemporary use of the *ordinate volens* argument but does not otherwise address influence upon Sor María. Solaguren, "La doctrina mariológica de la 'Mística Ciudad de Dios,'" lxviii.

of the third *signum* of *In III Sententiarum*, dist. 19, in which Christ, Mary, and the angels occupy different *signa* altogether. Serrano divides the first *signum ad extra* into logical sub-moments, with Christ (a) predestined as head of the Mystical Body, (b) as the first predestined among brethren, and (c) the cause of all others' predestination. We see a similar, albeit less ornately realized, concern in Francisco del Castillo Velasco (†1641), who appended a treatise *De praeservatione Virginis Matris* to the 1641 edition of his two-volume commentary on Scotus's commentary on the third book of the Lombard's *Sentences*.[58] Like the other theologians suggested by Father Martínez Moñux, Castillo Velasco wrote in defense of the definability of the dogma of the Immaculate Conception. Since Pope Gregory XV extended Pope Paul V's censure of preaching against the Immaculate Conception to private teaching in 1622, Castillo Velasco confidently censures Thomists, like Bandelli and Spina, who condemn the Immaculate Conception along with Protestants such as Hushusius, Chemnitz, and Calvin.[59] He notes that the Immaculate Conception, being the common teaching of theologians, was even defended by Thomas Aquinas in his small commentary on the Angelic Salutation, and he commends Dominicans such as Catharinus, Viguerius and John of St. Thomas for vigorously defending the Blessed Virgin against the attacks of other Dominicans.[60] Like most Scotists, Sor María included, Castillo Velasco bases his arguments for the absolute predestination of Christ and Mary—and by extension the definability of the dogma of the Immaculate Conception—on the eighth chapter of Proverbs (especially 8:22), the first three chapters of Genesis (especially 3:14-15), and the mystical interpretation of the Psalms and the Song of Songs.

Castillo Velasco follows the position of Gallus, Quaresmio, and Mastri on the interpretation of the second *signum* in *In III Sententiarum*, dist. 19.[61] According to Castillo Velasco: in the first logical moment, God knows

58. Castillo Velasco, "De praeservatione Virginis Matris," 456–549.

59. Ibid., disp. 2, pars 1, nn. 4–5, 497.

60. Ibid., disp. 2, pars 2, nn. 19–20, 499–500.

61. Ibid., disp. 4, qu. 2, nn. 10–12, 536–37. Castillo Velasco arranges these *signa* in direct contrast to those of Ambrosius Catharinus, Francisco Suárez, Sanchez Lucero, and Juan Bautista Lezaña, who suppose some *debitum* in Mary, viz: in the first moment *ad extra* God decrees Christ in both His substance and His circumstances; in the second, the Blessed Virgin; in the third, creatures and the world; in the fourth, the predestination of the elect and the (negative) reprobation of the damned; in the fifth, Adam and Eve as the moral and physical heads of the human race with the Virgin Mary included in the law of Adam; in the sixth, the permission of sin; and in the seventh, Christ's redemption. The arrangement that Castillo Velasco presents is heuristic; in truth, the views of these authors (and many others who advanced arrangements of the *signa*) are significantly more complex in many cases. That said, the chief differences

himself as the highest good and thus know all of the goods that he can create via his *scientia simplicis intelligentiae*; in the second, God knows all creatures that he will create through his *scientia visionis*; in the third moment, God predestines all to grace and glory, first Christ with the highest grace and glory coeval with his rational soul, then the angels, men, and women, noting (like others before him), that God foresees the possible reprobation of those who reject his grace only negatively; in the fourth moment, God decrees the moral unity of the human race in Adam and foresees the fall of his posterity; in the fifth, he decrees that Christ shall suffer as a remedy for Adam's sin.[62] In other words, Castillo Velasco assumes Scotus's arrangement of the *signa* in *In III Sententiarum*, dist. 19, to be sufficient to the task at hand; he merely thinks that one should interpret Scotus to refer to the *scientia visionis* in the second *signum*. In this, Castillo Velasco is a book end of sorts to the tradition of Rada and Fabri.

Other Mariologists, such as Francisco Guerra (†1657) and Tomás Francés Urrutigoyti (†1682), were more creative in their interpretation of the *signa*. They see Scotus less as a master whose texts need to be reconciled and more a guide for their own, more elaborate arrangements. Guerra, for example, has God knowing and loving himself in the first moment; knowing all possibles in the second; predestining Christ in the third; decreeing the hypostatic union for Christ in the fourth; decreeing the highest possible grace to his humanity in the fifth; decreeing the particular endowments of his actual humanity in the sixth; predestining the blessed Virgin in the seventh; the angels in the eighth; the visible world in the ninth.[63] Guerra goes on to enumerate other *signa*, with redemption listed as the tenth

---

between them, of course, are (first) that Mary is not, on the Scotist account, included in the law of Adam and (second) that God decrees the circumstances of the incarnation only after its substance.

62. It bears noting in this respect that Juan Sendín Calderón (†1676), the theologian who wrote the definitive theological commentary on the *Mística ciudad de Dios*, explicitly rejects Castillo Velasco's treatment of God's *scientia simplicis intelligentiae*. In the first moment, according to Sendín Calderón, God knows himself as the highest good; in the second, he knows all creatures via his *scientia simplicis intelligentiae*; in the third, however, he sees the fittingness of the hypostatic union also via his *scientia simplicis intelligentiae*; in the fourth, he sees via his *scientia visionis*, the predestination of those he elects, with the predestination of Christ as the exemplary cause of the predestination of others, and—in a merely negative manner—the reprobation of those who shall sin; in the fifth, God deigns in his mercy and charity to reconcile the world to himself through his holy death. Cf. Sendín Calderón, *Opus theologicum*, tract. 6, controv. 1, sect. 8, 383–87, here 383–84. On the career of Sendín Calderón, see Fabre, "Juan Sendín Calderón," 271–303.

63. Guerra, *Maiestas gratiarum ac virtutum omnium Deiparae Virginis Mariae*, lib. 2, tract. 2, disp. 1, frag. 3, nn. 16–17, 421.

signum; Christ passible as the thirteenth; and the permission of sin as the fourteenth.[64] Guerra, then, like Juan Serrano, gives Mary her own place in the divine plan, represented by a separate *signum*. Urrutigoyti also has an interesting arrangement of the *signa rationis* in terms of God's actions *ad extra*.[65] Urrutigoyti believes that in the first instant God foreordains Christ as the head of the mystical body; in the second he predestines the Virgin Mary to be his mother; in the third he constitutes Adam to be the moral head of his posterity; in the fourth God foresees the fall of all who shall proceed from Adam by way of seminal generation; in the fifth, he foresees the fallen determinately in the mode in which they shall exist, but the Virgin is not included; in the sixth moment, he decrees Christ *in carne passibili*, preserving the Virgin from any *debitum peccati*; in the seventh, he decrees the Virgin's passibility and death; and in the last moment, he decrees all of the circumstances of time and place that shall give rise to their actions. In this respect, Urrutigoyti continues the general trend of Serrano and Guerra to grant the Blessed Virgin a separate *signum*. Like Francisco Guerra, too, Urrutigoyti creatively divides the *signa* in order to advance his own theological agenda. At this point, however, after surveying the major Scotists writing between 1600 and 1660, I think it fair to say that there are probably as many different arrangements of the *signa rationis* as there are Scotists.

There are elements of several—if not all—of these various arrangements of the *signa rationis* in Sor María's own. Recall it in outline: in the first moment, God knows himself as one whose perfections might be shared; in the second, God decrees to communicate his perfections as gifts; in the third, God decrees the Incarnate Word in three sub-moments (a) his divine composition (b) his perfections to be imitated and (c) his free worship of God his Father; in the fourth moment, God decrees all of the graces that he will bestow upon humanity (a) first to the humanity of Christ (b) then to the Blessed Virgin and (c) finally the very world itself; in the fifth, he decrees the creation, predestination, and negative reprobation of the angels; and in the sixth, he decrees the creation, predestination, and negative reprobation of human beings, which includes the foresight of their sin.

The first thing that stands out in Sor María's presentation is its detail. Like Hieronymus Gallus, Francisco Guerra, or Tomás Francés Urrutigoyti, she has clearly designed her arrangement with a purpose. Sor María's arrangement, however, cannot be reduced to any of the aforementioned

64. Guerra's list is either incomplete or mis-numbered. From it, however, we can gather that Guerra represents one of the Franciscan minority who believes Christ to be predestined as redeemer before the prevision of sin.

65. Urrutigoyti, *Certamen scholasticum expositivum argumentum pro Deipara*, sect. 9, sub. 6, nn. 241–42, 72.

Scotists. Arguably more complex than all but Guerra's, Sor María's arrangement incorporates elements of each of the principal texts of the Subtle Doctor along with the insights from each of other syntheses. With Quaresmio and the Mariologists generally, she arranges the *signa rationis* to invert the natural, supernatural, and hypostatic orders first proposed by Cardinal Cajetan, and (again like the Mariologists) Sor María deliberately places the Blessed Virgin among the *signa*. Sor María also includes the creation of the world, a detail taken from the fourth logical moment in Scotus's *In III Sententiarum*, dist. 32, which appears to have been a special preoccupation of Spanish Scotists, particularly Guerra and Urrutigoyti. Sor María also takes care to note the importance of freedom in her arrangement, like Gallus and Fabri. Sor María does not merely repeat these details, however. In fact, she treats them with no small amount of scholastic ingenuity. Scotus, for example, merely indicates the role of the sensible world as the remote means of attaining our salvation, which Urrutigoyti rightly recognizes as the necessary context and circumstances in which God's plans shall unfold. In contrast, Sor María, by placing the creation of the world in the supernatural order of God's endowments, provides what might (with some anachronism) be called a genuinely "cosmic" view of creation. Sor María improves in a similar manner upon Fabri, who rightly places the free exercise of our wills in a logical moment subsequent to our predestination. Sor María, however, locates true human freedom in Christ's own worship of the Father. More to the point, Sor María appears to have taken a stand on the controverted issue of the second *signum*, following the tradition of Castillo Velasco, Gallus, Quaresmio, and Mastri. To what degree, then, did any of these sources influence Sor María or the *Mística ciudad de Dios* directly?

As Father Martínez Moñux has already pointed out, the great Jesuit Juan Martínez de Ripalda, the Carmelite Raimundo Lumbier y Ángel, and Tomás Francés Urrutigoyti, were all active in Navarre. Sor María would likely have heard of the first two and indeed might well have read or conversed with Urrutigoyti. Urrutigoyti clearly designs his arrangement to argue that Mary is wholly without any *debitum peccati*—a position that Sor María shares, to be sure—but there simply is not enough similarity in their arrangements of the *signa* to suspect any direct influence. If we compare Sor María to other possible sources mentioned by Fathers Martínez Moñux and Solaguren—assuming Sor María to have read them or heard their views repeated—we hardly fare better. Volpi's arrangement of the *signa* is far simpler than Sor María's own. Despite his boundless appetite for controversy, too, Volpi did not become embroiled in the inter-Scotist controversy concerning whether God knows all possible creatures via his *scientia simplicis intelligentiae* during the second *signum*. If we take this intra-Scotist controversy as a point of departure, it would appear that the chief candidates for influence upon Sor María are Castillo Velasco, Gallus, Quaresmio, and Mastri. Sor María's arrangement of the *signa rationis* does not match any of these arrangements exactly. What if we take a different criterion? Among those who explicitly distinguish the hypostatic, supernatural, and natural orders, we find Sor María with Guerra, Quaresmio, and Mastri (at least implicitly). Among those who distinguish the Blessed Virgin with her own *signum*, we find her with Serrano, Guerra, and Urrutigoyti. If we look at those who include God's "non-election" of the reprobate in *In III Sententiarum*, dist. 19, we find Sor María more in line with Castillo Velasco.

We need not find any single source of inspiration on the *Mística ciudad de Dios*. One can, however, make a relatively good case for circumstantial influence, whether through reading, listening, or personal conversation. If we remove Mastri (as being both late and geographically remote) and Hieronymus Gallus (as being relatively obscure in comparison to the other theologians we have discussed), one finds Sor María in the general ambit of Juan Serrano, Francisco del Castillo Velasco, Francisco Guerra, Francisco Quaresmio, and Tomás Francés Urrutigoyti. Urrutigoyti's arrangement, while creative, is wholly unlike Sor María's in form and content. The presentations of the *signa rationis* by Serrano, Quaresmio, and Castillo Velasco are fairly perfunctory and show little of the creativity of Sor María's. These considerations bring Sor María closer to Guerra, who, like Sor María, subdivides his treatment of the Incarnation in to three different moments, includes the supernatural endowments of Christ's human soul, and places a special emphasis on the world God creates for the exercise of his powers. Still, were Sor María to have copied Guerra's arrangement, she would have numbered the *signa* differently and, more to the point, would have presumably followed his presentation of God's *scientia simplicis intelligentiae*. In this respect, Sor María appears to have been influenced by Francisco del Castillo Velasco.

By a process of elimination, I am inclined to think that Francisco Guerra and Francisco del Castillo Velasco are at least remote sources for Sor María's arrangement of the *signa rationis* in the *Mística ciudad de Dios*. Overall, her treatment is closest in form and content to Guerra's, but she departs from him in important respects. Two things, however, might give us reason to think that Castillo Velasco is the among Sor María's sources. First, there is the similarity in certain details: Sor María repeats Castillo Velasco's minority position, which locates God's *scientia simplicis intelligentiae* in the first *signum* and his *scientia visionis* in the second *signum*, as well as his note on the negative election of the reprobate. One might reasonably object that Castillo Velasco does not reserve a separate *signum* for the Blessed Virgin. If Castillo

Velasco cannot be included in the group of those who distinguish the Blessed Virgin with her own *signum*, however, it is only because he wished to restrict himself to the text of *In III Sententiarum*, dist. 19, and he expressly laments that Duns Scotus did not consider the Blessed Virgin in his own arrangement. Secondly—and more significantly—Castillo Velasco is at most only one step removed from Sor María. He lists among the most important *ex professo* treatments of the definability of the dogma of the Immaculate Conception, and the last person to influence his own teaching, one Juan de Soría, which is to say, a Juan de Ágreda.[66] Although this last bit of information is merely circumstantial, it is, if nothing else, more substantial than the similar sources mentioned by Father Martínez Moñux.

Sor María does not appear to have repeated the teaching of any particular Scotist, whatever the manner in which she learned the *signa rationis* or other scholastic arguments commonly used to advance the absolute predestination of Christ and the Immaculate Conception of the Blessed Virgin Mary. My tentative suggestion is that her arrangement of the *signa rationis* was inspired by Francisco Guerra, corrected with the teaching of someone in the circle of Francisco del Castillo Velasco, and touched up with Sor María's own theological genius. That she did not merely repeat the teachings of previous Scotists, however, gives us reason to think that Sor María might have been better read than many suppose. Had Sor María merely copied a single teacher or treatise, in all likelihood her teaching would match one of those above. Should she have done so well, we might expect her treatment of this highly technical debate to match it *verbatim*; should she have been less capable in the arts of memory, we might expect her treatment to be less sure, if not to contain outright mistakes. Had Sor María played the magpie, in other words, gathering things willy-nilly from sermons and personal conversations, it seems unlikely that she would have produced such an expert synthesis, for there is not a single element of the several treatments above that does not appear in her own, skillfully condensed and expounded with no small amount of scholastic ingenuity. Of course, for one whom God so readily and frequently gifted with the miracle of bilocation—even to the deserts of West Texas—it would have been a small thing to visit the lecture halls surreptitiously to hear the debates of the learned masters. And there remains, too, the very real possibility that these things were revealed to Sor María by God, who is without doubt a Scotist, at least with regards to the Immaculate Conception of Mary his Mother.

66. Castillo Velasco, "De praeservatione Virginis Matris," disp. 2, pars 2, no. 21, 500.

Bibliography

Belluti, Bonaventura. *Disputationes de Incarnatione Dominica ad mentem Doctoris Subtilis.* Catanae: Apud Ioannem Rossi, 1645.

Bengoechea, Ismael. "'Vidas de la Virgen María' en la España del siglo XVII." *Estudios Marianos* 49 (1984) 59–103.

Calvo Moralejo, Gaspar. "El Escotismo de la 'Mística Ciudad de Dios' y su influencia en el processo de beatificación de la M. Ágreda." In *Giovanni Duns Scoto. Studi e ricerche nel VII centenario della sua morte*, 2:257–78. Roma: Antonianum, 2008.

———. "La Purísima Concepción de María en la 'Mística Ciudad de Dios' de la M. Ágreda." *Antonianum* 80 (2005) 85–117.

Campos, Julio. "Los Padres Juan de Palma, Pedro Manero y Pedro de Arriola y la 'Mística Ciudad de Dios.'" *Archivo ibero-americano* 26 (1966) 227–52.

———. "Para la historia externa de la 'Mística Ciudad de Dios.' Fray José de Falces, procurador de los libros de la M. Ágreda." *Salmanticensis* 6 (1959) 159–85.

———. "Para la historia interna de la 'Mística Ciudad de Dios.' Fray Andres de Fuenmayor, director espiritual de la M. Agreda." *Hispania* 18 (1958) 210–36.

———. "La Venerable Madre Ágreda y su obra en Navarra." *Analecta Calasanctiana* 14 (1965) 305–93.

Campos, Zótico Royo. *Agredistas y Antiagredistas, estudio histórico-apologético.* Totano [Murcia]: Tipografía de San Buena-Ventura, 1929.

Carol, Juniper B. *Why Jesus Christ? Thomistic, Scotistic, and Conciliatory Perspectives.* Manassas, VA: Trinity, 1986.

Castillo Velasco, Francisco del. "De praeservatione Virginis Matris." In *Subtilissimi Scoti Doctorum super tertium Sententiarum librum*, tom. 1. Antverpiae: Apud Petrem Bellerum, 1641.

Centini, Maurizio. *De Incarnatione Dominica disputationes theologicae ad mentem Scoti.* Messanae: Apud Ioannem Francisci Bianchi, 1637.

Colahan, Clark. *The Visions of Sor María of Ágreda: Writing Knowledge and Power.* Tucson: University of Arizona Press, 1994.

Duns Scotus, Ioannes. *R. P. F. Ioannis Duns Scoti Opera Omnia.* Lugduni: Sumptibus Laurentii Durand, 1639.

———. *B. Ioannis Duns Scoti Opera Omnia.* Civitas Vaticana: Typis Polyglottis Vaticanis, 1950—.

Fabre, Luis. "Juan Sendín Calderón, teólogo franciscano del siglo XVII." *Archivo ibero-americano* 33 (1930) 271–303.

Fabri, Filippo. *Disputationes Theologicae in Tertium Sententiarum.* Venetiis: Ex Officina Bartholomaei Ginami, 1613.

Fedewa, Marilyn H. *María of Ágreda, Mystical Lady in Blue.* Albuquerque: University of New Mexico Press, 2009.

Gallus, Hieronymus. *Tomus prior in Tertium Sententiarum Subtillissimi Doctoris Ioannis Duns Scoti Opus de Ineffabili Incarnationis Mysterio.* Mediolani: Apud Ioannem Ambrosium Sirturum, 1645.

Guerra, Francisco. *Maiestas gratiarum ac virtutum omnium Deiparae Virginis Mariae.* Hispali: Apud Johannem de Ribera, 1659.

Llamas, Enrique. *La Madre Ágreda y la Mariología del Vaticano II.* Salamanca: Kadmos, 2003.

————."'La Mística Ciudad de Dios': Una Mariología en clave de 'Historia de Salvación.' De la Madre Ágreda al Concilio Vaticano II." In *La Madre Ágreda, una mujer del siglo XXI*, 155–88. Soria: Universidad Internacional Alfonso VIII, 2000.

————. *Venerable Mother Agreda and the Mariology of Vatican II*. Translated by Peter Damian Fehlner. New Bedford, MA: Academy of the Immaculate, 2006.

María de Jesús de Ágreda. *City of God: The Divine History and Life of the Virgin Mother of God Manifested to Mary of Agreda for the Encouragement of Men*. Translated by Geo. Blatter. Chicago: W. B. Conkey, 1912-13.

————. *Mística ciudad de Dios. Vida de María milagro de su omnipotencia y abismo de la gracia. Historia divina y vida de la Virgen Madre de Dios, Reina y Señora nuestra, María Santíssima, Restauradora de la Culpa de Eva y Medianera de la Gracia, dictada y manifestada en estos últimos siglos por la misma Señora a su esclava Sor María de Jesús, abadesa indigna de este convento de la Inmaculada Concepción de la villa de Ágreda para nueva luz del mundo, alegría de la Iglesia Católica y confianza de los mortales*. Introducción, notas y edición por Celestino Solaguren, con colaboración de Ángel Martínez Moñux, y Luís Villasante. Madrid: N.p., 1970.

Martínez Moñux, Angel. "La Inmaculada Concepción en la 'Mística Ciudad de Dios' de la Madre Ágreda." *Verdad y Vida* 22 (1964) 645–65.

————. "María signo de la creación, receptora de los méritos de Cristo. La cooperación mariana a la redención según la 'Mística ciudad de Dios.'" *Verdad y Vida* 26 (1968) 135–78.

Mastri, Bartolomaeo. *Disputationes Theologicae in Tertium Librum Sententiarum*. Venetiis: Apud Valvasensem, 1661.

Mendía Lasa, Benito. "En torno al problema de la autenticidad de la 'Mística Ciudad de Dios.'" *Archivo ibero-americano* 165-168 (1982) 391–430.

Mendía Lasa, Benito, and Artola Arbiza, Antonio. *La Ven. M. María de Jesús de Ágreda y la Inmaculada Concepción. El proceso eclesiástico a la "Mística Ciudad de Dios."* Ágreda: N.p., 2004.

Molina Prieto, Andres. "El culto mariano de imitación en la 'Mística Ciudad de Dios' de la venerable Sor María de Jesús de Ágreda." *Mariología* 49 (1984) 223–50.

Quaresmius, Franciscus. *De sacratissimis D. N. Iesu Christi quinque vulneribus*. Venetiis: Sumptibus S. Combi et J. Lanor, 1652.

Rada, Juan de. *Controversiarum theologicarum inter S. Thomam et Scotum super Tertium Sententiarum Librum*. Venetiis: Apud Ioannem Guerilium, 1618.

Sendín Calderón, Juan. *Opus theologicum*. Compluti: Ex Officina Francisci Garcia Fernandez, 1699.

Serrano, Juan. *De immaculata prorsusque pura sanctissime semperque Virginis Genetricis Dei Marie conceptione*. Neapoli: Ex Typographia Regia Aegidii Longhi, 1635.

Urrutigoyti, Tomás Francés de. *Certamen scholasticum expositivum argumentum pro Deipara*. Lugduni: Sumptibus Philippi Borde, 1660.

Volpi, Angelo. *Sacrae Theologiae Summa Ioannis Duns Scoti Doctoris Subtilissimi*. Neapoli: In Collegio Laurentii Regente, 1646.

Wolter, Allan B. "John Duns Scotus on the Primacy and Personality of Christ." In *Franciscan Christology: Selected Texts, Translations, and Introductory Essays*, edited by D. McElrath, 139–82. St. Bonaventure: Franciscan Institute, 1980.

14

Charity in the Church—Charity in the Eucharist

J.A. Wayne Hellmann, OFM Conv.

Prologue

While I was yet a student in Rome during the exciting years of the Second Vatican Council, the first dissertation I read was *The Role of Charity in the Ecclesiology of St. Bonaventure*[1] by Fr. Peter Damian Fehlner OFM Conv. Reading his dissertation inspired my interest in the theology of St. Bonaventure. Little did I realize that several years later, many conversations with him in his office at St. Anthony on the Hudson Seminary near Albany, NY would inspire and guide me in the writing of my own dissertation on St. Bonaventure, now translated into English, *Divine and Created Order.*[2] I am therefore happy to offer some reflections on this occasion to honor the years of work and profound theological insight Fr. Peter has brought and continues to bring to the table, even these many years later.

Introduction

Following the title of this essay, I will first review and draw from Fr. Peter's dissertation and illustrate the specific points he makes as he builds his case to demonstrate that charity is at the heart of Bonaventure's understanding of the mystery of the Church. Then, in the second part, I will draw from St. Bonaventure's own treatment of the Eucharist found in Book Four of his *Commentary on the Sentences*. I likewise hope to demonstrate that charity is

---

1. Peter D. Fehlner, *The Role of Charity in the Ecclesiology of St. Bonaventure*.
2. J.A. Wayne Hellmann, *Divine and Created Order in Bonaventure's Theology*.

at the heart of the Eucharist. Out of this, I hope to argue that charity in the Church and charity in the Eucharist are two sides of the same coin.

Part One: Charity in the Church

Fr. Peter's *Role of Charity in the Ecclesiology of St. Bonaventure* has for more than fifty years been on my bookshelf. I would never let it leave my office. It had been a long time since I had occasion to re-read it, until my preparation for this presentation. What a wonder it was to read his text again. I noticed that points I had underlined in pencil many years ago would be the same points I would underline today. In fact, some of these are about to appear below.

The first underlined text is found in the early part of the dissertation where he describes the then contemporary approaches to understand the Church. He writes: "The insistence on the role of the Church as a sign and sacrament of everlasting life for her members tends to make of the Church an instrument, rather than the realization of salvation itself."[3] The last part of that sentence I had underlined twice! It was precisely in those years I was learning about the Church as sacrament.

Here I sensed, however, something deeper going on, opening the door to the mystical. Fr. Peter explains that although in the world, the Church transcends the world. It is rooted elsewhere, in a social order that transcends the world, the life of the Triune God. That which transcends and unites is simply charity. Then he advances that "Bonaventure affirms unequivocally that the bond of unity in the Church is charity."[4] To support this, he cites Bonaventure: "Through the nature of charity we are all united, it is in other gifts of grace we are distinguished and ordered."[5] Fr. Peter continues to explain: "One who has charity is a member of the Church; one who does not have it, but can acquire it is potentially a member of the Church. One who does not have it, and cannot acquire it, e. g. the devil, is simply outside ecclesiastical unity.[6]

Peter admits this principle can seem problematic in terms of the organic structure of the Church on earth, but without now going into this, he states categorically that "nowhere does Bonaventure ever modify his

3. Fehlner, *Role of Charity*, 10.

4. Ibid., 36.

5. "*Per naturam enim caritatis omnes unimur, sed per dona alia gratiarum . . . distinguimur et ordinamur.*" Bonveture, 4 *Sent.*, d. 24, p. 1, a. 2, q. 1, ad. 1 (IV, 615a).

6. Cf. IV *Sent.*, d. 5, a. 1, q. 1, ad. 4 (IV, 121b); III *Sent.*, d. 28, a. un., q. 3, ad. 4 (III, 627b).

affirmation that charity is the radical principle of unity of the One Mystical Body of Christ, in any of its modes or ages of existence."[7]

How does Peter substantiate this principle? He writes: "Bonaventure's view of charity is primarily centered around the uncreated gift of charity, or the gift of the Holy Spirit, wherever, whenever, and in whatever degree and state the Church or mystical body of Christ is actualized. . . . So the dimension of the Church follows the dimensions of divine charity."[8]

The charity, rooted in the life of goodness, found in the heart of the Triune God, is the same charity that is the radical principle of unity in the one mystical body of Christ. This, of course, means the charity in the Church flows from, and based upon, the missions of the Son and the Holy Spirit. From this point, after introducing charity as the radical principle of unity in the Church, the dissertation moves to explicate this in the mission of the Son and then in the mission of the Holy Spirit.

Mission of the Son

Bonaventure writes that the principle of the Incarnation is the genesis of the sacramental principle of communion in the Church. Peter develops this. He writes:

> For in virtue of the incarnation the flesh becomes the sign and instrument of the salvation of the spirit, the visible of the invisible, the human of the divine; in turn the divine is manifested in and through the human, indeed the flesh and the body. For this reason the sacraments by which the Church is founded and formed come forth from the side of Christ; they are a continuation of this mystery of mediation.[9]

There is, therefore, a kind of circumincession between the divine and human natures in the life of Christ; and so in the life of the Church in its sacramental communion, there is a "kind of circumcision between corporal and spiritual, the external and internal, the human and divine in the Church."[10] So we are to lead not only our own human lives, but divine lives. The visible character of Christ's mission is the point of departure for incorporation into his mystical body, the Church.

7. Fehlner, *Role of Charity*, 41.

8. Ibid., 45.

9. Ibid., 53–54.

10. Ibid., 54.

The life giving influence of Christ in so far as he acts through his divine nature is first of all interior and invisible. But this life, received by the Christian, is received from Christ, not only as God or divine, but also as man or human. Vital, efficacious contact with the humanity of Christ is made most effective at that point with the body of Christ and with the grace manifested through that body. This happens in all the sacraments, but most especially in the Eucharist. Here again, there is circumincession of visible and invisible: the principle of the Incarnation and the principle of the sacramental life of the Church. The human body which Christ assumed is point of contact for admission of members into the Church, into a life which is divine.

Peter begins to conclude his reflection on Bonaventure's understanding of the mission of the Son. He makes clear that the mission of the Son in his incarnation must be continued in a visible and also in an invisible manner. The sacrament of Order serves as a visible guarantee of proper form for communicating divine life sacramentally. The mediating mission of Christ in his flesh, as sacramental and visible principle, to communicate his own invisible divine life, is foundational for the constitution of the Church and its visible communion. However, the Body of Christ is not the radical and final principle of unity in the one mystical Body. This belongs to the mission of the Holy Spirit.

Mission of the Holy Spirit

The mission of the Son is completed and fulfilled in the mission of the Holy Spirit. The Son's visible mission—visible incorporation of others into his mystical Body—points toward the invisible mission of the Holy Spirit. The life and love of the Son shared in his humanity—the formation of the Church from his side—is ordered toward and completed in the invisible and intimate share of that same life of love found within the *nexus* of the love between the Father and Son. Or, to put it another way, the Father adopts us through his Son in terms of the initiation of adoption, but in terms of its consummation, it is through the Holy Spirit.

The inner and invisible unity of the Church, therefore, is the Holy Spirit, as gift of uncreated charity. Fr. Peter writes:

> According to Bonaventure this inner unity of the Church permeating every facet of her existence in one way or another above all consists in charity, to be ascribed in a particular way to the Holy Spirit who is given God to unite the Church.[11]

11. Ibid., 74.

In this charity, in this spiritual communion, the inner life and unity of the Church is fulfilled. This gift is given through the Passion of Christ's suffering, death, and resurrection, when his heart was opened in obedience to the Father. From there, from his side on the cross, the goodness of the Divine Spirit from within the heart of God flowed out upon us and established the inner communion of the Church as intimate divine charity. And so the unity of the Church is not simply social, nor simply sacramental, but *sui generis*, invisible, mysterious and unique. This gift of the Holy Spirit is rather the intimacy of charity of the divine relationships themselves, the divine *nexus*, the sacred *vinculum*. Peter concludes: "The inner unity of the Church, then, is inexplicable apart from a consideration of that charity which is proper to the Holy Spirit."[12]

In his third chapter on the Mission of the Spirit, Peter develops an incredibly beautiful insight—the relation of the mission of the Spirit and the vocation of the Mother of God—a thematic he subsequently continued to develop throughout his life. He writes that the relation between the mission of the Holy Spirit and the vocation of Mary elucidates the inner nature of the unity of the Church. The unique excellence of her dedicated intimacy with God is the work of the Holy Spirit and therefore a union of charity. Filled with the grace of the Spirit, she partakes in a special way of the fecundity of that eternal goodness, the fountain head of the procession in the Trinity, the very communication of the divine good by the Father to the Son and the Spirit. This is symbolized by her virginity, which is unique, because it is also fecund. "The intimacy of this union is the work of the Holy Spirit, and therefore fundamentally a union of charity."[13]

Finally, to conclude the first part of this essay, I let Peter speak directly from the last section of his dissertation:

> The role of charity in the Church is to unite her, to make of her a communion, because the nature of charity is communicative; and because the nature of the Church is ultimately resolved into a participation in the life of the Trinity, her inner unity is above all one of charity.[14]

Thus, the Church can now be seen as not simply an instrument of salvation, rather, as Peter drawing out Peter's argument, the Church, if true to the consummation of the mission of the Spirit, is already realization of salvation itself.

12. Ibid., 77.
13. Ibid., 78.
14. Ibid., 160.

Part Two: Charity in Eucharist

Before proceeding to the specific questions of charity in the Eucharist, it could be helpful to draw from Bonaventure's first two distinctions on "sacraments in general" as found in Book Four of is *Commentary on the Sentences.*[15] His insights in those first two distinctions have implications for consideration of the Eucharist.

It is interesting to note, at least from a contemporary perspective, that Bonaventure's arguments for the institution of sacraments begin not in reference to actions or specific directions by Christ. Rather his argument initially turns to God's mercy for us and to our need for help to overcome the brokenness of sin. Sacraments provide the way to health (*salus*). Sacraments are simply fitting for God's love for us and fitting for our need of God's love. Sacraments are actually not necessary on the part of God, and not absolutely necessary for those who desire salvation. However, they "are advantageous"[16] for cultivating a deeper internal life of grace.

It is God, not the sacraments in and of themselves, who effectively causes invisible grace in the soul. The external visible sacraments dispose one to the grace God wishes to give, in view of fidelity to his Covenant. Bonaventure explicitly writes that one can say sacraments "cause" grace, only, however, in the sense of an extended kind of meaning. He emphasizes, in line with Hugh of St. Victor, that sacraments are important for training, discipline, and cultivation of desire for God's grace. They thereby ultimately provide entrance into a deeper interior mystical life.

In this context, Bonaventure moves forward with both Augustine and Hugh of St. Victor that a sacrament is a "sign of something sacred" and is "instituted for the sake of signifying." He emphasizes this: ". . . sacramental medicine has, of its integrity, signification. This is common to all the sacraments."[17]

Important to note here is the importance Bonaventure places on the external sign, that is, its natural signification (as rooted in creation), confirmed by institution (the word spoken). Both are points of departure for understanding the unique grace God gives in a specific sacrament. It is almost as if Bonaventure is saying the external sign flows from the mediating visible mission of Christ in his humanity and the internal grace received is from the invisible mission of the Holy Spirit.

---

15. Bonaventure, *Commentary on Sentences: Sacraments.*

16. Ibid., 47.

17. Ibid., 52.

He explicitly warns that to understand a sacrament one does not move backward from the internal grace received to the external sign.[18] Rather, to understand a sacrament, one moves forward from the external sign as the starting point. The external sign that signifies and points toward the invisible grace would be much like the visible mission of the Son as the starting point for the invisible mission of the Spirit. All of this means the specific visible sign is pivotal for identifying, understanding, and experiencing the specific internal grace received.

Then, about institution! Bonaventure follows the *De Sacramentis* of Hugh of St. Victor when he addresses this question: "Because the time for the remedy began at the fall, advanced in the Law, and was consummated in the Gospel, all three ages are appropriate for their institution, but yet only more or less appropriate."[19] Bonaventure concludes, then, that it is appropriate that sacraments be instituted in different times, according to the salvific needs found in the different periods of salvation. As a result of this, he identifies Baptism and Eucharist, along with Order mainly as an adjunct to Eucharist, as the three sacraments instituted by Christ in the New Law of the Gospel.

Now let us examine some specifics on the Eucharist, as found in distinctions eight to thirteen.

Bonaventure easily argues that the Eucharist is a sacrament of the New Law. There are two reasons. First, it contains the true body of Christ. Second, the effect of the Eucharist is the bond of charity. Bonaventure brings forward the theology of Augustine identifying the *res*, or the final effect and reality of the Eucharist is the *vinculum caritatis*. Often in reference to the Eucharist, he quotes Augustine: *O Sacramentum pietatis! O signum unitatis! O vinculum caritatis!* The bond of charity is proper only to the New Law. He will argue that the Eucharist does not initially establish the bond of charity. This is initiated in Baptism. The Eucharist deepens the unity of charity already present in the soul. In fact, the presence of charity is a pre-requisite for a deepening of that charity.

And so charity is actually a prerequisite so that the Eucharist can obtain its end, a deepening of that same prerequisite, the bond of charity. In fact, charity along with faith is the prerequisite for every sacrament, but most especially for the Eucharist. Bonaventure takes his lead from Peter Lombard: "There are three things in this sacrament: the visible species, the true body of Christ, and the mystical body." And so as Bonaventure understands Peter Lombard, the visible sign of bread is the *sacramentum* and the

18. See ibid., 53.
19. Ibid., 85.

true body of Christ contained therein is the *res*. However, the *res* of the body of Christ also has the further characteristic of a sign, namely, *sacramentum*. This is because sacramental body of Christ points toward and signifies the mystical body, which in turn is the fullness and final reality or *res* of the sacrament of the Eucharist.

Bonaventure, however, changes Lombard's final end, or the final and full *res* of the sacrament of the Eucharist from the "mystical body" to "charity." In other words, Bonaventure dives deeper into the unifying bond within the mystical body, which is charity. The sacrament of the Eucharist takes us ever deeper into the mystery of God's love where we are connected ever more deeply within the *vinculum caritatis*.

This has implications as well for even deeper understanding of the external sign of bread, the *sacramentum tantum*. The Eucharistic food is a sign of love. The sharing of food and drink is a natural sign of love and friendship. This was especially true at the Last Supper "since upon departing it is appropriate for one to show signs of love and remembrance."[20] The visible food or external sign signifies the body of Christ that nurtures and heals. The sacramental body of Christ is the internal *res* of the external sign or *sacramentum*, but the *res* of the body of Christ is also a further sign and thereby also a further *sacramentum*. This means the true body of Christ, in turn, points to an even deeper reality beyond itself to the reality of participation in the charity that is the gift of the Spirit, the *nexus*, the *vinculum* or bond of charity. The Spirit, uncreated charity, is the full and final *res* of the sacrament of the Eucharist.

What is interesting here is that although the above threefold manner of understanding dimensions (*sacramentum tantum, res et sacramentum, res tantum*) of the Eucharist pre-date Bonaventure, Bonaventure's emphasis on the Augustinian notion of *vinculum caritatis* as the *res tantum*, the consummation and final purpose of the Eucharist, does not appear earlier. It is neither in Peter Lombard nor in Hugh of St. Victor, two of his principal sources. Alexander of Hales connects *caritas* with the Eucharist, but Bonaventure outdoes Alexander in his development of charity as the ultimate reason and consummate purpose of the Eucharist.

In this context Bonaventure also picks up on the Augustinian notion of the two ways of Eucharistic eating or drinking: sacramentally and spiritually. If a person is not disposed interiorly, or if even opposed to Christ, but yet has faith, that person sacramentally receives the true body of Christ, but he or she eats only with the mouth. If a person is disposed in charity and desire, he or she eats not only the body of the Lord sacramentally, but

20. Ibid., 188.

such a person eats spiritually and thereby and is thus incorporated more deeply into the unity of charity. This person eats with the heart. To eat only sacramentally with the mouth, but not with the heart, means one does not participate in the grace given in the Eucharist. The purpose of the Eucharist is not achieved. To eat spiritually, disposed in charity, is the only way to know the fruit of Eucharistic participation and thereby know the fullness of its purpose, an ever deepening and broadening charity. In distinction nine, Bonaventure himself speaks directly to this reality:

> Spiritual chewing is reflection on the food, namely the flesh of Christ offered for us with respect to the price of our redemption and with respect to food as our refreshment. Swallowing is reached when one reflects with the love of charity and is joined to what is reflected upon. In this way one is thus swallowed into the body, and when one is swallowed into the body, one is refreshed and made more similar. . . . To the end that someone eats spiritually, two things are required: reflection of faith and affection of charity. . . . Therefore, not just any sort of faith is sufficient, but of necessity faith operating through love.[21]

Thus affection of charity is required for spiritually eating and drinking of the Eucharist and for participation in the final *res* of the sacrament of the Eucharist, which is an ever deepening incorporation into that bond, the charity of the gift of the Spirit. In this sense the true body of the Lord is indeed the mediator (*res et sacramentum*) of the final *res*, the Uncreated gift of the Spirit connecting us within the very heart of a loving and merciful God.

Later Bonaventure again raises a pertinent point when he raises the question whether both species belong to the integrity of the sacrament. With his general emphasis on the importance of the external sign, he affirms the positive. Both species pertain to the integrity of the sacrament. "The *res* of the sacrament, charity, is not expressed in either of them *per se*, but rather in both of them together." He develops this further: ". . . perfect refreshment is not in the bread alone nor in the wine alone, but in both."[22] For those who eat spiritually, only the bread and wine together signify and point toward the immense charity of God, the *vinculum caritatis*.

21. Ibid., 217–18.
22. Ibid., 268.

Conclusion

It is no surprise that Bonaventure emphasizes personal preparation before partaking in the Eucharist. Its final goal is mystical union in the Uncreated gift of the Holy Spirit, divine charity. Thus, there must be practice of charity in action as well an on-going cultivation of charity within the affections of the heart, if one is to eat spiritually with the heart to deepen one's life into the Eucharistic mystery of charity. Eucharist takes us to the heart of an ecclesiology of charity. It is where the ecclesiology of charity is fully realized and thus the "realization of salvation itself."

Bibliography

Bonaventure. *Commentary on the Sentences: Sacraments.* Translation, introductions, and notes by J.A. Wayne Hellmann, OFM Conv., Timothy R. LeCroy, and Luke Davis Townsend. St. Bonaventure, NY: Franciscan Institute, 2016.

———. *Opera Omnia.* Edited by PP. Collegii S. Bonaventurae, 10 vols. Quaracchi: Ad Claras Aquas, 1882–1902.

———. *Tomus IV: In Quartum Librum Sententiarum.* In *Opera Omnia,* vol. IV, edited by PP. Collegii S. Bonaventurae. Quaracchi: Ad Claras Aquas, 1889.

Fehlner, Peter, D. *The Role of Charity in the Ecclesiology of St. Bonaventure.* Rome: Editrice "Miscellanea Francescana," 1965.

Hellmann, J.A. Wayne. *Divine and Created Order in the Bonaventure's Theology.* Translated with an appendix by Jay M. Hammond. St. Bonaventure, NY: Franciscan Institute, 2001.